Instructor's Edition
Becoming an Academic Writer

Instructor's Edition
Becoming an Academic Writer
A Modern Rhetoric

Joseph M. Moxley
University of South Florida

D. C. Heath and Company
Lexington, Massachusetts   Toronto

Address editorial correspondence to

D. C. Heath and Company
125 Spring Street
Lexington, MA 02173

Acquisitions Editor: Paul A. Smith
Developmental Editor: Linda M. Bieze
Production Editor: Heather L. Garrison
Designer: Kenneth Hollman
Production Coordinator: Richard Tonachel
Permissions Editor: Margaret Roll

Published simultaneously in Canada.

Printed in the United States of America.

International Standard Book Number: 0-669-24496-1 (Student Edition)
0-669-24497-X (Instructor's Edition)

Library of Congress Catalog Number: 93-71416

10 9 8 7 6 5 4 3 2 1

PREFACE

Students come to college with a broad range of writing experiences. During their high school years, some may have been asked to write critical analyses and research papers while others may have focused more on personal writing. There also may be some students who have dealt with relatively few formal writing assignments during their pre-college years. Outside school, some have had jobs where they performed specific job-related writing tasks. Regardless of their diverse backgrounds, college students are engaged in a process of *becoming*: they are becoming more aware of the complexity of these scholarly conversations; becoming more sensitive to the interrelationships between ideology, research methods, and argument; becoming, in a word, educated.

Generally, even the most accomplished students arrive at college needing to change or adapt many of their practices and notions about what writing is, how it is done, and what it should look like. In order to succeed in the academic environment, they may need to re-examine their writing processes. (In some cases they may not even be aware that they do indeed follow any writing process.) They will probably need to learn what sorts of written discourse a college curriculum requires. Many find they can no longer merely offer personal memories or emotional responses to issues, as they had in the past. Rather, they must now engage issues, questions, and topics in an "academic" manner, one that deals thoughtfully and critically with subjects that have been considered carefully and debated for many years as well as with subjects that represent the major issues of our day. Last, student writers become aware, sometimes painfully, that there are certain conventions, practices, and methods of inquiry that they must master. In short, for these students and because of these various needs, I have written this book.

Becoming an Academic Writer: A Modern Rhetoric is a concise, practical textbook to help students develop skills and master the forms of writing for college audiences. While developing this book, I was guided by the assumption that students can best cultivate their skills by writing regularly in a variety of academic voices to a wide spectrum of college audiences and purposes, by reading and critiquing professional and student writing samples, and by receiving supportive criticism from their peers and writing instructors.

In the initial college composition class, *Becoming an Academic Writer* can help students recognize their innate abilities to develop and shape ideas by writing and can aid them in honing those abilities for the special demands of college writing. So that students can understand what academic readers expect from them, this book presents the conventions for writing in the academic genres that they will need to use in their course work and professional lives, such as process reports, persuasive arguments, and research reports. The book also shows students how successful academic writers use all the stages of the writing process to shape their thoughts for particular audiences. Finally, the book models for students the critical questions that successful academic writers ask themselves when developing their documents.

While this practical textbook is grounded in modern composition research and theory, I have also tried to create an enjoyable and interesting book that will spark substantive discussions in your writing classroom. Having field-tested this book in my classes over the past four years, I am confident that the essays on multiculturalism, racism, gender bias, the environment, crime, and related issues will evoke student interest, lively discussions, and solid academic writing in your classes.

What Makes This Book Special?

Becoming an Academic Writer **provides a complete guide to establishing a writing community.** Thanks to modern composition theory, we are well aware of the theoretical importance of working in groups. We know collaborative work helps students transcend their own perspectives and better perceive the needs of readers and prepares students for the collaborative work expected of them in many careers. Yet from our experience in the classroom, we also know that many students feel unprepared to offer meaningful comments about their peers' documents. Sometimes students are skeptical about the group process; sometimes they are unaccustomed to helping each other improve; sometimes they are unsure of themselves as critics; and sometimes they are afraid of receiving or giving honest criticism. Unfortunately, even textbooks that place collaborative work at the heart of the writing classroom tend to fall short when it comes to showing students *how* they can establish a climate of trust and substantively critique one another's documents.

Beyond offering the usual guidelines for working with groups and explaining to students why they are asked to work together, I provide numerous sample dialogues of students working collaboratively to improve one another's manuscripts. These dialogues illustrate the range of commentaries that individuals can provide about a single document and also show *how* an author can ask peers to stay focused on critiquing a document. Then, by subsequently showing how students have revised their manuscripts in response to their peers' comments, I demonstrate how students can distinguish useful commentaries from less useful ones.

Becoming an Academic Writer **demystifies academic writing conventions.** This book presents the conventions for writing the documents that students will face in their academic and professional careers, such as biographies, analytical reports, persuasive essays, and research-based essays. So that students will have a better sense of what instructors look for when grading student documents, sample criteria-based evaluation sheets are provided in each of the writing-assignment chapters. Rather than suggesting that there is one ideal way to structure (or evaluate) each of these genres, I present the academic conventions as flexible alternatives. The fourteen professionally written essays and twenty-one student-written essays further illustrate the scope and elasticity of these conventions.

Becoming an Academic Writer **develops the rhetorical stance of students-as-writers.** This book illustrates that writing is a rhetorical act, that *how* and *what* students write is affected by their classroom culture and broader college or university setting, and that all writing must derive directly and specifically from particular purposes and must be directed toward particular audiences. *Becoming an Academic Writer* focuses attention on the circumstances and impulses that propel the process and impinge on the product in the writing classroom. This book addresses questions that students want answers to, such as *"What do my teachers want from me? How can I give teachers what they want?"*

The readings and assignments serve as catalysts for students to concentrate on the interrelationship between composing styles and discourses, purposes, audiences, and contexts. Each writing assignment offers guidelines for defining audience, voice, purpose, and context.

Each of the writing-intensive chapters in *Becoming an Academic Writer* **provides extensive prewriting, writing, collaborating, revising, and editing exercises to help students develop, refine, and polish manuscripts.** Unlike other process-oriented texts that take hundreds of pages to *tell* students about composing strategies, I *show* students concisely how they can employ these strategies to produce effective reports. As a result of their reading and writing, students learn that writing is not merely a vehicle for transmitting information, but a way of thinking about issues.

Becoming an Academic Writer **shows students how to read and think critically.** This book shows how successful academic writers use their knowledge of academic conventions to read and critique biographies, analytical reports, persuasive reports, research-based reports, and other academic documents. Throughout the text, sample questions are offered for critiquing the professional and student models, for generating subjects to write about, and for discovering original ideas. The chapters and assignments encourage students to adopt a questioning attitude, to separate fact from opinion, to analyze assumptions and evidence, to examine logical connections between ideas, to synthesize material from various readings, to argue cogently and persuasively, and to imagine and explore alternatives.

Becoming an Academic Writer **demonstrates the principles of Rogerian communication.** This book offers a complete guide to negotiating differences. I do not cast Carl Rogers' strategies for negotiating consensus between antagonistic positions as simply another form of persuasion. True to the spirit of Rogers' ideas, I teach students to avoid browbeating readers with emotional, ethical, and rational arguments when readers are so emotionally tied to an issue that they are unwilling to change their position. Instead of assuming that modern readers can be swayed by incontrovertible evidence and reasoning, I show students how to identify and appreciate rhetorical circumstances that will require authors to set aside their pride and focus on building consensus. The Rogerian approach should be particularly refreshing for writing instructors who are weary of the overly contentious (and often simplistic) tone of traditional academic argument.

Becoming an Academic Writer **provides a comprehensive description of research techniques.** When chapters on library research follow chapters on autobiography, analysis, persuasion, and other genres, students often have misconceptions about how the research process can relate to these other genres. For example, many students erroneously believe research involves only summarizing secondary sources; some students believe they cannot present their own thoughts on a subject; some believe research precludes arguing a position passionately, often resulting in dead, pedantic writing. Therefore, rather than presenting research-report writing as one of many aims, this book clarifies that library research can be a powerful *prewriting tool* that should be considered whenever a writer addresses important or contentious issues. As a result, a chapter on library research appears early in the text, before any writing assignments. Then, when presenting the writing assignments, I show students how to distinguish between topics that will require outside documentation and those that can be explicated on anecdotal information or common-sense reasoning.

This book provides a comprehensive review of library-research techniques, including, for example, how to use CD ROM technology and how to paraphrase, summarize, and quote sources according to the Modern Language Association style. Numerous exercises are provided in the textbook and *Instructor's Guide* to help students schedule their work load and correctly summarize, paraphrase, and quote sources.

Becoming an Academic Writer **provides a thorough description of field-research techniques.** Perhaps the most distinctive feature of this book is its comprehensive treatment of field-based research techniques. I offer detailed instructions for interviewing authorities, for constructing useful questionnaires, and for conducting naturalistic research based on ethnographic methods because I have found that students become excited about writing and research when they conduct field research. As the writing samples provided in this book suggest, field research can help students find answers to the problems that they face in their daily lives and understand how different cultures shape behavior and perceptions about reality and future possibilities.

Becoming an Academic Writer **encourages students to take a realistic view of writing development.** This book attempts to inspire and reassure students who seek immediate improvement. By reviewing professional writers' comments about their development and by reminding students of all that is involved in composing, I provide students with the background information they need to take a realistic view of their writing development. Additionally, so that they can avoid repeating the same errors again and again, I challenge students to write about their peers, and instructor's criticisms of their writing, and to speculate about how the process they use in their writing influences the ultimate quality of their documents.

The *Instructor's Guide* for *Becoming an Academic Writer* concisely presents classroom strategies and reviews modern composition pedagogy. Rather than needing to wade through hundreds of pages to find practical classroom suggestions, instructors can quickly determine how to teach the writing assignments by referring to Linda Sarbo's *Instructor's Guide*. This brief manual offers sample syllabi, suggestions for how to handle the student paper load, daily procedures for engaging students in classroom discussions, additional collaborative writing assignments, and exercises to help students break library and field research into smaller, more manageable steps. Even experienced instructors of writing will benefit from Sarbo's review of goals and methods of responding to student writing, such as tape-recorded responses and portfolio grading.

How This Book Is Organized

"Introduction—For the Student" summarizes prewriting, drafting, collaborating, revising, and editing strategies. This chapter also encourages students to identify the rhetorical principles that shape the design and development of all writing.

Part I, "How to Get the Work Done," provides the background material students need to overcome procrastination and develop documents worth reading. Chapter 1 challenges students to analyze the myths they have about composing, reviews the working habits and attitudes of successful academic writers, offers guidelines for working with peer-review and peer-editing groups, and discusses how to develop a writing and research notebook. Chapter 2 explains library research strategies and offers a review of the guidelines for citing sources according to the Modern Language Association style of documentation.

Part II, "The Writing Portfolio," presents ten distinct academic genres: biographical and autobiographical essays; reports of subjects, processes, and cause-and-effect relationships; persuasive and negotiation essays; and reports based on library research, questionnaires, and ethnographic research.

All the chapters in "The Writing Portfolio" are organized in the following way:

> A brief introduction defines the genre and discusses its usefulness and
> scope across the academic disciplines.
> Two to four writing samples are provided as examples of the genre.
> Critical reading questions are provided for each sample to help focus
> classroom discussions and help students learn to read critically.

The conventions of the genre are introduced in more detail, and these conventions are then used to critique the professional and student samples.

Numerous writing assignments are provided and students are cautioned to further define their context, audience, purpose, and voice to complete any assignment in the genre.

Prewriting and drafting strategies that are especially helpful for developing the genre are introduced. (For example, students are encouraged to draw a map of their home town if they plan on writing about a childhood memory.)

Revising and editing strategies are presented to help students critique their work and their peers' work.

A variety of collaborative learning exercises are provided to help students critique one another's documents. (Some chapters provide discussions of students working in groups and some chapters show how students respond to instructor's criticisms to improve their documents.)

Additional writing samples are provided near the conclusion of each chapter to give students a better sense of the range of voices and purposes encompassed by the genre.

Each chapter concludes with questions that challenge students to identify major strengths and weaknesses in their writing. Students are encouraged to keep a written record of errors that typically intrude on the overall success of their documents.

Part III, "How to Revise and Edit your Work," presents more detailed information about the revising and editing strategies of successful writers than is provided in the writing-assignment chapters. As a result, you will routinely want to instruct students to review certain parts of these chapters when they are having difficulty polishing their manuscripts. In particular, Chapter 11 explains how to systematize revision so that substantive questions are addressed before editorial ones, and it explains how students can ensure that their paragraphs are logically constructed. This chapter also offers six techniques students can use to edit their sentences to ensure that they are emphatic and concise. Finally, Chapter 12 reviews the conventions for using commas, dashes, colons, semicolons, and apostrophes.

Acknowledgments

Throughout the time that I have worked on this project, I have been guided by the reactions of my undergraduate students who have used this book in manuscript form. I am particularly indebted to the students who worked so diligently and creatively to produce the essays and research reports that appear in this text. I am also sure that this book would not have been completed without the reviewers who so kindly and thoroughly critiqued numerous drafts of this work. I feel fortunate to have worked with so many talented people on this project, and I wish to thank the following people in particular for their helpful commentaries: James E. Barcus, Baylor University; Lynn Dianne Beene, The University of New Mexico; the late Stephen H. Goldman, of The University of Kansas; Martin J. Jacobi, Clemson University; Sarah Liggett, Louisiana State University; George Otte, Baruch College; Delores K. Schriner, Northern Arizona State University; Margot Soven, La Salle University; William E. Tanner, Texas Woman's University; Victor Villanueva, Jr., Northern Arizona University; Michael Vivion, University of Missouri, Kansas City; and William F. Woods, Wichita State University.

I am especially indebted to Paul Smith, Senior Acquisitions Editor, for encouraging me to develop this project, Linda M. Bieze, Developmental Editor, for helping me to polish the book, and Heather Garrison, Production Editor, for bringing this project from manuscript to bound book. I also wish to thank Linda Sarbo, who has written the *Instructor's Guide*. Finally, I thank my wife, Pat Hemmens, and children, Lauren Kelly and Craig Joseph.

J.M.

B R I E F   C O N T E N T S

CONTENTS

4. Analyzing Subjects and Processes   87

5. Analyzing Causes and Effects   124

8. Writing Reports Based on Library Research   225

9. Writing Reports Based on Interviews and Questionnaires   269

6. Writing Persuasively   157

7. Solving Problems by Negotiating Differences   192

10. Writing Reports Based on Ethnographic Methods 310

Part 3 How to Revise and Edit Your Work 351

11. How to Make Substantive Revisions 353

12. How to Use Correct Punctuation   371

Index   381

Introduction—For the Student

Being able to express yourself in writing is fundamental to your success in school and most professional careers. In school, instructors expect you to critique documents, analyze concepts, provide evidence for assertions, present credible arguments, and conduct field-based and library-based research. Later, your professional and financial success will be directly linked to your ability to develop and communicate ideas, to synthesize and report other people's ideas, to persuade people through your writing, to research subjects, and to develop original ideas.

Being able to communicate with others in school and beyond is clearly an important reason for working on your writing. This book is designed to help you achieve that goal. Yet the research and insights of numerous scholars have demonstrated that writing is more than just a powerful mode of communication. When writing, we often experience what professionals call the "Eureka Phenomenon"—a moment characterized by intellectual excitement and passion in which we *discover what we want to say and how we want to say it.* In addition, writing about difficult concepts can enhance comprehension and recall. Creative people often say, "Put it in writing," because ideas are best evaluated only after they are written. When ideas are presented on a page, they can be reexamined, confirmed, or refuted. Writing helps us understand other people because it challenges us to imagine other people's lives and thoughts and anticipate their responses to ours. Through library- and field-based research, we learn about human behavior, world events, research, and innovative ideas. As a result, we may become more empathic, thoughtful, broad-minded and self-reflexive. These are all important aspects of creative, critical thinking.

Understanding Thinking and Writing Processes

Prewriting, drafting, collaborating, revising, editing, and evaluating criticism—these are the composing strategies that empower authors to discover and communicate ideas. Studies of professional and student writers at work have demonstrated that the amount of time we give to each of these activities depends on a variety of factors, such as our personality, schedule, writing habits, and the genre of the writing task. These strategies and how they interact are explored in more detail below.

Prewriting Strategies

As children many of us heard the classic fable about the tortoise and the hare. The moral of the story is that rushing straight from point A to point B is not always the swiftest way to the destination. Sometimes it makes sense to pause for a few moments and ask yourself, "Do I really want to go there? What obstacles can I expect to encounter? Do I need to take a compass and a map? Is the path well marked? What provisions am I likely to need along the journey?"

Like many children's tales, "The Tortoise and the Hare" has implications for adults, too. For even though logic tells us that we can save time by quickly writing a first draft, we in fact might manage our time more effectively by doing some preliminary prewriting. The term *prewriting* refers to the planning and research that you do before writing. It also involves analyzing your *communication situation*, which you can do by asking yourself rhetorical questions, such as "Who is my audience? What is my purpose? What sort of judgments do I want my readers to make about my personality based on the voice that I project?" Prewriting also includes tentative attempts at organizing ideas based on preconceptions (or schemas) about how readers expect the document to be organized. In other words, authors draw on their experience as readers and writers to identify a sense of what *conventions* exist for how particular documents should be shaped. For example, people who have read widely know that a report that attempts to persuade readers to take action on an issue will have a different from a narrative about a memorable person or event.

Prewriting can be especially difficult because it requires authors to play the role of *believer* and *doubter* at the same time. When prewriting, authors must set aside doubt and believe that their ideas will gain substance with additional research and drafting, yet they must also doubt the value of their ideas and question the relevance of the subject matter for an intended audience.

It is no secret to most students that procrastination can also play a role in the writing process—particularly in the early stages before an idea is fleshed out. Many of us routinely procrastinate when we take on new writing assignments. During prewriting, other activities, even unpleasant ones like doing the laundry, somehow become remarkably attractive and important. Sometimes we can get off to a good start on a project, then hit a writing block and stumble back into delaying tactics. As suggested by the following student, procrastination can become a negative force:

> I started writing the introduction at 10:00 Tuesday night. At 10:30 I watched Entertainment Tonight. After the show, I went to the kitchen to get a snack. When I sat down at my desk with my food and my scratch paper in front of me, I noticed it was 11:07. I could not resume my writing at such an odd time. I had to begin either half past the hour or on the hour—nothing in between. So I cleaned my room a bit and thumbed through the TV Guide to see what else was on. At 11:30 I watched David

Letterman and wrote during the commercials, composing nearly a paragraph. After the show, I took a No-Doz, finished the paragraph, and went to bed.*

The urge to procrastinate can stifle the voices of even accomplished thinkers and writers. However, this inclination is not always pernicious. In fact, studies of prominent scientists, engineers, business people, and artists have suggested that procrastination can be a vital part of the creative process. "Sleeping on an idea" or letting a subject "cook" for a few hours can be a healthy way of putting the unconscious to work. Few of us can routinely march productively from A to Z. Sometimes we need to wander around some and allow ideas to bump up against each other before we can express them through language. Of course, just because procrastination often plays a vital role in the writing process does not mean that you can seriously regard sunning yourself for hours by the pool as hard work! As with other activities, *balance* is the key. After extensive periods of hard work, you can give yourself time off, time to recharge your energies and critical faculties, all the while keeping an eye and ear open to new ideas about problems that you are facing in your writing.

Drafting Strategies

Drafting refers to the process of putting words on a page, typing words into a computer, or dictating words onto a tape. The key to successful drafting is to suspend judgment on the quality of the ideas and to write without stopping. No matter how poor your initial attempts seem to be, you need to trust that elegant expressions, words, and passages will eventually emerge from the rough draft through revision.

Collaborating Strategies

Contrary to the myth of the isolated author in the garret, most successful academic and professional writers do *not* work in isolation. Many writers get their best ideas in discussions with friends or from reading. Working collaboratively is not cheating; discussing alternative ways to develop drafts with supportive peers is a fundamental way of making meaning.

Revising Strategies

Revision involves making *global changes*—that is, substantive changes in the content and organization of a document. Revision is *not* a simple matter of correcting the spelling of a few words. Instead, for instance, experienced writers sometimes discard the first five pages of a six-page essay. Writers toss paragraphs around, experiment with innovative beginnings, chase down

*Ronald, Kate and Jon Volkmer. "Another Competing Theory of Process: The Students." *Journal of Advanced Composition* 9 (1989): 83–96.

fleeting thoughts and feelings. Revision can be a passionate, chaotic, and dynamic activity that is driven as much by feeling as by intellect. Writers measure what they have written against their intellect and an internal feeling, a felt sense, about how the ideas should be formed. Instead of holding on to the old, they risk playing with new possibilities, new forms, and new ideas.

Rather than viewing revision as a form of punishment or merely as an act of polishing ideas, good writers consider revision to be an opportunity to develop their thinking. When facing tough writing assignments, they rarely expect to produce a final copy after writing just one or two drafts. Like an alley cat stalking its prey, successful writers are patient and ruthless. Comforted by the knowledge that few people express their ideas perfectly without practice, they expect to revise. They understand that revision is an inevitable step in the process of making meaning. And while experienced writers realize that no simple formula can be used to revise all drafts, they do agree that revision is best characterized as a questioning stance toward the world and their words. They use critical questions to find cracks and crannies, places where they need to develop or clarify their thinking. In their relentless pursuit of clearly expressed, well-developed ideas, they find *soft spots*—that is, passages that need to be focused or discarded or amplified. They ruthlessly ask "So what?" and "Who cares?" and reexamine, because they know reconsidering a line or a metaphor or even a word may give birth to a new idea or to reconsideration of what has been written. As playwright Neil Simon remarked, in writing you can practice until you hit the ball out of the park, whereas in baseball it's fairly easy to strike out. Because successful writers want to knock the cover off the ball, they reshuffle their pages and reread their work with the hope of finding and correcting flawed reasoning, underdeveloped thinking, and poor word choices.

Editing Strategies

Editing involves making *local changes.* Once they are satisfied that a text effectively communicates the substance of their ideas in an emphatic way, successful writers read sentence by sentence, word by word, and identify grammatical, mechanical, and format errors. When editing, authors trim down overblown phrases and replace inexact words. Although readers may disagree about how best to revise a written document, they usually will have little difficulty agreeing on editing. In fact, editing is one of the few times when you can be fairly sure that the changes you make are correct ones. We can all usually agree, for example, when a sentence needs a question mark or that a compound subject takes a plural verb.

Evaluating Criticism

The final writing activity for most students is submitting their work to peers and teachers, just as the final act for professional writers is submitting the completed product to bosses or editors. Criticism can often be painful, so it is understandable that many of us try to avoid hearing or thinking much about our critics' comments. Nevertheless, as illustrated throughout this book, your growth as a writer is largely dependent on your ability to learn from your mistakes and to improve drafts in response to feedback from thoughtful peers and instructors.

What Controls How We Compose Documents?

Individuals differ in how they write documents. Some people, for instance, tend to be terrific procrastinators, while others are prolific planners. Extensive planners may spend days discussing ideas with friends and reading essays about their subject before feeling even remotely prepared to write. In contrast, some people prefer not to plan at all. Instead of talking with others, reading, drafting outlines, or setting a schedule, they prefer to begin writing immediately and rely on later revisions to help them sort out their thoughts and plans. Finally, as you may know from experience, there are some gifted people who have learned to balance the need to plan with the need to dive in. They discover their purpose and form both as they prepare and as they proceed.

The Communication Situation

Writers differ in the extent to which they procrastinate, plan, and revise. We also know that the *communication situation* of a document significantly affects how writers compose. Every document you write—as well as *how* you write— is shaped in response to a communication situation. For every writing project you face, you can best determine what you want to say and how you want to say it by analyzing the three components of your communication situation: audience, purpose, and voice. As the diagram below suggests, changes in one component will require adjustments in the others as well, because the communication situation is an interactive phenomenon.

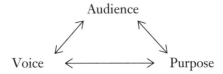

Your Audience. To be an effective writer, you must use language that is audience-centered, not writer-centered. In other words, you need to transcend your own perspective and consider the needs and interests of your readers. Transforming a writer-centered draft into an audience-centered draft can be one of the most exciting but frustrating challenges that you face as a writer.

When you begin a project and while you are revising it, you can save time and write a more effective draft by answering the following questions:

1. Who is your *primary audience?* A teacher? a parent or loved one? fellow students? a politician? a university committee? a broad, general audience such as subscribers to a weekly magazine like *Time?*

2. Does your document have multiple audiences? Can you discern an important *secondary audience?* If so, how will you account for the needs of this audience? Should you have separate sections in your document that address the needs of these different audiences?

3. How knowledgeable are your primary and secondary audiences about your subject? What concepts or terms will you need to define for these audiences? What level of education does your primary audience have?

4. What factors impinge on how your audience will feel about your subject? For instance, are you addressing someone who is overcome by grief or emotional problems?

Because experienced authors are accustomed to developing new ideas while writing, they expect that their answers to the above questions may change as they revise a document. For instance, writers are not always sure whom they are writing for when they begin a project. Sometimes their ideas about their *external audience* (that is, the people who will read the work) change as they work with the material.

Furthermore, it is not uncommon for successful writers to ignore thoughts about their external audience at the start of a project. During the preliminary stages of writing, some people become discouraged and intimidated by thoughts of who will eventually read their work. To avoid thinking about their instructor or classmates, they prefer to concentrate on first developing an idea or argument so that it makes sense to them. When addressing a difficult subject, some writers may be so concerned with developing the material for themselves that they don't want to pause or complicate matters by questioning what others would think about the subject. They may even write a few drafts before questioning how their words and ideas will affect readers.

You will not always be able to make informed guesses about your audience's level of education, knowledge about the topic, or interest in it. When this occurs, you need to rely on an *internalized, imaginary audience.* For example, even when you know the people for whom you are writing—such as friends, an instructor, or a boss at work—you may not know their exact opinions about your subject. Also, you will occasionally write to broad, general audiences that include people with diverse attitudes toward your subject. From observations of writers at work and from accounts of their processes, we know that successful writers carry on dialogues with themselves about their subject and about how different readers will likely respond to it. In other words, they invoke a sense of audience by asking themselves, "Now what would my audience think about this example? I wonder if I can assume that my audience knows about this information?" By asking these sorts of questions as they develop ideas and evaluate passages, authors call on their past reading and writing experience in order to create an internalized, imaginary audience.

Purpose. Until you know your *primary purpose* for writing, you cannot know what information to leave in, what to leave out, or even how to best organize a document. Of course, some academic documents have multiple purposes. A persuasive essay about date rape, for example, may have paragraphs that inform, paragraphs that persuade, paragraphs that threaten, and paragraphs that request information. However, on a more global level, most texts can be said to have one primary purpose.

Because of the generative nature of the writing process, your sense of the primary purpose for a document will often become clearer once you have written a few drafts. Yet because the effectiveness of a document is chiefly determined by how well you focus on addressing a primary purpose, you can save time by identifying your purpose as early as possible. Try answering the following questions when you are unsure about your purpose for a document:

1. What is your primary purpose for writing? For instance, are you attempting to analyze a subject, to explain a cause-and-effect relationship, or to persuade an audience about your position?

2. Do you have competing or conflicting purposes for writing this document? If so, should the document be separated into two papers?

3. What crucial information should you emphasize to affect your audience? You may want to shock, educate, or persuade your readers, for instance.

4. How can you organize the document to emphasize key information that suits your purpose?

Voice, Tone, and Persona. *Voice* and *tone* refer to an author's attempt to project to readers a sense of his or her personality and feelings about the subject. In turn—because what authors hope to convey is not always precisely what readers receive—these terms also refer to readers' perceptions of the author's personality and feelings about the subject. As you probably know from past experience, it is quite possible for a writer to believe that he or she is presenting a logical, coherent account, while readers might consider that same account to be scattered and superficial. Sometimes readers can have difficulty understanding an author's message because they dislike the author's voice or tone.

If *voice* reflects the author's true personality, then in contrast, the term *persona* refers to an author's use of a literary mask to hide his or her true opinion about a matter. For example, if you were writing about how you act while waiting in long lines, you might want to honestly inform your reader that you become a raging lunatic, that your heart rate doubles, and that you can keep calm only by doing sit-ups and push-ups. Yet if you are not proud of this Type-A tendency, you might present the persona of a patient person who has mastered the ability to meditate calmly and think deeply about important issues when forced to wait in a seemingly endless line.

Just as listeners get a sense of your personality by observing how you dress and act and by listening to the tone of your voice, readers make judgments about your personality and feelings regarding a subject based on what and how you write. Even when you avoid use of the first person and personal references, readers make judgments, rightly or wrongly, about what kind of person you are and about your professional abilities. Readers make assumptions about how clever and fair a thinker you are by noting such things as the quality of your reasoning, the words you choose, and the way you format your text. Even little things like spelling and punctuation errors can give the reader a sense of who you are and how you feel about the subject. By noting an author's examples, organization, and word choices, we might say, for example, that he or she displays an opinionated or logical or emotional persona.

The vitality of a writer's voice or persona often has a tremendous influence on readers' responses. Sometimes, for example, readers say they enjoy a text because an author seems straightforward and personable. In contrast, sometimes readers dislike a book because the author seems stuffy or cold-hearted. As an example of the latter, note the "computer tone" in the following letter, which I received after the birth of my first child:

> Thank you for cooperating with the Hospital Stay Certification component of your Health Insurance Policy. The company has been notified of the patient's emergency admission. The information submitted has been reviewed and a length of stay has been assigned. This emergency stay is certified for two days.
>
> We remind you that the review of your hospital stay was limited to determining the appropriate length of stay for the emergency admitting diagnosis and did not question medical necessity. We further remind you that payment of benefits is still subject to the terms of your Health Insurance Policy.

Surely this is an impersonal, mechanical way to say that my newborn would be covered by my insurance policy—a fact that I already knew. Although the letter was signed by a woman, it seems certain to have been written by a computer. If I had called this woman on the phone, she probably would have said something like, "Congratulations on the birth of your baby. As you already know, your insurance covers expenses for two days of hospitalization up to 90 percent. Enjoy that little one!" One message, two very different voices.

The challenge of juggling apparently unrelated ideas can be so great that you may overlook your voice or tone. When attempting to explain complex ideas and processes, you may understandably focus your critical energies on being coherent and logical. Yet, you must also remember that readers are people too, and they are likely to be swayed as much by their sense of how credible you are as by the logic of your argument. One trick that writers use to gauge the voice in a document is to read a manuscript aloud or to speak it into a tape recorder and then listen to how they sound. You may also find it useful to consider the following questions when evaluating the effectiveness of your voice and persona:

1. What inferences about my personality do I want my readers to make? Given my audience and purpose, is it appropriate to express my feelings about this subject? Would it be more appropriate for me to project a strong, passionate tone, or should I try to appear more objective?

2. Based on what I have written, what sense about my personality or feelings about the subject will readers be likely to infer?

3. Have I used any words or examples that are emotionally charged and likely to alienate my readers? What personal examples should I add or delete to help my readers better understand me and my message?

How This Book Is Organized

The organization of this text is based on the following assumptions: you can best improve your writing by writing, by reading other people's writing, by having your manuscripts criticized by a variety of people, and by critiquing other people's writing.

The opening two chapters in Part I, How to Get the Work Done, offer background material about the writing process and research strategies. In particular, Chapter 1 illustrates the working habits and attitudes that can enable you to achieve your writing goals. This chapter also offers suggestions for working with your peers as editors so that your efforts at collaboration are productive. Chapter 2 presents time-saving library search strategies and offers a brief review of the guidelines for citing sources according to the Modern Language Association style of documentation.

The chapters in Part II, The Writing Portfolio, are designed to engage you in various writing projects. Chapters 3 through 5 present the conventions for writing autobiographical and biographical essays and reports of processes, subjects, and causes and effects. Chapters 6 through 10 cover how to argue persuasively, how to negotiate settlements between opposing factions, and how to write reports based on library research, interviews and surveys, and ethnographic methods. Each chapter in Part II provides numerous writing samples by both professional and student authors. Strategies for overcoming writing blocks and for developing original ideas are presented in each chapter. These should provide you with a healthy alternative to giving in to avoidance behaviors, such as polishing the chrome on your car. In particular, each chapter suggests prewriting, drafting, organizing, revising, and editing strategies that you can use to develop substantive documents without wasting valuable time.

The chapters in Part III, How to Develop an Effective Style, focus on specific composing strategies. To help you attack your manuscripts with the critical eye of an experienced editor, Chapter 11 reviews a variety of revising and editing strategies, featuring how professional authors revise and highlighting the critical questions that experienced academic readers consider when evaluating texts. The next chapter provides detailed examples of well-organized paragraphs and explains how you can ensure that your paragraphs are logically constructed and well developed. This chapter also offers six techniques for editing sentences to make them emphatic and concise. Finally, chapter 12 reviews punctuation conventions.

How Can You Facilitate Your Own Writing Development?

This book is filled with sound writing advice that you can use to write documents more efficiently, effectively, and painlessly. By analyzing the examples of writing included in this book, you should have a better sense of what college instructors expect when they review your work. The samples of student review groups will give you a sense of how you can use group work to improve your writing. Also, accounts of students discussing their drafts will show you how to critique your peers' drafts tactfully.

Ultimately, however, your success as a writer is determined by your own willingness to work hard, to experiment with new approaches, to solicit criticism from supportive readers, and to give yourself room to make mistakes. Use your time in school now to better ensure your later success. When prewriting, try to keep any perfectionist tendencies in check. Allow yourself to explore new ways to form ideas and learn to harness the generative, meaning-making function of language. When revising, be critical of your work, but remember that you are critiquing one particular project, not your total development as a writer. Underline sentences and highlight passages in your work that you are not sure about and then ask your instructor for guidance. When critiquing your own work or reviewing your peers' comments about your drafts, remember that writing is a lifetime apprenticeship. If you remain patient, trust your intuition and intellect to help you discover what you want to say, and keep writing, then you will steadily improve as a writer. Most important of all, trust the process. Know that, with work, ideas can gain clarity and grace.

Part 1

How to Get the Work Done

The Attitudes and Work Habits of Successful Academic Writers

What is your fantasy of how writers work? Do you believe that writers are unusually talented people who write in lonely garrets and occasionally—like those lucky $35 million lottery winners—write a novel, or a nonfiction book, or even a screenplay that hits the jackpot? Do you imagine writers doing research by cruising the Bahamas in a private yacht and hanging out with movie stars and power brokers at the Full Moon Golf and Racket Club?

As someone who is determined to become a competent, confident writer, it is important for you to start by analyzing your attitudes about writing. After all, your attitude about writing and your assumptions about how writers work can limit your imagination and the quality of your finished product. You can debunk a truckload of myths about writing by analyzing how you write, how your peers write, and how professional writers write.

Writing Myths*

Below are eleven of the common myths that many of us hold about writers. To help you identify blind spots—that is, opinions and attitudes you hold that you are not even conscious of—you should discuss these misconceptions with friends outside of class and with your peers in class. You should also explore in writing (or in your writer's journal, if you have one) any attitudes and myths you tend to subscribe to that might interfere with your writing success.

Writers Are Born Rather Than Nurtured

Or, writers are unusual, especially intelligent people. *Reality:* Perhaps a few people are born with a special ability to express themselves through language. Yet ability without desire or experience nets an empty page. Despite count-

---

*The material on the working habits of successful academic authors is adapted from "If Not Now, When?" *Writing and Publishing for Academic Authors.* Ed. Joseph M. Moxley. Lanham, MD: University Press of America, Copyright 1992 by University Press of America. Reprinted by permission.

less attempts, researchers have been unable to prove that writers are uniquely intelligent or original. What is unique, however, is that writers discipline themselves to write and revise. When their thoughts are muddy, successful writers persist until they achieve clarity.

Writers Always Enjoy Writing

Reality: Even professionals agonize about their writing from time to time. For example, Sue Lorch, an accomplished writing teacher and author, writes,

> I do not like to write. Most people to whom I reveal this small, personal truth find it exceedingly odd, suggesting by their expressions that I ought either to repair my attitude or develop the discretion necessary not to go around telling people about it. Apparently these people hear my confession as an admission of fraud. Because my professional life centers on the written word—on producing it, interpreting it, teaching it, and teaching others to teach it—people assume that I should enjoy writing. Not at all. I inevitably view the prospect of writing with a mental set more commonly reserved for root canals and amputations: If it must be done, it must be done, but for God's sake, let us put it off as long as possible.*

Although experienced writers may dislike the act of writing, they know, nonetheless, that if they are to develop ideas, they need to put their pen to the page or their fingers to the keyboard. Like the forty-niners prospecting for gold in the Sierras, many of us write with the hope of eventually experiencing the "Eureka Phenomenon"—the inspirational moment when our passion finds form and we discover what we want to say by writing.

Gifted Writers Are Overflowing with Ideas

Reality: Experienced writers do not have a monopoly on good ideas. Like most other people, they suffer through long, weary days when good ideas seem as rare as a lunar eclipse. Even on the worst days, however, they have faith in the creative process; their experience tells them that the chaos and frustration of early drafting will subside once a few drafts are written. Also, they look outside of themselves for ideas by reading extensively, observing their world, and building relationships with people.

Writing Is a Lonely Craft Conducted Best by Introverts

Or, only a weak writer seeks help from others. *Reality:* Contrary to the myth of the lonely writer in the garret, you do not need to chain yourself to a desk in order to create. Writing need not be a solitary, lonely act. In fact, writers

---

*Lorch, Sue. "Confessions of a Former Sailor." In *Writers on Writing*. Ed. Tom Waldrep. New York: Random House, 1985. 165–172.

who do not enjoy working in isolation either coauthor essays or they make arrangements with friends to meet together and write on their separate subjects. Others find it useful to write in noisy college cafeterias. And even if you do your best writing in a quiet room away from other people, you can probably do your best revising by observing how your words influence actual readers. When you can no longer find fault with your manuscript, there's nothing more invigorating than sharing it with trusted peers.

In business settings, authors often coauthor corporate reports and interoffice memoranda. Even the stereotypical author in the garret is responding line by line to how his or her words are likely to be received by the intended reader. Most writers routinely seek advice from colleagues and editors.

Writers Work Best at Their Desks

Reality: Thoughts about what you are going to write about do not only occur when you are sitting at your desk. If you are receptive to sudden insights, you will find that some of your best ideas originate when you are puttering about in the world, playing golf, or driving in busy traffic. Studies of the creative processes of scientists and artists suggest that our most innovative breakthroughs occur in the slack moments between work and play, so you would be wise to keep a notepad or tape recorder handy to record promising thoughts.

Writers Are Most Critical When They Are Planning and Drafting

Reality: When they are just beginning a writing project, experienced writers ignore doubts about the quality of their ideas. They often set aside questions about how best to organize their ideas or whether their rough drafts contain grammatical and mechanical errors. Experienced writers understand that it is impossible to evaluate the originality of an idea based on a first or second draft.

Truly Skilled Writers Rarely Revise

Or, quality writing always develops spontaneously; revision is a form of punishment inflicted by nit-picking teachers. *Reality:* Professional writers do not perceive revision as merely a process of correcting errors; instead, they value revision as a method for developing and discovering their ideas.

Once Written, the Word Is Final

Reality: Sure, when you submit your finished essays to your teachers, you should believe in what you have said. Ideally, your essays represent your best thinking on your subject. However, you should feel free to change your mind when reviewing your work at a later date. In fact, your teachers want to help you recognize that thinking is an ongoing process. Rigid thinkers, like rigid writers, are characterized by bitterness and sarcasm rather than invigorated by the challenges of an everchanging world.

It Is Inappropriate to Use "I" in Writing

Reality: You *should* use the first person when you are discussing personal experiences and when you want your readers to understand that the ideas in the text are your ideas or your opinions. Because the "I" voice is so integrated with the insightful, energetic inner voice that helps us create, you might find it useful to write all your first drafts in the first person. Later on, if required by your communication situation, you can remove or rework the first-person references.

The First Paragraph of Every Essay Should Define Your Thesis

Reality: Rigid rules about structuring ideas need to be shattered when serious thinking is going on. No single structure or format can satisfy diverse audiences and purposes. When you are revising your work, you will want to respond to the conventions for structuring ideas that exist for your specific communication situation.

Teachers Care Primarily about Grammar, Punctuation, and Spelling

Reality: More than anything else, your teachers care that you have thought deeply about a subject and written about it in such a way that they can understand your thinking. Your teachers are much more concerned with the quality and depth of your ideas than with spelling, grammatical, or punctuation errors. However, because stylistic errors can intrude on your reader's understanding of your subject, teachers understandably are concerned with these sorts of errors as well.

How Can You Succeed as a Writer?

Many of us fear that reflecting too much about how we write could dampen our creative abilities. Yet budding writers need not stumble about in the dark, hoping to find the light switch. From anecdotal accounts of writers at work and from modern research that has analyzed writers' composing processes, we have learned that successful writers often share similar attitudes and work habits. Of course, imitating their practices and attitudes does not guarantee success. We are *not*, after all, producing nuts and bolts. Yet if we don't put our heads down and do the work, if we don't adopt the attitudes and work habits of other successful writers, how can we hope to be creative and productive? Below are several positive writing habits that you may wish to develop.

Establish a Comfortable Place to Write

If possible, find a quiet place where all your needed writing tools—such as a personal computer, dictionary, and paper—are set up. To help you focus on the work at hand, I recommend finding a place that is reasonably free of distractions. For example, you may find it helpful to be away from temptations like the phone, television, refrigerator, radio, stereo, magazines, and books.

Determine Your Most Energetic Time of Day

> A writer is not so much someone who has something to say as he is someone who has found a process that will bring about new things he would not have thought of if he had not started to say them.
>
> *William Stafford*

You will probably find it easier to establish a regular writing schedule if you can write during your most energetic time of day. I strongly recommend that you try getting up an hour earlier each day to write. The advantage of morning writing is that you are fresh from the night's sleep. Also, once the words are written, you won't need to feel guilty about procrastinating all day and the responsibility of writing will not hover over you. Not everyone's "body clock" is the same, of course. You may prefer to write in the evening; that is fine so long as you are able to produce meaningful work.

> In fact I think the best regimen is to get up early, insult yourself a bit in the shaving mirror, and then pretend you're cutting wood, which is really just about all the hell you are doing—if you see what I mean.
>
> *Lawrence Durrell*

> It's important to try to write when you are in the wrong mood or the weather is wrong. Even if you don't succeed, you'll be developing a muscle that may do it later on.
>
> *John Ashbery*

When circumstances prevent you from writing at your best time of day, however, do not use this as an excuse not to write at all. Even ten minutes of freewriting at your worst time of day is better than no writing.

Establish a Regular, Reasonable Writing Schedule

> Writers are not born nor made, but written.
>
> *William Matthews*

You can overcome the impulse to procrastinate by establishing reasonable goals. For example, you should not expect to write an A-level or even a C-level essay in a single session, but it *is* reasonable for you to write a solid introduction or to develop one point of your essay in a single session. Each time you begin a new project, you should evaluate how much time you can devote to completing the document. Then set realistic goals for completing first, second, and third drafts.

Each time you complete a writing session, map out the agenda for your next session. Because revision can be a never-ending process, you need to train yourself to stop working on a topic by setting self-imposed deadlines— deadlines that allow you sufficient time to engage in a variety of rewriting activities.

> You know when you think about writing a book, you think it is overwhelming. But, actually, you break it down into tiny little tasks any moron could do.
>
> *Annie Dillard*

If you find it difficult to maintain your schedule of goals, use the reward system. Allow yourself a treat or indulge in a pleasurable activity—a hot fudge sundae or a relaxing swim—but only after you successfully complete a specific goal.

Listen to the Messages You Give to Yourself When Writing

Writing can be discouraging. After hours of effort, you can end up with a product that absolutely fails to express what you intended. Plus, the feedback and criticism of your classmates and teachers can be depressing. When there is a large gap between what you said and what you meant to say, you can easily get down on yourself, telling yourself that you are not a good writer and that you will never be good at writing.

As with other activities, however, you need to shut off the negative voice within you and trust the generative nature of language to help you find exactly what you want to say. You must have confidence that your writing will be concise, coherent, and persuasive, given enough time and effort.

Whenever you become discouraged about your writing or about your potential as a writer, you must remember that successful authors did not become competent overnight. In fact, for most people, learning to write well is a lifelong process, an apprenticeship.

Be Flexible

Unlike a chef who follows a single recipe for preparing chocolate cheesecake, writers lack a single *modus operandi*. Sometimes you may need to write 30 drafts and other times a single draft will do. Sometimes you should dictate your ideas; sometimes you should write them on the computer; sometimes you should scratch them out carefully with a pencil.

Instead of expecting yourself to write perfect first drafts or to develop your best ideas before writing, you need to learn to trust the generative nature of composing. By being flexible and open minded, you will sometimes discover your most innovative ideas in progress, because language generates thought. In fact, what you learn as you write will sometimes contradict your preliminary hunches, so be prepared to revise accordingly.

Pursue Interesting Subjects

Whenever possible, try to choose writing topics that interest you, topics that are extensions of your academic, professional, and personal life. For example, if you enjoy flying airplanes or collecting rare books or scuba diving or meeting new people, then that is what you should write about. Try to select topics and projects that build on past projects and that are extensions of your daily activities and academic interests.

When you are assigned a topic that at first appears uninteresting, develop commitment to the task by immediately involving yourself in the subject. Granted, some subjects never become interesting, but you can usually find some rewards in reshaping topics in creative ways. Most subjects can be made engaging once you explore their parameters by drafting freewrites, by discussing them with peers, and by researching them.

Organize Your Ideas and Your Reading Notes

Maintaining organized files for all of your classes can be an important time-saver. By keeping a list of ideas or drafts of essays that might be worth developing and by organizing reading notes, you will have less trouble generating subjects to write about. (The last section of this chapter provides a more complete discussion of how to keep a Writing and Research Notebook.)

Work on More Than One Project at a Time

Because professional writers find it difficult to critique a manuscript immediately after they have written it, they tend to work on more than one project at a time. The advantage of this approach is that when you get bored by a writing task, yet know that it needs still more work before being submitted, you can turn your attention to another assignment and return to revise the original project later, when you can look at it more critically.

Develop a Mutual Assistance Society

Going public—sharing your writing with friends and classmates—can help motivate you to get the work done and help you judge whether or not your writing successfully communicates your ideas. However, avoid weak egos who seize on your vulnerability as an opportunity to crush you and to document all of the ways that they think the piece should be written. Also, avoid dominating the discussion defensively when others share their reactions. Just listen. Of course, you should not submit your writing to others if you consider the work complete and truly do not want criticism.

Write with a Word Processor

Writers who work on a word processor enjoy tremendous advantages over those who still work with pens, pencils, or typewriters. Because word processors reduce the drudgery of retyping pages, and because whole sections of writing can be moved around in a computer file, writers can more easily make global, substantive changes. In an odd way, the printed word on the screen seems more transitory, more fluid, making it all that much easier to cut out words and introduce new ones. And subsequent drafts can be printed on paper at the touch of a finger. Students often remark that it's easier to critique their ideas once they are printed because the printed text seems less personal. Also, by making copies of files under different names, writers can easily return to earlier drafts (although frankly writers seldom do this, just as old lovers may keep photographs of each other but they rarely schedule rendezvous).

Most word-processing programs are easy to learn, and some are so simple that you can master them in minutes without even consulting a manual. In addition, new style analyzers (such as NotaBene, Rightwriter, or Grammatik) examine a text's readability (according to the Flesch, Flesch-Kincaid, and Gunning scales) and offer advice on usage, punctuation, and style.

Because of the many advantages inherent in composing with a word processor, I strongly recommend that you either invest in your own personal computer or, if possible, use your school's computer laboratory. Of course, however, you don't have to use a word processor to revise well. Shakespeare certainly didn't have the benefit of modern technology. Word processors simply make revising easier, just as Edison's electric light bulb was an improvement over candlelight for nighttime reading.

Write Daily

Successful writers do not wait until they are inspired to write. That's why it is a truism among successful student and professional writers that writing involves 99 percent perspiration and 1 percent inspiration.

> I'm not sure I understand the process of writing. There is, I'm sure, something strange about imaginative concentration. The brain slowly begins to function in a different way, to make mysterious connections. Say, it is Monday, and you write a very bad draft, but if you keep trying, on Friday, words, phrases, appear almost unexpectedly. I don't know why you can't do it on Monday, or why I can't. I'm the same person, no smarter, I have

nothing more at hand. . . . It's one of the things writing students don't understand.

Elizabeth Hardwick

When asked how they develop ideas, professional writers often explain that regular writing becomes an addictive activity that enables them to develop new ideas. As they work on Project A, they get ideas for Projects B through Z! If you write regularly, you will generate more creative ideas than if you write only sporadically.

Making time for writing on a regular basis does not necessarily mean that you will have less time for your other classes, family, and social activities. After all, working a little each day instead of putting whole projects off until the weekend will leave your weekends freer for other activities. Rather than giving in to procrastination and letting the responsibility to write haunt every pleasurable moment, try little dosages of writing at a time. Ultimately, after a training period in which you need to force yourself to write, you will find writing has its own rewards and you will soon look forward to composing.

On days when disaster strikes—when the rain leaks through the roof of your writing site or a bad storm knocks out the electricity—you should still try to contribute something to your writing, even if it is a single sentence written hastily on a napkin or spoken into a tape recorder.

Talk Over Ideas with Peers and Teachers

Evaluating your work, your peers' work, and published writing can be extraordinarily complex. Unlike a math question that has a single correct answer, the criteria for excellence in writing vary according to your communication situation. In other words, what constitutes excellence depends in large part on the writer's audience, purpose, and voice. For example, you would use different standards to judge the success of an editorial on the plight of the homeless, a love letter, or a final exam essay for a course on economic theory.

Because the criteria that readers will use to evaluate your work shift according to changes in your communication situation, no ideal standards of excellence can be defined. As a result, your instructors cannot provide you with prose models or formulas that will help you write in all situations. There are no perfect essays that you can mimic.

The process of evaluating manuscripts is doubly complicated by the subjective nature of reading and interpretation. As you have probably noticed when you have shared your work with teachers and friends, different readers often draw conflicting conclusions about a text's purpose or quality. Editors of professional journals and magazines often ask three critics to examine a manuscript for publication because they need a third vote to break the tie. For example, a reader who likes the persona that you project in your prose and who agrees with your opinion on the subject may look for the best in your papers, whereas a reader who disagrees with your thesis or who finds your tone in an essay to be pedantic or condescending may be more inclined to note places where you have failed to provide sufficient evidence. If your ideas are based on theories that your readers hold as self-evident truths, then those readers are likely to think of you as remarkably commonsensical; readers who have a different theoretical base will probably be more inclined to dismiss you and your work as misguided.

Some authors find discussions with trusted colleagues to be an invaluable way of developing and polishing ideas. University professors, for example, frequently attend scholarly conferences so that they can discuss ideas with editors and other scholars. Some authors do not feel comfortable beginning a new project until they have discussed their ideas with others. In contrast, some authors prefer to keep silent about their writing goals until they have completed a draft or two.

Regardless of whether they use the input of others before writing, all serious writers share their drafts and completed products with critics. For most writers, accepting criticism is a way of life. Seasoned writers learn to appreciate tough criticism because they know a thorough evaluation means that they are being treated with professional respect.

At first, you may find it painful to receive criticisms of your manuscripts from your peers or instructor, but with practice you will learn what every writer knows: you can develop more original ideas and produce more effective documents by sharing your work with others. With practice, you will learn not to be emotionally distressed by what may seem to be unkind remarks. Remember that constructive criticism is not a personal attack, even though it may seem that way when you first hear it. Instead of immediately dismissing people's suggestions or trying to argue with them, try to thank them for being honest and conscientious enough to seriously evaluate your work. With even more practice, you will learn to respond to and benefit from tough criticism.

Of course, sometimes you will need to reject a reviewer's comments. Though well intended, some people just miss the mark when reviewing your work, and others are so overly critical that you are too overwhelmed and defensive to consider their comments seriously. While you should always contemplate the advice of your critics, you need not agree with all of their comments.

In a writing course you have a superb opportunity to have your work read and evaluated by your peers. Rather than merely imagining how a potential audience might respond to your work, you can meet in a circle with a few of your classmates and discuss your ideas for writing projects or evaluate drafts. As you exchange your ideas, however, keep the following guidelines in mind:

1. Appoint someone in your group to keep track of discussion time so that each writer's work receives roughly the same amount of attention.

2. Do not try to transform the peer-review workshop into a collaborative writing exercise. There simply isn't time in most peer group situations to solve every problem that people raise. Instead, consider the group's

ideas and suggestions as a whole and later you can attempt to revise accordingly.

3. Bring work to the group that is worthy of consideration. Offering hastily scribbled notes is as much an insult as coming to a birthday party without a gift. If you are not ready to share your work, then let your teacher know so that he or she can give you an alternative assignment. It really isn't fair to offer criticism to others if you are not in a position to receive it as well.

4. When it's your turn to have your work reviewed, identify for the group any particular issues, problems, and questions that you have. For example, let them know if you are uncomfortable with your voice or purpose, and give them a sense of how complete you believe your essay is. Telling your peers that you are open for advice and criticism—if it's true—helps break the ice. Once the members in your group begin to respond to your work, however, remain silent and *listen* until they are finished offering suggestions, questions, or observations. After all, your current purpose is *not* to argue about what you meant to say, but to learn how your peers perceived what you meant. You should feel free to interrupt the flow only if their discussion wanders off course or to ask questions that will clarify their criticisms.

5. Each writer should read his or her piece aloud to the other members in the group. Although this may seem awkward or time-consuming at first, you will find that hearing writing helps you revise writing! Remember also to speak slowly when you read your work aloud. Although you are very familiar with your work, your peers are hearing it for the first time.

6. Expect a little confusion. Responding to writing is much like writing itself: sometimes you need to stumble around a while before you can accurately identify and articulate the problem that you have perceived.

7. When criticizing a peer's manuscript, remember that authorship is ownership. Your proper role is consultant, not coauthor. When the purpose of the writer's work is unclear, do not necessarily assume that you know exactly what the writer hopes to do. Instead of explaining how you would revise the manuscript, focus on explaining your response to it. Point out places in your peers' writing that don't seem effective, even if you cannot suggest exact ways to improve them. After all, when a document is still in rough form, you cannot presume to know what the writer ultimately will do with it. For many of us, there is an enormous gap between rough and final drafts. As readers we need to respect this distinction and provide the sort of commentary that will encourage authors to develop manuscripts in ways that they believe are appropriate.

8. Speak to each other. Remember that you were a reader long before you were a writer and that it is much easier for all of us to critique other people's manuscripts than our own. Draw on your background as a reader to identify weak passages. If you are unsure about what a passage means,

tell the author and explain the nature of your confusion. Nothing is gained if you do not elaborate on your impressions and thoughts. And don't neglect to praise well-written work. Point out the strengths as well as the weaknesses of each manuscript.

9. Avoid global, general comments like, "I think the paper is good." Although somewhat helpful, general responses are usually too vague to help your peers improve their work. Whenever possible, try to isolate your comments to particular aspects of your peer's text.

10. When concluding a review of a peer's manuscript, group members should try to summarize their most important criticisms. Because reasonable people can still disagree about the quality of a manuscript after much discussion, group members should not feel that the critique went poorly if they cannot reach consensus about how to best improve a document. It's normal and acceptable for some disagreement to exist about the best ways to improve a draft.

Maintain a Writing and Research Notebook

Unlike a journal that records daily events in a chronological order, a *Writing and Research Notebook** is organized by subject categories. By organizing your ideas and plans in a three-ring binder, you can gather together related insights, which can in turn stimulate your thoughts on different ideas. Such a notebook can help you identify a specific research question, organize your reading notes, draw inferences from what you read, and construct a bibliography. Following are some recommendations for compiling your research notebook, section by section.

A Writing Log

Because you can sometimes feel as if you are being unproductive even when you are researching sources or doing reading that will lead to writing, you may find it useful to keep a log of the work that you have completed and the ideas you have developed (see Sample Log Sheet). The advantage of a log is that it can help motivate you to work on a project even when you are in a slump and unsure of how to proceed.

A Schedule of Writing Goals and Research Decisions

You can use this section to decide which subjects to pursue and to outline the amount of time you will probably need to set aside for prewriting and

---

*This material on developing a writing and research notebook is adapted from *Publish, Don't Perish: The Scholar's Guide to Academic Writing and Publishing*, by Joseph M. Moxley. Copyright © 1992 by Greenwood Press, an imprint of Greenwood Publishing Group, Inc. Westport, CT.

Sample Log Sheet

Date	Hours Worked	No. of Words Written	Goals
1. 11/20	1.25	500	I need to talk with friends about the stresses they experience. What symptoms of stress do they experience—talking aloud, nightmares, panic attacks?
2. 11/21	2.0	1,000	I need to find articles and research authorities in the library. I should start with *PsycLit* and the *Social Science Citation Index.*
3. 11/25	4.0	750	Need to read the 10 articles I collected yesterday. Perhaps I should experiment with the double-entry format discussed in *Becoming an Academic Writer.*
4. 11/27	.30	1,000	Finish taking notes from sources in double-entry format.
5. 11/28	3.0	2,000, wrote first draft	I want to interview some students in my dorm. I should ask Julie and Dave how their counseling is helping them get over the stress.
6. 11/29	2.0	1,000, integrated interviews into report	I want to get Julie and Dave to read this draft. That way I can see if I represented their ideas fairly.
7. 12/1	1.0	3,000	Have draft reviewed by peers in class.
8. 12/3	2.00	2,700, edited earlier draft for economy	Need to check to see that my sources are cited correctly. Can readers clearly determine when I am quoting, paraphrasing, and citing sources?
9. 12/5	1.0	2,500 = final word count	Need to edit final draft and submit for grading.

revising (see Sample Writing and Research Goals). Because writing is typically not a step-by-step process, you will probably want to routinely revise your goals for research, writing, and anticipated due dates. To help develop a realistic schedule, you may find it useful to ask the following questions.

1. How much time can I spend on selecting a topic?

2. When will I have identified the major sources that I will need to consult before writing a solid draft? What sources may be difficult to obtain?

3. When can I develop a tentative description of my communication situation?

Freewriting and Self-reflexive Writing

In this section you can freewrite about any subjects that you choose, including *self-reflexive writing*, or writing about writing. Psychologists and composition theorists have found that writing about the problems we are experiencing with different writing projects and writing about specific revising goals can be a powerful way to overcome blocks and improve as writers. Below are a few questions that may help you gain insight into counterproductive writing behaviors.

1. What changes can you make in your life that will help you accomplish your writing goals? How can you schedule more time to write?

Sample of Writing and Research Goals

Tentative Title: Chill Out! Seven Proven Techniques for Overcoming Stress

Tentative Purpose: Identify ways to overcome stress.

Tentative Audience: College students

Peer Support: Do I know someone who might have some interesting information about the subject? Who would be a good critic of any of my drafts?

Schedule for Completing Drafts: Week 1, complete library research. Week 2, complete reading essays and books and taking notes in double-entry form. Write a rough draft. Week 3, interview some friends with the literature review in mind. Write a second draft. Week 4, have solid draft reviewed by peers in class. Edit for economy and submit report for grading.

2. What are your writing "rituals"? What is the best time of day for you to write? Where do you like to write? The crowded cafeteria? The quiet study? How does your writing space influence your writing? Have you ensured that you have the materials on hand necessary to do your rituals?

3. What changes can you make in your environment that will help you achieve your writing goals?

4. What self-talk can you identify that intrudes on your productivity? For example, does a small voice within you whisper that your ideas lack originality, or that the teacher or editor will dislike your manuscript? Do you tell yourself that you lack the time or ability necessary to get the work done?

5. What social supports can you establish to promote regular writing? Can you arrange, for example, to discuss ideas for writing projects with informed friends? Do the people whom you live with respect your need for quiet time when developing projects? Do you know people who can provide you with encouragement when you are feeling discouraged about the worthiness or potential of an idea?

6. What myths about writing or scholarly research do you hold that intrude on regular writing? What changes in *how* you write will help you achieve your writing goals?

7. How is regular writing influencing your attitude about yourself as a writer? Or, if you're having difficulty writing regularly, why do you think this is so?

8. How has rejection in the past influenced your perception of yourself as a writer? How has the fear of rejection influenced what you write about?

9. In what ways do you attempt to work with your intuition when writing? If an unrelated thought occurs to you when you are writing, do you try to ignore the thought or do you pursue it and question how and if it relates, after all, to your subject? When revising, are you willing to reject what you have written and start fresh with a new organization or a new thought as necessary?

Reading Notes and Thoughtful Excerpts

In this section you can keep a record of the memorable and intriguing quotations that you come across in your reading. If you have read any other guidelines for academic writing, then you probably know that textbook authors commonly recommend that you keep reading notes and bibliographical references on 4-by-6-inch cards. The great advantage of using cards is that they can be shuffled and reordered as you organize your manuscript.

However, as an alternative to the card system, you can make photocopies of any material you expect to use in your final draft. This will allow you to reread the essays and highlight key points at your convenience. Of course, to save money, to avoid being overwhelmed by material, and to get you thinking seriously about your topic, you need to be selective about which resources are worth photocopying.

Using the Double-entry Form. One very effective technique for avoiding note-bound prose is to respond to powerful quotations in what writing theorist Ann Berthoff calls the *double-entry notebook form.* As you can see from the following sample, the double-entry form shows the direct quotation on the left side of the page and your response to it on the right. There are two advantages to this technique: first, it helps you think about your subject; second, it helps you step away from your sources and discover your own approach and voice.

They [i.e. creative ideas] may indeed occur at times of relaxation, or in fantasy, or at other times when we alternate play with work. But what is entirely clear is that they pertain to those areas in which the person consciously has worked laboriously and with dedication. *Purpose* in the human being is a much more complex phenomenon than what used to be called will power. Purpose involves all levels of experience. We cannot *will* to have insights. We cannot *will* creativity. But we can *will* to give ourselves to the encounter with intensity of dedication and commitment. The deeper aspects of awareness are activated to the extent that the person is committed to the encounter.
Rollo May, *The Courage to Create*, 46

I'm absolutely certain that Rollo May is right: total involvement in the "encounter" of the creative process is crucial for the emergence of the Eureka moment.

Unfortunately, I think, too many people are too uncomfortable about the intrusion of the disruptive "right brain" or "unconscious." They dislike the creative process because of the fear of chaos and of failure.

How, then, can we encourage people to "submerge" themselves, to lose themselves in an idea or feeling, long enough to experience the Gestalt, the felt sense, the joy, the bliss, the *jouissance?* If students could only experience this passion for the creative process, they would learn that writing is not a boring, mechanical process of filling in completed thoughts into preestablished modes of discourse.

New Writing and Research Ideas

The heart of a successful notebook, this is the place for you to keep a record of your best ideas. Rather than ignoring the innovative ideas for new writing projects that occur when you are in the middle of another assignment you can keep a record of your new ideas in this section.

Your thoughts about your subject are likely to change as you read more about your subject, discuss your ideas with peers and your teacher, freewrite ideas about your topic, and write preliminary drafts. Even if you begin with a solid idea about what you want to say and how you want to say it, you should be willing to sabotage your plans if more fruitful ideas come your way and sufficient time remains to develop them. In addition, you may have insights about how you are actually researching or writing your document. For example, while writing a paragraph on page 8 of a research study, you realize that the way you phrased your research question in your journal or in an earlier draft of your report no longer accurately reflects your intentions. It's okay to restate your thesis to keep pace with what you're learning.

The Latest Drafts of Your Reports

Because innovative ideas about your subject and ways to structure your report may occur when you are not working on the project, you should always keep your notebook handy and your notebook should always contain the most recent draft of your documents. Whenever insights occur or you find yourself with some unexpected spare time, you can record and revise conveniently.

Thought-provoking Articles

After you have been maintaining a notebook for a short while, it will be bulging at the seams and you will need to remove unimportant material and file it in another appropriate place. Although you will not have space to store many outside articles, you may want to keep one or two of the most helpful articles in your notebook so that you can get to them easily when you are looking for inspiration. Ultimately, however, you will probably find it more useful to file articles and printed documents in their own three-ring binders or file folders.

A Working Bibliography

Because you will need to list the references that you have consulted in a bibliography at the end of any researched document, you should carefully keep track of the sources you use while conducting research. It can be quite annoying and frustrating to be forced, after completing your research and writing, to return to the card catalog or periodical shelves to retrieve the information you need to properly cite these works. This frustration intensifies when you discover that other people have subsequently checked out your materials.

As soon as possible, check to ensure that you understand the form of documentation that you will need to follow. (See Chapter 2 for a review of the Modern Language Association [MLA] style for documenting sources.) Then be sure that you record on the copy of the photocopied material all of the bibliographical facts that you will need to cite in the bibliography—such as the author's name, the journal name and volume number, or the book title name and publisher; the city and date of publication, if available; and the page numbers. Fortunately, in most scholarly journals and some commercial magazines, this information is already printed on the title page of each essay. If it isn't, you had better record it now; otherwise, you may need to retrace your steps.

A Record of Humorous Anecdotes

When I hear or read something that I think is funny, I often write it down. I generally keep this notebook section for my own amusement, but I do enjoy sharing these anecdotes with friends and students. For example, here are two entries that I wrote this morning after hearing them on the radio:

> In Seattle, Washington, last night a criminal was arrested for breaking and entering. Apparently the criminal broke into a furniture store and then he fell asleep on a recliner. In the morning, the employees took the gun out of the criminal's hand and then called the police.

> On the border of Mexico and Texas last night, two criminals were arrested for possession of cocaine. Apparently, the criminals had so much cocaine that their car was riding on its axle.

A Record of Powerful Dreams

Many people keep a record of their dreams because they believe that dreams tap their unconscious and can help them identify and solve problems. While discovering earth-shattering ideas in your dreams may seem as improbable as a subplot from a Star Trek movie, you may find recording your dreams to be a surprisingly useful writing activity, as do these celebrated authors:

> Dreams have been useful in my writing as springboards for creativity. Upon awakening, I reach for a pad and pencil lying on the bedside table and record what I can remember.
>
> *Milli Frisch Meyer*

> I dream a lot of dreams and most of them are comic and I wake up laughing. But I've dreamed many nights the next scene of a novel I'd been working on, in great detail, even dialogue and details. One time just in a couple of dreams (which solved a novel) and in my last one, almost every night for months, full dreams, half-dreams between sleep and waking, or in a kind of daze. It's nice to get to the typewriter with half your work done.
>
> *Robert Penn Warren*

> The waking mind, you see, is the least serviceable in the arts. In the process of writing one is struggling to bring out what is unknown to himself. To put down merely what one is conscious of means nothing, really gets one

nowhere. Anybody can do that with a little practice, anybody can become that kind of writer.

Henry Miller

Since you are probably accustomed to ignoring dreams, you may have some difficulty remembering them, let alone recording them. There are a few procedures you can follow to train yourself to recall dreams. First, keep a notebook by your bed and remind yourself when you go to bed to remember your dream in the morning. Then, when you wake up, do not open your eyes. Instead, concentrate on remembering as much as possible of your dream. Without trying to interpret it, record everything that you can remember from your dream.

A Collection of Powerful Metaphors

If you, like me, want to incorporate more figurative language into your prose, you may find it useful to keep a collection of compelling metaphors that you come across in your daily reading. For example, this image struck me when I came across it recently:

> Should we worry about protecting some insignificant plants and insects when we need to feed, clothe, and house our own species? The truth is, like mountaineers roped together on a steep cliff, we depend utterly on the survival of other species.

G. Jon Roush

I recorded it in my "Metaphors" section, for use whenever or wherever I may need it.

Categorizing Your Notebook

There is nothing sacred about the categories for organizing a Writing and Research Notebook. For instance, you may not want to keep a section that records funny moments in your life. You may, instead, want to dedicate your energies to understanding a decision that you need to make—notes and plans and thoughts related to a certain career choice, for instance.

Every writer needs to select the categories that will help him or her develop personally meaningful questions and pursuits. For example, here are the alphabetical categories of F. Scott Fitzgerald's notebooks: (A) Anecdotes; (B) Bright Clippings; (C) Conversation and Things Overheard; (D) Description of Things and Atmosphere; (E) Epigrams, Wise Cracks and Jokes; (F) Feelings & Emotions (without girls); (G) Descriptions of Girls; (H) Descriptions of Humanity (Physical); (I) Ideas; (J) Jingles and Songs; (K) Karacters; (L) Literary; (M) Moments (What people do); (N) Nonsense and Stray Phrases; (O) Observations; (P) Proper Names; (R) Rough Stuff; (S) Scenes and Situations; (T) Titles; (U) Unclassified; (V) Vernacular; (W) Work References; (Y) Youth and Army.

As you can see, Fitzgerald's categories are entirely different from the ones that I have suggested. Ultimately, you need to develop the categories that will help organize and stimulate your thinking. If you are interested in developing your own personality and in understanding and overcoming your limitations, you may find it helpful to consult Ira Progoff's provocative and innovative book *At a Journal Workshop.* Progoff provides detailed guidelines for establishing categories for writing that are designed to help people set goals and develop self-understanding. Examples of his categories include,

Dialogue with Works	Working with Our Dreams
Dialogue with the Body	Dialogue with Society
Dialogue with Events	Inner Wisdom Dialogue
Situations and Circumstances	Now: The Open Moment

Here are some of the categories that students in my classes have used in their journals:

School	Advertisements
Jobs	In-Class Writing
Places of Interest	Responses to In-Class Activities
Events of Interest	Powerful Life Conclusions
Personalities of Myself and Others	(brought on by personal
Insecurities	experience)
Sports and Leisure	Responses to Reading
Family and Friends	Conversations
Moral and Social Issues	Movie Reviews
Descriptions of Class Members	Death
Research Topics	Poetry
Women/Men	Significant Quotes
Movies	

Although the thought of maintaining a Writing and Research Notebook may at first appear intimidating, you will probably be surprised to find that it is actually quite easy to keep one on a day-by-day basis. In the dozens of writing classes that I have taught over the past ten years, I can report that only one or two students each semester dislike the discipline. Indeed, the following comments are fairly representative of how most students feel after keeping a notebook for a semester:

> Writing these entries has helped me to remember important events from my childhood that I was not aware were buried in my subconscious; in particular, I have thought of several special moments that I shared with my maternal grandmother and have made a record of them. I now have a written record and can reread them years from now when perhaps my memory becomes faulty, and I am no longer able to recall them with ease.

Another bonus of journal writing is the discipline it has imposed on me to write frequently. I enjoy writing, but I have always found excuses not to do so because I allowed other responsibilities to take precedence. Since journal writing has been a class requirement, its importance has been elevated because I see it as an obligation (not a negative).

Do you ever notice how important something seemed to you in high school and now that you look back on that you think, "God, I sure acted stupid back then!"? Doesn't it sort of make you wonder if what you consider important now is really stupid, especially if you were to look back on it in say, 10 years? What then is truly important?

Journal writing has helped me get a better perspective on my life and problems.

I used the journal to let out emotions and thoughts. The journal was like a person I would talk to whenever I needed someone to talk to.

I used my journal to help myself study for exams in other subjects. This is something I never used to do—take notes on chapters—and I found it to help.

I think the more you write, the more you enjoy it, the more easily you can come up with ideas.

I've learned that I have a lot of hidden opinions and feelings about issues that I usually don't get a chance to express. Consequently, in this class, I have an outlet to express my ideas in a creative and structured way. By writing a little each day, I am able to think more about what I feel which, in turn, helps me to become a better writer.

Maintaining a Writing and Research Notebook can help you write regularly, set goals, establish priorities, and organize your scholarly endeavors. If you tend to be a disorganized writer, the notebook can provide an invaluable focus for creative ideas. Although you can succeed without such a notebook, maintaining one can give you some control over what and how you write.

CHAPTER TWO

How to Use the Library and Document Sources

For some student writers, the word "research" is associated with tedious hours in the library pursuing a boring topic. However, conducting research can be a rewarding adventure—an excellent, ongoing way to develop new ideas and research questions.

As repositories of our collective knowledge, libraries offer fertile ground for hunting and gathering ideas. Admittedly, the tremendous amount of information in modern libraries can be overwhelming, particularly if you are just becoming accustomed to the research process. Actually doing the writing—that is, synthesizing ideas from all of those different sources by developing a voice and purpose—is already tough enough, and when combined with the task of finding suitable sources, it can truly feel overwhelming. Yet you can reduce not only the amount of time and effort it takes to research material but also your anxiety about the research process by familiarizing yourself with the tools of the library.

Venturing into unknown territory, you need a compass and survival tools. This chapter introduces the tools you will need to explore information in research libraries using a variety of reference materials, such as encyclopedias, bibliographies, periodical indexes, the card catalog, and on-line and CD-ROM computer indexes.

Strategies for Gathering Research Material

The first step in any writing project is determining a specific topic. To help narrow your topic, you may find it useful to gather some general background information. This process can help you locate some valuable sources to consult. To obtain a few essential facts and to gain a sense of the "dialogue" that is transpiring among scholars and researchers about your topic, try consulting general encyclopedias and dictionaries, or, if appropriate, specialized encyclopedias and dictionaries. Of course, because college instructors tend to frown on research studies that merely summarize encyclopedia entries, you will want to avoid relying heavily on encyclopedias. Nevertheless, when beginning a research project, reading one succinct entry in an encyclopedia—such as the *Encyclopedia Britannica, Encyclopedia Americana,* or *Collier's Encyclopedia*—can save you tremendous time. Rather than poring through a stack of books to get a general sense of the scope of your topic, you will find in encyclopedias and dictionaries concise summaries of significant facts, experiments, and theories related to your subject. Also, general and specialized encyclopedias and dictionaries often list important works and bibliographies, thereby providing you with solid preliminary leads for further research. To access the information available in a general encyclopedia, check the encyclopedia's subject index. To determine whether an encyclopedia or dictionary is published on your subject, check the card catalog. Below is a list of a few popular specialized encyclopedias and dictionaries.

> *Black's Law Dictionary*
> *Dictionary of the History of Ideas*
> *Encyclopedia of Banking and Finance*
> *Encyclopedia of Pop, Rock, and Soul*
> *Harper Dictionary of Modern Thought*

To obtain specific facts and figures that are based on the United States Census and other demographic research, consult the *Statistical Abstract of the United States.* On a broader scale *The World Almanac* can also provide invaluable data. If you need to find information about a person's background, try consulting *Biography and Genealogy Master Index* or *Biographical Dictionaries.*

Finding a bibliography—a listing of what has been published on a subject—can be a terrific timesaver. As a result, it is definitely worth your effort to check the *Bibliographic Index,* which is designed to refer researchers to bibliographies or books that have bibliographies in them. Because the *Bibliographic Index* does not provide a cumulative listing of bibliographies, however, you may need to review several past years to find bibliographies related to your topic. Also, once you find one relevant article or book that contains a bibliography, you can always follow up on its sources. A third way to find bibliographies on your topic is to check the subject card in the card catalog and select books that include bibliographies.

Using the Card Catalog

You can hunt for information on your topic by consulting the card catalog. In many modern libraries, the bulky file drawers containing the 3-by-5-inch cards have been replaced by space-saving computer terminals. Regardless of how the information is stored, all card catalogs list books in three different ways: (1) according to the author's name; (2) according to the title of the book; and (3) according to the subject under which the book is categorized. If you are unsure about which subject headings your topic is likely to be listed under, you can check the *Library of Congress Subject Headings* (LCSH), generally located near the card catalog.

Although the information on the author, subject, and title cards is roughly the same, the advantage of working with subject cards is that these cards contain a list of other subject categories under which a given book is listed. Consequently, you can consult these other subjects to obtain more titles—that is, more books—on your subject. Also, subject cards tell you whether particular books contain a bibliography of sources on your subject.

Consulting Periodicals, Indexes, and Abstracts

If your subject addresses a contemporary issue, then you should rely more on periodicals—that is, contemporary magazines, newspapers, and scholarly journals—than on books. To discover articles on your subject among the thousands of magazines and journals published each year, you can consult periodical indexes. When you are unsure about the best reference works for your specific subject, consult *Ulrich's International Periodicals Directory*. This volume contains a comprehensive list of the periodicals that are available in the various fields. Additional resources to consult for periodicals are Sheehy's *Guide to Reference Books* or Katz's *Magazines for Libraries* or McCormick's *The New York Times Guide to Reference Materials*.

Periodical indexes are reference books that contain lists of citations to articles in specific periodicals. For example, if you are pursuing a popular subject, you can review the *Reader's Guide to Periodical Literature* to find whether any articles on your subject have been published in over a hundred popular magazines. But if you are writing about a more specialized or academic topic, you may need to find the periodical index that references the journals and magazines in which your subject is likely to appear. Such indexes include the following:

Accountants' Index
Applied Science and Technology Index
Art Index
Biography Index
Biological and Agricultural Index
Book Review Index
The Business Index
Business Periodicals Index
Comprehensive Dissertation Abstract Index
Criminology Index
Current Index to Journals in Education

Education Index
Engineering Index
Environment Abstracts and Index
Essay and General Literature Index
Humanities Index
Index to Legal Periodicals
Music Index
New York Times Index
The Newspaper Index
The Philosopher's Index
Psychological Abstracts

Using Computerized Databases*

Computerized databases may be the most exciting innovation in library science since the invention of the printing press. Essentially, via computer modems, on-line indexes can put you in touch with countless essays, books, pamphlets, and statistics. Presently, you can consult over 500 on-line databases. For example, if you have access to either *InfoTrac* or *The Magazine Index*, which are on-line periodical indexes, you can use effective *descriptors*— that is, subject categories—to command the computer to search through over a thousand contemporary magazines and generate a list of essays on your subject.

In turn, CD-ROM (compact disc–read only memory) indexes resemble the on-line versions except that the information is stored on CDs, thereby enabling users to sidestep the $35–150 hourly charge for on-line databases like *Chemical Abstracts*. CDs, which were introduced in 1983, can store as many as 550 million characters, or the equivalent of 275,000 double-spaced typed pages.

If you have never used the CD-ROM indexes, then you will probably come away shocked and delighted by their potential. Rather than shuffling through mountains of books and periodicals and becoming distracted by tangential or irrelevant ideas, you can sift through a world of information in minutes by accessing the appropriate databases. CD-ROM databases allow you to print the full bibliographic citation for published materials. In addition, many of the databases provide excellent abstracts, which can also be printed and which allow you to determine whether a particular source will be useful to you. Also, many of the CD-ROM databases allow you to save the results of your research on a floppy disk so that you can take this information home and review it in the quiet and peace of your office (provided, of course, that you have an IBM-compatible computer system that uses DOS).

Although they differ in searching procedures, most databases require you to guide the search by selecting specific descriptors. For example, to find the most appropriate descriptors for ERIC (Educational Resources Information Center), you should consult the *Thesaurus of ERIC Descriptors*. Fortunately, many databases use the same vocabulary of descriptors as those provided in *The Library of Congress Subject Headings*, and there are some similarities among systems regarding searching procedures. *Online Searching: A Dictionary and Bibliographic Guide* offers a comprehensive review and exhaustive glossary of terms that are now used by on-line and CD-ROM databases. Incidentally, if you wish to sidestep the process of identifying a list of descriptors—that is, synonyms for each concept that you hope to research—

*The material on how to use CD-ROM databases is adapted from "Why Use Computerized Databases?" *Writing and Publishing for Academic Authors*. Ed. Joseph M. Moxley. Lanham, MD: University Press of America. Copyright 1992 by University Press of America. Reprinted by permission.

you can try a general search by introducing a particular subject or author's name. For example, if you use the word "ethnography" as a general term, the database will offer a thousand or so entries of sources that use that term in the title or abstract. By randomly reviewing a few of these references, you can note what descriptors these titles are filed under.

As you take advantage of on-line and CD-ROM indexes to lighten the load of conducting research, you will sometimes feel as if you have an army of research assistants working for you. For example, within seconds the *Social Science Citation Index* allows you to find all of the essays, books, or book reviews that have been written on a particular subject. You can then limit the scope of your search (or, as librarians would call it, your set) by requesting only those published materials that have appeared in certain journals or years. Once you have narrowed your subject, you can then take a look at each entry. This step will provide you with information regarding the full bibliographical context for each given book, essay, or review. In addition—and I know this is hard to believe—you will be told how many times this particular essay or book or review has been quoted by other scholars. Then, if you wish, you can review what these other scholars have had to say about this particular source. In addition, you will be told how many references this particular source used. And most remarkable, within seconds you can also take a look at each of these references to determine whether or not you would like to review these additional sources. Given the remarkable capabilities of CD-ROM databases, you can see why more and more researchers depend on them to locate all of the essays written by a particular scholar or to determine what studies are being referred to most frequently or to obtain a complete listing of all of the articles on a subject that have been cited in prominent journals.

Because they are a relatively recent invention, CD-ROM databases are often less comprehensive than their on-line counterparts. Yet if your subject addresses a relatively recent issue, you should probably use the CD-ROM version because it will not cost you money and because you will get immediate results. In other words, you can immediately print the abstracts and citations that are likely to be of use to you.

If your research is in a very specific area for which your library has no databases, you should consult *CD-ROMS in Print: An International Guide*, compiled by Norman Desmarais (Meckler Corporation, Westport, CT 06880). You can count on most modern research libraries to have the following popular CD-ROM databases available:

> *ABI/Inform* provides the citations and abstracts of articles from over 800 business and management journals. Coverage: 1971 to present.
> *Compact Disclosure* can provide you with financial and management information on over 12,000 public companies. This information is extracted from annual and periodic reports filed with the Securities and Exchange Commission.

Compendex Plus provides bibliographic citations and abstracts from the world's significant engineering and technological literature. It includes journals, books, and selected government reports. Coverage: 1986 to present.

Dissertation Abstracts International contains bibliographic citations and abstracts of doctoral dissertations as well as some master's theses completed at over 500 North American and many European universities. Coverage: 1980 to present.

ERIC contains bibliographic citations and abstracts of journal articles and documents (conference papers, reports, government documents) on educational subjects and related topics in the social sciences. Coverage: 1971 to present.

MLA International Bibliography provides bibliographical data on 3,000 journals, monographs, and book collections on scholarship in literature and modern languages.

NTIS is an index to government-sponsored research, development, and engineering plus analyses prepared by federal agencies, their contractors, or grantees. Coverage: 1980 to present.

PsycLIT contains bibliographic citations and abstracts of journal articles in psychology and related subjects. Coverage: 1974 to present.

Science Citation Index is an index to the journal literature of the sciences covering 3,300 journals across 100 scientific disciplines. Coverage: 1985 to present.

Social Science Citation Index is an index to the journal literature of the social sciences covering 1,400 journals across 50 disciplines. Coverage: 1986 to present.

Using Current Contents

Another recent innovation in library research is *Current Contents* on diskette. Like its printed version, *Current Contents* allows you to review the tables of contents of thousands of scholarly journals. Thus, within seconds, you can learn whether editorials, letters, reviews, or articles have been written on your subject. Also, like the CD-ROM databases, *Current Contents* provides full bibliographic descriptions of all indexed articles. For your convenience, you can also print these materials or save them to a floppy disk, and review them on your own PC.

Government Publications

You may also find it useful to discover whether the United States Government Printing Office (GPO) has published any research reports, pamphlets, or statistics on your subject. The GPO, along with United Nations organizations, prints countless essays, pamphlets, and research studies on the law, history, and such everyday subjects as growing herb gardens. To determine whether the government has published useful information on your subject, try consulting any of the following indexes in the Government Documents Section of your library: *The Monthly Catalog to the United States Government Publications*, the *Public Affairs Information Service Bulletin*, or the *American Statistics Index*.

Serendipity

Finally, you should not overlook the role of luck in the research process. After you have consulted the card catalog and have located your book in the stacks, take a moment to browse. Sometimes surprisingly useful sources come about as a result of good fortune.

Don't be embarrassed to seek help from librarians. Throughout the research process, feel free to consult with librarians as well as with your teacher. Of course, librarians are busy professionals, and you cannot expect them to do your research for you. But they are trained to help you find all of the sources that you will need.

MLA Conventions for Documenting Sources

Most of your professors will expect you to follow the conventions for documenting sources established by the Modern Language Association (MLA). By studying the following MLA guidelines you learn how to document books and articles written or edited by single or multiple authors and how to document sources from newspapers, popular magazines, and interviews with authors. Although this information will become most important to you in the final stages of writing a paper, you should be aware of these conventions in the preliminary stages of conducting research so that you can record all the information you will need to successfully complete your report.

According to the MLA style, you should place quotation marks around direct quotations that are less than five lines long and weave these excerpts into the language of the text. Rather than using footnote numbers and requiring a reader to flip to a bibliography section in the back of the essay or to look at a footnote at the bottom of the page to find the author of the source, you are expected to provide in parentheses the name of the author or the source that you are citing in your text, along with the page number of the quotation. When the author's name is unavailable, use the name of the government agency or the title of the work. Below, these and additional special considerations are explained so that you will know how to cite sources in the body of your text. This discussion is followed by guidelines for constructing a Works Cited section, which you are expected to provide at the conclusion of your report.

Although I have attempted to address most of the problems that students face when writing research reports, the following is still an incomplete account of the MLA conventions and formats for documenting sources. You may need to refer to the *MLA Handbook for Writers of Research Papers, Third Edition*, edited by Joseph Gibaldi and Walter S. Achert, for more specific information. For additional information about when to offer direct quotes and how to summarize and paraphrase secondary sources, see Chapter 8.

How to Document Sources in Your Text

Single Author Format. As illustrated in the following examples, you can mention the author's name as part of your discussion or you can place the author's name in parentheses along with the page number of the original source immediately following the cited material.

1. Place short direct quotations in quotation marks and put the author's name and page number in parentheses.

   Example: "A typical adult needs about eight hours of shut-eye a night to function effectively. By that standard, millions of Americans are chronically sleep deprived, trying to get by on six hours or even less" (Toufexis 79).

Note that there is no comma separating the author's name from the page number of the quotation. Further, the documentation—that is, the author's name and source page number—appears outside the quotation marks but inside the period that closes the sentence.

Because critical readers tend to be skeptical, they might wonder who Toufexis is and on what research she states her claim. If so, these readers could flip to the Works Cited section at the end of your report and discover that Toufexis' essay appeared in *Time* magazine, which clearly goes a long way in establishing her credibility. However, you could save your reader this trouble and help establish your source as credible by providing Toufexis's name and some background about the scope and nature of her essay, as illustrated in the following format and example.

2. Use the author's name in your text along with the quoted material; put only the page numbers for the quotation in parentheses. To promote the author's credibility, mention any pertinent institutional affiliations (such as universities or magazines) or degrees (such as M.D. or Ph.D.) inside the text.

   Example: According to Anastasia Toufexis, a writer for *Time* magazine, "millions of Americans are chronically sleep deprived" because they try to get by on six hours rather than eight hours (79).

Format for Citing Paraphrased or Summarized Material. As explained in detail in Chapter 8, you will often want to paraphrase or summarize secondary sources. It is usually better to paraphrase—that is, to communicate someone else's ideas in your own words—than to directly quote authority after authority. Merely retyping direct quotation after direct quotation proves only that you can type (or hire a good typist). Essays with extensive direct quotations tend to lack vigor, clarity, or originality. In addition, you will sometimes find it useful to summarize the gist of an entire book or article.

Whenever you paraphrase or summarize, you want to be extremely careful that your reader is aware that you are indebted to the secondary source. You can acknowledge your indebtedness by mentioning the name of the author or by placing the author's (or authors') name(s) in parentheses near the information that you have paraphrased.

> **Example:** Many adult Americans would probably be surprised to know that they are endangering their health by sleeping less than eight hours a night (Toufexis).

Anonymous Author Format. Even when the author of a source is unknown, you can still acknowledge your reliance on other works, as illustrated by the following examples. Place a shortened version of the title either in the text or in parentheses near the information that you have paraphrased. When directly quoting, you do not need to put a comma between the title and page number when the title appears in the parentheses.

> **Example:** Indeed, tropical rainforests have given us many of the everyday items we take for granted. "One in four prescription drugs is derived from rainforest species, including 70% of known anticancer agents" ("Facts" 3). Drugs to control childhood leukemia, Hodgkin's disease, malaria, hypertension, heart ailments, and arthritis come from rainforest species as do irreplaceable anesthetics for serious surgery and birth control medicines ("Facts").

> **Example:** According to an article on "Ecosystems" that appeared in the *Encyclopedia Britannica*, a rainforest is determined by the location and its level of rainfall. The rainforests are found in the "seasonless tropics" (1031) where it is always hot and moist, and they commonly receive over 70 inches of rain per year. These two factors are present in South America, Africa, and South East Asia, and rainforests have flourished there virtually untouched for 60 million years (1031).

When using the title instead of an author's name, remember to place quotation marks around titles of articles and underline the titles of books, periodicals, and newspapers.

Two Author Format. Whenever a source has two authors, you can place both authors' names either in the text or in parentheses, as illustrated in the following examples:

Example: The Greenhouse effect is likely to change rainfall patterns, raise sea levels 4 to 7 feet by the year 2100, and increase the world's mean temperature 2.7 to 8 degrees Fahrenheit by the year 2050 (Brown and Flavin 16).

Example: Brown and Flavin assert that the Greenhouse effect is likely to change rainfall patterns, raise sea levels 4 to 7 feet by the year 2100, and increase the world's mean temperature 2.7 to 8 degrees Fahrenheit by the year 2050 (16).

Three or More Author Format. For sources written by three or more people, you should name only the first author followed by the abbreviation "et al.," which means "and others."

Example: A similar and earlier study of British students' writing samples, completed by James Britton et al., suggested that British students' academic opportunities for creative expression diminish as students grow older.

Documenting Sources from Governments and Corporations. Although there are some differences in how you list government and corporate sources in your Works Cited section, the in-text references are essentially the same as for authors. Use the name of the sponsoring corporation or the governmental body just as you would use the name(s) of the author(s) of a text.

Example: Independent research studies suggest that non-ionizing electromagnetic fields may cause or promote cancer (New York State Power Lines Project; Wertheimer and Leeper; Milham; Finnish Cancer Registry).

Material That Has Been Edited, Translated, or Compiled. When you are citing material that has been edited, compiled, or translated, you should mention the author's name in your text or in parentheses and supply appropriate page references. Credit is given the individuals who revised, edited, translated, or compiled the material in your Works Cited section, but not in the text body or text citations.

Example: According to Abraham Maslow, "All people in our society (with a few pathological exceptions) have a need or desire for a stable, firmly based, usually high evaluation of themselves, for self-respect or self-esteem, and for the esteem of others" (21).

Quoting Secondary Sources. When conducting research, you will routinely come across quotations in your sources that would be useful to cite in your report as well. When this occurs, do your best to obtain the original source to ensure that it was quoted or paraphrased accurately. For example, if you were reading Abraham Maslow's seminal text *Motivation and Personality* and were struck by a thought-provoking excerpt from a work by Freud or an interesting paraphrase of a study by Freud, you would be wise to check a translation of Freud's piece to ensure that Maslow had cited or paraphrased him properly. Taken to the extreme, a truly rigorous scholar would check Freud's original work in German. Naturally, following this research trail can be time-consuming, yet this is the only way that you can be absolutely sure that you are not misinterpreting an original source. Information can obviously become diluted and transformed when it passes from person to person.

Of course, time limitations and problems securing original sources often prevent us from being so rigorous. In addition, sometimes the quotations we want to repeat are unavailable in written form, such as when the author has interviewed authorities or conducted a survey of attitudes. As a result, we will sometimes need to rely on "secondary source material." Fortunately, the MLA guidelines permit us to account for secondary sources by using the abbreviations "qtd. in" for "quoted in." Place the "qtd. in" abbreviation in parentheses with the page number and name of the author of the source that you are citing.

> **Example:** According to David Dinges, a psychologist at the University of Pennsylvania, "Human error causes between 60% and 90% of all workplace accidents, depending on the type of job. And inadequate sleep is a major factor in human error, at least as important as drugs, alcohol and equipment failure" (qtd. in Toufexis 78–79).

Power Quoting Format. In order to demonstrate that they have read widely or that numerous scholars believe the same thing to be true, authors often cite more than one source to support a single point. Separate the different citations with semicolons and place these references either inside the text or parenthetically outside the text.

> **Example:** Using the *Shostrom Personality Orientation Index,* Seeman, Nidlich and Banta; Nidlich, Seeman and Dreskin; and Hjelle found a two month change in meditators with respect to positive improvement in self-actualization, spontaneity, and self-acceptance. Hjelle found anxiety decreases on the *Bendig Scale* as did Lazar, Farwell and Farrow. . . . Replications using the same test with the same results have also been made (Davis; Nidich, Seeman, and Seibert; Stern; and Kory and Hufnagel).[47]

Incidentally, although quoting multiple sources to drive home a point can be an impressive indicator of thorough research, this technique can backfire on you. After all, a long list of authors' names isn't terribly readable. Moreover, if many authors have said or found the same thing to be true, you should consider whether this information can be taken as part of the general knowledge of your field. Finally, if by oversimplifying you lump researchers together who would in fact disagree with each other, then an educated reader would find you guilty of misrepresentation—or, worse yet, of reductionism.

Multiple Works by a Single Author Format. When you cite multiple works by the same author (or authors), you can identify which source you are paraphrasing or quoting by incorporating the author's name and a short version of the title of the work you are citing in the text and placing the page number in parentheses following the reference. Or you could provide all of this information in the parentheses.

> **Example:** Paul Brodeur, a staff writer at *The New Yorker* for 31 years and author of *Currents of Death: Power Lines, Computer Terminals and the Attempt to Cover Up Their Threat to Your Health* (Simon and Schuster) recently argued that "millions of Americans are still at risk" because of the dangers of low-level electromagnetic radiation:
>
>> Evidence is building that exposure to low-level electromagnetic radiation that is given off by power lines, electric blankets, video display terminals (VDTs) and even some electric clocks can cause cancer, birth defects, miscarriages and other health problems. ("Hidden" 9)
>
> **Example:** Brodeur further asserts that school administrators would be wise to put some thought into how computers are placed in classrooms:
>
>> The students should sit no closer than 28 inches from the front of their screens. *Reason:* Some VDTs—particularly large, color modes—emit strong magnetic fields close to the screen.
>>
>> Great care also should be taken that children sit at least three or four feet from the *sides* and *backs* of neighboring VDTs. The fields that radiate out the sides and backs of VDTs are even stronger than those given off by the screens. ("Protect Yourself" 11)

Note that because the above two examples are longer than five lines, they are placed in "block quotation" format, and the parenthetical source information is placed outside the closing period.

Block Quote Format. If your quotation is five or more lines long, then you need to set it off from your text. Indent the quotation ten spaces from the left margin, double-space the lines, and provide the citation in parentheses at the end.

> **Example:**
>
>> One of the most surprising recent discoveries concerns the sleep needs of adolescents. For years they were urged to get eight hours, the same as adults. No longer. Teenagers appear to require more than 9 1/2 hours. Carskadon found that to be the case when she studied a group of children every summer for seven years from the time they were ages 10 to 12 until they turned 17 to 19. During the experiments, the youngsters got 9 1/2 hours of sleep each night. In the beginning years of the study, they experienced no problems during the day, but after they reached puberty there was an increase in daytime sleepiness. (Toufexis 82–83)

Block quotations do not require opening and closing quotation marks. If you are quoting an entire paragraph, you may indent the first line. As mentioned above, the documentation—that is, the author's name and page numbers—appears outside the period that ends the block quotation, with no period following the parentheses.

Field Research Format. Interviewing authorities, surveying attitudes and behaviors, listening to music or watching television, conducting laboratory research, or observing events—these can all be forms of original "field" research, which require a different form of documentation from that used to cite printed material.

By weaving into your text some explanation of what you have done or observed when you were "in the field" generating original source material, you will avoid confusing your reader. For example, if you have interviewed a local surgeon at his office to investigate the costs and benefits of attending medical school, you should inform your readers of this in the text of your report. Likewise, if you measured the level of acidity in rain water outside your dorm room to provide additional information for your essay on acid rain, you should explain your strategy. Moreover, if you listened to ten best-selling contemporary CDs to research conceptions of modern love, you should tell your reader which songs and artists you consulted. Your teachers will also expect you to document your original research activities in your lists of Works Cited.

The MLA Style of Documenting Works Cited

At the end of your report, the MLA style requires you to provide a list of references in a Works Cited section, a comprehensive, alphabetical listing of all of the sources that you consulted as you prepared the text. This list should *not* include references to materials that are not cited in the report.

Begin your reference list on a new page and center the title, "Works Cited," at the top of the first page. Note that the numbering of your pages should continue from the last page of your report and, like the text itself, all entries should be double-spaced. However, unlike your text, the first line of each entry should begin at the left margin and subsequent lines should be indented five spaces.

As illustrated by the following diagram, there are three essential "chunks" of information that your teachers expect you to provide in a Works Cited entry, and these chunks are separated by periods:

Author's Name.	Title of Work.	Publication Information.

According to the MLA guidelines, put titles of articles in quotation marks and underline titles of books, periodicals, and newspapers. When publishers provide more than one place of publication, it is necessary for you to mention only the first source of publication listed by the publisher. For instance, if you were citing Ben Shahn's *The Shape of Content*, which is published by Harvard UP (UP is an abbreviation for University Press), then you do not need to mention London, England, because Cambridge, Massachusetts, is listed in the book as the first place of publication.

Finally, when publication information is missing in the original source, you need to let your reader know that the omission isn't an oversight on your part by using the following abbreviations: n.p. (no place of publication given), n.p. (no publisher given), n.d. (no date of publication given) and n. pag (no pagination in source). To avoid unnecessarily long documentation, use standard abbreviations for periodicals and publishers. For instance, rather than writing D. C. Heath and Company or Harcourt Brace Jovanovich, Inc., you can write Heath or Harcourt.

Format for Listing Books

One Author

Rose, Michael. <u>Lives on the Boundary: The Struggles and Achievements of America's Underprepared</u>. New York: Free Press, 1989.

Two or Three Authors

Strunk, W., Jr., and E. B. White. <u>The Elements of Style</u>. 3d ed. New York: Macmillan, 1979.

Three or More Authors

Britton, James, et al. <u>The Development of Writing Abilities</u>. London: Macmillan, 1975.

Anonymous Author or Corporate Author(s)

Association of American Publishers. <u>An Author's Primer to Word Processing</u>. New York, 1983.

The University of Chicago Press. <u>Chicago Guide to Preparing Electronic Manuscripts for Authors and Publishers</u>. Chicago, 1987.

Government Author

New York. New York State Scientific Advisory Panel. <u>Biological Effects of Power Line Fields</u>. New York: New York State Printing Office, July 1, 1987.

United States. Library of Congress. Copyright Office. <u>How to Investigate the Copyright Status of a Work</u>. Washington, D.C: GPO, 1977.

> Note: GPO is an abbreviation for "Government Printing Office."

More Than One Book by Same Author

Pascal, Blaise. <u>Pascal's Pensees</u>. New York: Dutton, 1956.

———. <u>The Provincial Letters</u>. New York: Random, 1941.

Note: Use the title of the work to place successive works by the same author(s) in alphabetical order; use three hyphens rather than repeating the author's name to indicate multiple works.

One Editor, Compiler, or Translator

Wilson, Joseph M., ed. <u>Major Writing Theorists in America</u>. Illinois: NCTE, 1989.
Note: The abbreviation "ed." for editor can be replaced by the appropriate abbreviation for a compiler or translator—that is, "comp." or "trans."

Two or Three Editors

Mersky, Roy M., Robert C. Berring, and James K. McCue, eds. <u>Author's Guide to Journals in Law, Criminal Justice, and Criminology</u>. Author's Guide to Journals Series. New York: Haworth, 1977.
Note: Only the first author's name is reversed.

Citing an Author's Work in an Edited Collection

Minot, Stephen. "How We Come to Know What We Know." <u>Major Writing Theorists in America</u>. Ed. Joseph M. Wilson. Illinois: NCTE, 1989.

Citing a Translation or Edited Test

Vygotsky, Lev. S. <u>Thought and Language</u>. Ed. and trans. Eugenia Hanfmann and Gertrude Vakar. Cambridge, England: MIT P, 1962.

Format for Listing Articles

One Author in a Professional Journal

Bailey, Herbert S., Jr. "On the Future of Scholarly Communication." <u>Scholarly Publishing</u> 17 (1986): 251–254.

Two or Three Authors in a Professional Journal

Denham, Alice, and Wendell Broom. "The Role of the Author." <u>Scholarly Publishing</u> 12 (1981): 249–258.
Brown, Lester R., and Christopher Flavin. "The Earth's Vital Signs." <u>State of the World</u> (1988): 5 +.
Note: Use the "+" symbol when pages following the first page of the article do not appear in consecutive order.

Articles in Weekly or Bi-weekly Magazine

Toufexis, Anastasia. "Drowsy America." <u>Time</u> 17 Dec. 1990:78+.

Articles in Monthly or Bi-monthly Magazine

Rubin, Lillian B. "Sexual Pursuit! How We Play the Game." <u>MS</u> May 1989: 40–43.

Anonymous Author or Corporate Author

Rainforest Action Network. "Facts Sheet No. 1 About Rainforests." N.p. Mar. 1989.

International Committee of Medical Journal Editors. "Uniform Requirements for Manuscripts Submitted to Biomedical Journals." <u>Annals of Internal Medicine</u> 96 (1982): 766–770.

Newspaper Articles

Royko, Mike. "Readers Are Just Plain Mad." <u>The Tampa Tribune</u> 2 Jan. 1991: A8.

Anonymous or Corporate Newspaper Articles

New York Times Report. "Bush Team Plans Iraq Strategy." <u>The Tampa Tribune</u> 2 Jan. 1991: A1+.

"Tax Panel Should Address Report's Questions with Boldness." <u>The Tampa Tribune</u> 2 Jan. 1991: A8.

Encyclopedias or Dictionaries

"Ecosystems." <u>Encyclopedia Britannica</u>, 1991 ed.

Note: When possible, provide the author's name for entries in encyclopedias.

Published Interviews

Hemingway, Ernest. "Interview with George Plimpton." <u>Writers at Work: The Paris Review Interviews</u>, Second series. Ed. George Plimpton. Middlesex, England: Penguin, 1963: 215–240.

Format for Listing Unpublished Sources

Computer Programs

<u>The Best of Educorp</u>. Computer software. Macworld, 1985. Macintosh, disk.

<u>Willmaker 4</u> Computer software. Berkeley, CA: Nolo Press, 1992. Macintosh, disk.

Lectures

Williamson, Ron. Address. Should Americans Fight Iraq? Northwood University. Chicago, 14 Jan. 1991.

Letters

Feldman, Larry. Letter to the author. 8 May 1990.

Personal Interviews

Wilson, John. Telephone interview. 8 June 1991.

Smith, Paul. Personal interview. 12 Dec. 1992.

A Television or Radio Program

"Is Your Fruit Safe?" narr. John Read, prod. Judy Leidigger, dir. Michael T. Babbass, <u>Environment Review</u>, Environment News Network, Tampa, 11 May 1992.

Part 2

The Writing Portfolio

Writing Autobiographies and Biographies

As we age, we invariably wonder who and what experiences shaped us. One of our most elemental impulses is to define and explore the self. We try to understand who we are and who we can be by examining how we respond to different situations and people. Sometimes we wonder what other people think of us and wonder why we behave the way we do. Sometimes we are perplexed and feel inner discord because our self-images don't fit with what other people or society seem to expect of us. When we feel the urge to make changes in our lives, we often find that reflecting on our experiences is a prerequisite for change. As Abraham H. Maslow remarks in his thought-provoking book on human development, *Personality and Motivation*, "One cannot choose wisely for a life unless he dares to listen to himself, his own self, at each moment of life."

Yet it is quite possible to live an unexamined life, to live without clearly articulating what we think or believe. Most of us know people who never question why women are treated differently from men in our culture, why racism exists, why we need to spend as much money as we do on the nation's defense budget. Some people assume that poverty and the inequitable distribution of wealth are inevitable by-products of our capitalistic society. As suggested by the popularity of diet books and the prevalence of eating disorders, some people believe that only thin people are beautiful, while heavy people are lazy, sluggish, and undesirable. And—as satirized by the bumper sticker "The one who dies with the most toys wins"—many people assume that success means attaining and flaunting wealth as opposed to devoting time and energy to one's family or important social causes. As these examples demonstrate, we have a tendency to perceive social, political, and cultural values as "givens"—as immutable facts of life.

A college education can increase your ability to analyze experiences, to empathize with others, and to understand how cultural assumptions shape behavior. One of the primary reasons for becoming educated is to learn to evaluate your beliefs and to question how others may be trying to manipulate you. Perhaps more than any other medium, the blank page offers you the best opportunity to examine your assumptions and to explore the conflicts in your life.

Because autobiography involves reflecting about who you are and why you make decisions as you do, you may not see immediately how it relates to typical academic writing, which generally focuses on subjects other than the self. On a practical level, however, autobiographical writing engages many of the same thinking strategies required by other forms of writing. For example, when writing an autobiography, you will probably explore causes and effects, hypothesize about developmental steps, and perhaps even persuade a reader about the rightness of your actions. More importantly, on a broader level, we should note that all writing—all knowing—is to some degree autobiographical. Without personal relevance, much information can seem inane and trivial. Most educators agree that we learn best when we relate new information to what we already know, and some experts in writing theory believe that expressive, autobiographical writing plays a part in all writing, including academic writing.

This chapter challenges you to explore in writing a powerful moment in your life, a moment when you reconsidered who you wanted to be and who you are. For those of you who would prefer not to discuss autobiographical experiences, an alternative assignment is provided: you can interview someone else and then write his or her biography—that is, a narrative about another individual's experiences. Excerpts from autobiographies and biographies are provided throughout the chapter to give you a sense of the range of different topics that are available. In addition, to show you how students can work together to improve a peer's text, several drafts of one student's autobiography are provided along with his peers' suggestions for revision.

Writing Samples

In the following essay, Brent Staples, an assistant editor at *The New York Times*, writes about how fellow pedestrians find his presence to be intimidating on dark city streets.

Black Men and Public Space*

Brent Staples

My first victim was a woman—white, well dressed, probably in her late twenties. I came upon her late one evening on a deserted street in Hyde Park, a relatively affluent neighborhood in an otherwise mean, impoverished section of Chicago. As I swung onto the avenue behind her, there seemed to be a discreet, uninflammatory distance between us. Not so. She cast back a worried glance. To her, the youngish black man—a broad six feet two inches with a beard and billowing hair, both hands shoved into the pockets of a bulky mili-

1

---

*From *Harper's*, December, 1986. Reprinted with the permission of the author.

tary jacket—seemed menacingly close. After a few more quick glimpses, she picked up her pace and was soon running in earnest. Within seconds, she disappeared into a cross street.

That was more than a decade ago. I was twenty-two years old, a graduate 2 student newly arrived at the University of Chicago. It was in the echo of that terrified woman's footfalls that I first began to know the unwieldy inheritance I'd come into—the ability to alter public space in ugly ways. It was clear that she thought herself the quarry of a mugger, a rapist, or worse. Suffering a bout of insomnia, however, I was stalking sleep, not defenseless wayfarers. As a softy who is scarcely able to take a knife to a raw chicken—let alone hold one to a person's throat—I was surprised, embarrassed, and dismayed all at once. Her flight made me feel like an accomplice in tyranny. It also made it clear that I was indistinguishable from the muggers who occasionally seeped into the area from the surrounding ghetto. That first encounter, and those that followed, signified that a vast, unnerving gulf lay between nighttime pedestrians—particularly women—and me. And I soon gathered that being perceived as dangerous is a hazard in itself. I only needed to turn a corner into a dicey situation, or crowd some frightened, armed person in a foyer somewhere, or make an errant move after being pulled over by a policeman. Where fear and weapons meet—and they often do in urban America—there is always the possibility of death.

In that first year, my first away from my hometown, I was to become 3 thoroughly familiar with the language of fear. At dark, shadowy intersections, I could cross in front of a car stopped at a traffic light and elicit the *thunk, thunk, thunk, thunk* of the driver—black, white, male, or female—hammering down the door locks. On less traveled streets after dark, I grew accustomed to but never comfortable with people crossing to the other side of the street rather than pass me. Then there were the standard unpleasantries with policemen, doormen, bouncers, cabdrivers, and others whose business it is to screen out troublesome individuals *before* there is any nastiness.

I moved to New York nearly two years ago and I have remained an avid 4 night walker. In central Manhattan, the near-constant crowd cover minimizes tense one-on-one street encounters. Elsewhere—in SoHo, for example, where sidewalks are narrow and tightly spaced buildings shut out the sky—things can get very taut indeed.

After dark, on the warrenlike streets of Brooklyn where I live, I often see 5 women who fear the worst from me. They seem to have set their faces on neutral, and with their purse straps strung across their chests bandolier-style, they forge ahead as though bracing themselves against being tackled. I understand, of course, that the danger they perceive is not a hallucination. Women are particularly vulnerable to street violence, and young black males are drastically overrepresented among the perpetrators of that violence. Yet these truths are no solace against the kind of alienation that comes of being ever the suspect, a fearsome entity with whom pedestrians avoid making eye contact.

It is not altogether clear to me how I reached the ripe old age of twenty- 6 two without being conscious of the lethality nighttime pedestrians attributed to me. Perhaps it was because in Chester, Pennsylvania, the small, angry industrial town where I came of age in the 1960s, I was scarcely noticeable against a backdrop of gang warfare, street knifings, and murders. I grew up one of the good boys, had perhaps a half-dozen fistfights. In retrospect, my shyness of combat has clear sources.

As a boy, I saw countless tough guys locked away; I have since buried 7 several, too. They were babies, really—a teenage cousin, a brother of twenty-two, a childhood friend in his mid-twenties—all gone down in episodes of bravado played out in the streets. I came to doubt the virtues of intimidation early on. I chose, perhaps unconsciously, to remain a shadow—timid, but a survivor.

The fearsomeness mistakenly attributed to me in public places often has 8 a perilous flavor. The most frightening of these confusions occurred in the late 1970s and early 1980s, when I worked as a journalist in Chicago. One day, rushing into the office of a magazine I was writing for with a deadline story in hand, I was mistaken for a burglar. The office manager called security and, with an ad hoc posse, pursued me through the labyrinthine halls, nearly to my editor's door. I had no way of proving who I was. I could only move briskly toward the company of someone who knew me.

Another time I was on assignment for a local paper and killing time 9 before an interview. I entered a jewelry store on the city's affluent Near North Side. The proprietor excused herself and returned with an enormous red Doberman pinscher straining at the end of a leash. She stood, the dog extended toward me, silent to my questions, her eyes bulging nearly out of her head. I took a cursory look around, nodded, and bade her good night.

Relatively speaking, however, I never fared as badly as another black- 10 male journalist. He went to nearby Waukegan, Illinois, a couple of summers ago to work on a story about a murderer who was born there. Mistaking the reporter for the killer, police officers hauled him from his car at gunpoint and but for his press credentials would probably have tried to book him. Such episodes are not uncommon. Black men trade tales like this all the time.

Over the years, I learned to smother the rage I felt at so often being 11 taken for a criminal. Not to do so would surely have led to madness. I now take precautions to make myself less threatening. I move about with care, particularly late in the evening. I give a wide berth to nervous people on subway platforms during the wee hours, particularly when I have exchanged business clothes for jeans. If I happen to be entering a building behind some people who appear skittish, I may walk by, letting them clear the lobby before I return, so as not to seem to be following them. I have been calm and extremely congenial on those rare occasions when I've been pulled over by the police.

And on late-evening constitutionals I employ what has proved to be an 12 excellent tension-reducing measure: I whistle melodies from Beethoven and

Vivaldi and the more popular classical composers. Even steely New Yorkers hunching toward nighttime destinations seem to relax, and occasionally they even join in the tune. Virtually everybody seems to sense that a mugger wouldn't be warbling bright, sunny selections from Vivaldi's *Four Seasons*. It is my equivalent of the cowbell that hikers wear when they know they are in bear country.

Critical Reading Questions

1. What is Staples's primary purpose in writing this essay?
2. How has Staples accounted for his audience's likely attitudes about his subject?
3. How would you describe Staples's voice in this piece? What details does he offer to establish his voice? If you were in his position, do you believe that you would try to establish a similar tone?
4. How does Staples attempt to hook your interest in his introduction?
5. What information has Staples provided to help you appreciate the seriousness of his subject?

Our parents play a profound role in shaping who we are and what we think we can realistically expect out of life. Perhaps for this reason, students and professional authors often enjoy writing about their parents. The following autobiography is excerpted from Russell Baker's award winning book *Growing Up*, which won the Pulitzer Prize for autobiography in 1982.

Growing Up*
Russell Baker

I began working in journalism when I was eight years old. It was my mother's 1
idea. She wanted me to "make something" of myself and, after a level-headed appraisal of my strengths, decided I had better start young if I was to have any chance of keeping up with the competition.

The flaw in my character which she had already spotted was lack of 2
"gumption." My idea of a perfect afternoon was lying in front of the radio rereading my favorite Big Little Book, *Dick Tracy Meets Stooge Viller*. My mother despised inactivity. Seeing me having a good time in repose, she was powerless to hide her disgust. "You've got no more gumption than a bump on a log," she said. "Get out in the kitchen and help Doris do those dirty dishes."

My sister Doris, though two years younger than I, had enough gumption 3
for a dozen people. She positively enjoyed washing dishes, making beds, and

*From *Growing Up*, pp. 17–27. Copyright © 1982, used with permission of Congdon & Weed, Inc., Chicago.

cleaning the house. When she was only seven she could carry a piece of short-weighted cheese back to the A&P, threaten the manager with legal action, and come back triumphantly with the full quarter-pound we'd paid for and a few ounces extra thrown in for forgiveness. Doris could have made something of herself if she hadn't been a girl. Because of this defect, however, the best she could hope for was a career as a nurse or schoolteacher, the only work that capable females were considered up to in those days.

This must have saddened my mother, this twist of fate that had allocated 4 all the gumption to the daughter and left her with a son who was content with Dick Tracy and Stooge Viller. If disappointed, though, she wasted no energy on self-pity. She would make me make something of myself whether I wanted to or not. "The Lord helps those who help themselves," she said. That was the way her mind worked.

She was realistic about the difficulty. Having sized up the material the 5 Lord had given her to mold, she didn't overestimate what she could do with it. She didn't insist that I grow up to be President of the United States.

Fifty years ago parents still asked boys if they wanted to grow up to be 6 President, and asked it not jokingly but seriously. Many parents who were hardly more than paupers still believed their sons could do it. Abraham Lincoln had done it. We were only sixty-five years from Lincoln. Many a grandfather who walked among us could remember Lincoln's time. Men of grandfatherly age were the worst for asking if you wanted to grow up to be President. A surprising number of little boys said yes and meant it.

I was asked many times myself. No, I would say, I didn't want to grow up 7 to be President. My mother was present during one of these interrogations. An elderly uncle, having posed the usual question and exposed my lack of interest in the Presidency, asked, "Well, what *do* you want to be when you grow up?"

I loved to pick through trash piles and collect empty bottles, tin cans 8 with pretty labels, and discarded magazines. The most desirable job on earth sprang instantly to mind. "I want to be a garbage man," I said.

My uncle smiled, but my mother had seen the first distressing evidence 9 of a bump budding on a log. "Have a little gumption, Russell," she said. Her calling me Russell was a signal of unhappiness. When she approved of me I was always "Buddy."

When I turned eight years old she decided that the job of starting me on 10 the road toward making something of myself could no longer be safely delayed. "Buddy," she said one day, "I want you to come home right after school this afternoon. Somebody's coming and I want you to meet him."

When I burst in that afternoon she was in conference in the parlor with 11 an executive of the Curtis Publishing Company. She introduced me. He bent low from the waist and shook my hand. Was it true as my mother had told him, he asked, that I longed for the opportunity to conquer the world of business?

My mother replied that I was blessed with a rare determination to make 12 something of myself.

"That's right," I whispered.   13
"But have you got the grit, the character, the never-say-quit spirit it 14
takes to succeed in business?"
My mother said I certainly did.   15
"That's right," I said.   16
He eyed me silently for a long pause, as though weighing whether I 17
could be trusted to keep his confidence, then spoke man-to-man. Before taking a crucial step, he said, he wanted to advise me that working for the Curtis
Publishing Company placed enormous responsibility on a young man. It was
one of the great companies of America. Perhaps the greatest publishing
house in the world. I had heard, no doubt, of the *Saturday Evening Post?*

Heard of it? My mother said that everyone in our house had heard of the 18
Saturday Post and that I, in fact, read it with religious devotion.

Then doubtless, he said, we were also familiar with those two monthly 19
pillars of the magazine world, the *Ladies Home Journal* and the *Country Gentleman.*

Indeed we were familiar with them, said my mother.   20
Representing the *Saturday Evening Post* was one of the weightiest honors 21
that could be bestowed in the world of business, he said. He was personally
proud of being a part of that great corporation.

My mother said he had every right to be.   22
Again he studied me as though debating whether I was worthy of a 23
knighthood. Finally: "Are you trustworthy?"

My mother said I was the soul of honesty.   24
"That's right," I said.   25
The caller smiled for the first time. He told me I was a lucky young man. 26
He admired my spunk. Too many young men thought life was all play.
Those young men would not go far in this world. Only a young man willing
to work and save and keep his face washed and his hair neatly combed could
hope to come out on top in a world such as ours. Did I truly and sincerely
believe that I was such a young man?

"He certainly does," said my mother.   27
"That's right," I said.   28
He said he had been so impressed by what he had seen of me that he was 29
going to make me a representative of the Curtis Publishing Company. On
the following Tuesday, he said, thirty freshly printed copies of the *Saturday
Evening Post* would be delivered at our door. I would place these magazines,
still damp with the ink of the presses, in a handsome canvas bag, sling it over
my shoulder, and set forth through the streets to bring the best in journalism,
fiction, and cartoons to the American public.

He had brought the canvas bag with him. He presented it with reverence 30
fit for a chasuble. He showed me how to drape the sling over my left shoulder
and across the chest so that the pouch lay easily accessible to my right hand,
allowing the best in journalism, fiction, and cartoons to be swiftly extracted
and sold to a citizenry whose happiness and security depended upon us soldiers of the free press.

The following Tuesday I raced home from school, put the canvas bag 31
over my shoulder, dumped the magazines in, and, tilting to the left to balance
their weight on my right hip, embarked on the highway of journalism.

We lived in Belleville, New Jersey, a commuter town at the northern 32
fringe of Newark. It was 1932, the bleakest year of the Depression. My father
had died two years before, leaving us with a few pieces of Sears, Roebuck furniture and not much else, and my mother had taken Doris and me to live
with one of her younger brothers. This was my Uncle Allen. Uncle Allen had
made something of himself by 1932. As salesman for a soft-drink bottler in
Newark, he had an income of $30 a week; wore pearl-gray spats, detachable
collars, and a three-piece suit; was happily married; and took in threadbare
relatives.

With my load of magazines I headed toward Belleville Avenue. That's 33
where the people were. There were two filling stations at the intersection
with Union Avenue, as well as an A&P, a fruit stand, a bakery, a barber shop,
Zuccarelli's drugstore, and a diner shaped like a railroad car. For several
hours I made myself highly visible, shifting position now and then from corner to corner, from shop window to shop window, to make sure everyone
could see the heavy black lettering on the canvas bag that said *The Saturday
Evening Post*. When the angle of the light indicated it was suppertime, I
walked back to the house.

"How many did you sell, Buddy?" my mother asked. 34

"None." 35

"Where did you go?" 36

"The corner of Belleville and Union Avenues." 37

"What did you do?" 38

"Stood on the corner waiting for somebody to buy a *Saturday Evening* 39
Post."

"You just stood there?" 40

"Didn't sell a single one." 41

"For God's sake, Russell!" 42

Uncle Allen intervened. "I've been thinking about it for some time," he 43
said, "and I've about decided to take the *Post* regularly. Put me down as a regular customer." I handed him a magazine and he paid me a nickel. It was the
first nickel I earned.

Afterwards my mother instructed me in salesmanship. I would have to 44
ring doorbells, address adults with charming self-confidence, and break down
resistance with a sales talk pointing out that no one, no matter how poor,
could afford to be without the *Saturday Evening Post* in the home.

I told my mother I'd changed my mind about wanting to succeed in the 45
magazine business.

"If you think I'm going to raise a good-for-nothing," she replied, "you've 46
got another think coming." She told me to hit the streets with the canvas bag
and start ringing doorbells the instant school was out next day. When I
objected that I didn't feel any aptitude for salesmanship, she asked how I'd

like to lend her my leather belt so she could whack some sense into me. I bowed to superior will and entered journalism with a heavy heart.

My mother and I had fought this battle almost as long as I could remem- 47
ber. It probably started even before memory began, when I was a country child in northern Virginia and my mother, dissatisfied with my father's plain workman's life, determined that I would not grow up like him and his people, with calluses on their hands, overalls on their backs, and fourth-grade educations in their heads. She had fancier ideas of life's possibilities. Introducing me to the *Saturday Evening Post*, she was trying to wean me as early as possible from my father's world where men left with their lunch pails at sunup, worked with their hands until the grime ate into the pores, and died with a few sticks of mail-order furniture as their legacy. In my mother's vision of the better life there were desks and white collars, well-pressed suits, evenings of reading and lively talk, and perhaps—if a man were very, very lucky and hit the jackpot, really made something important of himself—perhaps there might be a fantastic salary of $5,000 a year to support a big house and a Buick with a rumble seat and a vacation in Atlantic City.

And so I set forth with my sack of magazines. I was afraid of the dogs that 48
snarled behind the doors of potential buyers. I was timid about ringing the doorbells of strangers, relieved when no one came to the door, and scared when someone did. Despite my mother's instructions, I could not deliver an engaging sales pitch. When a door opened I simply asked, "Want to buy a *Saturday Evening Post*?" In Belleville few persons did. It was a town of 30,000 people, and most weeks I rang a fair majority of its doorbells. But I rarely sold my thirty copies. Some weeks I canvassed the entire town for six days and still had four or five unsold magazines on Monday evening; then I dreaded the coming of Tuesday morning, when a batch of thirty fresh *Saturday Evening Post*s was due at the front door.

"Better get out there and sell the rest of those magazines tonight," my 49
mother would say.

I usually posted myself then at a busy intersection where a traffic light 50
controlled commuter flow from Newark. When the light turned red I stood on the curb and shouted my sales pitch at the motorists.

"Want to buy a *Saturday Evening Post*?" 51

One rainy night when car windows were sealed against me I came back 52
soaked and with not a single sale to report. My mother beckoned to Doris.

"Go back down there with Buddy and show him how to sell these maga- 53
zines," she said.

Brimming with zest, Doris, who was then seven years old, returned with 54
me to the corner. She took a magazine from the bag, and when the light turned red she strode to the nearest car and banged her small fist against the closed window. The driver, probably startled at what he took to be a midget assaulting his car, lowered the window to stare, and Doris thrust a *Saturday Evening Post* at him.

"You need this magazine," she piped, "and it only costs a nickel." 55

Her salesmanship was irresistible. Before the light changed half a dozen 56 times she disposed of the entire batch. I didn't feel humiliated. To the contrary. I was so happy I decided to give her a treat. Leading her to the vegetable store on Belleville Avenue, I bought three apples, which cost a nickel, and gave her one.

"You shouldn't waste money," she said. 57

"Eat your apple." I bit into mine. 58

"You shouldn't eat before supper," she said. "It'll spoil your appetite. 59

Back at the house that evening, she dutifully reported me for wasting a 60 nickel. Instead of a scolding, I was rewarded with a pat on the back for having the good sense to buy fruit instead of candy. My mother reached into her bottomless supply of maxims and told Doris, "An apple a day keeps the doctor away."

By the time I was ten I had learned all my mother's maxims by heart. 61 Asking to stay up past normal bedtime, I knew that a refusal would be explained with, "Early to bed and early to rise, makes a man healthy, wealthy, and wise." If I whimpered about having to get up early in the morning, I could depend on her to say, "The early bird gets the worm."

The one I most despised was, "If at first you don't succeed, try, try 62 again." This was the battle cry with which she constantly sent me back into the hopeless struggle whenever I moaned that I had rung every doorbell in town and knew there wasn't a single potential buyer left in Belleville that week. After listening to my explanation, she handed me the canvas bag and said, "If at first you don't succeed . . ."

Three years in that job, which I would gladly have quit after the first day 63 except for her insistence, produced at least one valuable result. My mother finally concluded that I would never make something of myself by pursuing a life in business and started considering careers that demanded less competitive zeal.

One evening when I was eleven I brought home a short "composition" 64 on my summer vacation which the teacher had graded with an A. Reading it with her own schoolteacher's eye, my mother agreed that it was top-drawer seventh grade prose and complimented me. Nothing more was said about it immediately, but a new idea had taken life in her mind. Halfway through supper she suddenly interrupted the conversation.

"Buddy," she said, "maybe you could be a writer." 65

I clasped the idea to my heart. I had never met a writer, had shown no 66 previous urge to write, and hadn't a notion how to become a writer, but I loved stories and thought that making up stories must surely be almost as much fun as reading them. Best of all, though, and what really gladdened my heart, was the ease of the writer's life. Writers did not have to trudge through the town peddling from canvas bags, defending themselves against angry dogs, being rejected by surly strangers. Writers did not have to ring doorbells. So far as I could make out, what writers did couldn't even be classified as work.

I was enchanted. Writers didn't have to have any gumption at all. I did 67
not dare tell anybody for fear of being laughed at in the schoolyard, but
secretly I decided that what I'd like to be when I grew up was a writer.

Critical Reading Questions

1. What theme unifies this autobiography?
2. How would you describe Baker's tone? What words and examples does
   he use to create the tone?
3. How does Baker's use of specific details and dialogue contribute to the
   success of this piece?

In the following autobiography, student writer Bernice Geradts makes
an unexpected connection between a personal experience and a distant memory. Until she began freewriting about her memories, Geradts had never
understood why she tended to feel overly hostile when strangers invaded her
personal space.

The Invisible Circle

Bernice Geradts

Today's program on *Geraldo*: "Invasion of Personal Space." Great! Another 1
vague topic with speakers no one could relate to. Yet, I could have been one
of the guests on that show. Being a guest on the *Geraldo* show was not part of
my thoughts three years earlier during our cooking class at hotel school. My
concentration then was focused on the *baverois* we had to make that day.

I had an assigned partner; Jiska was her name. Jiska adored cooking and 2
often got excited over the little things in life, like when the gelatin congealed
or when she was allowed to choose the flavor of *baverois* she was going to
prepare. Her excitement always resulted in one thing—a painful punch to
my arm.

I could easily deal with an enthusiastic assigned partner. That was not 3
the problem. Her punches were what bothered me. These provoked me to
explode into a rage. My outbursts surprised me. Was there really a reason for
me to react in such a fashion? After cooking class I went home to my room
and racked my brain to find the reason for my aggressive behavior.

That night as I was writing in my journal at my desk, my thoughts and 4
pen went far back to a childhood vacation in Greece. The memories warmed
my heart, and I felt myself being transported back to the colorful, flowery
hallway in that Greek hotel in Athens.

My little companions and I were playing hide-and-go-seek again. This 5
time I decided to outsmart them all by going to the floor below the one
where we were playing. I giggled out loud, proud of my wonderful idea,
knowing my friends would never find me there. As I skipped down the hall

I did not notice that one of the hotel room doors had opened. Suddenly, out of nowhere, a figure stood in front of me. Looking up, I could see a massive man with a stomach so large that his shirt buttons seemed to want to jump loose from the pressure of his huge body. His face was as red as a tomato, his jet black eyes were flashing in all directions, and his mouth moved with an incredible speed, emitting a sound that thundered through the hallway.

I was overwhelmed and could not move. My mouth fell open as I stared 6 at this man. What was he saying? Did he think that I could understand a word of what I presumed to be Greek? Sweat was dripping from his temples as his arms jerked in every direction. Suddenly, one of his arms came my direction, and I could feel a burning, tingling sensation on my cheek—the Greek had hit me! He did this several times, yet before I could scream or dart away, he disappeared.

What happened next was a blur; I still cannot quite remember. I only 7 recall that I rolled up into a little ball in a corner of the hallway under an old desk, tears rolling down over my burning face.

I was so young at that time that I could easily erase the tears, along with 8 the Greek man, from my memory; except I could never quite conquer the anger I bore against anyone who hit me. Eight years later, as I sat with my journal at my desk, I came to understand that anger. I realized why Jiska's friendly punches had threatened my personal space. If I had been a guest on Geraldo's show, I would have warned people to be careful who they punch in a friendly way because they may "hit" a memory which has been kept in the shadows.

Critical Reading Questions

1. What theme unifies this autobiography?
2. What concrete details and sensory language does Geradts provide to help you visualize and understand her experience?
3. How would you describe Geradts's voice in this piece? What examples or words does she use to establish this tone?

Because first-person accounts of memorable experiences can be so gripping and entertaining, some accomplished authors enjoy writing biographies of other people's lives. You are probably all familiar, for instance, with the "autobiographies" of celebrities that are actually written by professional "ghost writers." One advantage to writing someone else's biography is that it increases your sensitivity to the ways in which different cultures and events have shaped others' lives. As illustrated below, you can write biographies by interviewing other people and then telling their stories as if you were them.

The following biography of Nora Quealey, written by Jean Reith Schroedel, presents a powerful account of one woman's work experience on a truck assembly line. This biography is excerpted by Schroedel's book *Alone in a Crowd* (1985), a compendium of oral histories of working-class women that Schroedel undertook when she was an undergraduate at the University of Washington.

Nora Quealey*
Jean Reith Schroedel

I was a housewife until five years ago. The best part was being home when ₁ my three kids came in from school. Their papers and their junk that they made from kindergarten on up—they were my total, whole life. And then one day I realized when they were grown up and gone, graduated and married, I was going to be left with nothing. I think there's a lot of women that way, housewives, that never knew there were other things and people outside of the neighborhood. I mean the block got together once a week for coffee and maybe went bowling, but that was it. My whole life was being there when the kids came home from school.

I never disliked anything. It was just like everything else in a marriage, ₂ there never was enough money to do things that you wanted—never to take a week's vacation away from the kids. If we did anything, it was just to take the car on Saturday or Sunday for a little, short drive. But there was never enough money. The extra money was the reason I decided to go out and get a job. The kids were getting older, needed more, wanted more, and there was just not enough.

See, I don't have a high school diploma, so when I went to Boeing and ₃ put an application in, they told me not to come back until I had a diploma or a G.E.D. On the truck line they didn't mind that I hadn't finished school. I put an application in and got hired on the spot.

My dad works over at Bangor in the ammunition depot, so I asked him ₄ what it would be like working with all men. The only thing he told me was if I was gonna work with a lot of men, that I would have to *listen* to swear words and some of the obscene things, but still *act* like a lady, or I'd never fit in. You can still be treated like a lady and act like a lady and work like a man. So I just tried to fit in. It's worked, too. The guys come up and they'll tell me jokes and tease me and a lot of them told me that I'm just like one of the guys. Yet they like to have me around because I wear make-up and I do curl my hair, and I try to wear not really frilly blouses, see-through stuff, but nice blouses.

We had one episode where a gal wore a tank top and when she bent over ₅ the guys could see her boobs or whatever you call it, all the way down. Myself and a couple other women went and tried to complain about it. We wanted personnel to ask her to please wear a bra, or at least no tank tops. We were

---

* From *Alone in a Crowd: Women in the Trades Tell Their Stories*, 1985, pp. 91–97. Reprinted by permission of Temple University Press.

getting a lot of comebacks from the guys like, "When are you gonna dress like so-and-so," or "When are *you* gonna go without a bra," and "We wanna see what *you've* got." And I don't feel any need to show off; you know, I know what I've got. There were only a few women there, so that one gal made a very bad impression. But personnel said there was nothing they could do about it.

But in general the guys were really good. I started out in cab building 6 hanging radio brackets and putting heaters in. It was all hand work, and at first I really struggled with the power screwdrivers and big reamers, but the guy training me was super neato. I would think, "Oh, dear, can I ever do this, can I really prove myself or come up to their expectations?" But the guys never gave me the feeling that I was taking the job from a man or food from his family's mouth. If I needed help, I didn't even have to ask, if they saw me struggling, they'd come right over to help.

I've worked in a lot of different places since I went to work there. I was in 7 cab build for I don't know how long, maybe six months, eight months. Then they took me over to sleeper boxes, where I stayed for about two-and-one-half years. I put in upholstery, lined the head liners and the floor mats. After that I went on the line and did air conditioning. When the truck came to me, it had hoses already on it, and I'd have to hook up a little air-condition-pump-type thing and a suction that draws all the dust and dirt from the lines. Then you close that off, put Freon in, and tie down the line. Then I'd tie together a bunch of color-coded electrical wires with tie straps and electrical tape to hook the firewall to the engine. Sometimes I also worked on the sleeper boxes by crawling underneath and tightening down big bolts and washers. Next they sent me over to the radiator shop. I was the first woman ever to do radiators. That I liked. A driver would bring in the radiators, and you'd put it on a hoist, pick it up and put it on a sling, and work on one side putting your fittings on and wiring and putting in plugs. Then they bounced me back to sleeper boxes for a while and finally ended up putting me in the motor department, where I am now. The motors are brought in on a dolly. The guy behind me hangs the transmission and I hang the pipe with the shift levers and a few other little things and that's about it. Except that we have to work terribly fast.

I was moved into the motor department after the big layoff. At that time 8 we were doing ten motors a day. Now we're up to fourteen without any additional help. When we were down, the supervisor came to me and said we had to help fill in and give extra help to the other guys, which is fine. But the minute production went up, I still had to do my own job plus putting on parts for three different guys. These last two weeks have been really tough. I've been way behind. They've got two guys that are supposed to fill in when you get behind, but I'm stubborn enough that I won't go over and ask for help. The supervisor should be able to see that I'm working super-duper hard while some other guys are taking forty-five minutes in the can and having a sandwich and two cups of coffee. Sometimes I push myself so hard that I'm actually in a trance. And I have to stop every once in a while and ask, "What did I do?" I don't even remember putting parts on, I just go from one to the other, just block everything out—just go, go, go, go. And that is bad, for myself, my own sanity, my own health. I don't take breaks. I don't go to the bathroom. There's so much pressure on me, physical and mental stress. It's hard to handle because then I go home and do a lot of crying and that's bad for my kids because I do a lot of snapping and growling at them. When I'm down, depressed, aching, and sore, to come home and do that to the kids is not fair at all. The last couple of days the attitude I've had is, I don't care whether I get the job done or not. If they can't see I'm going under, then I don't care. And I'll take five or ten minutes to just go to the bathroom, sit on the floor, and take a couple of deep breaths, just anything to get away.

The company doesn't care about us at all. Let me give you an example. 9 When we were having all this hot weather, I asked them please if we couldn't get some fans in here. Extension cords even, because some guys had their own fans. I wasn't just asking for myself, but those guys over working by the oven. They've got a thermometer there and it gets to a hundred and fifteen degrees by that oven! They've got their mouths open, can hardly breathe, and they're barely moving. So I said to the supervisor, "Why can't we have a fan to at least circulate the air?" "Oh, yeah, we'll look at it," was as far as it went. We're human. We have no right to be treated like animals. I mean you go out to a dairy farm and you've got air conditioning and music for those cows. I'm a person, and I don't like feeling weak and sick to my stomach and not feel like eating. Then to have the supervisor expect me to put out production as if I was mechanical—a thing, just a robot. I'm human.

You know, I don't even know what my job title is. I'm not sure if it's 10 trainee or not. But I do know I'll never make journeyman. I'll never make anything. I tried for inspection—took all the classes they offered at the plant, went to South Seattle Community College on my own time, studied blue-printing, and worked in all the different areas like they said I had to. I broke ground for the other girls, but they won't let me move up. And it all comes down to one thing, because I associated with a black man. I've had people in personnel tell me to stop riding to work with the man, even if it meant taking the bus to and from work. I said no one will make my decisions as to who I ride with and who my friends are. Because you walk into a building with a person, have lunch with him, let him buy you a cup of coffee, people condemn you. They're crazy, because when I have a friend, I don't turn my back on them just because of what people think. What I do outside the plant after quitting time is my own business. If they don't like it, that's their problem. But in that plant I've conducted myself as a lady and have nothing to be ashamed of. I plant my feet firmly and I stand by it.

Early on, I hurt my neck, back, and shoulder while working on sleeper 11 boxes. When I went into the motor department I damaged them more by working with power tools above my head and reaching all day long. I was out for two weeks and then had a ten-week restriction. Personnel said I had to go back to my old job, and if I couldn't handle it I would have to go home. They wouldn't put me anywhere else, which is ridiculous, with all the small parts areas that people can sit down and work in while they are restricted. My doctor said if I went back to doing what I was doing when I got hurt, I had a fifty-fifty chance of completely paralyzing myself from the waist down. But like a fool I went back. Some of the guys helped me with the bending and stooping over. Then the supervisor borrowed a ladder with three steps and on rollers from the paint department. He wanted me to stand on the top step while working on motors which are on dollies on a moving chain. I'd be using two press-wrenches to tighten fittings down while my right knee was on the transmission and the left leg standing up straight. All this from the top step of a ladder on rollers. One slip and it would be all over. I backed off and said it wouldn't work. By this time I'd gotten the shop steward there, but he didn't do anything. In fact, the next day he left on three weeks' vacation without doing anything to help me. I called the union hall and was told they'd send a business rep down the next day. I never saw or heard from the man.

Anyhow, I'm still doing the same job as when I got hurt. I can feel the 12 tension in my back and shoulder coming up. I can feel the spasms start and muscles tightening up. Things just keep gettin' worse and they don't care. People could be rotated and moved rather than being cramped in the same position, like in the sleeper boxes, where you never stand up straight and stretch your neck out. It's eight, ten, twelve hours a day all hunched over. In the next two years I've got to quit. I don't know what I'll do. If I end up paralyzed from the neck down, the company doesn't give a damn, the union doesn't give a damn, who's gonna take care of me? Who's gonna take care of my girls? I'm gonna be put in some moldy, old, stinkin' nursing home. I'm thirty-seven years old. I could live another thirty, forty years. And who's gonna really care about me?

I mean my husband left me. He was very jealous of my working with a lot 13 of men and used to follow me to work. When I joined the bowling team, I tried to get him to come and meet the guys I worked with. He came but felt left out because there was always an inside joke or something that he couldn't understand. He resented that and the fact that I made more money than he did. And my not being home bothered him. But he never said, "I want you to quit," or "We'll make it on what I get." If he had said that I probably would have quit. Instead we just muddled on. With me working, the whole family had to pitch in and help. When I come home at night my daughter has dinner waiting, and I do a couple loads of wash and everybody folds their own clothes. My husband pitched in for a while. Then he just stopped coming home. He found another lady that didn't work, had four kids, and was on welfare.

It really hurt and I get very confused still. I don't have the confidence 14 and self-assurance I used to have. I think, "Why did I do that," or "Maybe I shouldn't have done it," and I have to force myself to say, "Hey, I felt and said what I wanted to and there's no turning back." It came out of me and I can't be apologizing for everything that I do. And, oh, I don't know, I guess I'm in a spell right now where I'm tired of being dirty. I want my fingernails long and clean. I want to not go up to the bathroom and find a big smudge of grease across my forehead. I want to sit down and be pampered and pretty all day. Maybe that wouldn't satisfy me, but I just can't imagine myself at fifty or sixty or seventy years old trying to climb on these trucks. I've been there for five years. I'm thirty-seven and I want to be out of there before I'm forty. And maybe I will. I've met this nice guy and he's talking of getting married. At the most, I would have to work for one more year and then I could stay at home, go back to being a housewife.

Critical Reading Questions

1. What questions do you think Jean Schroedel asked Nora Quealey as she developed this biography?

2. How does your sense of Nora Quealey change as you read through the account? What changes in tone do you perceive in the biography?

3. What details about Quealey's work does Schroedel provide to give readers a sense of its rigorous nature?

4. In what ways does Quealey exercise direct control over her destiny? How does Quealey's background determine what is possible for her to achieve?

5. Which of Quealey's negative job experiences would you attribute to her gender and which would you attribute to the nature of her work—that is, to working on a truck assembly line? Have you faced, or do you know other women who have faced, similar experiences when attempting to work in male-dominated professions?

Analyzing Pertinent Conventions

There is no one ideal way to develop and structure autobiographical or biographical essays. In other words, no perfect structure or formula exists into which you can simply pour your thoughts. As with other writing projects, you determine the best way to shape your essay by asking whom you are writing to, what your purpose is, and what persona or voice you should attempt to project. For example, an autobiographical essay intended to persuade college students not to drive while drunk would take on a very different shape from one that describes the death of a parent to a general audience. Based on past reading experiences, however, autobiographical writers and academic readers do share a few expectations about how autobiographies are shaped. Of course, no writing instructor or textbook can describe *exactly* how your autobiography should be formed, but the following guidelines are worth considering when you plan and revise your work.

Establish an Appropriate Voice or Persona

The success of your autobiography or biography hinges on how authentic and engaging your voice is to the reader. Because our voice is so much a part of us, we can easily overlook how much it influences readers. Successful writers, however, understand that the effectiveness of an autobiography depends on the appeal of the author's voice. For example, Brent Staples's essay, which appears earlier in this chapter, is a powerful condemnation of modern American culture. Certainly, African-American men should not have to whistle to walk downtown, and all African-American men should not be treated as criminals. Yet to avoid alienating readers who happen to be white, he establishes a sympathetic and analytical tone. Although he rightfully challenges people to consider that African-American men are feared and mistrusted—"it is the equivalent of the cowbell that hikers wear when they know they are in bear country"—he also acknowledges that "black males are drastically over-represented among the perpetrators of that violence." His thoughtful and compassionate voice subsequently helps draw his readers' attention to the plight of the African-American male.

Although there is a tendency to do so, you do not need to reveal your "inner self" in an autobiography. Instead, you may wish to project a *persona*—that is, you can project a personality or "mask" that doesn't truly reveal who you are. For example, for satirical or humorous purposes, you could encourage readers to think that you are especially naive and innocent. Or, you could project the image of someone who is as tough as nails when you are really soft and generous. You could even assume the persona of someone of the opposite sex. Also, if you decide to write a biography, then you will want to assume the voice and style of your subject.

Use Narrative Order and Flashback

Autobiographical essays typically follow a chronological order in which a conflict or problem is introduced and then explored through a series of events and examples. In Brent Staples's essay, he recalls his first "victim" from "more than a decade ago," when he was only twenty-two, and he then moves chronologically through time to the present day.

Occasionally, authors present a flashback in the introduction, which essentially introduces the older, more mature voice of the narrator and sets up the conflict that will drive the story. For example, Russell Baker begins his brilliant autobiography, *Growing Up*, in the voice of a mature adult, a loving son who is eager to look back on his mother and speculate about how she influenced his life:

> We all come from the past, and children ought to know what it was that went into their making, to know that life is a braided cord of humanity stretching up from time long gone, and that it cannot be defined by the span of a single journey from diaper to shroud.

I thought that someday my own children would understand that. I thought that, when I am beyond explaining, they would want to know what the world was like when my mother was young and I was younger, and we two relics passed together through strange times. I thought I should try to tell them how it was to be young in the time before jet planes, superhighways, H-bombs, and the global village of television. I realized I would have to start with my mother and her passion for improving the male of the species, which in my case took the form of forcing me to "make something of myself."

Lord, how I hated those words. . . .

Hook Your Reader

In the introduction of an autobiography, you may want to grab your readers' attention with a suspenseful statement or an unusual situation. An opening sentence like "My first victim was a woman" in Staples's essay is intended to surprise and pique the curiosity of a reader. Don't underestimate the importance of your opener.

Place the Reader in a Particular Setting

Generally speaking, readers are more interested in the human element—that is, the characters and tension that drive the narrative—than the setting. However, you still need to provide some information about the setting or context in which your autobiography takes place. If readers are to understand why you have acted as you have, then you must clarify the *scene* or *situation* in which you are experiencing the act that is being discussed. For example, great generosity or stinginess has quite different implications when it occurs in the context of appalling poverty or tremendous wealth. In a subtle way, background information provides *verisimilitude*—that is, it enables readers to believe in you and your story and to more easily imagine themselves in your shoes.

If your readers are to thoroughly relive a pivotal moment in your life, then you need to provide descriptive, sensory language. Examine, for instance, how Russell Baker engages your senses and uses numerous descriptive details so that you can better imagine his world:

> Morrisonville was a poor place to prepare for a struggle with the twentieth century, but a delightful place to spend a childhood. It was summer days drenched with sunlight, fields yellow with buttercups, and barn lofts sweet with hay. Clusters of purple grapes dangled from backyard arbors, lavender wisteria blossoms perfumed the air from the great vine enclosing the end of my grandmother's porch, and wild roses covered the fences.
>
> On a broiling afternoon when the men were away at work and all the women napped, I moved through majestic depths of silences, silences so immense I could hear the corn growing. Under these silences there was an orchestra of natural music playing notes no city child would ever hear. A

certain cackle from the henhouse meant we had gained an egg. The creak of a porch swing told of a momentary breeze blowing across my grandmother's yard. Moving past Liz Virts's barn as quietly as an Indian, I could hear the swish of a horse's tail and knew the horseflies were out in strength. As I tiptoed along a mossy bank to surprise a frog, a faint splash told me the quarry had spotted me and slipped into the stream. Wandering among the sleeping houses, I learned that tin roofs crackle under the power of the sun, and when I tired and came back to my grandmother's house, I padded into her dark cool living room, lay flat on the floor, and listened to the hypnotic beat of her pendulum clock on the wall ticking the meaningless hours away. . . .

Decide on a Focus

In four, or ten, or even a hundred pages, an autobiographer cannot tell the complete story of his or her life. Although you may want to link together different experiences that illustrate a unifying theme, you will find this essay easier to write if you focus on a specific moment of time. If you skip over entire years in single sentences and if no single theme appears to connect the events, chances are that you need to limit the scope of your presentation.

Writing Assignments

If you feel uncomfortable writing about autobiographical experiences, you may want to consider writing in response to one of the following assignments:

1. Interview someone whom you have always been curious about. Inquire about important moments in this person's life and choose one of them to illustrate biographically.

2. Read several biographies of one famous person, like Benjamin Franklin, Malcolm X, or Katharine Hepburn. Write a brief biography of an important moment in that person's life.

Although you may already have thought of a significant moment in your life to write about, you should still consider other topics before committing to one event. After all, by the time most of us have reached college, we have met a number of extraordinary people and have been in a variety of unusual situations that have had effects on our lives, so you should avoid grasping at the first subject that comes to mind. To decide what kinds of religious, moral, personal, or political experiences have led to major changes in your personality, outlook, commitments, profession, or world view, try responding to the following questions.

1. How did the way your parents raised you influence who you are? What has been the effect on your life of being brought up in a religious or nonreligious environment? If your parents divorced, how did the break affect you? How did where you grew up influence who you are now? In

what ways did your family or neighborhood shape the person you are today?

2. Have you ever observed an unusual event that you believe others would be curious about? Have you seen a tornado, or hurricane, or car accident? (If you can isolate an unusual experience to write about, you have a great advantage over an author who is working to make the ordinary seem unusual. Readers' curiosity about how others live their lives makes them appreciate being introduced to unusual settings, people, and processes.)

3. Why are you driven or not driven to succeed? What experiences and people have encouraged or discouraged you? Who has been the most influential person in your life?

4. In what important ways have other people's image of you affected how you behave or think? To what degree are others' images of you accurate?

5. What experiences and people have taught you that you should be generous (or thrifty)? How have your attitudes about money influenced your past decisions?

6. Do you belong to a specific social, sexual, or political group? How has your membership in this group shaped your personality?

7. What has been your most exciting moment as a college student? Can you remember sitting through your first hour-long exam? What was your first impression of your roommate?

8. Have you ever done anything that you were really embarrassed about? What happened and why do you think you acted as you did? What have you learned as a result of this experience?

9. Has anyone ever totally let you down? In retrospect, have you been able to understand why the person failed to fulfill your expectations? Have you ever known anyone who chose a difficult career path or life-style? How has your experience with this person influenced your life and career goals?

Prewriting and Drafting Strategies

The following strategies can help you avoid procrastination, develop ideas, and begin drafting.

Analyze Your Communication Situation

Autobiographies differ from other kinds of writing in that you may at first want to ignore your audience's needs and interests. After all, the impulse to explore a memory is often founded more on a desire to understand oneself rather than to communicate with readers.

Although you may not consider your readers while writing preliminary drafts, you will eventually need to question whether they will fully understand your experience. We read autobiographies and biographies because we are interested in other people's experiences and in how others make sense of their lives. Occasionally we read to understand how a prominent historical figure, businessperson, artist, or scientist achieved success, and sometimes we read to understand how other people overcome day-to-day challenges. The autobiographer's attempt to inform or amuse or even persuade an audience is what distinguishes autobiographical writing from more private journal writing.

Stir Your Memory

If you are writing about a childhood experience, you may wish to charge your memory by drawing a map of your hometown. Include all of the significant people and places you can recall. If you are writing about an influential person in your life, try to find some pictures of him or her to help you remember that person more vividly.

Freewrite

Rather than trying to write a draft of your biography or autobiography in your head, try writing without stopping for ten to fifteen minutes. Just let your memories of important experiences flow onto the page. When freewriting, do not pause to reread your sentences critically. In fact, don't even attempt to compose in complete sentences. Momentarily try to dismiss concerns for grammar, mechanics, and even content. Then, once your hand cramps or the ten to fifteen minutes are up, reread your free-association effort and see what passages seem worth developing in a second freewrite.

At first, freewriting may seem to be mechanical and awkward. After all, most of us tend to trust the critical voice within us, and it does seem more natural to reread and mentally rehearse our ideas. In the preliminary stages of drafting a document, you must remember that you need to "break a few eggs to make an omelet," that generating ideas involves confronting chaos and taking risks. Freewriting can help you develop ideas that you probably would not have considered if you had used more rigid forms of thinking. In a game of pool, when there are still a lot of balls on the table, a clever shot can send them ricocheting in all directions and some drop in the pockets. In the same way, when you write quickly and freely, you will get lucky: new ideas will pop perfectly into place. The momentum of freewriting can allow you to discover meaning, to compare different ideas, and to explore potential relationships. In addition, freewriting can be a significant time-saving device. In fifteen minutes, you can generate as many as 200 to 400 words instead of struggling in vain to write a perfect first draft.

To transform freewrites into first-rate academic documents, Peter Elbow has suggested that you *loop* from one freewrite to the next. Looping essentially involves rereading a freewrite to identify statements worth developing and ideas that are emerging. Highlight sections that seem to have merit, cross out sections that make no contribution, and copy ideas that appear interesting but are unrelated to your immediate subject onto a separate page. Finally, and this is the most crucial step in freewriting, write a summary statement, one that captures the gist of the freewrite or the direction the freewrite appears to be moving in. Write this summary statement at the top of a sheet of paper and freewrite again with this statement in mind. After conducting three freewrites, you will have produced 1,200 to 2,000 words in about 45 minutes. People who have experimented with this technique generally report that much of what is created in the later freewrites is usually quite useful.

Meditate

Being able to write well requires that you can concentrate and focus on a subject for a sustained period of time. Unfortunately, finding the time to be reflective and giving yourself the space to let your ideas flow are often difficult in today's world. As a student, you have tremendous pressures on you. Many of you must work at full-time jobs, raise children, and attend school simultaneously.

To help you reach the reflective mood that is so important to clear thinking, you may find it useful to meditate. This doesn't necessarily mean that you need to chant a mantra and stare blissfully at a vase of roses. Instead, it means that you can listen to some environmental music—such as waves breaking across a rocky beach—or merely sit still and breath deeply, while attempting not to think about any particular subject. After relaxing in this manner for a short while—say fifteen minutes—you are likely to feel more refreshed, focused, and ready to write.

Revising and Editing Strategies

Because autobiographical and biographical essays are so personal, you may have some difficulty identifying weaknesses in early drafts. The primary challenge of revising autobiographical essays is to escape the angst of your experience and become a writing critic. In order to become a tough critic, give yourself ample time to let the draft "cool." If possible, set the essay aside for a full day, then reread it, asking yourself the following questions:

1. Have I provided enough background information to enable my readers to understand why I and the people whom I am writing about respond as we do to the circumstances I am describing?

2. Will my readers understand the conflict or problem that I am addressing? Does my autobiography or biography seem focused, or am I trying to report too many experiences?

3. Is my language straightforward and clear? Have I avoided excessive abstract words? Can I use more concrete words? Can I help my readers visualize my experience by appealing more to their senses?

4. Is the autobiography well organized? Would a different ordering of events be more forceful?

5. What sort of voice or persona am I presenting in the essay? Have I been successful in maintaining this voice or persona throughout the essay?

6. Is my writing economical? Can I combine and edit some of the sentences to make them more vigorous?

7. Is the essay grammatical and mechanically correct? Are there specific errors I tend to make that I haven't yet checked for, such as subject-verb agreement, pronoun agreement, run-ons and fragments, or needless tense shifts?

Before submitting your work to classmates or your instructor, you should also refer to Chapters 11 and 12. By experimenting with the revising and editing strategies discussed in these chapters, you can revise your autobiography at the textual, paragraph, and sentence levels.

Collaborative Learning

To give you an example of how a writer's purpose can evolve through a peer writing workshop, consider how student writer Herb McKendry revises his essay in response to his peers' suggestions and his own concerns. You can sharpen your own editorial skills by critically reading the following draft and then comparing your criticisms with those of McKendry's peers as they worked together in an in-class peer group.

Untitled (Second Draft)

Herb McKendry

Father, not all people are aware of the burden put on a man who is disabled; 1 who has eight hungry, dirty, miserable kids; who has a wife who is constantly sick with something; who has to depend on welfare checks and food stamps to make ends meet; and who has no chance of getting a job—any job. I can understand how the stress from so many problems could be over-bearing, how the pressure would lead to regret, frustration, and anger.

Father, I do not envy your life. If life were a card game, you've certainly 2 been dealt a horrible hand—most people would fold, but you would not. Not many people realize the pain of a responsible man who never enjoys the success of his efforts, wants and hope; the budget balanced; the cabinets full; the car nice and new; the closets filled with decent clothes; the house clean and respectable; the wife loving and healthy; and the kids safe and warm.

Not many people are able to see how fragile a child really is, how they depend on your support of their behavior, how needy they are of your unconditional touch and approval, how innocent and gentle they really are, and how directly their growth reflects your treatment of them. 3

Father, you know the burden and pain of being a frustrated responsible man. I know the burden and pain of being your child. I saw your hopes for an easier life with every cigarette you smoked, every beer your drank, and every word you yelled. Although it was hard, I could see your love for me with every slap, kick, and scream. As a child, I remember hating myself for making you mad. I truly believed that a spanking with a belt, or being put in a linen closet for several days, or telling my teachers that my bruises were caused by my clumsiness was just punishment for being an inconsiderate, guilty child. Physically, your children are almost all grown, but emotionally we are still your kids waiting for our father's gentle hug, soft word and warm touch. Now as an adult, with help from therapy, I realize we were not guilty children. 4

No child needs to suffer from someone else's inability to deal with stress. Child abuse is wrong and inexcusable. 5

When a parent finds him or herself in a situation where the stress and frustration becomes overwhelming to a point that the safety of any child is threatened, he or she should have enough love and concern to seek outside intervention. This solution is not difficult. Between grandparents, aunts and uncles, in-laws, neighbors and friends or even day cares, a person can be found to care for the child while the frustrated parent finds peace. Many areas even offer an emergency day care program which is set up for this specific problem at no cost to the parent. 6

Solutions to this human disgrace can be summarized in one word: love. Any parent who truly loves his child cannot fathom the thought of abuse. Therefore, any parent who does abuse their child desperately needs professional help. 7

Loving a child is easy for a healthy parent. It is unfortunate that I look back at my childhood with shame and regret, despite all your efforts. There is one consolation, though, my children have the best daddy. 8

Writers at Work: Round 1

Although the following is not an exact record of the exchange that occurred when McKendry presented his autobiography to his peer group, it is fairly representative of the kinds of comments that he received:

"Wow, this really seems honest and forceful," said Molly McLeod. "I like the part when you talk about how people don't realize how fragile children are. It's hard to understand how people can be so brutal, you know?"

"Yeah, it's powerful," said John Barber. "But you might want to work on the spelling and grammar a little bit. The word "truly" has only got one 'l.' I don't know about the word 'dad,' though. Should it be capitalized?"

"Well, I don't know, but I'm gonna check all that stuff later. I mean, I know that there are a lot of errors and all, but I think there's something even more important that's missing, but I don't know what it is. I just feel it's not right, you know? I'm dissatisfied with it, but I can't figure out what's wrong, and it's driving me crazy. I mean, I really wanted to write about this topic. I've thought about this for a long time, but I'm not sure that I really have an audience for it. To be totally honest, I wrote this for myself, not for an audience. I'm not sure if it's what the teacher wants, you know."

"Well, I can see how you're a little unsure about your audience," Mike said. "Throughout most of the piece you seem to be talking directly to your Dad. Then later on you start talking to other people. I think you should decide if this piece is for your Dad or if it's for other people."

"Nah, I don't think so," Jennifer said. "I think that even when he addresses his Dad, he's still writing for people in general about child abuse."

"Well, I think it's really good," Bill said. "The only part that bugged me was the fourth paragraph." Bill pointed at his copy of Herb's autobiography and said, "When you say, 'I could see your love for me with every slap, kick, and scream,' I'm kind of confused. It seems to me that you would want to hit back, you know? I just don't get that part. I mean, how could you love your Dad when he was being so terrible?"

Herb stared at his essay for a moment and then said, "Yeah, well, that's how I felt. Well, I guess that's one of the peculiar things about being abused. You see, I've been in group counseling, so now I know how common these feelings are."

"Well, that's really interesting. Maybe you should explain why you felt that way, for people who haven't been abused."

In response to these diverse suggestions from his peers, McKendry produced the following revision:

Guilty Children

Herb McKendry

Father,   1

Not all people are aware of the burden put on a man who is disabled; who has   2
eight hungry, miserable, dirty kids; who has a wife who is constantly sick with
something; who has to depend on welfare checks and food stamps to make
ends meet; and who has no chance of getting a job—any job. I can understand how the stress from so many problems could be over-bearing, how the
pressure could lead to regret, frustration, and anger.

Father, I do not envy your life. I really admired you for trying so hard   3
because I knew not many people realize the pain of a responsible man who
never enjoys the success of his efforts, wants, and hope; who never enjoys the
budget balanced, the cabinets full, the car nice and new, the closets filled
with decent clothes, the house clean and respectable, the wife loving and
healthy, and the kids safe and warm.

Father, you know the burden and pain of being a frustrated responsible 4
man. I know the burden and pain of being your child. I tried to see your
hopes for an easier life with every cigarette you smoked, every beer you
drank, and every word you yelled by attributing it to stress. Although it was
hard, I tried to see your love for me with every slap, kick, and scream.

Father, you didn't realize how fragile us kids really were, how dependent 5
on your support of our behavior, how needy we were of your unconditional
touch and approval, how innocent and gentle we really were, and how directly our growth reflects your treatment of us.

As a child, I remember hating myself for making you mad. I truly 6
believed that a spanking with a belt, or being put in a linen closet for several
days, or telling my teachers that my bruises were caused by my clumsiness
was just punishment for being an inconsiderate, guilty child. I remember seeing other kids in school who were always happy and full of spirit. I remember
praying to God for that spirit too, but I never really could. I also remember
trying to save the doomed, frail spirits of my brothers and sisters. Now that
time has passed. Physically we have all grown, but emotionally we are still
your kids, waiting for your gentle hug, soft word, and warm touch. Now as an
adult, with help from therapy, I realize we were not guilty children.

If you are like my father—that is, if you have such great difficulties deal- 7
ing with stress that you abuse your children—I ask that you seek counseling.
When you find yourself in a situation where the stress and frustration
becomes overwhelming to a point that the safety of any child is threatened,
please seek outside intervention. This solution is not difficult. Between
grandparents, aunts and uncles, in-laws, neighbors and friends, or even day
care centers, you can find a person to care for the child while you seek peace.
Many areas even offer an emergency day care program which is set up for
this specific problem at no cost to you.

Writers at Work: Round 2

In response to the suggestions of his peers, Herb McKendry revised his autobiography and brought a copy of his third draft to the group for a second
review a week later. After reading his revised essay out loud to his group
members, Herb asked them what criticisms they could suggest. Below is a
sample of the advice that they gave him:

"Well, I can see that you corrected all of the misspellings and punctuation
errors," John said. "I think you'll get an 'A' on it for sure."

"Yeah, I like the change you make to the part when you talk about how
you felt when your Dad hit you."

"Thanks, guys, but listen—I'm still worried about my audience. Do
you like what I did with the final paragraph. What do you think Mike? Did
I improve the audience?"

"Well, I don't think I should criticize this piece. I mean, I can't write
this well."

"No, really, I'm curious about what you think. I've been thinking about what you said on Tuesday about working on the audience. I tried to broaden it, you know."

"Well, to be totally honest," Mike said, "I don't think you need that final paragraph. I think that makes your piece sound like an advertisement or something. As far as I'm concerned, you've said everything you need to with that last line, 'Now, as an adult, with help from therapy, I realize we were not guilty children.' I think that's a terrific final line given your story. This is really an amazing story, Herb, but I'd definitely cut out that last paragraph."

PEER REVIEW WORKSHOP

Naturally, as a reviewer you should try to answer any of the questions that your peer has asked you to consider when critiquing his or her work. You should also be sensitive to your peer's willingness to listen to what you have to say. The best way to do this is to ask how detailed you should be when reviewing his or her work. Use the following questions as a guide to evaluating your peers' work:

1. Does the essay appear to be focused around a single experience or theme? What are the major conflicts experienced by the author?

2. What voice or persona do you sense in the work?

3. Can you identify any passages that seem confusing or vague?

4. Has the author used concrete, sensory language? Do any passages stand out as particularly powerful in this regard?

Additional Writing Samples

In *Lives on the Boundary: The Struggles and Achievements of America's Underprepared*, Mike Rose offers a compelling description of his own life. Beyond portraying his personal experiences as a vocational student (who would have been assigned to honors courses if his file hadn't been confused with that of another student), Rose launches a vigorous attack on American education. The following passage is from Rose's opening chapter, "I Just Wanna Be Average."

I Just Wanna Be Average*

Mike Rose

Students will float to the mark you set. I and the others in the vocational classes were bobbing in pretty shallow water. Vocational education has aimed

---

* From *Lives on the Boundary: The Struggles and Achievements of America's Underprepared*, pp. 26–29. Copyright © 1989 by Mike Rose. Reprinted with the permission of The Free Press, a division of Macmillan, Inc.

at increasing the economic opportunities of students who do not do well in our schools. Some serious programs succeed in doing that, and through exceptional teachers—like Mr. Gross in *Horace's Compromise*—students learn to develop hypotheses and troubleshoot, reason through a problem, and communicate effectively—the true job skills. The vocational track, however, is most often a place for those who are just not making it, a dumping ground for the disaffected. There were a few teachers who worked hard at education; young Brother Slattery, for example, combined a stern voice with weekly quizzes to try to pass along to us a skeletal outline of world history. But mostly the teachers had no idea of how to engage the imagination of us kids who were scuttling along at the bottom of the pond.

And the teachers would have needed some inventiveness, for none of us 2 was groomed for the classroom. It wasn't just that I didn't know things—didn't know how to simplify algebraic fractions, couldn't identify different kinds of clauses, bungled Spanish translations—but that I had developed various faulty and inadequate ways of doing algebra and making sense of Spanish. Worse yet, the years of defensive tuning out in elementary school had given me a way to escape quickly while seeming at least half alert. During my time in Voc. Ed., I developed further into a mediocre student and a somnambulant problem solver, and that affected the subjects I did have the wherewithal to handle: I detested Shakespeare; I got bored with history. My attention flitted here and there. I fooled around in class and read my books indifferently—the intellectual equivalent of playing with your food. I did what I had to do to get by, and I did it with half a mind.

But I did learn things about people and eventually came into my own 3 socially. I liked the guys in Voc. Ed. Growing up where I did, I understood and admired physical prowess, and there was an abundance of muscle here. There was Dave Snyder, a sprinter and halfback of true quality. Dave's ability and his quick wit gave him a natural appeal, and he was welcome in any clique, though he always kept a little independent. He enjoyed acting the fool and could care less about studies, but he possessed a certain maturity and never caused the faculty much trouble. It was a testament to his independence that he included me among his friends—I eventually went out for track, but I was no jock. Owing to the Latin alphabet and a dearth of *R*s and *S*s, Snyder sat behind Rose, and we started exchanging one-liners and became friends.

There was Ted Richard, a much-touted Little League pitcher. He was 4 chunky and had a baby face and came to Our Lady of Mercy as a seasoned street fighter. Ted was quick to laugh and he had a loud, jolly laugh, but when he got angry he'd smile a little smile, the kind that simply raises the corner of the mouth a quarter of an inch. For those who knew, it was an eerie signal. Those who didn't found themselves in big trouble, for Ted was very quick. He loved to carry on what we would come to call philosophical discussions: What is courage? Does God exist? He also loved words, enjoyed picking up big ones like *salubrious* and *equivocal* and using them in our conversations—laughing at himself as the word hit a chuckhole rolling off his tongue. Ted didn't do all that well in school—baseball and parties and testing the courage he'd speculated about took up his time. His textbooks were *Argosy* and *Field and Stream*, whatever newspapers he'd find on the bus stop— from the *Daily Worker* to pornography—conversations with uncles or hobos or businessmen he'd meet in a coffee shop, *The Old Man and the Sea.* With hindsight, I can see that Ted was developing into one of those rough-hewn intellectuals whose sources are a mix of the learned and the apocryphal, whose discussions are both assured and sad.

And then there was Ken Harvey. Ken was good-looking in a puffy way 5 and had a full and oily ducktail and was a car enthusiast . . . a hodad. One day in religion class, he said the sentence that turned out to be one of the most memorable of the hundreds of thousands I heard in those Voc. Ed. years. We were talking about the parable of the talents, about achievement, working hard, doing the best you can do, blah-blah-blah, when the teacher called on the restive Ken Harvey for an opinion. Ken thought about it, but just for a second, and said (with studied, minimal affect), *"I just wanna be average."* That woke me up. Average?! Who wants to be average? Then the athletes chimed in with the clichés that make you want to laryngectomize them, and the exchange became a platitudinous melee. At the time, I thought Ken's assertion was stupid, and I wrote him off. But his sentence has stayed with me all these years, and I think I am finally coming to understand it.

Ken Harvey was gasping for air. School can be a tremendously disorient- 6 ing place. No matter how bad the school, you're going to encounter notions that don't fit with the assumptions and beliefs that you grew up with—maybe you'll hear these dissonant notions from teachers, maybe from the other students, and maybe you'll read them. You'll also be thrown in with all kinds of kids from all kinds of backgrounds, and that can be unsettling—this is especially true in places of rich ethnic and linguistic mix, like the L.A. basin. You'll see a handful of students far excel you in courses that sound exotic and that are only in the curriculum of the elite: French, physics, trigonometry. And all this is happening while you're trying to shape an identity, your body is changing, and your emotions are running wild. If you're a working-class kid in the vocational track, the options you'll have to deal with this will be constrained in certain ways: You're defined by your school as "slow"; you're placed in a curriculum that isn't designed to liberate you but to occupy you, or, if you're lucky, train you, though the training is for work the society does not esteem; other students are picking up the cues from your school and your curriculum and interacting with you in particular ways. If you're a kid like Ted Richard, you turn your back on all this and let your mind roam where it may. But youngsters like Ted are rare. What Ken and so many others do is protect themselves from such suffocating madness by taking on with a vengeance the identity implied in the vocational track. Reject the confusion and frustration by openly defining yourself as the Common Joe. Champion the average. Rely on your own good sense. Fuck this bullshit. Bullshit, of course, is everything you—and the others—fear is beyond you: books, essays, tests, academic scrambling, complexity, scientific reasoning, philosophical inquiry.

The tragedy is that you have to twist the knife in your own gray matter 7 to make this defense work. You'll have to shut down, have to reject intellectual stimuli or diffuse them with sarcasm, have to cultivate stupidity, have to convert boredom from a malady into a way of confronting the world. Keep your vocabulary simple, act stoned when you're not or act more stoned than you are, flaunt ignorance, materialize your dreams. It is a powerful and effective defense—it neutralizes the insult and the frustration of being a vocational kid and, when perfected, it drives teachers up the wall, a delightful secondary effect. But like all strong magic, it exacts a price.

Critical Reading Questions

1. What does Rose mean by the opening sentence of this passage, "Students will float to the mark you set"? What evidence does Rose provide to support this assertion?

2. How would you describe Rose's tone in this document? How does this essay differ from those presented at the beginning of this chapter?

3. What descriptions of his classmates does Rose provide to help you develop a mental image of these students?

4. What assumptions about audience does Rose appear to be making in this passage?

In the following biography, Shelli Boyd, a student writer, illustrates the horror of date rape. To write this biography, Boyd interviewed a young woman with whom she worked at a local restaurant.

Welcome to Tampa
Shelli Boyd

Nationwide attention has been focused on the crime of acquaintance rape 1 through the much publicized trials of Mike Tyson, William Kennedy Smith, and the local case of Carl Allison. Thanks to the victims who find the courage to come forward, date rape is being recognized as a problem that must be addressed. However, for every woman possessing the strength to face her attacker as well as the public's often unfounded preconceptions, there are many more who, for various reasons, suffer in silence. This is the story of one such woman.

Four years ago when "Sarah" was a freshman at USF, she was raped by a 2 man she met in a bar. She told no one, fearing her family and friends would not understand and would somehow blame her. Consequently, the man was never apprehended and Sarah lives with the shame experienced by the victims of the crime. She agreed to tell her story under the condition that her real name be withheld.

My Story

I was 19 years old when I came to Tampa. I moved from Atlanta, Georgia, over the Christmas season, so that I could attend USF in the spring. I didn't know that many people and I was really homesick when school started. I used to call home all the time and beg my mom and dad to come and get me, but they said I should give it a semester, that I would get used to it.   3

My new roommate partied all the time and I rarely saw her the first couple of weeks I was here. She and a group of friends went out drinking all the time, and I was excited when she invited me to go with them one night. We went to this club downtown that was so packed I wanted to leave the moment we got there. My roommate and her friends seemed to know everybody, while I just kind of hung back, feeling very out of place. After a while, I decided to leave. My roommate said she could find another ride, and that's when *he* came up.   4

I was wearing a Georgia Bulldogs sweatshirt and he asked me if I went to school there. When I told him I was from Atlanta, he said he was from there, too. We talked about some clubs there, and other spots that I used to hang out at, and he had been to all of them. I was so happy to run into someone from home that I really let my guard down. We talked for a long time—he told me that he didn't like Tampa that much either at first, but if I gave it some time I would love it. We even talked about carpooling to Atlanta over spring break, or maybe just going up there for one weekend.   5

When I look back, I feel I should have seen some sign, some sort of clue as to what he had in mind, but I didn't. He seemed harmless. He was kind of cute, and he seemed really easy going. I must have had "victim" written all over me: I was lonely as hell, I didn't know that many people, and I was very naive.   6

I finally decided to leave again. I was really glad to run into someone from home, but it seemed to make my homesickness that much worse. He tried to get me to stay, but I lied and said that I had an early class and had to go. He asked if he could walk me out, but I said no, that he didn't have to do that. He started insisting that he walk me to my car, that it wasn't safe for a girl to walk around by herself. "Tampa's not very safe," he kept saying, and I remember thinking that he was probably right.   7

We left the club and walked through the parking lot to my car. There were several people hanging out in the parking lot talking and laughing, and I said to him, "See? I would have been just fine," and he said, "You can never tell." When we got to my car, we talked a little while and then he started kissing me. I let him kiss me, but I made him stop when he started trying to touch my breasts. He said he was sorry, and we started kissing again. He kept trying to touch me, but whenever I asked him to stop, he would. Some peo-   8 ple came walking by, and I told him I was embarrassed. He asked if I wanted to get inside my car. I said no, that I really should be going home, and then he asked if I would give him a ride to see if his roommate's car was still there. He said that he hadn't seen his roommate in a while and just wanted to make sure that he hadn't been stranded or anything.

At that moment, I guess I sensed something. I didn't want to give him 9 a ride, but I didn't want to be rude either. I said OK, and we got in my car. He directed me around the parking lot and onto this little side street. He told me to turn and we ended up in this little dead-end alley way. Before I knew what was happening, he turned off my engine and took the keys.

"What are you doing?" I remember asking, and he just smiled. He 10 grabbed me and started kissing and groping me under my sweatshirt. I started screaming and hitting him, but he covered my mouth and pulled me into the backseat where he started ripping at my clothes. He kept saying that I wanted it, that I wanted him to do this to me. I couldn't believe it. I could not believe this was happening. He said that I had been teasing him all night, and asking for this, and he was going to give it to me.

The whole thing seems like a dream. I see it in my mind as if it happened 11 to someone else. I guess I was in shock or something, but I kind of removed myself from the picture. The worst part, worse than the pain or the fear, was the degradation. I was nothing but a piece of meat to him. He did not see me as a human being with feelings or emotions, he saw me as something less than human. The look on his face and the sounds he was making as he raped me made me feel like I was less than human. My self-esteem was and still is shattered.

I didn't tell anyone about that night. I felt so stupid for letting him in my 12 car. I was ashamed to tell my parents. I knew they would feel responsible since I begged them to let me come home and they said no. I don't know how I made it through the semester; my grades were really bad and at times I was suicidal, but I survived. It's been four years since I was raped, and I still have a hard time at night. I sometimes dream about it and I wake up crying. I'm trying to put the whole thing behind me and go on, but it's not easy. I now know that I should have gone to the police, but at the time I really did think it was my fault. I thought that I had led him on in some way, and even if I didn't, there was no way to prove it. It would have been his word against mine. I only hope that he hasn't done the same thing to someone else.

Critical Reading Questions

1. How does Boyd's overview of this biography influence how you read her essay?

2. What specific details about "Sarah's" experience does Boyd provide to help you visualize and understand the rape?

3. How has Boyd organized her account of her friend's experience? What alternative ways of organizing this document can you devise?

4. What one or two suggestions for improving this essay would you offer to Boyd if she sought your aid?

Evaluating Criticism

Once you receive your essay back from your instructor, take a moment to reflect on the nature of any problems that your instructor identified in it. Look, for example, to see whether your content was well developed. Did you present your narrative using a coherent organization? Did you provide the details about the people and scene that readers need to understand and empathize with your experience? Was your voice appropriate—vigorous, objective, passionate? If your instructor noted numerous grammatical and mechanical errors, do you understand how to avoid these kinds of errors in the future?

Historians and philosophers are fond of saying that those who do not learn from history are doomed to repeat it. This observation is equally valid in regard to your development as a writer. Rather than putting yourself down for making errors, remember that you are in school to learn. Focus on the most important shortcomings your instructor found in this essay and then work to avoid these problems in your next assignment.

Analyzing Subjects and Processes

Analysis involves breaking a subject into discrete parts so that it can be better understood. You practice analysis whenever you try to solve a problem or think critically about a subject. Deciding what college to attend, what major to specialize in, whom to spend time with, where to live, how to study, how to use your free time—making decisions such as these requires you to exercise your analytical abilities. Solving everyday problems involves breaking a problem down into discrete parts, prioritizing, and weighing options—all of which are forms of analysis.

At the most elementary level, all writing involves analyzing and reporting information. Definitions of subjects, reports of processes, autobiographies, persuasive arguments, in-class essays, research reports, letters to loved ones, business correspondence—all of the writing that we do requires that we break a subject down into its component parts so that readers can understand it better.

Being able to analyze subjects and events is crucial to your success in virtually every college course. Your literature professor may ask you to analyze how a character's personality evolves throughout a novel. Science instructors may ask you to write a lab report that illustrates how different chemicals interact. Biology teachers may assign papers on Darwin's theory of evolution. Physics instructors may require you to explain Einstein's theory of relativity. Education instructors may ask you to explain Vygotsky's model of cognitive development. Engineering instructors may ask you to describe how solar heating works or how sound is changed into electrical signals. Analytical thinking is obviously an important part of college work, and especially writing.

Analytical writing can have any of several purposes. When your primary purpose for writing is to answer the question "What is it?" you are writing a *subject analysis*. In turn, when you are writing to answer "How can I do this?" or "How is this done?" you are writing a *process analysis*. There are two distinct types of process analyses: *prescriptive process reports* and *descriptive process reports*. Prescriptive reports are instructions; they explain in chronological order how something should be done so that readers can do it. In contrast, descriptive reports clarify how a process occurs so that readers can understand it better. Many descriptive processes are too complicated to be separated into chronological order. The following processes, for example, are too complex to be explained simply and sequentially: how children acquire language, how adolescents adopt moral standards, how people's self-images change as they age, how loving relationships evolve or deteriorate, how our sense of time changes with age, how adults confront death and dying. Although academic readers tend to enjoy intelligent discussions of such sophisticated processes, they dislike superficial explanations.

Writing Samples

In the following essay, student Michael Miller analyzes his strengths and weaknesses as a writer. To avoid being vague in his self-assessment, Miller reviewed essays that he had written in high school and college.

Say What?

Michael Miller

Evaluating one's own writing process is arduous, and without the help of my 1 old essays I am not quite sure I could have done it. By noting the comments my instructors made in response to my essays in high school and college classes, I have realized something that I had never considered before: different papers involved different writing and rewriting processes. Because the essays that I studied were written so long ago, I also felt that I could be more objective in critiquing them and in considering the value of my teachers' commentaries. Thus, in addition to helping me get a better sense of different ways to write essays, studying my old essays helped me identify several important strengths and weaknesses.

Initially I had trouble remembering exactly how I developed my papers, 2 but after reading old papers, I could easily recall the processes I used to develop them. I soon noted that if I were writing a serious persuasive paper, involving hard facts, I would provide structure and sound support for a thesis that I was already aware of, but if I were writing a creative narrative piece, I would not always know how it would turn out until I had finished the first draft and read what I had written. The discovery of these different writing processes helped me to better understand that, although effective writing processes are of paramount importance, writing is not an exact science and processes will never be exactly the same.

By reviewing my old essays, I have found that my most consistent 3 strength is tone. In the past my teachers have described tone as the writer's style, personality, or even tone of voice. A writer's tone can vary as much as that of a speaker. With proper tone, the writer can overcome many of the disadvantages of the written word and add inflection and personality that are normally found only in the spoken word. However, unlike many other writing skills, tone is difficult to properly develop. For example, if a writer is having a problem with grammar or even something more complex like making transitions, there are specific exercises for mastering these skills. Tone, on the other hand, is very subtle; precise word choice and careful phrasing are key elements in creating a certain tone and, although the textbook can assist, tone is only truly developed through much practice and reading of other writers.

More than anything else, rereading my essays has helped me discover my 4 weaknesses as a writer. Fortunately, I have found that, over the years, my problems with grammar and syntax have dwindled to a minimum. However, I have noticed a recurring problem. Time after time, my graded papers are returned with remarks such as "clarify," "unclear," or "explain." Obviously, I have been doing something wrong; after careful analysis, I have managed to define the problem. I quite simply expect too much from the reader. I repeat the mistake of assuming that readers think just as I do, and that they understand broad inferences and vague statements in my writings. This results in a confused reader and a frustrated writer.

Fortunately, in this case, I can agree with the philosopher Dewey in that 5 "a problem defined is half solved." Now that I realize that my writing is vague, I can take steps to correct it. In fact, just being aware of the problem will help somewhat; however, to completely overcome the problem will require strategy. Hence, I have decided to develop a heuristic system to ensure that support and explanation will be given to all of my statements, and inferences will be eliminated. Consequently, the reader will always be able to follow my line of thought or reasoning. The heuristic approach is as follows:

1. What does it mean?
2. Did you give details?
3. Did you give examples?
4. Can it be more clear?
5. Will the reader understand your meaning?

I am confident that, by applying each of these questions to my writing, the 6 vagueness problem will be solved. But I also realize that improving one's writing is a never-ending process, and solving one problem only leaves the writer more time to devote to another aspect of the writing process.

Critical Reading Questions

1. In what ways does Miller say the kind of writing he does influences how he writes? In what ways are your writing habits similar?
2. Miller explains that his greatest fault as a writer is his tendency to be vague. Where in this draft do you find that diagnosis to be true?
3. How would you describe Miller's tone in this piece? What specific words or examples contribute to this tone?
4. Do you share any of Miller's strengths or weaknesses as a writer? Have you ever reviewed any of your essays that were graded in previous

courses? What strengths and weaknesses do you believe you would find if you did?

In the following passage, Alfie Kohn, a contributing editor to *Psychology Today*, summarizes communication research that has analyzed differences between how males and females communicate. Because Kohn is writing for a commercial, mainstream magazine, he does not provide traditional academic footnotes. Yet he carefully avoids taking credit for other researchers' work by citing the names and university affiliations of those he reviews.

Girl Talk—Guy Talk*

Alfie Kohn

"Hey, y' know what?"   1

"Mmmm?"   2

"I was walking near that, um, new construction site? Near the bank?"   3

"Yeh."   4

"Well, this kinda crazy guy comes up to me, you know? I'm, like, ready 5 to run for the bank."

"Huh."   6

"It's really *amazing* that these people approach you in broad daylight, 7 don't you think?"

"I know. I was at the movies once and some bum started asking me for 8 money."

"Really? What happened?"   9

With this imaginary dialogue, enter the stereotypical world of men's and 10 women's speech, in which men tend to dominate conversations, interrupt or shift the topic to one they prefer, and in which women—by adopting a questioning, tentative tone—work hard to gain men's attention.

In fact, a decade's worth of research has shown that men and women in 11 our culture use distinctive styles of speech and also tend to play different roles when talking with one another. More recently, researchers have moved away from examining men's and women's language in the abstract, preferring to scrutinize the actual settings, such as courtrooms and physicians' offices, in which conversation takes place. Although some researchers now suggest that speech patterns are as much a function of social status as of gender, studies have confirmed definite sex differences in diverse situations.

Boston College sociologist Charles Derber has studied the roles that 12 men and women take on in conversation and has found that men often shift conversations to their preferred topics, whereas women are more apt to respond supportively. In a study of married couples, Derber found that the wife gave more active encouragement to her husband's talk about himself,

---

* From *Psychology Today*, February 1988. Copyright 1988 by Alfie Kohn, reprinted by permission of the author.

while the husband "listened less well and was less likely to actively 'bring her out' about herself and her own topics."

In fact, men often interrupt outright, and they do this far more fre- 13 quently than women do, several studies have shown. Candace West and Don Zimmerman, sociologists at the University of California, recorded a number of two-party conversations. When men spoke with men or women with women, there were relatively few interruptions, and those that did occur were balanced between the two speakers. When men conversed with women, however, not only did more interruptions occur, but 96 percent of them involved men interrupting women.

From her doctoral research in sociology at the University of California, 14 Santa Barbara, Pamela Fishman concludes, "Both men and women regarded topics introduced by women as tentative [whereas] topics introduced by the men were treated as topics to be pursued. The women . . . did much of the necessary work of interaction, starting conversations and then working to maintain them."

Closely connected to conversational roles is the matter of styles of 15 speech. Linguist Robin Lakoff, of the University of California, Berkeley, along with many other researchers, has pointed to questioning as a distinctive characteristic of women's speech. Specifically, women:

- Ask more questions. Fishman's analysis of tape-recorded conversations between professional couples found that the women asked nearly three times as many questions as the men.

- Make statements in a questioning tone. ("I was walking near that, um, new construction site?") The rising inflection, Lakoff says, suggests that the speaker is seeking confirmation even though she may be the only one who has the necessary information.

- Use more tag questions. Adding a brief question at the end of a sentence (". . . don't you think?") suggests doubt or encourages the listener to respond. Not all studies have confirmed Lakoff's assertion that women use more of these, however.

- Lead off with a question. Starting a conversation this way ("Hey, y' know what?") is intended to ensure a listener's attention. This device and others led West and Zimmerman to note that there are "striking similarities" between the conversations between men and women and those between adults and children.

- Use more "hedges" or qualifiers ("kinda") in their speech and also rely on intensifiers ("really"). The latter, which can refer not only to the choice of words but to the emphasis with which they are pronounced (*"amazing"*), tell the listener "how to react," according to Lakoff. "Since my saying something by itself is not likely to convince you," Lakoff observes, "I'd better use double force to make sure you see what I mean."

The implications of these findings have been the subject of considerable 16 discussion, particularly among feminists. That women express their thoughts more tentatively and work harder to get someone's attention probably says something about their conversational experience with men—experience along the lines of what Derber, Fishman, West and Zimmerman have documented. Moreover, women may have internalized men's assumptions that what they have to say isn't very interesting or intellectually rigorous. This hesitancy then becomes the norm for "proper" feminine speech. Lakoff deplores this situation, noting that "a woman is damned if she does and damned if she doesn't." She is "ostracized as unfeminine by both men and women" if she speaks directly and assertively but dismissed "as someone not to be taken seriously, of dim intelligence, frivolous" if she adopts the traditional style and role.

While it may be a disadvantage in our society, "women's language" has 17 features that many believe should be preserved. Requesting rather than commanding, attending to others' needs in a conversation and listening more effectively are seen by many as valuable social skills. Linguist Sally McConnell-Ginet of Cornell University urges women to adopt a conversational style that doesn't sacrifice sensitivity but "nevertheless doesn't make you sound as if you have less commitment to your beliefs than you have." The issue, she adds, is not just "how women should change the way they speak, but how men should change the way they listen."

In the last few years, researchers have also begun to look at how a partic- 18 ular setting can influence patterns of speech. "There's been a change from looking at discrete elements of language [and toward] interaction—the whole situation," says Cheris Kramarae, professor of speech communication at the University of Illinois. We're "studying language in context."

Viewing language in concrete situations has led some researchers to 19 argue recently that speech is at least as much a function of social status as of gender. Duke University anthropologist William O'Barr pored over 10 weeks' worth of trial transcripts and discovered that a witness's occupation and experience on the stand told more about speech patterns than whether the witness was a man or woman did. "So-called women's language is neither characteristic of all women nor limited only to women," O'Barr writes in his book *Linguistic Evidence.* If women generally use "powerless" language, he adds, this may be due largely "to the greater tendency of women to occupy relatively powerless social positions" in American society.

Occupation—or at least situational context—also proved the dominant 20 factor in a study of day-care workers by psychologist Jean Berko Gleason of Boston University. "Male day-care teachers' speech to young children," she points out, "is more like the language of female day-care teachers than it is like that of fathers at home."

Finally, West spent five years exploring conversational dynamics among 21 male and female physicians and patients at a Southern family-medicine practice. Since physician and patient provide a clear example of a relationship between two people of unequal status, West could determine whether interruptions reflected status or gender. The answer: Both played a part. Overall, physicians interrupted patients more often than the reverse, but female physicians were interrupted more when they had male patients. "It appears," West concludes, "that gender can take precedence over occupational status in conversation."

At the same time, gender differences in speech may simply reflect power   22 relations between men and women in general. Maryann Ayim, who teaches education at the University of Western Ontario, puts it this way: "If females are more polite and less aggressive than males in their language practices, if they are more supportive and less dominant, this is hardly shocking, for it simply reflects the reality in every other sphere of life."

Critical Reading Questions

1. Why does Kohn begin his summary with a sample dialogue? Is this introduction effective?

2. What assumptions does Kohn present to explain the differences between male and female speech? Do you find any of these assumptions to be specious?

3. In what ways does your personal experience refute or support the differences in communication patterns summarized by Kohn?

4. How would you describe Kohn's tone in this piece?

The following selection is excerpted from the introduction to Gail Sheehy's book *Passages*. At first Sheehy's observations may appear to be unsupported generalizations; note, however, that she attempts to support these generalizations about life-style patterns through the remainder of her 560-page book. (To identify life-style patterns, Sheehy reviewed psychological literature and interviewed 115 adults.)

Passages*

Gail Sheehy

Although I have indicated the ages when Americans are likely to go through   1 each stage, and the differences between men and women where they are striking, do not take the ages too seriously. The stages are the thing, and most particularly the sequence.

Here is the briefest outline of the developmental ladder.   2

* From *Passages*, copyright © 1974, 1976 by Gail Sheehy. Used by permission of the publisher, Dutton, an imprint of New American Library, a division of Penguin Books USA Inc.

Pulling Up Roots

Before 18, the motto is loud and clear: "I have to get away from my parents." 3
But the words are seldom connected to action. Generally, still safely part of
our families, even if away at school, we feel our autonomy to be subject to
erosion from moment to moment.

After 18, we begin Pulling Up Roots in earnest. College, military service, 4
and short-term travels are all customary vehicles our society provides for the
first round trips between family and a base of one's own. In the attempt to
separate our view of the world to the contrary—"I know exactly what I
want!"—we cast about for any beliefs we can call our own. And in the process
of testing those beliefs we are often drawn to fads, preferably those most
mysterious and inaccessible to our parents.

Whatever tentative membership we try out in the world, the fear haunts 5
us that we are really kids who cannot take care of ourselves. We cover that
fear with acts of defiance and mimicked confidence. For allies to replace our
parents, we turn to our contemporaries. They become conspirators. So long
as their perspective meshes with our own, they are able to substitute for the
sanctuary of the family. But that doesn't last very long. And the instant they
diverge from the shaky ideals of "our group," they are seen as betrayers.
Rebounds to the family are common between the ages of 18 and 22.

The tasks of this passage are to locate ourselves in a peer group role, a 6
sex role, an anticipated occupation, an ideology or world view. As a result, we
gather the impetus to leave home physically and the identity to begin leaving
home emotionally.

Even as one part of us seeks to be an individual, another part longs to 7
restore the safety and comfort of merging with another. Thus one of the
most popular myths of this passage is: We can piggyback our development by
attaching to a Stronger One. But people who marry during this time often
prolong financial and emotional ties to the family and relatives that impede
them from becoming self-sufficient.

A stormy passage through the Pulling Up Roots years will probably facil- 8
itate the normal progression of the adult life cycle. If one doesn't have an
identity crisis at this point, it will erupt during a later transition, when the
penalties may be harder to bear.

The Trying Twenties

The Trying Twenties confront us with the question of how to take hold in 9
the adult world. Our focus shifts from the interior turmoils of late adoles-
cence—"Who am I?" "What is truth?"—and we become almost totally pre-
occupied with working out the externals. "How do I put my aspirations into
effect?" "What is the best way to start?" "Where do I go?" "Who can help
me?" "How did you do it?"

In this period, which is longer and more stable compared with the pas- 10
sage that leads to it, the tasks are as enormous as they are exhilarating: To
shape a Dream, that vision of ourselves which will generate energy, aliveness,

and hope. To prepare for a lifework. To find a mentor if possible. And to form the capacity for intimacy, without losing in the process whatever consistency of self we have thus far mustered. The first test structure must be erected around the life we choose to try.

Doing what we "should" is the most pervasive theme of the twenties. 11 The "shoulds" are largely defined by family models, the press of the culture, or the prejudices of our peers. If the prevailing cultural instructions are that one should get married and settle down behind one's own door, a nuclear family is born. If instead the peers insist that one should do one's own thing, the 25-year-old is likely to harness himself onto a Harley-Davidson and burn up Route 66 in the commitment to have no commitments.

One of the terrifying aspects of the twenties is the inner conviction that 12 the choices we make are irrevocable. It is largely a false fear. Change is quite possible, and some alteration of our original choices is probably inevitable.

Two impulses, as always, are at work. One is to build a firm, safe struc- 13 ture for the future by making strong commitments, to "be set." Yet people who slip into a ready-made form without much self-examination are likely to find themselves *locked-in.*

The other urge is to explore and experiment, keeping any structure ten- 14 tative and therefore easily reversible. Taken to the extreme, these are people who skip from one trial job and one limited personal encounter to another, spending their twenties in the transient state.

Although the choices of our twenties are not irrevocable, they do set in 15 motion a Life Pattern. Some of us follow the locked-in pattern, others the transient pattern, the wunderkind pattern, the caregiver pattern, and there are a number of others. Such patterns strongly influence the particular questions raised for each person during each passage, and so the most common patterns will also be traced throughout the book.

Buoyed by powerful illusions and belief in the power of the will, we com- 16 monly insist in our twenties that what we have chosen to do is the one true course in life. Our backs go up at the merest hint that we are like our parents, that two decades of parental training might be reflected in our current actions and attitudes.

"Not me," is the motto, "I'm different." 17

Catch-30

Impatient with devoting ourselves to the "shoulds," a new vitality springs 18 from within as we approach 30. Men and women alike speak of feeling too narrow and restricted. They blame all sorts of things, but what the restrictions boil down to are the outgrowth of career and personal choices of the twenties. There may have been choices perfectly suited to that stage. But now the fit feels different. Some inner aspect that was left out is striving to be taken into account. Important new choices must be made, and commitments altered or deepened. The work involves great change, turmoil, and often crisis—a simultaneous feeling of rock bottom and the urge to bust out.

One common response is the tearing up of the life we spent most of our   19
twenties putting together. It may mean striking out on a secondary road
toward a new vision or converting a dream of "running for president" into a
more realistic goal. The single person feels a push to find a partner. The
woman who was previously content at home with children chafes to venture
into the world. The childless couple reconsiders children. And almost everyone who is married, especially those married for seven years, feels a discontent.

If the discontent doesn't lead to a divorce, it will, or should call for a seri-   20
ous review of the marriage and of each partner's aspirations in their Catch-30
condition. The gist of the condition was expressed by a 29-year-old associate
with a Wall Street law firm:

"I'm considering leaving the firm. I've been there four years now; I'm   21
getting good feedback, but I have no clients of my own. I feel weak. If I wait
much longer, it will be too late, too close to that fateful time of decision on
whether or not to become a partner. I'm success-oriented. But the concept of
being 55 years old and stuck in a monotonous job drives me wild. It drives me
crazy now, just a little bit. I'd say that 85 percent of the time I thoroughly
enjoy my work. But when I get a screwball case, I come away from court saying, 'What am I doing here?' It's a *visceral* reaction that I'm wasting my time.
I'm trying to find some way to make a social contribution or a slot in city
government. I keep saying, 'There's something more.'"

Besides the push to broaden himself professionally, there is a wish to expand   22
his personal life. He wants two or three more children. "The concept of a home
has become very meaningful to me, a place to get away from troubles and relax.
I love my son in a way I could not have anticipated. I never could live alone."

Consumed with the work of making his own critical life-steering deci-   23
sion, he demonstrates the essential shift at this age: an absolute requirement
to be more self-concerned. The self has new value now that his competency
has been proved.

His wife is struggling with her own age-30 priorities. She wants to go to   24
law school, but he wants more children. If she is going to stay home, she
wants him to make more time for the family instead of taking on even wider
professional commitments. His view of the bind, of what he would most like
from his wife, is this:

"I'd like not to be bothered. It sounds cruel, but I'd like not to have to   25
worry about what she's going to do next week. Which is why I've told her
several times that I think she should do something. Go back to school and get
a degree in social work or geography or whatever. Hopefully that would fulfill her, and then I wouldn't have to worry about her line of problems. I want
her to be decisive about herself."

The trouble with his advice to his wife, is that it comes out of concern   26
with *his* convenience, rather than with *her* development. She quickly picks
up on this lack of goodwill: He is trying to dispose of her. At the same time,
he refuses her the same latitude to be "selfish" in making an independent
decision to broaden her own horizons. Both perceive a lack of mutuality. And
that is what Catch-30 is all about for the couple.

Rooting and Extending

Life becomes less provincial, more rational and orderly in the early thirties. 27
We begin to settle down in the full sense. Most of us begin putting down
roots and sending out new shoots. People buy houses and become very
earnest about climbing career ladders. Men in particular concern themselves
with "making it." Satisfaction with marriage generally goes downhill in the
thirties (for those who have remained together) compared with the highly
valued, vision-supporting marriage of the twenties. This coincides with the
couple's reduced social life outside the family and the in-turned focus on raising their children.

The Deadline Decade

In the middle of the thirties we come upon a cross-roads. We have reached 28
the halfway mark. Yet even as we are reaching our prime, we begin to see
there is a place where it finishes. Time starts to squeeze.

The loss of youth, the faltering of physical powers we have always taken 29
for granted, the fading purpose of stereotyped roles by which we have thus
far identified ourselves, the spiritual dilemma of having no absolute answers—any or all of these shocks can give this passage the character of crisis. Such thoughts usher in a decade between 35 and 45 that can be called the
Deadline Decade. It is a time of both danger and opportunity. All of us have
the chance to rework the narrow identity by which we defined ourselves in
the first half of life. And those of us who make the most of the opportunity
will have a full-out authenticity crisis.

To come through this authenticity crisis, we must reexamine our pur- 30
poses and reevaluate how to spend our resources from now on. "Why am I
doing all this? What do I really believe in?" No matter what we have been
doing, there will be parts of ourselves that have been suppressed and now
need to find expression. "Bad" feelings will demand acknowledgement along
with the good.

It is frightening to step off onto the treacherous footbridge leading to 31
the second half of life. We can't take everything with us on this journey
through uncertainty. Along the way, we discover that we are alone. We no
longer have to ask permission because we are the providers of our own safety.
We must learn to give ourselves permission. We stumble upon feminine or
masculine aspects of our natures that up to this time have usually been
masked. There is grieving to be done because an old self is dying. By taking
in our suppressed and even our unwanted parts, we prepare at the gut level
for the reintegration of an identity that is ours and ours alone—not some
artificial form put together to please the culture or our mates. It is a dark passage at the beginning. But by disassembling ourselves, we can glimpse the
light and gather our parts into a renewal.

Women sense this inner cross-road earlier than men do. The time pinch 32
often prompts a woman to stop and take an all-points survey at age 35. Whatever options she has already played out, she feels a "my last chance" urgency

to review those options she has set aside and those that aging and biology will close off in the *now foreseeable* future. For all her qualms and confusion about where to start looking for a new future, she usually enjoys an exhilaration of release. Assertiveness begins rising. There are so many firsts ahead.

Men, too, feel the time push in the mid-thirties. Most men respond by 33 pressing down harder on the career accelerator. It's "my last chance" to pull away from the pack. It is no longer enough to be the loyal junior executive, the promising young novelist, the lawyer who does a little *pro bono* work on the side. He wants now to become part of top management, to be recognized as an established writer, or an active politician with his own legislative program. With some chagrin, he discovers that he has been too anxious to please and too vulnerable to criticism. He wants to put together his own ship.

During this period of intense concentration on external advancement, it 34 is common for men to be unaware of the more difficult, gut issues that are propelling them forward. The survey that was neglected at 35 becomes a crucible at 40. Whatever rung of achievement he has reached, the man of 40 usually feels stale, restless, burdened, and unappreciated. He worries about his health. He wonders, "Is this all there is?" He may make a series of departures from well-established lifelong base lines, including marriage. More and more men are seeking second careers in midlife. Some become self-destructive. And many men in their forties experience a major shift of emphasis away from pouring all their energies into their own advancement. A more tender, feeling side comes into play. They become interested in developing an ethical self.

Renewal or Resignation

Somewhere in the mid-forties, equilibrium is regained. A new stability is 35 achieved, which may be more or less satisfying.

If one has refused to budge through the midlife transition, the sense of 36 staleness will calcify into resignation. One by one, the safety and supports will be withdrawn from the person who is standing still. Parents will become children; children will become strangers; a mate will grow away or go away; the career will become just a job—and each of these events will be felt as an abandonment. The crisis will probably emerge again around 50. And although its wallop will be greater, the jolt may be just what is needed to prod the resigned middle-ager toward seeking revitalization.

On the other hand. . . . 37

If we have confronted ourselves in the middle passage and found a 38 renewal of purpose around which we are eager to build a more authentic life structure, these may well be the best years. Personal happiness takes a sharp turn upward for partners who can now accept the fact: "I cannot expect *anyone* to fully understand me." Parents can be forgiven for the burdens of our childhood. Children can be let go without leaving us in collapsed silence. At 50, there is a new warmth and mellowing. Friends become more important than ever, but so does privacy. Since it is so often proclaimed by people past midlife, the motto of this stage might be "No more bullshit."

Critical Reading Questions

1. Do the steps in Sheehy's description of a typical American's life cycle sound valid to you? Have you ever experienced any of the stages she describes or do you know other people who seem to be living out a life pattern similar to that defined by Sheehy?
2. What assumptions does Sheehy appear to be making about her audience? Does she assume that her readers will accept her insights at face value?
3. How do Sheehy's quotations from actual people help establish her credibility?
4. Has this essay given you any insights about how your choices now can influence your opportunities later on?
5. How do changes in technology and economics affect patterns of social behavior? In what ways do you think men and women have chosen new life patterns since Sheehy wrote her book in the 1970s? What changes do you expect in the future?

Analyzing Pertinent Conventions

No one correct way or one ideal model exists to shape an analysis of subjects or processes. Nevertheless, there are a number of conventions that typify how analytical reports are organized. Instead of regarding the following points as an absolute formula, consider them to be rough guidelines.

Introduce the Significance of the Subject

In most of the academic writing that you do in college as well as the professional writing that you will do later in your career, you will want to proceed from *given information*—that is, ideas and assumptions that you know your reader believes—to *new information*—that is, the material that you will educate the reader about. When the significance of the subject or process you are analyzing is not immediately apparent, or "given," you will need to educate your readers about its importance. For example, notice in the following sample how Michael Talbot provides the background information in the introduction to his essay "Ecological Lawn Care," which appeared in *Mother Earth News*:

> By 1984, the United States applied more synthetic chemical fertilizers on
> its lawns than India applied on *all* its food crops. According to the Environ-
> mental Protection Agency, an estimated 65 million pounds of herbicides,
> insecticides and fungicides were applied around homes and gardens,
> with another 165 million pounds used on industrial, commercial and
> government landscapes—much of this on the nation's lawns, playfields,

parks and cemeteries. Other studies indicate that urban and suburban residents are now subjected to more pesticide exposure than their rural counterparts, in spite of the heavy use of pesticides in agricultural areas.

By sensitizing his audience to the scope of this problem, Talbot has increased the likelihood that they will read his essay. Without this clarification, his readers might be less likely to follow the steps he goes on to outline for growing healthy lawns without pesticides.

Present a Clear Thesis and Forecast Your Organization

Because they know readers can choose not to read their work, careful writers treat their audience with respect. Successful writers avoid confusion about their purpose and subject because a confused reader won't stay around long.

Readers can comprehend and recall information better when authors provide an overview of the main points of the document before launching into a detailed analysis of these issues. Likewise, sentences that explain a text's organization help readers understand information better. In other words, readers appreciate it when writers tell them what we are going to tell them, tell them, and then tell them what we have told them. As a result, experienced authors often provide a brief overview of the purpose of the document through a *thesis statement*. They also rely on *forecasting sentences* that highlight how the text is organized and what the reader should pay most attention to. Now this does not mean that you begin every college essay with a thesis statement such as "The purpose of my essay is to explain 1, 2, 3, 4," nor do you need to *always* say, "I will make these four points below: 1, 2, 3, and 4." For instance, Michael Miller did not need to write, "The purpose of my essay is to discuss my strengths and weaknesses as a writer." Instead, he immediately began analyzing his strengths and weaknesses because he knew his readers would infer his purpose. You can best determine whether you need to explicitly state your purpose by analyzing your communication situation. If your audience is likely to find your subject complicated and difficult to understand, then your audience may appreciate explicit thesis and forecasting statements. In testing situations, when instructors have numerous essays to read, explicit thesis and forecasting statements can help instructors quickly assess whether you have understood the essay questions and addressed them adequately. In contrast, when readers will probably find your subject simple or when they are reading for pleasure, you may want to simply imply your thesis. In most academic contexts, though, you are better safe than sorry: when in doubt, state your thesis (while avoiding the clichéd language, "My purpose in this essay is . . .").

Focus on Developing Your Ideas

Anecdotes, examples, facts, and statistics are the lifeblood of an effective academic report. Unlike friends who don't mind vague generalizations in an informal discussion, academic readers expect you to provide careful reasoning and substantive evidence to support controversial assertions. As the author, you are responsible for defining terms with which your reader is unfamiliar, for offering examples that will help your readers understand your subject, and for providing evidence for your conclusions.

Because skilled academic readers are sensitive to instances in which authors make unsupported generalizations, you would be wise to use qualifiers that limit the scope of your observations. For example, in the introduction to *Passages*, Gail Sheehy does not claim that all adults go through the same developmental stages at the same time. Instead, she warns *against* "mechanistically" interpreting the major life steps that she has defined. Sheehy limits the scope of her work by acknowledging that we all have "an individual inner dynamic that can never be precisely coded."

You can also aid comprehension by comparing and contrasting your subject to other subjects with which the reader is already familiar. For example, in his introduction to Cuban cooking, Eduardo Valdez, a student writer, describes how that island's cuisine has evolved over a five-hundred-year period from a collaboration among cultures:

> The food of Cuba is part native Indian, part European, and part African. It is distinct, however, from the foods of other islands with similar origins. For example, Jamaica also served as a base for pirates. It was also settled by Europeans and their unwilling African slaves. Yet the two cultures share few food tastes; Jamaican food is stewed and "jerked," while Cuban food is often fried or roasted. Jamaican food traditionally favors curries and hot peppers, while Cuban food uses garlic, onions, oregano, bay leaves, etc. A popular Jamaican meat is goat; the hands down Cuban favorite is pork.
>
> Cuban, Mexican, and Spanish foods are often mistakenly lumped together. The cultures share a language and a common origin, but few food tastes. A Cuban restaurant will not serve tacos or burritos. Tortillas are unknown to Cuban cooks. Jalapeno peppers are a punishment, not a condiment, to Cuban cooks. Sangria, to Cubans, is a waste of good wine. Island cooking styles are no more similar than Italian cooking is to French cooking.
>
> In Cuban culture, mealtimes are cherished institutions. It is a time for the family to come together, to communicate and share of themselves and of their food. No meal is given special significance; breakfast, lunch and dinner are each given equal importance. In the United States, the late meal, dinner, is the largest and most formal of the day. In Europe, especially Spain, France, and Italy, the midday meal (what we call "lunch") is the main meal of the day.

Establish an Appropriate Voice

When analyzing processes and subjects, you are the expert communicating to the less informed. To establish a credible voice, you will need to provide substantive content and organize the material in a logical way.

The degree to which you reveal your personality on the page varies according to your style and communication situation. Some authors feel uncomfortable using "I"—that is, writing with the first-person pronoun. When you want to keep the spotlight on the information that is being presented, not on yourself as presenter, you will want to "disappear" from the page as much as possible. Generally speaking, the more technical the subject, the less present is the authorial "I." For example, an engineer writing a professional document about the nuclear-power production process would include few if any first-person references. However, some use of the first person can be entirely appropriate even in conservative and technical communication situations. A few anecdotes and personal references can enliven your reader's interest in the subject, which is particularly important when informing readers about "dry" material.

Even when your communication situation requires you to omit all of the first-person references in your document, you still may find it useful to write rough drafts in the first person. The expressive, narrative voice can play an important part in critical thinking, so you should not try to edit it out of existence. Below is the opening paragraph to Melissa Henderson's essay on babies born to cocaine-addicted mothers. Note how Henderson's revision of her freewrite omits the obtrusive "I" references, yet still reflects her horror and anger.

First Draft: I was really shocked to learn that 55,000 crack babies were born in 1991. I think the mothers of these babies should be put into jail for their cruelty. It's disgusting to me that these mothers would let their babies suffer so much. I think it's so sad how these babies cry constantly. I'm so horrified by how these babies shake so hard that they rub their limbs raw and bruise their heads. I think it's really terrible that these poor babies can't look in other people's eyes because it's too overwhelming for their sensitive nervous systems.

Second Draft: Approximately 55,000 crack babies were born last year. The effect of mother's use of crack on fetuses differs. Some mothers' blood pressure reaches such high levels that the placenta tears away from the lining of the uterus, causing a "no-fuss" abortion. Those that survive are often born with underdeveloped intestinal tracts and missing fingers. Crack can also damage the fetus's central nervous system, resulting in babies who avoid contact with others and suffer from such severe tremors that they rub their limbs raw. Given the severity of these symptoms, I think the mothers of these babies should be prosecuted as criminals.

Consider Using Visuals

In both subject analysis and process analysis, consider using visuals to clarify complicated points, to emphasize significant results, and to offer a shorthand version of the gist of the information you are reporting. In addition to tables and figures, a vivid photograph or drawing can often drive home an important point. For example, if you were writing about world hunger, a picture of children rummaging through a garbage heap in a third-world country could be a powerful complement to ten paragraphs of statistics illustrating the scope of this problem.

When describing a process, authors sometimes highlight the chronology by providing a flow chart, which essentially is a pictorial representation of the major steps, as illustrated on page 104.

Place Information in a Logical Order

When writing about subjects or problems, authors often discuss the parts of the subject or major issues of the problem according to their level of importance. Because you could lose the interest of your reader at any point, you should generally place the most important aspects of your analysis first. For example, if you were writing about SADD—Students Against Drunk Driving—you might first want to mention the number of students on your campus who have died as a result of alcohol-related accidents. Second, you could mention the number of students nationwide who have died because they drove while intoxicated or were hit by a drunk driver. Third, you might want to give the statistics about how many people in the future are predicted to die as a result of drunk drivers. Fourth, you could discuss SADD's lobbying efforts with the state legislatures and the federal Congress. Fifth, you could give some information about what SADD does on your campus and make a few suggestions about what students can do to combat this terrible problem.

When analyzing a physical process, you will usually present the necessary steps in chronological order. You can also aid comprehension by grouping the steps in major stages, particularly when the process is long or complex. To help ensure clear communication, you might number the important steps in the process. Also, you can use helpful transitional words to cue your readers to the flow: first, second, next, then, now, at this point, finally.

Use Images and Metaphors for Emphasis and Clarity

Metaphors and images can help readers perceive commonplace objects and ideas in new ways. As an example, consider the comparison that Diane Peterson, a student writer, makes of writing to the states of matter:

> Writing seems to resemble the states of matter: solid, liquid, gas. At times, writing, like ice, possesses its own form and resists change. It is splintered when its form is changed by an external force. At other times, writing, like water, flows into and readily accepts externally imposed form: genre. Also, writing, like gas, can become nebulous like a cloud, constantly shifting its form, suggesting new possibilities. At all times, writing remains changeable. Form can change, ideas can change, method of expression can change. Writing can reflect the writer's external world. Like ice, writing can reflect external reality clearly, hiding its depth. Like water, writing can reflect the

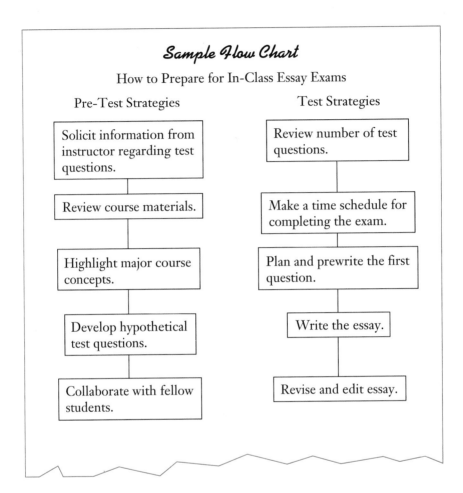

Sample Flow Chart

How to Prepare for In-Class Essay Exams

Pre-Test Strategies · Test Strategies

- Solicit information from instructor regarding test questions.
- Review course materials.
- Highlight major course concepts.
- Develop hypothetical test questions.
- Collaborate with fellow students.

- Review number of test questions.
- Make a time schedule for completing the exam.
- Plan and prewrite the first question.
- Write the essay.
- Revise and edit essay.

external world and simultaneously provide a clear view of its interior. Ripples or waves may change the view we see. Or writing may be like a vapor, present but unseen, clear but unclear, as water vapor refracts light. Does writing simply reflect the writer's background, task, intention, etc., or does writing refract and separate these elements? Or both? As I examine writing, it seems to be laced with inherent contradictions, to form, dissipate, and reform somehow changed.

Sometimes a metaphor "has legs." In other words, you may learn something new about subject A by comparing it to subject B. In the best of circumstances, metaphors expand your thinking, as suggested by the following example, in which a student writer uses an extended metaphor to explain his growth as a writer:

In order to make a more personal introduction to my writing, I would ask that you allow me the exercise of trying to create an extended metaphor. While it may seem a bit pretentious and flamboyant, I would like to compare my creative imagination to an orchid tree, which when grown from a seed takes at least seven years of stimulated growth before it can produce its first intricately pleasing contribution to nature—a full blossom. I, like an orchid tree growing in a naturally random environment, have endured the droughts and wintry dispositions of many teachers and other mentally influential people. Likewise, I have also been exposed to the fertile floods of stimulus from authors and other influential persons. I, like the orchid tree, have grown for years unaware of that which I have the potential to produce. My consciousness has finally, fed and enriched by the rich radiant sunlight of education, begun to bud. My blossoms are yet pale, small, and fall from my branches both easily and prematurely. The searing beams of radiance that dance across my leaves and soak into my consciousness are constantly deflected and filtered by the imposing shade of societal obligations and time-consuming responsibilities.

I suggested that I have started to bloom. This may sound somewhat egotistical, but allow me to qualify my suggestion with some critical modifications. To begin with, some of my blossoms have been quite pale in color, suffering perhaps from a lack of creative fertilization. Yet other blossoms have been so verdantly rich in color that the intricate detail, which makes the blossom so pleasing to the mind's eye, has been engulfed and obscured by the superfluity of florid color. It is also not uncommon for a chilling breeze on several days or numbing shade to cause immature blossoms in my mind to wither and die. In short, my orchid tree is far from being a perfect specimen.

Mention Safety Warnings

If there are any important safety warnings for the process you are analyzing, you should mention them *before* they become pertinent. For example, if you were explaining how to install track lighting, you would want to be clear from the start about when to turn off the electricity. To catch the impatient reader's attention, you might even want to set the warning off from the rest of the text by underlining it or placing it in bold or capital letters.

Review for Grammatical and Mechanical Correctness

Critical readers never miss clues that an author is truly committed and addressing a subject that he or she cares about. Readers can judge a writer's commitment by assessing whether he or she has paid careful attention to words, as well as to organization and support. Prose that has been put together carelessly, that lacks a vigorous voice, that contains flaws in reasoning, grammar, and syntax annoys readers. These sorts of problems tell readers that the writer doesn't care enough about the topic to polish it, or worse, they undercut the writer's authority and may even give the reader the sense that the writer is uneducated.

Writing Assignments

You will probably have an easier time writing an analysis of a subject or process if you can select a topic that interests you. Rather than rushing to make a choice, discuss some possibilities with your instructor, classmates, and friends.

However, writers are not always free to choose their own subjects, to address concerns that they feel strongly about. Your teacher may very well assign a topic that differs significantly from one that you might select. While some subjects may never be fascinating to you, you may be surprised to find that an apparently boring subject can actually become quite interesting once you have worked on it for a while. Furthermore, the trick to getting a project done quickly and efficiently is to begin work on it immediately. If you procrastinate because you don't like the topic and make it seem like a huge task to begin writing, you may become blocked and anxious.

When deciding which of the following analytical writing topics to choose, consider whether you will need to do research in the library or whether you will be able to use only your own experiences and observations. Check with your teacher to see whether you are expected to consult with library sources or interview authorities.

1. What are some of the major pressures that college students face? What social, economic, and familial pressures do you and your friends experience?

2. What causes couples to break up? What stresses do young couples experience that interfere with and destroy supportive relationships?

3. What do you believe you need to do to improve as a writer? What could your teacher and peers do to help you meet your writing goals? What are your greatest strengths and weaknesses as a writer? Besides your teachers, what other audiences have you written for? For example, have you ever written for your peers or for people who are less informed on a subject than you?

4. What social, political, or environmental issues concern you? What are the long-term implications of drug use in the inner city? What are the social, personal, or economic consequences of teenage pregnancy, doctor-assisted suicide, or the breakdown of the family? What are the major problems with our nation's educational system?

5. What are your strongest skills? Are you a terrific debater? a strong swimmer? an excellent cross-country runner? a gifted salesperson? a sharp job interviewee? Write about your skill so that your readers will be able to master it or appreciate it.

6. Do you have any unusual hobbies that others might wish to try? For example, do you grow roses, train animals, or tie flies? Write a brief report that explains exactly how a novice could become involved in your hobby.

7. Let us suppose that you have been promoted from the position of technician to manager. So that the person who replaces you will know what to do, your boss has asked you to write an updated job description. Prioritize your duties from most important to least important, and then write a detailed account of your responsibilities so that your replacement will know what to do and when to do it.

Prewriting and Drafting Strategies

The following prewriting strategies can help you avoid procrastination and develop promising first drafts.

Consider Your Communication Situation

You may need to write several rough drafts before you have a solid sense of your audience and purpose. However, you can usually save time by giving some thought at the outset about whom you are writing to and what their specific needs and attitudes are likely to be. To better define your communication situation, you may find it useful to review the questions for analyzing purpose, audience, and tone that were presented in the introduction to this book.

Practice Close Observation

If you choose to write about a subject or process that can be observed, you may want to play the role of a detective who needs to report back to a client or group of interested people. Go out into the field and make your observations as discreetly as possible.

Draft and Informal Outline

To develop the details that will help your readers understand your subject, you may find it useful to consider the following questions and then write an informal outline based on your answers:

1. What major parts or features make up this object or concept?
2. What does the subject look, feel, sound, taste, or smell like?
3. What are the distinguishing characteristics of the subject?
4. In what categories can the parts be placed?
5. What other objects or concepts is the subject similar to or different from?
6. How do these parts work in isolation or in connection to the other parts?

Similarly, when you are analyzing a process, you may find it useful to construct an outline in response to the following questions:

1. Why is this process important?
2. How many major steps comprise the process?
3. What are the important safety warnings?
4. What does step 1 consist of?
5. What does step 2 consist of?
6. What does step 3 consist of?

Draw a Pie Diagram

If you are describing or analyzing a subject, try drawing a pie diagram that identifies the major aspects of the subject. Because you can allocate bigger pieces of the pie to particularly crucial elements, you can use pie diagrams to estimate visually how much time or what portion of the report you will spend addressing each aspect of your subject.

Revising and Editing Strategies

To enable you to shift effectively from creator to critic, let as much time as possible pass before evaluating each draft of your work. Even skilled writers have difficulty challenging their ideas and identifying redundant or underdeveloped passages. For example, once you have written a solid draft of a process analysis, try to complete the process (or, better yet, have someone else complete it) based on your instructions.

Ask Critical Questions

As you write and revise, give special attention to the following questions because they highlight problems that frequently occur with student analyses of subjects or processes.

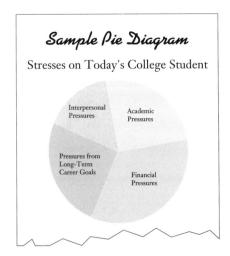

Sample Pie Diagram

Stresses on Today's College Student

Interpersonal Pressures

Academic Pressures

Pressures from Long-Term Career Goals

Financial Pressures

1. Have I provided the details that my audience will need in order to understand the subject? What changes can I make to simplify my presentation of the subject?

2. Is my essay unified by a clear purpose or thesis? Have I presented sufficient forecasting statements so readers will understand the organization of the essay? Have I subsequently followed the organization I promised in the introduction? Have I mixed together stages that should be kept separate? Have I neglected any important steps?

3. How well developed is the content? Are all important terms and concepts well defined? What additional comparisons, illustrations, or analogies could I add?

4. Will readers find fault with my logic? Have I provided sufficient information for readers to understand my reasoning?

5. Have I made the report visually appealing? Would readers better understand how I have organized my information if I used more subheadings, tables, flow charts, or other visual aids?

6. Is my writing economical? Can I combine and edit some of the sentences to make them more vigorous?

7. Is the report grammatically and mechanically correct? Are there any specific errors that I tend to make that I haven't yet checked for, such as subject-verb agreement, pronoun agreement, or needless tense shifts?

In addition to these questions, you should refer to the guidelines on editing and punctuation in Chapters 11 and 12 before submitting your work to classmates or your instructor.

Collaborating Strategies

Writers differ in regard to when they prefer to solicit outside criticism. Some people like to discuss project ideas with trusted associates before and during writing, some prefer to keep their projects private until they have written a good draft, and some prefer to thoroughly exhaust a project—that is, to do absolutely everything in their power to make the manuscript perfect—before sharing it with critics.

Sample Peer Revision

The best way to become comfortable and effective at critiquing and being critiqued by your peers is to do it often. There is simply no substitute for a "baptism by fire." When critiquing your peers' work, remember that it is much easier to critique than to invent, that we can draw on our background as readers, and that we can be more objective when evaluating our peers' work than when critiquing our own.

To give you a sense of how writers can use diverse feedback from peers to improve a manuscript, I have presented below the opening paragraphs of

Michael Miller's second draft of "Say What?" which appeared at the beginning of this chapter. In addition, I have presented the comments that Miller's peers gave to him when he shared this draft with them. Before noting his peers' suggestions, consider what you would tell Miller if he sought your help.

> Evaluating one's own writing process is arduous, and without the help of my old essays I am not quite sure I could have done it. Rereading previously graded materials provided assistance throughout this enormous task. To begin with, the comments of instructors over a period of years helped identify consistent strengths and weaknesses, and also the fact that I had not read the papers in a while allowed me to view them objectively for the first time. My old essays even helped identify my writing processes. Initially I had trouble remembering exactly how I developed my papers, but after reading an old paper I could easily recall the process I used to develop it.
>
> In following the above procedure to recall a writing process, I came upon a surprising realization: my writing processes were an almost direct result of the types and topics of the papers. Different papers involved different writing and rewriting processes. If I were writing a serious persuasive paper, involving hard facts, I would have provided structure and sound support for a thesis that I was already aware of, but if I were writing a creative narrative piece, I was not always certain how it would turn out until I had finished the first draft and read what I had written. The discovery of these different writing processes helped me to better understand that, although effective writing processes are of paramount importance, writing is not an exact science and processes will never be exactly the same.

Although the following account of Miller's peer-review group is not an exact rendition, it does reflect the kinds of suggestions that his peers made. Some peer-review groups have as many as seven members; Michael's only had three during this session: Judy Leidigger, Molly Walton, and Robert Henderson.

> "Wow, I think this is really good," Judy said. "I like your introduction."
>
> "Yeah," said Robert, "and you have a good voice too. You seem honest and hard working. I'll bet you'll get an A on this."
>
> "Well, that would be great," Michael said. "But I do know it still needs work. Do you guys have any ideas about how I can make it better?"
>
> "Well," said Judy, "you do seem to be going in a lot of different directions in that first paragraph. I guess I first thought you were going to talk about your strengths and weaknesses, so I was a little surprised when you talked about the different ways you compose your assignments. Maybe all you need to do is work on the order of what you're going to talk about."
>
> "Yeah, you may be right. That makes sense."
>
> "Well, I think it's great," said Molly. "I wouldn't change a thing."
>
> "Well, I think it's great too, but it seems like it still needs some focus, you know?" said Judy. "I mean, I'm not so sure that you should say that this assignment was such an enormous task—particularly after saying that it was an arduous process. I mean it wasn't that hard was it?"
>
> Michael laughed along with Judy. "Yeah, you're right. That sounds a little too self-serving, doesn't it."

Because there is a limit to how much time your peers and teachers can give to critiquing your work, you may want to wait to share your work until you have completed a fairly solid draft. But don't wait too long! After all, you don't want your project so near completion that you are going to ignore recommendations for change. Because many of your peers will feel uncomfortable about critiquing your work, try to put them at ease by encouraging their honest responses. Reassure them that it is still a "work in progress," and invite input by noting a few questions you have about the document.

PEER REVIEW WORKSHOP

Try to answer the questions that your peers have asked you to consider. Also, be sensitive to the intensity and depth of response that your peers have requested or implied that they want. There is no reason to force your opinion on people who are unwilling to listen to it. While some of your peers may appreciate—though not enjoy—your scrutiny of their work, others could find any constructive remarks to be devastating. Remember to prioritize your critique. Point out the most substantial faults you perceive and identify specific passages that exhibit these weaknesses. Avoid absolute statements, such as, "Your organization is impossible to follow and your conclusion should be the introduction." After all, reasonable people do tend to disagree about how to improve a text. Thus, instead of providing absolute statements, soften your commentaries by using "I messages"—that is, "I had difficulty following your organization," "I think your conclusion may make a better introduction than your present one."

To help identify weak spots in the manuscript, ask yourself the following questions when reading:

1. Are there any points in the discussion where you are confused or where you think additional support needs to be provided? What information do you believe the author should add before submitting the report for a grade?

2. If the author is attempting to describe *what* something is, do you believe that he or she has effectively defined the subject? What additional appeals to your senses can the author make? What information does the author need to provide before you thoroughly understand him or her?

3. If the author is attempting to explain *how to do* something, is enough information presented for you to do it? Are you unclear about any of the necessary steps or the order in which they occur? In what ways can the author simplify the subject matter?

4. Do you think the report is well organized? Is the report unified by a single controlling purpose or thesis? Does the introduction give you an accurate sense of what the report is about? Are sufficient forecasting statements provided? Does the author actually accomplish what he or she promised to do in the opening forecasting statements?

5. Do you think the report is likely to interest the author's intended readers? What changes could the author make to appeal more to the interests of readers?

Additional Writing Samples

In the following essay, Patricia Jody, a student writer, analyzes the rationale for revising the nation's educational program to better account for the contributions of minorities. Jody did considerable library research and completed more than a dozen revisions before being satisfied with the following draft.

Multiculturalism

Patricia Jody

Multiculturalism is the movement that is seeking to incorporate new voices   1
into the literary canon and current curricula. It seeks to validate the non-white, non-male perspective; it rejects the male experience as the norm, or universal experience. A seemingly unlikely champion of multiculturalism is Stanly Fish, a Milton scholar, who teaches at Duke University. He welcomes the added perspectives and believes that there is much to be gained by acknowledging and valuing diversity.

Linda Brodkey, a professor of English at the University of Texas at   2
Austin, developed a course to aid graduate assistants who were teaching Freshman English. The focus of the course was to be "writing about difference." In order to provide the students with a common core of examples of argumentation and style, Brodkey chose case law studies on Title VII of the Civil Rights Act, which says it is the employer's responsibility to provide a workplace free of sexual harassment, and Title IX of the 1979 Education Amendment. Title IX prohibits discrimination in educational institutions which receive federal funds. The legal rhetoric was readily available to all students, and furnished an intellectual field to draw upon, to encourage the students to examine assumptions, and to model debate styles in their own writing. The syllabus based on these materials was presented to the English department faculty and was approved in a 46–11 vote. One of the dissenting faculty members was Professor Alan Gribben. After losing in the democratic process in his department, Gribben went to the NAS, the National Association of Scholars, an organization formed solely to combat multiculturalism, and the local press. He charged that Brodkey's course was an attempt to "politically indoctrinate" students. He referred to the course as "oppression studies." Gribben succeeded in destroying the course.

Popular magazines such as *Newsweek, Time,* and *U.S. News and World*   3
Report have reported "raging controversies" on campuses across the country. *U.S. News and World Report* described colleges and universities as being "under siege" (*"Science and Society"* 10). While the events in Texas certainly

illustrate radical right *his*trionics, the actual debate seems much more restrained. The war-torn imagery of college campuses seems to be another of the many distortions surrounding this issue.

Here at the University of South Florida, multiculturalism is frequently 4 a topic of conversation among the faculty in the English Department. These conversations generally support the inclusion of the new voices with the traditional canon. At least that is the perception of one member of the faculty. This individual and many other faculty members try to incorporate female, black, and Hispanic authors into their courses. The English Department re-evaluated the Master and Ph.D. exams, and a new question, from either World Literature, African or Native American Literature, is now included on the comprehensive exam. This inclusion generated no major objections.

Among students at the University of South Florida, multiculturalism 5 does not seem to be the burning issue that the popular press has reported. This is evidenced by the results of an informal survey that I conducted at the Tampa campus. The purpose of the questionnaire was to take the pulse, at USF, regarding this issue. About forty students, ranging in age from early 20s to mid-40s participated. They represented majors from several colleges on campus. Most seemed concerned with the monetary impact of multiculturalism—the cost for additional courses—and any graduation delay caused by adding additional requirements. While many did not want to support this issue with their time or money, most had no objection to *incorporating* multiculturalism into existing classes. Also, many were not opposed to *substituting* diversity courses into the curriculum. The *St. Petersburg Times* reported in their March 22, 1992 issue that USF plans to include courses that deal with gender and race issues, ethics, and international affairs in a new set of undergraduate requirements. It is hoped that the interdisciplinary courses will enable the students to think in broader perspectives.

The campus newspaper, the *Oracle*, features the "Nothing Left" column, 6 written by Robert Hoffman. He regards multiculturalism as a "fraud perpetrated by the outcasts of society" (5). He describes American culture as being white, Christian, and male. He believes multiculturalism springs from a bitterness on the parts of blacks and women, because they have no place in American culture. This column generated quite a few responses, including one from the chair of the anthropology department.

In a sense, Hoffman may have a point. Women, blacks, Hispanics, 7 Asians, and Native Americans are not charmed by the notion that they have no place in American culture. They would indeed like their contributions acknowledged. When their efforts to have these achievements honored and accepted are labeled as fraud, or they are dismissed as misfits, resentment and rebelliousness is the response.

Proponents of multiculturalism would like to see the history books 8 reflect the contribution of the Cherokee during the War of 1812, for example. This history lesson would reflect Junaluska's saving of Andrew Jackson's life at the Battle of Horseshoe Bend. This chapter would also consider Jackson's failure to remember his Cherokee friends and the result-ing "Trail of Tears," the tragic Cherokee march to Oklahoma, after losing their land in the mountains of western Carolina. The English classes might read *The Education of Little Tree* by Forrest Carter, a Native American.

The contributions of the so-called misfits are many (Wallace). Weaving 9 their participation into the curriculum might include teaching that Alain Locke was the first black Rhodes scholar, and that he studied at Oxford, the University of Berlin, and Harvard. It might teach that Ralph Bunche was the first black to win the Nobel Peace Prize. Students might learn that Dr. Charles Drew pioneered processes for storing blood plasma. Or, that Lise Meitner pioneered the splitting of the atom but dissociated herself from the bomb. Or, that Rosalind Franklin's notebook was stolen and "mysteri-ously" Watson and Crick received an unauthorized copy of this notebook, which was crucial to their assembly of the double helix model of DNA. Or, that Mrs. Einstein did the math formulas for $E=MC^2$ and received half of the Nobel Prize money in her divorce from Albert, because of her con-tribution.

The goal of multiculturalism is to prevent the valued accomplishments 10 and histories of its citizens from being ignored. If we teach students about the genuine contributions of women, blacks, and Native Americans in math, science, history, and literature, perhaps we can lessen the racism and sexism in American culture. Celebrating diversity does not destroy or negate the achievements of white males, it honors the skills and experiences of all the participants.

──────────────── **Works Cited** ────────────────

Harper, James. "USF May Weave Multicultural Lessons into Classes." *St. Petersburg Times* 22 Mar. 1992: 3B.

Hoffman, Robert. "The Multicultural Movement Is a Fraud Perpetrated by Outcasts." *Oracle* 8 Oct. 1991: 5.

Terry, Wallace. "Do You Know These Famous Americans?" *Parade Magazine* 4 Feb. 1990: 6–7.

Unknown. "Science and Society, Tough Times on Campus." *U.S. News and World Report* 12 Apr. 1991: 10.

Critical Reading Questions

1. How would you describe Jody's tone in this piece—as speculative? argu-mentative? objective? rational? What information does she provide and how does she organize her information to establish this tone?

2. How would Jody's voice and tone differ if the information in the con-cluding paragraphs were placed in the introductory paragraphs?

3. What are the goals of multiculturalism as defined by Jody?

4. What assumptions do you think Jody makes about her audience's likely acceptance or rejection of multiculturalism?

5. If Jody sought your aid in improving her essay, what suggestions would you make?

In the process analysis below, Tracey Williams's desire to critique her drafts in search of the perfect résumé has given us an example of a hardworking student writer at work.

The Evolution of a Résumé

Tracey Williams

The first impression an employer gets of you is through your résumé. We 1 graduating seniors know that. We also know the importance of a résumé's appearance. It must be clearly organized and error-free. The format should guide the reader's eye to the more significant qualifications of the student. Unfortunately, as well-prepared as we may be for our field, having the greatest talent in the world is useless unless you know how to sell it. A well-prepared résumé can get your foot in the door.

The résumé I currently use is quite different from the first one I wrote 2 in a composition course. Although that assignment was the basis for the résumé I actually send to potential employers, it is useless to me now. After growing and improving from many revisions, it now does exactly what a résumé is supposed to do: portray me as a skilled professional with writing experience. As I learned more about my field (and about myself—skills, interests, strengths, and weaknesses), I gradually made changes in my résumé. In the future, I may also make changes according to the needs of a potential employer. *There is, in short, no such thing as a perfect, permanent résumé.*

So, when do you begin the process of creating a résumé? I made my first 3 attempt while I was still a year away from graduation. To be honest, that early start was actually an assignment in my technical writing class. I felt that since I still had a year to go before graduating, I hadn't yet accumulated enough significant writing experience to build a résumé. So, using the recommendations from our course text, I went "by the book," and ended up with the chronological résumé (see Figure 1). This résumé has a good appearance, but offers little else. The emphasis is more on what I've been doing rather than on the skills I have.

It looks pretty good, doesn't it? I thought so, and so did my instructor. 4 I received an "A" on it, and, satisfied that that was out of the way, I completely forgot about it. I assumed I was off to a strong start, and with a few minor revisions my résumé would be ready for use when I graduated. I was wrong.

Lesson number one: A résumé should not read like a job application. The draft 5 in Figure 1 says enough about where I've worked and gone to school, but very little about skills I have which qualify me for a technical writing position. This major error was pointed out to me during a résumé workshop provided by my university. Although a chronological résumé should include an employment and education history, it also needs to represent important skills, experience or accomplishments.

To prepare for a new and improved résumé, the workshop instructor 6 suggested I make a list of job responsibilities and skills I already have (past or present) and to apply them to a professional writing position. How was I supposed to do that? My only jobs had been in the restaurant business and surely those skills wouldn't apply, would they? My instinct was to try to place emphasis on my extended education and to downplay my "unrelated" job experience which I incorrectly thought would be a hindrance. The résumé on page 118 came of my efforts (see Figure 2).

This functional résumé is more practical. It lists job and classroom skills 7 that increase my credibility as a skilled professional.

This is an example of a functional résumé rather than a chronological 8 résumé. Its advantage is that the employer can focus directly on the skills I have, not just on where I learned them. I used classroom as well as job experience to come up with the "accomplishments." The problem with this résumé is its lack of information about my background. It's at the other extreme from my first résumé.

Lesson number two: A good résumé is a combination of both job background and 9 *pertinent skills.* I composed the next résumé in an attempt to combine the best of both the chronological and functional styles (see Figure 3).

The major revision to this draft is the addition of sections to highlight 10 skills and job-related experiences. I took a copy of this résumé to Shari Greenburg, a USF career counselor, for critiquing. She thought it was basically a good résumé, but suggested several improvements.

Lesson number three: A résumé should highlight strengths and accomplish- 11 *ments.* The sample in Figure 3 doesn't emphasize my G.P.A. or honors at all. Shari suggested I add a section to highlight my educational achievements. She also recommended that I stress certain areas by underlining. The next résumé is the improved, updated version because it combines work history with significant skills, but also highlights educational accomplishments and special skills (see Figure 4).

Notice in this revision how I have underlined my computer experience 12 and job titles. The management and training experience is now obvious at a glance. Many positions require the use of a computer/word processor, and the fact that I have such experience is now apparent. (In fact, as a personal note, I strongly recommend that students take advantage of any computer user services available on their campus. The last potential employer I spoke with made it a point to find out if I had any computer experience. It's one less detail they'll have to train you for.)

The "interests" and "references" sections are not necessary. However, 13 they can and should be used to fill vacant space on the page to give the résumé a balanced appearance. Other categories such as "special skills" or "geographical preference" can also be used. The résumé in Figure 4 not only

Figure 1

Tracey Lee Williams
3508 Obispo Street
Tampa, FL 33629
Tel.: 813-555-4195

Career Objective
To work in the field of technical communications as a writer or editor and eventually gain training or supervising responsibilities.

Education

1989–present	University of South Florida
	Currently pursuing a Bachelor's degree in Professional/Technical Writing. Graduation date: May 1991. Current grade point average: 3.80 of a possible 4.00.
1987–1989	Hillsborough Community College, Tampa, Florida
	Majored in Education. Left shortly before completion of degree to pursue career in restaurant management. Grade point average: 3.25 of a possible 4.00.
1978–1980	Bainbridge Junior College, Bainbridge, Georgia
	Completed majority of basic studies. Grade point average: 2.60 of a possible 4.00. Majority of college expenses earned through part-time work (twenty hours per week).

Employment

1985–present	J. B. Winberie Restaurant, Tampa, Florida
	Began as preparation cook and have since worked as a line cook, server, and trainer. Responsibilities include designing and writing an agenda of job duties and set-up instructions for service employees.
1980–1984	Domino's Pizza, Inc., Pompano Beach, Florida
	Began as a delivery person and later completed trainee program for management. Acted as manager for two stores and supervised the opening of a third store. Responsibilities included controlling inventory, completing payroll, scheduling, training new employees and manager trainees, handling cash sales in excess of $20,000 weekly, and cross-training all employees.
1978–1980	Bainbridge Junior College, Bainbridge, Georgia
	College work-study job as transcript clerk. Responsibilities included maintaining student files, posting grades, copying and mailing transcript requests, and starting files for new students.

Excellent references are available upon request.

Figure 2

Tracey Lee Williams
3508 Obispo Street
Tampa, FL 33629
813-555-4195

ACCOMPLISHMENTS

Management

- Directing the opening of a new unit, managing two others
- Increasing sales by 40 percent in less than six months
- Handling cash sales in excess of $20,000 weekly
- Interviewing, hiring, and training new employees and management trainees
- Planning and conducting employee meetings
- Maintaining product inventory
- Scheduling weekly shifts
- Cross-training all employees
- Delegating duties to others
- Solving problems with customers and employees
- Balancing daily register intake for bank deposit
- Developing expertise in using an adding machine
- Completing weekly payroll

Technical Writing

- Organizing and writing an agenda of job responsibilities for employees
- Formulating employee task instructions
- Composing lesson plans
- Devising memorandums for various situations
- Preparing an investigative report
- Planning and writing a proposal, feasibility report and progress report
- Completing process analysis and instructions for using office equipment
- Editing other students' work
- Using word processors
- Typing 40-50 wpm

Education

University of South Florida, Tampa, Florida
Currently pursuing a Bachelor of Arts degree in Professional/Technical Writing.
Planned graduation date: May, 1991
Current G.P.A.: 3.75 of a possible 4.00

Figure 3

Tracey Lee Williams
3508 Obispo Street
Tampa, FL 33629
813-555-4195

CAREER OBJECTIVE

To work in the field of technical communications as a writer or editor and eventually gain training or supervising responsibilities.

EDUCATION

University of South Florida, Tampa, Florida
B.A. in Professional/Technical Writing, May 1991   G.P.A. 3.80/4.00 Dean's List

Hillsborough Community College, Tampa, Florida
A.A. in Liberal Studies, June 1989   G.P.A. 3.00/4.00 Honor Roll

*Financed 70% of education expenses through full-time and part-time employment while maintaining high G.P.A.

Objective-related courses: Expository Writing, Technical Writing, Advanced Technical Writing, Advanced Composition, and Narration and Description. Society for Technical Communication. Member, Arts and Letters Honor Society.

Organized and wrote agenda of job responsibilities for employees; formulated employee task instructions; edited other students' work; devised memorandums for various situations; planned and composed investigative, progress and feasibility reports; completed cost analysis and estimate; developed process analysis and instructions; prepared trip report.

*All work completed on Macintosh IIcx, Word 4.0

CAREER-RELATED EXPERIENCES

Server/trainer, J. B. Winberie Restaurant, Tampa, FL   1985–present
Trained fifteen employees, assisted customers on a daily basis, worked efficiently under strict time constraints. Worked successfully with several coworkers at one time, remained calm and proficient under stressful conditions, promoted several times to positions requiring increasing responsibility.

Driver/Manager, Domino's Pizza, Inc., Pompano Beach, FL   1980–1984
Solved problems with customers and employees; increased sales by 40% in less than six months; directed the opening of a new unit and managed two others; handled cash sales in excess of $20,000 weekly; planned and conducted employee meetings; interviewed, hired and trained new employees; scheduled weekly shifts; cross-trained all employees; delegated responsibilities to others; promoted several times to positions requiring increasing responsibility.

met the satisfaction of the career counselor, but also illustrates the following qualities suggested in the *CPC Annual* used by the career resource center at the University of South Florida.

* *Industriousness and Ambition*—I met this standard when I pointed out, under Education Highlights, my self-reliance in financing my educational expenses. In the Career-Related Experience section, I also included any promotions, thus stressing my ambition and capabilities.

* *Cooperative Attitude*—A high G.P.A. indicates flexibility, as do memberships in organizations. These are both featured under Educational Highlights. In addition, any job experience involving working with others should be stressed under Career-Related Experience as I have done in the résumé in Figure 4.

* *Interest in the Work and Enthusiasm for the Employer's Product or Service*—The Career Objective presents your point of interest to the employer. I emphasized my interest and enthusiasm by listing relevant course work under Educational Highlights, including a section of Technical Writing Experience, and pointing out my word processing experience.

* *Orderly Business-like Mind*—A crisp, neat format is the first thing that will catch an employer's eye. An organized, error-free format tells the employer the candidate cares about quality work and has a pragmatic attitude.

When I finished the last résumé (see Figure 4), I thought it was nearly perfect. After so many improvements and revisions, I felt there was little room for improvement. In fact, I even sent a few out to potential employers. But, I wanted to make sure I had done all I could, so I returned to Shari. She thought it looked very nice, but pointed out further corrections to be made. So, we fine-tuned my résumé and ended up with the one in Figure 5. The advantage of this résumé is that it lists the Technical Writing and Career-Related Experiences in order of importance. 14

This résumé looks identical to the one in Figure 4, but there are a few significant differences. *Lesson number four: Sequence counts, so list your accomplishments in order of importance.* Shari suggested some changes in the Career-Related Experience area. I needed to make sure the skills most pertinent to my field were listed first. All of the experiences are now in a different order. I also placed a space between the two career-related experiences to make the distinction obvious. Also, because my title is more important than the days worked, we decided to shorten the Interests section as well. Four or five entries are sufficient. 15

I plan on using this résumé in my job search. As I gain more experience in my field, appropriate alterations can be made. I would like to stress that any job experience, no matter how trivial it seems, can benefit your résumé. Career counselors are trained to help you turn your skills from a brief summer job experience (or a lengthy career) into valuable assets to show off on your résumé. 16

Figure 4

Tracey Lee Williams
3508 Obispo Street
Tampa, FL 33629
813-555-4195

Career Objective

To work in the field of technical communications as a writer or editor and eventually gain training or supervising responsibilities.

Education

B.A., Professional/Technical Writing, University of South Florida, Tampa, May 1991
G.P.A. 3.80/4.00

A.A., Liberal Studies, Hillsborough Community College, Tampa, June 1989
G.P.A. 3.00/4.00

Education Highlights

- Financed 70% of education expenses through part-time and full-time work while maintaining a high G.P.A.
- Career-related course work: Expository Writing, Technical Writing, Advanced Technical Writing, Advanced Composition, and Narration and Description.
- Member Arts and Letters Honor Society, Society for Technical Communication.
- Dean's List and Honor Roll

Technical Writing Experience

Planned and composed investigative, feasibility, and progress reports; developed process analysis and instructions; organized and wrote agenda of job responsibilities for employees; formulated employee task instructions; successfully revised correspondence to increase reader comprehension; edited students' work; devised memorandums for various situations; prepared trip report.
   *All work completed on Macintosh IIcx, Word 4.0

Career-Related Experience

1985–present *Server/Trainer,* J. B. Winberie Restaurant, Tampa, Florida
Trained fifteen employees, assisted customers, performed efficiently under strict time constraints, worked successfully within a large group of coworkers, earned excellent rating on guest survey, remained calm and proficient under stressful conditions, promoted several times to positions requiring increased responsibility.

1980-1984 *Manager,* Domino's Pizza, Inc., Pompano Beach, Florida
Solved problems with customers and employees; increased sales by 40% in less than six months; directed opening of new unit and managed three stores; handled cash sales in excess of $20,000 weekly; planned and conducted employee meetings; interviewed, hired, and trained new employees and manager trainees; delegated responsibilities; promoted several times to positions requiring increased responsibility.

Interests

Reading, writing, cooking, aerobics, and music.

References

Available on request.

Figure 5

Tracey Lee Williams
3508 Obispo Street
Tampa, FL 33629
813-555-4195

CAREER OBJECTIVE

To work in the field of technical communications as a writer or editor and eventually gain training or supervising responsibilities.

EDUCATION

B.A., Professional/Technical Writing, University of South Florida, Tampa, May 1991
G.P.A. 3.80/4.00

A.A., Liberal Studies, Hillsborough Community College, Tampa, June 1989
G.P.A. 3.00/4.00

EDUCATION HIGHLIGHTS

- Financed 70% of education expenses through part-time and full-time work while maintaining a high G.P.A.
- Career-related course work: Expository Writing, Technical Writing, Advanced Technical Writing, Advanced Composition, and Narration and Description.
- Member Arts and Letters Honor Society, Society for Technical Communication.
- Dean's List and Honor Roll

TECHNICAL WRITING EXPERIENCE

Planned and composed investigative, feasibility, and progress reports; developed process analysis and instructions; organized and wrote agenda of job responsibilities for employees; formulated employee task instructions; successfully revised correspondence to increase reader comprehension; edited students' work; devised memorandums for various situations; prepared trip report.
    All work completed on Macintosh IIcx, Word 4.0

CAREER-RELATED EXPERIENCE

Server/Trainer, J. B. Winberie Restaurant, Tampa, Florida   (1985–present)
Trained fifteen employees, assisted customers, performed efficiently under strict time constraints, worked successfully within a large group of coworkers, earned excellent rating on guest survey, remained calm and proficient under stressful conditions, promoted several times to positions requiring increased responsibility.

Manager, Domino's Pizza, Inc., Pompano Beach, Florida   (1980–1984)
Solved problems with customers and employees; increased sales by 40% in less than six months; directed opening of new unit and managed three stores; handled cash sales in excess of $20,000 weekly; planned and conducted employee meetings; interviewed, hired, and trained new employees and manager trainees; delegated responsibilities; promoted several times to positions requiring increased responsibility.

INTERESTS

Reading, writing, cooking, aerobics, and music.

REFERENCES

Available on request.

————————————— Works Cited —————————————

Greenburg, Shari. February 18, 1991. Interview with author.
Munschauer, John L. "The Resume: How to Speak to Employers' Needs."
  CPC Annual 1:25, 1990–1991.

Critical Reading Questions

1. Has Williams provided a comprehensive description of the steps that she
   went through as she prepared the "perfect" résumé? Are you confused
   about any of these steps, or does she provide the details you need to follow her reasoning?
2. If Williams were in your peer-review workshop, what specific advice
   would you give to her to help her improve this process analysis report
   (*not* to help her improve her résumé)?
3. In what ways has Williams challenged beliefs that you have held about
   writing résumés?
4. How would you describe Williams's tone in this essay?

Evaluating Criticism

Now that you have written several reports and wintered the penetrating criticisms of your peers and instructor, you probably have a good sense of your
weaknesses as a writer. In the conclusions to earlier chapters, I have encouraged you to take a hard look at the criticisms your texts have earned and then
to try to discern any patterns of error. While I still believe that you can best
improve as a writer by identifying patterns in your critics' commentaries, I
also know that always focusing on the negative can become tedious and
depressing.

Sometimes you need to focus on the big picture—that is, on *your overall
development as a writer*. While you may still be making a variety of important
errors in your manuscripts, you are at the same time laying the groundwork
for future self-improvement. Remember, also, that the classroom provides
you with an opportunity to take risks and to learn from errors.

Now you can begin to widen the scope of your self-analysis. Instead of
focusing on identifying patterns of errors, look at the strengths of your essays.
Do readers, for instance, often suggest that you select important topics? Are
you gifted at presenting a vigorous voice? Do your words sway readers? Focus
on these and other positive questions. And consider your own development as
a writer. Ask yourself, for example, what you have learned about yourself as a
writer as a result of the prewriting, drafting, revising, or collaborating techniques that you are experimenting with. In what ways has your perception of
yourself as a writer (or person) changed as a result of a writing assignment?
How is offering criticisms of your peers' work, as well as receiving their cri-
tiques of your writing, improving your ability to work with others?

Analyzing Causes and Effects

We human beings ask "Why?" perhaps more than any other question. When we listen to the nightly news and hear about the violence plaguing our country, we ask, "Why does the United States lead the world in violent crimes?" When we read studies that indicate that 28 percent of women in America have been raped and that the occurrence of date rape is rising on college campuses, we ask, "Why is this happening?" When we read about environmental problems, such as the depletion of the ozone layer, we wonder, "Why don't we do something about it?" Whenever we make decisions in our daily lives, we ask ourselves, "Why should I do this?"

When writing to answer "What is *the effect*, or result, of this?" or "What is *the cause* of this?" you are writing a *causal analysis*—that is, a report that explores a cause-and-effect relationship. Analyzing causal relationships requires you to question how different parts and sequences interact with each other over time, which is often more difficult than reporting a chronological order of events, as you do when describing a process. Projects exploring how and why change occurs are among the most interesting writing assignments that you will tackle in school and in professional life.

On a daily basis, we seek to understand why events occurred by identifying the factors that led up to them. For example, if you were not doing well on your tests and homework assignments in chemistry, you might ask, "Did my high school chemistry class(es) sufficiently prepare me for this class? Am I studying long enough? Am I taking effective lecture notes? Am I paying too much attention to the course texts and too little to the instructor's lectures? How is my attendance? Is my part-time job interfering too much with my school work? Am I using my time to study effectively? Are some of my friends having a negative influence on my study habits? Am I taking too many courses or putting too much time into another course? What can I do to improve my memory or study skills?" After asking these and other questions, you would eventually be able to identify a variety of causes for your poor performance. And once you recognize the causal relationship, you can set about realistically to improve your chemistry grade.

In some instances you may be able to better explain an effect by distinguishing sufficient causes from necessary causes. A *sufficient cause* is one that *must* occur for the effect to take place. For instance, in order for someone to contract the AIDS virus, any of the following forms of contact is a sufficient cause: a previously infected patient's bodily fluids must enter the uninfected person's body through either an open sore, sexual contact, or a contaminated instrument, such as a needle. When describing a physical phenomenon, such as how acid rain is produced, you may have little difficulty identifying sufficient causes.

Yet when we face complicated questions and problems, we often are unable to identify sufficient causes so we must speculate about *necessary causes*—those causes that *can* result in the effect. For instance, no single cause precipitated the collapse of the Soviet Union, yet we could speculate that hunger, poor economic conditions, alienation from communism, and political corruption were all necessary causes. Because academic readers are sensitive to the complexity of most issues, they generally do not expect you to offer sufficient causes for complex problems. Instead, they expect you to speculate about possible causes and effects, while limiting the scope of your claims with qualifiers such as "usually," "may," "possible," "sometimes," or "most." No simple answer, no sufficient cause, can explain, for example, why some people become violent criminals or serial killers while others devote themselves to feeding the hungry or serving the helpless.

Writing Samples

Below, John VanLenten, a student writer, addresses the shock he experienced when a teacher vigorously critiqued one of his essays. Because VanLenten is discussing the effects of a personal experience, he did not find it necessary to consult library sources.

Another Kind of Victory

John VanLenten

This writing class is going to be *so* easy. That was my immediate impression 1 as I scribbled my first assignment for my narrative and descriptive writing class on the pad in front of me. "Due Weds., a one page paragraph on an object." My eyes rolled upward in disbelief. Composing descriptive paragraphs as a junior at a university seemed a definite regression.

After all, I had developed a cocky attitude toward writing, fostered by 2 my previous writing experiences as a high school and junior college student. Reactions to my compositions prior to entrance into the university consisted primarily of "A" grades, with generous and vague praise scattered throughout, usually in the form of "nice" and "good job!" After years of positive reinforcement, I felt extremely confident in my ability to write quickly and concisely.

Driving home after class, I thought about the new waterbed covering I 3 had recently purchased. A flamboyant description of the colors and textures would surely merit an "A." After an hour of devising a catchy introduction, raiding a thesaurus and slapping a concluding sentence on to the final product, I could visualize the bold red "A" in the paper's right corner.

A week later, the instructor distributed the graded papers at the begin- 4
ning of class. My eyes, trained to react with bored satisfaction rather than amazement at an "A" paper, were not accustomed to the felt tip "C" which confronted me. Red ink eclipsed the neatly typewritten page. "Vague" and "unclear" and "boring" took up residence where "nice" and "good job!" should have resided. I felt numb. Naturally, I believed, he misunderstood my intentions, and a "C" was my punishment for his inability to grasp my genius.

Since the instructor suggested scheduling conferences for those who 5
needed assistance on writing tasks, I adjusted my attitude and reluctantly took my place in line outside his office door the next day. Two other humiliated students stood in front of me, clutching papers which looked more like bloody towels than last week's assignment. Like me, they had probably done battle with their pride and lost. However, I still expected that an explanation of my approach to the subject would convince him to raise the grade to at least a "B." In ten minutes, I felt sure I would reach a compromise, if not achieve a victory.

Instead, I gained some experience much more valuable than an easy vic- 6
tory. Rereading my paper, he carefully explained each of his corrections. While previous teachers had rewarded a large vocabulary and neat margins with high grades, he pointed out that a series of adjectives wedged between trite introductory and concluding sentences deadened, rather than clarified, the images I sought to convey. "In other words," he told me, "if something is black, call it black—don't call it 'ebony.'" He reinforced my strong points and suggested that I really look at my subject. Careful personal observations would create a powerful paper, not the borrowing of sterile and inappropriate words for an SAT word list.

Leaving his office, I realized that I had received the first honest criticism 7
of my writing. While other writing teachers seemed blindly impressed, he had actually taken time to evaluate what I had attempted to say, and to pay attention to how I expressed it. All the "nice" and "good" "A" papers would never have taught me that.

Critical Reading Questions

1. How does VanLenten hook his reader's interest in the introduction?

2. Beyond the chronological review of a memorable autobiographical experience, what purpose or theme unifies the essay? What information does VanLenten provide to help readers understand why his teacher's criticism affected him as it did?

3. Throughout the essay, VanLenten uses images to invigorate his language. For example, in paragraph four he writes, "Red ink eclipsed the neatly typewritten page." What other images can you find, and how do these affect the tone of the manuscript?

4. VanLenten says he "adjusted his attitude" in preparation for his conference with his teacher. What kind of attitude do you think he had?

5. Have you ever had an experience similar to VanLenten's—that is, have you been shocked by criticism, then been taught a lesson by the experience?

After hearing from a friend about her being raped by a date, Shelli Boyd, a student writer, became interested in analyzing why date rape occurs. To gain some additional information on this subject, she reviewed several popular magazines such as *Glamour* and *Newsweek*, as well as several academic journals such as the *Psychology of Women Quarterly*.

What Causes Date and Acquaintance Rape?

Shelli Boyd

A man meets a woman for the first time in a bar and buys her a few drinks. 1 The woman is from out of town and not familiar with the area. After some witty conversation and a couple of slow dances, the man persuades the woman to leave with him under the guise of taking a walk outdoors. In his mind, he is assured of sex; in her mind they are just getting some fresh air. His apartment, unknown to her, happens to be close by, and he steers them in that direction. When they reach his residence, she declines his offer to come up, but relents when he explains he must get something from inside. Once the door is closed, he begins to kiss and push her in the direction of the bedroom. She politely demurs, but he will not stop. She struggles ineffectively and later tries to clamp her legs shut as he tries to get between them. The man forcibly has sex with the woman, and although she never screams, and he doesn't use a weapon, rape still occurs. The man rationalized his actions by placing blame on the woman: "If she was gullible enough to fall for that line then I am not responsible for what happened" (Jack M. 144).

The Date Rape Dilemma

The date rape dilemma begins with attitudes of men and women toward rape 2 and intercourse. Women are socialized into behaving in a passive and compliant manner making them "vulnerable to rape" whereas men are taught to be aggressive and are "expected to be the initiators of sexual activity" (Hall et al. 102). Males are pressured to "score" with females and apply a "success orientation to sex, conceptualizing sex in terms of striving for and achieving a goal" (Hall et al. 103).

The numbers of women who claim to have been raped while on a date or 3 in the company of someone they knew and trusted are surprising. A 1988 study of 795 college men and women at the University of North Carolina shows that as many as 1 in 10 college women surveyed believe that "she was physically forced" to engage in sexual intercourse, while 76 percent of the men surveyed were "accepting of forced sex in certain circumstances" such as "taking a woman on an expensive date" and "being led on by the woman" (Miller 553–554). While the number of women who claim to have been forced to have intercourse seems surprisingly high, the actual number of victims is more than likely even higher. Many victims do not come forward to report the crime for "fear of the public's disbelief" (Ward 129).

Society's preconceptions about date rape were witnessed during the tri- 4 als of William Kennedy Smith and Mike Tyson. Smith's accuser, an unwed mother with a history of three abortions and prior sexual abuse by a relative, was seen as a man-hater and a manipulator by the public due to her experiences of the past (Carroll et al. 19). Tyson's accuser, however, was a young beauty contestant, seemingly innocent and a "heroine: a young woman whose traumatic experience has been . . . the vehicle for a courageous and selfless stand against the sexual abuse of women and children in America" (Oates 61). The trials of these men and women "have confirmed what many women suspected all along: that when a man is accused of a sex offense, the woman goes on trial" (Barrett et al. 23).

Too often victims of rape blame themselves for the crime, and in cases of 5 date rape, others are quick to place blame on the victim as well. A woman's style of dress as well as the use of alcohol or drugs "increases perceptions of victim blame" while a "sexually inexperienced woman (or an elderly woman) will more often be accepted as an innocent victim" (Ward 128).

How can the problem of date and acquaintance rape be solved? One 6 avenue to explore is education. Males should be taught that it is never acceptable to use force or coercion to obtain sex, and females should be taught to become less passive and compliant. Sexual intercourse is a personal act of choice and both sexes need to learn to respect that. Sex is not a prize to seize at any cost, and force or coercion used in order to procure penetration does not elevate any man in status. On the contrary, rape debases man in the hierarchy of civilization.

Works Cited

Barret, Todd, et al. "Sex Crimes: Women on Trial." *Newsweek* 16 Dec. 1991: 22–23.

Carroll, Ginny, et al. "The Trial You Won't See." *Newsweek* 16 Dec. 1991: 19–20.

Hall, Eleanor, Judith Howard, and Sherrie Poezio. "Tolerance of Rape: A Sexist or Antisocial Attitude?" *Psychology of Women Quarterly* May 1986: 102–103.

M., Jack. "Seven Years Ago I Raped a Woman." *Glamour* Jan. 1992: 142–147.

Miller, Beverly. "Date Rape: Time for a New Look at Prevention." *Journal of College Student Development* Nov. 1988: 553–554.

Oates, Joyce. "Rape and the Boxing Ring." *Newsweek* 24 Feb. 1992: 60–61.
Ward, Colleen. "The Attitudes Toward Rape Victims Scale." *Psychology of Women Quarterly* Aug. 1988: 126–130.

Critical Reading Questions

1. Who, would you say, is Boyd's primary audience in this piece? Young college-age women? young men? anyone interested in date rape? If Boyd had selected a more narrow audience—such as just college-age men—what changes would she need to make in her tone or presentation?

2. Would you describe this piece as an objective or a persuasive account of the date rape problem? What specific passages cause you to rate the essay as you do?

3. What necessary causes does Boyd identify for the surprising frequency of date rape? What additional information might Boyd provide to substantiate her position?

4. If Boyd sought your aid on this manuscript, what two suggestions would you make for improving it?

In the following essay, "Big Mac and the Tropical Forests," Joseph Skinner argues that Americans are not thinking seriously about how their love of fast-food restaurants is linked to the destruction of the rain forests. Although this essay was published in 1985, the problems that Skinner outlines still exist today.

Big Mac and the Tropical Forests*

Joseph K. Skinner

Hello, fast-food chains.   1

Goodbye, tropical forests.   2

Sound like an odd connection? The "free-market" economy has led to   3
results even stranger than this, but perhaps none have been as environmentally devastating.

These are the harsh facts: the tropical forests are being leveled for com-   4
mercial purposes at the rate of 150,000 square kilometers a year, an area the
size of England and Wales combined.[1]

At this rate, the world's tropical forests could be entirely destroyed with-   5
in seventy-three years. Already as much as a fifth or a quarter of the huge
Amazon forest, which constitutes a third of the world's total rain forest, has
been cut, and the rate of destruction is accelerating. And nearly two thirds
of the Central American forests have been cleared or severely degraded since
1950.

Tropical forests, which cover only 7 percent of the Earth's land surface 6
(it used to be 12 percent), support half the species of the world's living things.
Due to their destruction, "We are surely losing one or more species a day
right now out of the five million (minimum figure) on Earth," says Norman
Myers, author of numerous books and articles on the subject and consultant
to the World Bank and the World Wildlife Fund. "By the time ecological
equilibrium is restored, at least one-quarter of all species will have disappeared, probably a third, and conceivably even more. . . . If this pattern continues, it could mean the demise of two million species by the middle of next
century." Myers calls the destruction of the tropical forests "one of the greatest biological debacles to occur on the face of the Earth." Looking at the
effects it will have on the course of biological evolution, Myers says:

> The impending upheaval in evolution's course could rank as one of the
> greatest biological revolutions of paleontological time. It will equal in scale
> and significance the development of aerobic respiration, the emergence
> of flowering plants, and the arrival of limbed animals. But of course the
> prospective degradation of many evolutionary capacities will be an impov-
> erishing, not a creative, phenomenon.[2]

In other words, such rapid destruction will vacate so many niches so 7
suddenly that a "pest and weed" ecology, consisting of a relatively few oppor-
tunistic species (rats, roaches, and the like) will be created.

Beyond this—as if it weren't enough—such destruction could well have 8
cataclysmic effects on the Earth's weather patterns, causing, for example, an
irreversible desertification of the North American grain belt. Although the
scope of the so-called greenhouse effect—in which rising levels of carbon
dioxide in the atmosphere heat the planet by preventing infrared radiation
from escaping into space—is still being debated within the scientific community, it is not at all extreme to suppose that the fires set to clear tropical
forests will contribute greatly to this increase in atmospheric CO_2 and thereby to untold and possibly devastating changes in the world's weather systems.

Big Mac Attack

So what does beef, that staple of the fast-food chains and of the North Amer- 9
ican diet in general, have to do with it?

It used to be, back in 1960, that the United States imported practically 10
no beef. That was a time when North Americans were consuming a "mere"
85 pounds of beef per person per year. By 1980 this was up to 134 pounds per
person per year. Concomitant with this increase in consumption, the United
States began to import beef, so that by 1981 some 800,000 tons were coming
in from abroad, 17 percent of it from tropical Latin America and three
fourths of that from Central America. Since fast-food chains have been
steadily expanding and now are a $5-billion-a-year business, accounting for

25 percent of all the beef consumed in the United States, the connections between the fast-food empire and tropical beef are clear.

Cattle ranching is "by far the major factor in forest destruction in tropical Latin America," says Myers. "Large fast-food outlets in the U.S. and Europe foster the clearance of forests to produce cheap beef."[3]

And cheap it is, compared to North American beef: by 1978 the average price of beef imported from Central America was $1.47/kg, while similar North American beef cost $3.30/kg.

Cheap, that is, for North Americans, but not for Central Americans. Central Americans cannot afford their own beef. Whereas beef production in Costa Rica increased twofold between 1959 and 1972, per capita consumption of beef in that country went down from 30 lbs. a year to 19. In Honduras, beef production increased by 300 percent between 1965 and 1975, but consumption decreased from 12 lbs. per capita per year to 10. So, although two thirds of Central America's arable land is in cattle, local consumption of beef is decreasing; the average domestic cat in the United States now consumes more beef than the average Central American.[4]

Brazilian government figures show that 38 percent of all deforestation in the Brazilian Amazon between 1966 and 1975 was attributable to large-scale cattle ranching. Although the presence of hoof-and-mouth disease among Brazilian cattle has forced U.S. lawmakers to prohibit the importation of chilled or frozen Brazilian beef, the United States imports $46 million per year of cooked Brazilian beef, which goes into canned products; over 80 percent of Brazilian beef is still exported, most of it to Western Europe, where no such prohibition exists.

At present rates, all remaining Central American forests will have been eliminated by 1990. The cattle ranching largely responsible for this is in itself highly inefficient: as erosion and nutrient leaching eat away the soil, production drops from an average one head per hectare—measly in any case—to a pitiful one head per five to seven hectares within five to ten years. A typical tropical cattle ranch employs only one person per 2,000 head, and meat production barely reaches 50 lbs./acre/year. In Northern Europe, in farms that do not use imported feed, it is over 500 lbs./acre/year.

This real-term inefficiency does not translate into bad business, however, for although there are some absentee landowners who engage in ranching for the prestige of it and are not particularly interested in turning large profits, others find bank loans for growing beef for export readily forthcoming, and get much help and encouragement from such organizations as the Pan American Health Organization, the Organization of American States, the U.S. Department of Agriculture, and U.S. AID, without whose technical assistance "cattle production in the American tropics would be unprofitable, if not impossible."[5] The ultimate big winner appears to be the United States, where increased imports of Central American beef are said to have done more to stem inflation than any other single government initiative.

"On the good land, which could support a large population, you have the   17
rich cattle owners, and on the steep slopes, which should be left in forest, you
have the poor farmers," says Gerardo Budowski, director of the Tropical
Agricultural Research and Training Center in Turrialba, Costa Rica. "It is
still good business to clear virgin forest in order to fatten cattle for, say, five
to eight years and then abandon it."[6]

(Ironically, on a trip I made in 1981 to Morazán, a Salvadoran province   18
largely under control of FMLN guerrillas, I inquired into the guerilla diet
and discovered that beef, expropriated from the cattle ranches, was a popular
staple.)

Swift-Armour's Swift Armor

The rain forest ecosystem, the oldest on Earth, is extremely complex and del-   19
icate. In spite of all the greenery one sees there, it is a myth that rain forest
soil is rich. It is actually quite poor, leached of all nutrients save the most
insoluble (such as iron oxides, which give lateritic soil—the most common
soil type found there—its red color). Rather, the ecosystem of the rain forest
is a "closed" one, in which the nutrients are to be found in the biomass, that
is, in the living canopy of plants and in the thin layer of humus on the ground
that is formed from the matter shed by the canopy. Hence the shallow-root-
edness of most tropical forest plant species. Since the soil itself cannot
replenish nutrients, nutrient recycling is what keeps the system going.

Now, what happens when the big cattle ranchers, under the auspices of   20
the Swift-Armour Meat Packing Co., or United Brands, or the King Ranch
sling a huge chain between two enormous tractors, level a few tens of thousands of acres of tropical forest, burn the debris, fly a plane over to seed the
ash with guinea grass, and then run their cattle on the newly created grasslands?[7]

For the first three years or so the grass grows like crazy, up to an inch a   21
day, thriving on all that former biomass. After that, things go quickly downhill: the ash becomes eroded and leached, the soil becomes exposed and hard-
ens to the consistency of brick, and the area becomes useless to agriculture.
Nor does it ever regain anything near its former state. The Amazon is rising
perceptibly as a result of the increased runoff due to deforestation.

Tractor-and-chain is only one way of clearing the land. Another   22
common technique involves the use of herbicides such as Tordon, 2, 4-D,
and 2,4,5-T (Agent Orange). The dioxin found in Agent Orange can be
extremely toxic to animal life and is very persistent in the environment.

Tordon, since it leaves a residue deadly to all broad-leaved plants, ren-   23
ders the deforested area poisonous to all plants except grasses; consequently,
even if they wanted to, ranchers could not plant soil-enriching legumes in the
treated areas, a step which many agronomists recommend for keeping the
land productive for at least a little longer.

The scale of such operations is a far cry from the traditional slash-and- 24
burn practiced by native jungle groups, which is done on a scale small
enough so that the forest can successfully reclaim the farmed areas. Such
groups, incidentally, are also being decimated by cattle interests in Brazil and
Paraguay—as missionaries, human rights groups, and cattlemen themselves
will attest.

Capital's "manifest destiny" has traditionally shown little concern for the 25
lives of trees or birds or Indians, or anything else which interferes with
immediate profitability, but the current carving of holes in the gene pool by
big agribusiness seems particularly short-sighted. Since the tropical forests
contain two thirds of the world's genetic resources, their destruction will
leave an enormous void in pool of genes necessary for the creation of new
agricultural hybrids. This is not to mention the many plants as yet undis-
covered—there could be up to 15,000 unknown species in South America
alone—which may in themselves contain remarkable properties. (In writing
about alkaloids found in the Madagascar periwinkle which have recently rev-
olutionized the treatment of leukemia and Hodgkin's disease, British bio-
chemist John Humphreys said: "If this plant had not been analyzed, not even
a chemist's wildest ravings would have hinted that such structures would be
pharmacologically active."[8] Ninety percent of Madagascar's forests have
been cut.)

But there is no small truth in Indonesian Minister for Environment and 26
Development Emil Salim's complaint that the "South is asked to conserve
genes while the other fellow, in the North, is consuming things that force us
to destroy the genes in the South."[9]

Where's the Beef?

The marketing of beef imported into the United States is extremely complex, 27
and the beef itself ends up in everything from hot dogs to canned soup. Fresh
meat is exported in refrigerated container ships to points of entry, where it is
inspected by the U.S. Department of Agriculture. Once inspected, it is no
longer required to be labeled "imported."[10] From there it goes into the hands
of customhouse brokers and meat packers, often changing hands many times;
and from there it goes to the fast-food chains or the food processors. The
financial structures behind this empire are even more complex, involving
governments and quasi-public agencies, such as the Export-Import Bank and
the Overseas Private Investment Corporation, as well as the World Bank and
the Inter-American Development Bank, all of which encourage cattle raising
in the forest lands. (Brazilian government incentives to cattle ranching in
Amazonia include a 50 percent income-tax rebate on ranchers' investments
elsewhere in Brazil, tax holidays of up to ten years, loans with negative interest rates in real terms, and exemptions from sales taxes and import duties.
Although these incentives were deemed excessive and since 1979 no longer

apply to new ranches, they still continue for existing ones. This cost the Brazilian government $63,000 for each ranching job created.)

Beef production in the tropics may be profitable for the few, but it is tak- 28 ing place at enormous cost for the majority and for the planet as a whole. Apart from the environmental destruction, it is a poor converter of energy to protein and provides few benefits for the vast majority of tropical peoples in terms of employment or food. What they require are labor-intensive, multiple-cropping systems.

The world is obviously hostage to an ethic which puts short-term prof- 29 itability above all else, and such catastrophes as the wholesale destruction of the tropical forests and the continued impoverishment of their peoples are bound to occur as long as this ethic rules.

--------------------------------- **Notes** ---------------------------------

1. Jean-Paul Landley, "Tropical Forest Resources," *FAO Forestry Paper* 30 (Rome: FAO, 1982). This UN statistic is the most accurate to date. For further extrapolations from it, see Nicholas Guppy, "Tropical Deforestation: A Global View," *Foreign Affairs 62*, no. 4 (Spring 1984).

2. There are amazingly few scientists in the world with broad enough expertise to accurately assess the widest implications of tropical deforestation; Norman Myers is one of them. His books include *The Sinking Ark* (Oxford: Pergamon Press, 1979). See also *Conversion of Moist Tropical Forests* (Washington, D.C.: National Academy of Sciences, 1980), "The End of the Line," *Natural History* 94, no. 2 (February 1985), and "The Hamburger Connection," *Ambio* 10, no. 1 (1981). I have used Myers extensively in the preparation of this article. The quotes in this paragraph are from "The Hamburger Connection," pp. 3, 4, 5.

3. Myers, "End of the Line," p. 2.

4. See James Nations and Daniel I. Komer, "Rainforests and the Hamburger Society," *Environment* 25, no. 3 (April 1983).

5. Ibid., p. 17.

6. Catherine Caufield, "The Rain Forests," *New Yorker* (January 14, 1985), p. 42. This excellent article was later incorporated in a book, *In the Rainforest* (New York: Knopf, 1985).

7. Other multinationals with interests in meat packing and cattle ranching in tropical Latin America include Armour-Dial International, Goodyear Tire and Rubber Co., and Gulf and Western Industries, Inc. See Roger Burbach and Patricia Flynn, *Agribusiness in the Americas* (New York: Monthly Review Press, 1980).

8. Qtd. in Caufield, "Rain Forests," p. 60.

9. Ibid., p. 100.

10. This is one way McDonald's, for example, can claim not to use foreign beef. For a full treatment of McDonald's, see M. Boas and S. Chain, *Big Mac: The Unauthorized Story of McDonald's* (New York: New American Library, 1976).

Critical Reading Questions

1. What would you say is the primary purpose of this essay?
2. What readers do you believe would be most interested in this essay?
3. How would you define Skinner's tone? What evidence does he provide to substantiate his argument that America's love of the fast-food diet is causally linked to the devastation of the rain forests?
4. What are some of the necessary or sufficient causes, according to the experts that Skinner cites, of the destruction of the rain forests? What are some of the effects of the destruction of the rain forest? How is the greenhouse effect related to Skinner's thesis?

Analyzing Pertinent Conventions

Follow Conventions for Introducing Your Topic

As discussed in Chapters 3 and 4, your introduction will generally highlight the significance of your topic and then proceed from given information—what the reader knows—to new information—what the reader doesn't know. Before you write a lengthy introduction, consider what information readers already take for granted.

As with reports of processes and subjects, you will often want to provide an *overview* of your purpose for writing about causes and effects and present *forecasting statements*—that is, sentences that clarify how the text is organized and what readers can expect. For example, note how the two opening sentences in "Big Mac and the Tropical Forest" immediately focus your attention on the causal connection that Skinner explicates throughout his essay:

> Hello, fast-food chains.
> Goodbye, tropical forests.

As this example demonstrates, you do not always state your purpose in a sentence like "The purpose of my essay is. . . ." Can you imagine how terribly boring it would be if all essays started in this manner? You also do not always need to mention explicitly how you have organized a document. For example, do you think the forecasting sentence (italicized) in the following introduction is necessary?

> Television presents our children with a world that is often different from their lives. Because young children cannot distinguish the imaginary world

from reality or distinguish right from wrong, we need to question what happens to children's thinking when they observe a cartoon figure like He-Man recover from a serious injury in seconds that would actually fatally wound a real-life person. *In this paper I will present the positive and negative effects of television on children.*

Many people think that TV is beneficial and necessary for the normal development of children. . . .

If you omitted that forecasting sentence, there would be no loss of meaning or confusion on the part of readers. Given the author's strong focus in the beginning line and the He-Man example, it is obvious that the author intends to explore the effects of television on children.

Also, you may want to avoid explicit thesis sentences and forecasting statements if your subject is likely to threaten the beliefs of your audience or if it is an inherently emotional subject. You may *occasionally* find it important to establish a credible persona first, by reviewing what your readers are likely to believe about a causal relationship, and then by stating your own opinion. For example, assume that I am writing an essay against spanking children. Now if you believe that spanking children is the proper way to discipline them, and if I claim in the introduction of the essay that spanking children may result in their becoming criminals, then you might assume that I am an oddball and dismiss my essay. Yet if I intelligently discuss some of the reasons why parents and psychologists recommend spanking, and then I introduce extensive research from prominent journals and reports that *all* violent criminals were spanked as children, you might be more willing to listen to my reasoning. (See Chapter 7 for a more complete discussion of how to handle communication situations that involve emotional and controversial topics.)

Focus on Developing Your Ideas

When analyzing causal relationships, you must question how different parts and sequences interact with each other over time. Rather than merely reporting the order of events in chronological fashion as we do when describing a process, we need to identify the specific reasons behind the effects or causes. This is often difficult because a single cause can result in different effects and an effect can have multiple causes. For example, even a simple effect such as a minor car accident can have multiple causes. Yes, we could say that John D. caused the accident because he was driving while intoxicated. Yet if we knew more about John D.'s state of mind—if we knew, for instance, that he wasn't watching where he was going because he was thinking about his wife's threat to leave him—then we could identify additional causes for the accident. It could very well be that he was exhausted after a sleepless night. Or perhaps his personal predicament had nothing to do with the accident: maybe the loss of his job that morning or his failure to have faulty brakes replaced is a more significant cause for the accident. If we get really carried away with our reasoning, we could say that his former employers were responsible. After all,

John D. would not have lost his job if the automobile manufacturer he worked for had not closed three of its American plants and moved manufacturing of some parts to plants in Mexico, Hong Kong, and Japan. In addition, we could also find potential causes for the accident by considering the other driver, Susan K. Maybe she rushed into the busy intersection expecting everyone else to make room for her because she was already late for an in-class exam. Perhaps if Susan K. had not drunk four pots of coffee, she would have been more mellow, more cautious, and less willing to risk her life to get to school on time.

Academic readers such as your instructors are quick to recognize shallow reasoning. As a result, you should avoid assuming a cause-and-effect relationship when the outcome could just as likely have been caused by chance. Academic readers are reluctant to assume causality between two actions because they are trained to identify *post hoc* ("after this") *fallacies*. Essentially a *post hoc fallacy* occurs when an author assumes Event B was caused by Event A simply because it followed Event A; the connection is false because it is equally possible that Event B was caused by some other factor. For example, let us suppose that Bill has been jilted by his girlfriend Laura. Because Laura argued with Bill last Friday night that he never spent any money on her and that she always has to pay for their dates, Bill might assume that she left him because he was cheap. However, this might not be the true reason for Laura's dumping Bill. In fact, it could be that Laura was tired of Bill's negative view of life. Perhaps she truly left Bill because she found him to be insensitive, boring, and uncommunicative.

Appeal to Your Readers' Senses

You can help your readers imagine your subject better by appealing to their senses. Whenever possible, describe how an object looks, sounds, tastes, feels, or smells. For example, in this excerpt from Carl Sagan's powerful essay on the effects of a nuclear war, "The Nuclear Winter," notice how Sagan appeals to our visual sense in his description of the effect of a single nuclear bomb on a city:

> In a 2 megaton explosion over a fairly large city, buildings would be vaporized, people reduced to atoms and shadows, outlying structures blown down like matchsticks and raging fires ignited. And if the bomb exploded on the ground, an enormous crater, like those that can be seen through a telescope on the surface of the Moon, would be all that remained where midtown once had been.

The lifeblood of effective writing is concrete and sensory language. A word, properly placed, can create a tone that angers or inspires a reader. Knowing the power of language to promote change, effective writers are selective in their use of *concrete words*—words that represent actual physical things like "chair" and "house"—and *sensory words*—words that appeal to our five senses. Selecting the right word or group of words is a crucial step in drawing your readers into your work so that they can fully understand your vision and ideas. Note the masterful use of concrete and sensory words in this passage from a *Newsweek* essay, "Don't Go in the Water":

> *"Black mayonnaise"*: The problem for most landlubbers, of course, is that most of the effects of coastal pollution are hard to see. Bays and estuaries that are now in jeopardy—Boston Harbor, for example, or even San Francisco Bay—are still delightful to look at from shore. What is happening underwater is quite another matter, and it is not for the squeamish. Scuba divers talk of swimming through clouds of toilet paper and half-dissolved feces, of bay bottoms covered by a foul and toxic combination of sediment, sewage and petrochemical waste appropriately known as "black mayonnaise." Fishermen haul in lobsters and crab [*sic*] covered with mysterious "burn holes" and fish whose fins are rotting off. Offshore, marine biologists track massive tides of algae blooms fed by nitrate and phosphate pollution—colonies of floating microorganisms that, once dead, strangle fish by stripping the water of its life giving oxygen.

In addition to selecting an abundance of distinctive concrete words (such as sediment, sewage, and nitrate) and sensory words (foul, burn holes, feces), the authors have used powerful images and metaphors. Note, for example, the clouds of toilet paper. Even more potent is the image of "black mayonnaise." Can you imagine biting into a sandwich spread with such poison?

Humanize Abstract Issues

No matter how technical your subject is, you should keep in mind that you are writing to other people. When you sense that *the human story* is being lost in abstract figures or academic jargon, consider adding an anecdote of how the problem you are discussing affects particular people. For example, Melissa Henderson began her report on the effect of crack on babies with the following portrayal of a newborn, which she composed after reading numerous essays about the effect of crack cocaine on human fetuses:

> Lying restlessly under the warm lights like a McDonald's Big Mac, Baby Doe fights with all of his three pounds of strength to stay alive. Because he was born prematurely, Baby Doe has an array of tubes and wires extending from his frail body which constantly monitor his heartbeat, drain excess fluid from his lungs and alert hospital personnel in the event he stops breathing. As he lies in the aseptic incubator, his rigid little arms and legs twitch and jerk as though a steady current of electricity coursed through his veins. Suddenly, without warning or provocation, he begins to cry a mournful, inconsolable wail that continues steadily without an end in sight. As the nurses try to comfort the tiny infant with loving touches and soothing whispers, Baby Doe's overwrought nervous system can no longer cope. Suffering from sensory overload, he withdraws into the security offered in a long, deep slumber. Welcome to the world, Baby Doe; your mother is a crack cocaine addict.

As you write drafts of your causal report, consider incorporating an anecdote—that is, a brief story about how people are influenced by your subject. For example, if you are researching the effects of a sluggish economy on our nation's poor, you might want to flesh out your statistics by depicting the story of how one homeless family lost their jobs, income, medical benefits, house, community, hope.

Establish an Appropriate Voice

Trying to communicate your subject in a coherent way can be so overwhelming that you forget to consider the influence of your voice or persona on the reader. When grappling with difficult issues and concepts, your prose can understandably become unclear, dull, or cluttered. Eventually, though, as you continue to revise your drafts and further refine your message, you need to cut away the superfluous words, redundancies, and needless abstractions. You can make your language more interesting and more understandable by eliminating needless jargon; passive voice; lengthy, redundant sentences; or pompous and archaic language.

Based on what you say, your readers will make judgments about whether you seem knowledgeable, educated, compassionate, angry, or confused. If you use excessive jargon, write extensively in the passive voice, fail to offer specific examples to illustrate your point, or do not elaborate on essential information, then some readers might consider you to be aloof or pompous, while others might assume that you are reluctant or unable to communicate.

Sometimes people believe they need to sound "academic" when they write; they don't think they can simply be themselves and write naturally. Rather than trying to simplify their prose, they reach for a thesaurus and select the least understood or most impressive-sounding word. Here's a sample of terribly technical language that a colleague of mine wrote to satirize the humorous elements of jargon-ridden prose:

> Health is generally benefited by the voluntary ingestion of 4000 to 5000 ml of hydrogen hydroxide in each 24 hour period, distributed more or less equally across the time period in 250 to 500 ml units.

Now when you read this, it may at first seem sophisticated, enshrouded as it is in pseudoscientific garb. Yet, properly translated into readable English, it simply says, "Drink eight glasses of water a day."

Pretentious jargon and obscure language can at first be intimidating because the authors appear to be implying that we *should* understand the message—"What, you don't understand this? Then you must be an idiot, eh?" However, college-educated, critical readers are rarely impressed by vague, abstract language. For example, what do you think of the following prose, which is excerpted from a draft of a graduate student's essay on language development?

> An oral language production system is the first one learned by children. The task of learning a written language production system occurs when children enter school. A noticeable difference between these two systems is the presence of a conversational partner. This difference is significant when you compare speaking and writing at the level of continuous discourse. Conversational partners provide constant cues, such as to elaborate, to clarify, to keep a goal in mind, to stay on the topic, etc. Evidence of children's dependence on conversational inputs when learning to write comes from observing effects of prompting children to continue, that is to take another conversational turn. Children are dependent to some extent on conversational interchange to develop a text. However, no conversational partner exists in written composition. Learning to write involves a transition from a language production system dependent on inputs from a conversational partner to a system capable of functioning autonomously. Without conversational supports, children have problems in thinking what to say, in making choices appropriate to a remote audience, in staying on the topic, and in producing an intelligible whole.

Clearly, this passage is weakened by jargon. A critical reader will wonder, for example, about the need for such terms as "oral language production system"; "continuous discourse"; or "conversational interchange." More insidious in this example, however, are the abundance of passive constructions and lack of people-oriented references. For example, who is doing the observing in the following sentence: "Evidence of children's dependence on conversational inputs when learning to write comes from observing effects of prompting children to continue, that is to take another conversational turn"? Also, take a look at the emptiness of the third sentence: "A noticeable difference between these two systems is the presence of a conversational partner." Even with rereading, it is unclear whether the "oral language production system" or the "written language production system" has "the presence of a conversational partner." Of course, the author could argue that everyone knows that conversation usually involves a dialogue between speakers while writing usually lacks such an exchange. Naturally, clever readers will see through the fog with a discerning eye and recognize that the writer's ideas are in fact relatively simple:

> Perhaps children don't learn to write until they enter school because writing demands more than speech. Whereas children can easily develop their ideas through dialogue—that is, by listening to queries and comments and suggestions from other speakers—they must conceptualize an audience when they write.

Ultimately, however, if you think about the gist of this writer's message long enough, it becomes so obvious that you wonder about the need to say it at all. Surprisingly, you will often find this to be the case: pedantic, long-winded speakers and writers are often hiding simple concepts behind verbal smoke screens. Thus, when you read, remember not to buy the snake oil! Be a critical reader.

Writing Assignments

Some of the essays suggested by the following questions can be based solely on your personal experience, some will require interviewing other people, and some will involve conducting library research. Before choosing a topic, you should check with your instructor to determine the scope of research that is expected of you. If you will need to substantiate a causal analysis with outside sources, you may find it useful to consult Chapter 2, How to Use the Library and Document Sources.

1. Can you recall circumstances that caused you to ask, "Why do things have to be this way?" Write about one of these perplexing instances.

2. What has been the effect of an invention in your lifetime? For example, what has been the effect of television, jet airplanes, nuclear weapons, fax machines, or personal computers on human relations and behavior?

3. What has been the effect of an important social change on your life or contemporary life in general? For example, how have the demographics of the baby boomers influenced competition in the workplace? How did the women's movement of the 1960s shape the opportunities that women have today? What would have happened to male-female relationships if "the Pill" hadn't been invented or been legalized? How has the trend from an industrial economy to a service economy influenced the current job market?

4. How did decisions about your upbringing affect who you are? What educational experiences or people deeply influenced you?

5. In what ways do you think a person's environment can influence his or her behavior? Have you ever known people who seem defined by their environment? What is the most unusual place you have ever been? How did the people in that place seem different from the people you know at home?

6. Has a particular historical or political event intrigued you? For example, how did the William Kennedy Smith 1992 rape trial or Anita Hill's and Clarence Thomas's 1991 testimony before the Senate Judiciary Committee influence the "war between the sexes"? Why did Iraq invade Kuwait in 1991? Why did the Iraqi people allow Saddam Hussein to stay in power after the "Mother of All Battles" became the "Mother of All Losses" in 1991? Analyze the factors that led up to the event you select as well as its effects, and write about it so that less informed readers will understand and appreciate it.

7. When you recall your writing background, what are the first writing memories that occur to you? Are they pleasant or unpleasant memories? How have these experiences shaped your current attitude about yourself as a writer?

8. How does your audience and environment influence the language that you use? For example, how would you describe a problem with your car differently to a mechanic, a teacher, a parent, and a friend?

Prewriting and Drafting Strategies

The following strategies can help you write a first draft of your cause-and-effect report.

Consider Your Communication Situation

Because writers often discover a richer and more compelling purpose for their documents once they have written a few drafts, you should not feel overly concerned if you are presently unsure about your exact purpose, audience, or voice. However, you will save yourself time now if you can summarize in a sentence the purpose of your analysis. For example, do you want to amuse your audience, to educate them, to persuade them about something?

As a student, much of your writing is understandably written specifically for your writing class and other classes. However, when you are writing for audiences other than your teachers, you might question where your essays would be likely to appear if they were published. Would your essay be appropriate for publication in a commercial magazine, a specialized newsletter, a professional journal, a campus magazine, or a student newspaper?

When the urge to procrastinate seems overwhelming, remember also that starting is half the battle. Once you freewrite, draw a cluster or pie diagram, or dictate a draft, you will gain a better sense of what you want to say and how you want to say it. Finally, if you truly wish to improve as a writer, set a firm schedule that motivates you to begin early and allows you sufficient time to thoroughly develop your ideas.

Ask Relevant Questions

Below are the primary questions that writers address when exploring *effects*. To begin drafting a focused document quickly, try using these questions to generate a rough outline of possible points:

1. What is the significance of the effect(s) for my intended readers? If there are multiple effects, do they occur in sequence or simultaneously?
2. What is the most important or most serious effect?
3. What is the second most important effect?
4. What additional effects are likely or possible?

When tracing *causes*, you may find the following questions to be useful:

1. What is the event or behavior that I am analyzing? What is its significance?

2. What are the possible causes for this effect? If there are multiple causes, do they have to occur in sequence or can they occur simultaneously? Define and prioritize the causes.

3. Have I properly distinguished sufficient causes from necessary causes?

4. Can I rank order the causes from the most probable to the least probable?

5. Have I presented pertinent additional causes?

Revising and Editing Strategies

When revising, remember that even accomplished authors find serious problems and errors in fifth, tenth, or even twentieth drafts. Yet rather than chastising themselves for missing the obvious, these authors recognize that writing is a learning experience. In fact, many people claim that they enjoy writing most when they discover new ideas while writing and come to reject previously held beliefs. The following strategies can help you effectively revise your writing.

Read Your Work Aloud

Before turning your work in to your instructor or your peers for criticism, you should read your text aloud. Not only will this technique help you spot faulty sentence construction and grammatical and spelling errors, but it will also help you identify gaps in reasoning. Another excellent way to evaluate your essay is to tape record your work and then listen to the recording. After you get over the unease of hearing yourself on tape, pay attention to your writing voice. Do you sound false, condescending, or wishy-washy? An even more effective technique is to have your classmates read your work aloud and then have them describe the persona that they hear.

Ask Critical Questions

In addition to experimenting with the revising and editing strategies discussed in Chapters 11 and 12, you should give special attention to the following questions because they highlight problems that frequently occur when student writers explore cause-and-effect relationships.

1. Have I provided the details that my audience will need in order to understand the subject? What changes can I make to simplify the presentation of the subject?

2. Is my essay unified by a clear purpose? Have I presented sufficient forecasting statements so readers will understand the organization of the essay? Have I subsequently followed the organization promised in the introduction?

3. How well developed is the content? Have I defined all important terms and concepts? What other comparisons, illustrations, or analogies could I add?

4. Will readers find fault with my logic? Have I provided sufficient information for readers to understand my reasoning? Are any of my conclusions *post hoc* fallacies?

5. Is the report visually appealing? Would readers understand my information better if I used more headings, tables, flow charts, or other visual aids?

6. Is my writing economical? Can I combine and edit some of the sentences to make them more vigorous?

7. Is the essay grammatical and mechanically correct? Are there any specific errors that I tend to make that I haven't yet checked for, such as capitalization or overuse of the passive voice?

Collaborating Strategies

Once you have reached a stage where you cannot improve your work any further without help, and once you are willing to listen to how other people respond to your writing, then you should turn your work over to people who are willing to review it critically. You can encourage and guide your critics by letting them know what troubles you about the manuscript and how much feedback you really want. Ask your readers to respond to the following questions after reviewing your essay.

PEER REVIEW WORKSHOP

1. Do you understand the cause-and-effect relationships that are presented? Do you believe the author has overstated the causal relationship? Can you think of other causes that could account for the effect, or other effects that could result from the cause?

2. Are there any points in the discussion at which you are confused or where you think additional evidence needs to be provided? What information do you believe the author should add before submitting the report for a grade?

3. In what ways could the writer make the report more interesting to his or her intended readers?

4. Do you think the report is well organized? Given the author's communication situation, do you believe the introduction should give readers more information about the report's content? Does the author actually accomplish what he or she promised to do in the introduction?

Additional Writing Samples

In the brief essay presented below, Carolyn Lutz, a student writer, explores the causes behind gender discrimination. Lutz initially became interested in researching this subject after writing a biography of a peer who had been propositioned by her professor.

Why Isn't There Gender Equity in Higher Education?

Carolyn Templeton Lutz

After several decades of the fight for equal rights between the sexes, most college students would hope that higher education has achieved gender equity. After all, because of the vehicle higher education represents—one of "higher" thought—it should be one of the areas in our society that is first to change. Yet, studies show disparate images of American higher education. 1

On the surface, it may appear as though few inequalities exist in the education of men and women. If anything, the small differences are disparaged: they are overlooked for the larger, more blatant issues of sexual discrimination. Yet, these seemingly insignificant differences in higher education add up to much larger problems with long-reaching ramifications that students carry into the business world. 2

According to studies which resulted from long-term observations of students' classroom behavior and interviews with students and teachers, researchers concluded that females tend to have less confidence in themselves and in their ability to succeed in challenging intellectual tasks. Females are more apt to interpret difficulty as an "indication of insufficient ability" (Markland 83). Females, usually, are more likely than males to avoid a task or subject after experiencing failure. This conclusion leads one to ask, "Why?" 3

Why do females tend to view themselves this way? Learning differences have a known effect upon academic achievement. Females usually develop better reading and formal language skills at an earlier age; yet, they typically avoid math and science courses (Markland). According to Susan Gabriel and Isaiah Smithson, editors of *Gender in the Classroom*, these learned behaviors are brought into the classroom from the American society; males and females are still being raised differently and taught differently. In many ways "it affects the ways they learn as much as it affects the rest of their lives" (Gabriel 8). And according to the American Association of University Women, females are subtly and overtly steered away from math and sciences. 4

These attitudes not only seem to have a long-term detrimental effect on females' self-esteem, but also on their academic accomplishments. While females certainly have the intellectual ability to do as well academically as males, they apparently don't receive, either from teachers or society, the encouragement and attention they may require to excel. 5

Perceptions of femininity and masculinity also play an integral part in   6
higher education. For instance, in *Gender and Subject in Higher Education*,
Thomas notes that the "perceptions of arts and sciences are shaped by
notions of femininity and masculinity" (36). The arts and the humanities are
considered more feminine and more subjective; the sciences are considered
more masculine and more objective. Thomas concludes that these perceptions only lead to stereotyping and discipline barriers: females and non-conformist males lean toward the arts and humanities; males and non-conformist
females lean toward the sciences. Thus, the stereotyping of education and
careers is perpetuated.

In the 1992 Spring edition of *Outlook: American Association of University*   7
Women, an Executive Summary outlines a comprehensive report, "How
Schools Shortchange Girls." Prepared by the Wellesley College Center for
Research on Women, the report encompasses the education experience of
girls. The results reveal many unsettling, often overlooked inequities in the
classroom. Listed below are the main points.

- Girls receive significantly less attention from classroom teachers than do
  boys.
- Sexual harassment of girls by boys—from innuendo to actual assault—in
  our nation's schools is increasing.
- The contributions and experiences of girls and women are still marginal-
  ized or ignored in many of the textbooks used in our nation's schools.
- Differences between girls and boys in math achievement are small and
  declining.
- The gender gap in science, however, is not decreasing and may, in fact, be
  increasing.
- Even girls who are highly competent in math and science are much less
  likely to pursue scientific or technological careers than are their male classmates.
- When scholarships are given based on the SAT scores, boys are more apt
  to receive scholarships than are girls who get equal or slightly better high
  school grades.
- Test scores can provide an inaccurate picture of girls' and boys' abilities.
  (2–5)

While many disparities still exist between male and female education, more   8
positive trends are beginning to surface. As recently as the early 1980s,
according to the 1991 *Statistical Abstract of the United States*, female enrollment in institutions of higher education began to surpass that of male enrollment. In fact, the projected figures for 1996 place female enrollment an
average of 14 percent higher than that of males. These recent trends and
projections in enrollment seem to imply that females are quickly trying to
catch up with males in the attainment of higher education. But to do so not

only involves the institutions of higher learning, but also the primary and secondary learning institutions and society as a whole. Attitude, biases, and pedagogy must challenge the traditional concepts of education and gender differences. Society must strive to view itself as a whole rather than separate genders. Then, and only then, may we answer "Yes" to the question, "Is there gender equity in higher education?"

Works Cited

"Executive Summary." *Outlook: American Association of University Women* Spring 1992.

Gabriel, Susan L., and Isaiah Smithson, eds. *Gender in the Classroom.* Urbana: U of Illinois P, 1990.

Markland, Michael, ed. *Sex Differentiation and Schooling.* London: Heinemann, 1983.

"New Protection for Campus Women." Editorial. *The Oracle* 2 Mar. 1992. p. 6.

Roeder, Karen. "Guest Column." *The Oracle* 17 Feb. 1992. p. 2.

Thomas, Kim. *Gender and Subject in Higher Education.* England: Soc. for Research into Higher Ed. & Open UP, 1990.

United States. *Statistical Abstract of the United States: 1991.* 111th ed. Washington, DC: GPO, 1991.

Critical Reading Questions

1. What are some of the causes Lutz presents for discrimination based on gender?

2. How would you describe Lutz's tone in this piece? What assumptions does she appear to be making about her audience?

3. If Lutz were in your peer review workshop, what advice would you give her for improving her essay?

In the following essay, G. Jon Roush speculates about the consequences of the rapid disappearance of living species. According to Roush, it was common in the past to lose one species a year, yet now we are losing one to three species every day.

The Disintegrating Web—The Causes and Consequences of Extinction*

G. Jon Roush

As soft and inescapable as sleep, the snow fell all winter long. It drifted against the trees and hills, filled the stream beds, buried the dens of

* From *The Nature Conservancy Magazine* (Nov./Dec. 1989).

burrowers. The Earth stayed cold all summer, as the white ground reflected the sun's heat back to the sky. Century after century, the snow deepened. Beneath the cool mantle, ice grew thousands of feet thick, until it began to move of its own weight, and the edge of frozen summer inched toward the Equator. Had the mean temperature cooled another two or three degrees, ice sheets advancing from each pole would have met and joined, wiping virtually all life off the planet.

As it was, by the time the glaciers began their slow retreat some 15,000 2 years ago, there had been carnage enough. In one brief 3,000-year period, North America alone lost 50 species of mammals and 40 species of birds to extinction. Scientists disagree about the causes. Some blame the ice and weather; others, human hunters.

Life on Earth is a chancy enterprise. At various times glaciers, volcanoes, 3 and perhaps even meteors and comets have razed the planet, contributing to the obliteration of countless species. Even without such cataclysms, extinction is a normal by-product of evolution. Estimates of the number of species on the Earth today range as high as 30 million or more, but 100 times that many have come into being and passed away since life first appeared on this planet.

Yet something unprecedented is going on now. We are at this moment 4 facing an ecological catastrophe unequaled in the history of the Earth. During the past 600 million years, the natural background rate of extinction has been about one species per year. Around the world now, the rate is estimated to be one to three species lost every day—perhaps as high as one species every hour—and the trend is accelerating. Scientists predict that by the early 21st Century, we will witness *several hundred extinctions per day*. Our grandchildren may live in a world with fewer than half the species of plants and animals populating ours.

With the possible exception of nuclear war, this torrent of extinction 5 may be the most serious threat ever to confront humankind.

Nature's Gifts

Should we worry about protecting some insignificant plants and insects when 6 we need to feed, clothe, and house our own species? The truth is, like mountaineers roped together on a steep cliff, we depend utterly on the survival of other species.

Almost half of all the pharmaceutical products that lessen our pain, con- 7 trol our diseases, and lengthen our lives are derived from other species. Most of them come from plants, and most of the rest come from "lesser" animals— the worms, reptiles, amphibians, insects, and fish that pass their lives unnoticed or even shunned by human beings. In the harsh company of predators and competitors, these plants and animals have evolved complex chemical mechanisms for healing their wounds, attracting their mates, digesting their food, poisoning their prey or their predators, finding safe refuge, or performing countless other life-saving tricks.

We are learning to use those chemicals for our own ends, whether to 8
produce penicillin from mold or heart-saving digitalis from the plant known
as foxglove. Although pharmaceutical scientists are increasingly adept at
creating new medicinal compounds, they cannot always replicate this vast
treasury of ready-made medicines. Some molecules are too complex or too
expensive to synthesize artificially, and so the species themselves must be
preserved if we are to benefit from their gifts.

Our understanding of this medicinal wealth remains pitifully small. 9
Although we make new discoveries continually, we have investigated only a
small percentage of the world's plants for their medicinal value. We lose more
species each day, and with each species, a universe of hidden possibilities.

Like our medicines, our store of food depends ultimately on the contin- 10
ued existence of wild species. The world's agriculture relies on only a few
species: one kind of soybean, two rices, two peas, and so forth. Resting on
such a narrow base, our most important foods are perilously vulnerable to
disasters like blight, pests, and drought, which could devastate whole human
populations. One of our most important defenses against such misfortune is
to reinvigorate domestic strains by hybridizing them with their wild cousins.

The only truly useless species is one that has become extinct. 11

The Disintegrating Web

But the importance of wild species goes far beyond their direct use by 12
humans. As more species become extinct, the living fabric of our planet is
becoming tattered, endangering whole natural systems and putting all of us
at risk. Even the local extinction of a species can change an entire ecosystem.
The people of Manaus have learned about that. Historically this Brazilian
city has received a third of its protein from fish. That is not surprising, since
Manaus sits on the banks of the Amazon River. What is surprising is that
most of those fish spend part of their lives not in the river but in the forest.
When the river floods each year, some species of fish follow the flood waters
and swim among the tree trunks, feeding on seeds and fruit. Three-fourths of
Manaus's fish diet has depended on those forest-foragers. Less forest means
fewer fish, and that means hard times for Manaus. By the time authorities
understood that relationship, all the large forests within 100 kilometers of
Manaus had been cut down.

These hidden chains of cause and effect can be subtle and intricate. Like 13
the people of Manaus, we usually find out about them only when it is too
late. Wisdom dictates that we proceed with care. Every time a species is lost,
others are jeopardized. A famous and particularly poignant example is *Calvaria major*, a tree on the island of Mauritius. *Calvaria* is also called the dodo
tree, because its fruit was an important source of food for the dodo. Dodos,
of course, were large, flightless birds that lived secure on their island for ten
million years with no predators—until Dutch sailors and colonists arrived,
along with their scavenging dogs and pigs. The trusting, slow-moving birds
were soon clubbed and harried to oblivion. But they did not die alone.

Curiously, after the last dodo died in 1680, no new dodo trees appeared. For some 300 years, one by one the world's only dodo trees grew old and died with no young trees to replace them. Finally in the 1970s, when only 13 ancient trees were left, Dr. Stanley Temple discovered the secret. The seed casings had to be crushed in the dodo's gravel-grinding craw before the seed could germinate. By force-feeding the seeds to turkeys, Dr. Temple was able to germinate three seedlings. Scientists have now developed artificial methods to abrade the dodo trees' seeds, but what sort of world are we making, when human beings must imitate dodos?

Avalanche Warning

Because of the web that connects all living things, the loss of any species can 14 bring unexpected consequences. Consider figs. Because figs are phenomenally prolific and nutritious, they are crucial for the support of an incalculable number of species. Almost all the 900 species of figs grow in tropical forests, where they are an essential food source for a large number of birds, insects, fish, turtles, and mammals. Figs are such a complete food that some species of bats eat almost nothing else.

Most of these fig-eaters help the trees by dispersing seeds throughout 15 the forest. But the friends of figs that count most are certain wasps. Without wasps, figs would become extinct. Wasps lay their eggs in the fruit of fig trees. The emerging wasps collect pollen from their host tree, and they carry that pollen to another tree where they deposit it along with the next generation of eggs. What makes the story astonishing is that with few exceptions, each of the 900 fig species can be pollinated by only one species of wasp.

Each of these wasp species is what some ecologists call a "keystone 16 species": a species on which many other species rely for their own continued existence. Removing one wasp species from the fig-regeneration cycle could set off a chain reaction of species loss. Fruit is the primary food source for about 75 percent of all vertebrate animals in the Amazon rain forest. For three months of every year, when most Amazonian fruit trees are barren, mammals and birds depend on only a few species for food, and of all those species, the most important are figs. No wasps, no figs. No figs, no spider monkeys, peccaries, or toucans. No monkeys or peccaries, no jaguars. And so forth.

That chain reaction exemplifies the most terrifying aspect of extinction. 17 Each time an ecosystem is reduced by one species, other species may be threatened, and the whole natural system may be weakened. As extinction continues, the chances for further extinctions multiply. In many systems we are already on the verge of an extinction avalanche, with hundreds or thousands of species at risk. Once the avalanche begins, some species will disappear quickly, and others may hang on for 200 or 300 years. Whatever the schedule, human intervention may slow the collapse and even rescue some species, but momentum will be on the side of annihilation.

The Costs of Ruin

Extinction is often expensive, and it grows exponentially more expensive as 18
it spreads. It may be fairly easy to substitute human labor for the work of a
single species like the dodo. But we do the work of whole systems at great
cost, like the cost of transporting food to Manaus.

More often than not, we cannot really replace natural systems, no matter 19
how much we spend. When Europeans settled the great grasslands of our
Midwest, their cattle replaced 30 million bison, as well as deer, elk, antelope,
and other grazers. These animals had evolved a complex bond with prairies
and prairie fires. Periodically, fires removed dead mulch and regenerated the
grasses, enriching the animals' diet. The animals, in turn, helped control the
fires by grazing the fuel and increasing the intervals between fires. A patchwork of grazed areas and grasses resulted, differing in size and timing in the
different prairie types. In all prairies, this patchwork supported a rich diversity of plants, mammals, birds, and insects.

To replicate those conditions and keep the plant communities healthy, 20
people now burn the prairies intentionally. But between fires, the dead grass
that the bison would have eaten accumulates, tinder for fires to be reckoned
with. So people must light more frequent controlled burns, which reduce
genetic diversity within species—another form of biological impoverishment.
Without bison, fire is an equal-opportunity leveler, helping tall plants out-
compete shorter plants for the light they both need. By grazing, trampling,
and wallowing, bison create patches of prairie that make fire less uniform and
give more plant species and populations a chance to flourish.

One solution is to reintroduce bison and other native grazers, as wildlife 21
experts are now doing on a few prairie preserves and refuges. But even this
solution has a problem: it works only on very extensive prairies, and there are
few remaining unplowed spaces big enough to recreate this dynamic interaction of bison, fire, and native prairie.

We are lucky that those grazers still exist and can provide their priceless 22
services on suitable lands. For smaller prairie remnants, the alternative is
more intensive human management, to compensate for natural processes that
cannot be restored.

Because of damage already done, protecting an ecosystem's endangered 23
species is often like nursing a ward of patients, each on the critical list and each
with a different, previously unknown disease. Such stewardship is usually
expensive. The more disturbed the habitat and the more diminished its species
diversity, the more costly protection is likely to be. Human beings must then
expend time, money, and ingenuity doing what nature once did for free. Of all
the costs resulting from extinction, the cost of protecting what is left may be
the greatest. The sooner we begin, the less expensive it is likely to be.

The Value of Worthless Things

Even if it could be proven that a certain species had no utility for us or our 24
descendants, and that it could be plucked from its ecosystem at no cost, we

would still be obliged to protect it for its sake and our own. To be fully human is to have a sense of moral responsibility. If we do not recognize the intrinsic worth of other species, and if we nonchalantly observe and abet their extinction, we become less than human.

This argument was developed most eloquently by Aldo Leopold in his 25 classic essay "The Land Ethic." He concluded that "a land ethic changes the role of *Homo sapiens* from conqueror of the land-community to plain member and citizen of it. It implies respect for his fellow members, and also respect for the community as such." A workable land ethic requires that we under-stand the consequences of our actions on other species. It further requires that we acknowledge the right of other species to continue their existence and to do so in a natural state.

But this gentle credo can be controversial when people's livelihood is at 26 stake. For example, because the Pacific Ocean's sea otter is a voracious eater of abalone and crab, it wins no popularity contests among commercial fisher-men. At one time, the sea otter had been hunted almost to extinction. By 1911 only about 1,000 of these winsome animals survived, but they were pro-tected and gradually came back. When the sea otter returned to its near-shore haunts, so did other species like the harbor seal and bald eagle. The reason? The sea otter is a keystone species. Among the otter's most favored delicacies are sea urchins, and sea urchins in turn are gluttons for kelp and sea grass. Unchecked, sea urchins will devour a kelp forest and look for more. But these sea weeds are essential habitat for many species of fish, which in turn feed seals and eagles. Without sea otters to control sea urchins, the system collapses.

We have no simple formula for balancing the interests of wage earners 27 against the benefits of a healthy ecosystem. It would be unjust, and politically unwise, to disregard those people whose subsistence may be disrupted by actions to prevent extinction. The future of the planet depends to a large degree on our success in creating economically and socially defensible strate-gies for doing the right thing.

Yet at root these issues involve more than economics. Two hundred 28 years ago, John Wesley, the founder of Methodism, declared that the Golden Rule applied to all creatures, even snakes, worms, toads, and flies. Surely we still measure the depth of our humanity by the breadth of our compassion. As Aldo Leopold summed it up, we need to "quit thinking about decent land-use as solely an economic problem. Examine each question in terms of what is ethically and esthetically right, as well as what is economically expedient. A thing is right when it tends to preserve the integrity, stability, and beauty of the biotic community. It is wrong when it tends otherwise."

Poison, Guns, and Aliens

Human beings cause extinction in four ways. First, we pollute the air, water, 29 and land. Each year we release hundreds of billions of tons of pollutants into the environment. Many are toxic and work their way up the food chain with lethal persistence. Others work indirectly, producing calamities like acid rain, ozone depletion, and global warming. As we transform the planet's chemistry and toy with its climate, we alter habitats everywhere, making life impossible for an increasing number of species.

Second, hunting and fishing for food, animal products, and sport has 30 rubbed out some of the most memorable species. From the time that human beings first crossed the Siberian land bridge into North America until human settlements had advanced through South America, the extinction of large, meaty mammals accelerated. As human beings moved through the hemisphere like an eraser across a blackboard, almost 40 percent of all mammals in South America and almost 30 percent of all mammals in North America became extinct. That coincidence has led many researchers to conclude that hunting was the primary cause of that wave of extinctions. Since 1600, every species of North American bird to become extinct has been at least partially the victim of hunting, as have large marine mammals like the Steller's sea cow, 11 species of tortoises, six species of West Indian lizards, and four species of snakes. The slaughter continues, as we kill rhinoceroses to sell their horns as an aphrodisiac, whales to make dog food, and leopards to make fur coats.

Third, when we introduce alien species into systems with few natural 31 defenses against them, those invaders may kill or crowd out native species. European starlings, introduced to the United States only a century ago, elbowed out American bluebirds by commandeering nesting sites. During World War II, Navy ships carried the brown tree snake from the Philippines to Guam, and that species has already devastated most of Guam's indigenous bird species. For example, in 25 years the number of Guam rails—a normally prolific bird—dropped from 40,000 to 18! Since 1850, 85 percent of Hawaii's endemic forest birds have become extinct or nearly so. Some were done in by avian malaria, spread by mosquitos from introduced birds in the 1820s. Others succumbed to roof rats introduced to Oahu between 1850 and 1870, and then, ironically, to mongooses brought in to control the rats.

In fact, Hawaii provides a regrettable number of examples of the dangers 32 of alien species. Because of its isolation and variety of terrain and climates, Hawaii has a great many species that are found nowhere else and are vulnerable to exotic competitors and predators. Possibly the best known rare plant on the islands is the silversword, which human collectors had severely plundered until a public education program helped bring the plant back. Unfortunately, the silversword's troubles were not over. It flowers only once during its lifetime, and then it is pollinated by only two species: a groundnesting bee and a flightless moth. An introduced Argentine ant now threatens both the bee and the moth. Wherever the Argentine ant is found, no silverswords reproduce. As is often the case, the silversword's extinction, if it happens, will not be an obvious and sudden cataclysm. The sad fate of many species is foretold only by the perpetual absence of offspring.

Extinction caused by invading species grows increasingly common. 33
These are not stories of marginal, poorly adapted species sliding gradually
toward extinction. Rather, they relate the quiet mayhem of a planet on which
natural barriers like mountain ranges, rivers, and oceans no longer have
force.

Losing Ground

Although pollution, hunting, and introduced species all contribute to extinc- 34
tion, the fourth cause is probably the most common and certainly the least
reversible. It is the direct destruction of habitat. The rule is simple and allows
no exceptions: every species must live somewhere, and no species can live
everywhere. Alligators cannot survive in Alaska, and polar bears would perish
in the Everglades. Often habitat needs are quite specific. Redwoods need
misting rain—not too much and not too little. Some birds need old or dead
trees, while others need young ones. Alter a species' habitat, and you have
probably weakened its grip on existence. Eliminate that habitat, and you have
almost certainly condemned the species to extinction. As human beings
develop the Earth—plowing its grasslands, cutting its forests, damming its
rivers, paving its soil—the planet's other inhabitants increasingly have no
place left to go.

We do not always need to destroy habitat completely in order to cause 35
extinction. Often it is enough simply to reduce its size or divide it into dis-
connected pieces. In 1914 the Panama Canal created Gatun Lake and turned
Barro Colorado into an island. That isolated remnant of a once vast habitat
could no longer support its rich diversity of species. In the 70 years following, at least 50 species of forest birds disappeared from the island. So did
predators like the panther, jaguarondi, and ocelot.

Tragic dramas like these are taking place on every part of the planet. 36
Every year in Brazil, an area of rain forest the size of Austria is cleared for
farming. This desecration is doubly tragic because in order to stay fertile, the
rain forests' thin soils need a constant cascade of organic matter from the forest vegetation. Once the forest is cut, the soil can sustain only a few years of
farming. To make room for a few years for a few species of crops or cattle
grazing, thousands of unknown species are lost forever.

The Only Defense: Ecosystem Protection

Not all endangered ecosystems are found in the tropics or in remote areas. 37
One of the rarest, for example, exists in New Jersey, the state with more people per square mile than any other. Several years ago, scientists with the
Squibb Corporation tackled an important problem. Whenever they produced a new antibiotic, bacteria had a disconcerting way of mutating to resist
it. They wanted a fail-safe defense against such subversion. Hoping for a new
class of antibiotics, they decided to go back to nature and collect samples of
promising microbes. They succeeded, but not where they expected. After
searching wetlands in Africa, Australia, and Brazil, they found pay dirt not

far from Squibb's New Jersey headquarters, in the muck of the banks of the Pine Barrens.

A wilderness mosaic of wetlands and upland forest, the New Jersey Pine 38 Barrens is a haven for a number of imperiled species. Because of the complexity of such diverse landscapes, no one part can be securely saved without saving the whole. For example, scientists believe that an extremely rare moth, Carter's noctuid moth, lays its eggs in the stems of the equally rare pine barren reed grass. One other site, in North Carolina, supports a small stand of the grass, but no moths have been found there. Apparently the moths need a large population of reed grass, but the grass will not grow in great numbers unless fires periodically remove surrounding trees and prepare the soil. Fortunately, fire is an important part of the Pine Barrens' ecology. In an area otherwise hospitable to oak, fires have kept this ecosystem predominantly pine, accounting for much of its unique mix of species. Since controlled burns can maintain this system while preventing large forest fires, biologists and fire experts are now cooperating to select areas for burning that will also accommodate the reed grass. If they succeed, they will strengthen the intricate web of a globally rare moth and a globally rare plant in a globally rare ecosystem.

Such poorly understood relationships abound in healthy ecosystems. No 39 one can predict exactly how the ecosystems or the species may be useful to mankind. Certainly no one could have predicted that hip-booted Squibb scientists would find a new and revolutionary class of antibiotics in the Pine Barrens. All we can predict is that the careless impoverishment of these systems through species loss will reduce humanity's own prospects for survival.

Only by protecting whole systems can we begin to stop the flood of 40 extinction. Zoos, gardens, seed banks, and other manufactured refuges for individual species can be crucial aids, but we cannot put our thumbs in every hole in the dike. It is perhaps conceivable that in some distant future, biologists will learn to clone complex living creatures from scraps of genetic material. By that time, however, the genetic cupboard will be half-bare, and besides, those cloned plants and animals are likely to have nowhere to live.

Critical Reading Questions

1. What important consequences of species impoverishment has Roush speculated about? What causes has he enumerated? Has he made compelling connections between the causes and the effects?

2. How would you define Roush's tone in this report? Are there passages that seem too emotional or not emotional enough to you? Which ones, and why?

3. How would you summarize this essay for someone who had not read it? How does Roush organize his essay in relation to the "keystone species" phenomenon?

4. What metaphors in Roush's report do you find particularly effective?

Evaluating Criticism

As discussed in the conclusion of the previous chapter, you can avoid repeating mistakes by taking a moment to examine the faults in your present manuscript. Because analyses of causes and effects make different intellectual demands on you than analyses of subjects or processes, your two essays may not reflect exactly the same kinds of errors. Nevertheless, you should attempt to identify patterns of error in both papers. Do you find, for example, that critics of both texts encourage you to focus more on your audience? Have you been urged to explore your material in greater depth? Are more examples and illustrations needed to support your claims and speculations? On the editorial level, do you continue overlooking pronoun agreement mistakes or making some other kind of common, careless error? Write down the four most serious problems that your teachers and critics have identified in your past work and then use the list as a reference when revising and editing the other essays you will write as you progress through this book.

Writing Persuasively

One of the more exciting and important aspects of language is that it allows you to persuade people to agree and to act. On a daily basis, we all deal with family, friends, acquaintances, and strangers who will try to persuade, or even manipulate, us. Buy me, trust me, believe in me—such is the chatter of routine life. According to some psychologists, we experiment with persuasion from the moment we realize as babies that people respond to us when we cry.

As a student, you frequently will be asked to present academic arguments, so you should be familiar with the principles of persuasion. Your sociology instructor, for example, may ask you to defend our courts' having two criminal justice systems—one for blue-collar criminals who use violence and another for white-collar criminals who commit "victimless" crimes. Your history instructor might require you to argue which philosopher had the greatest influence on the growth of democracy.

As a citizen, you will be also asked to respond to persuasive arguments: for or against increased taxes or our nation's foreign and social policies, for example. Politicians will try to convince you of the need for tougher immigration restrictions, for more money for education, for improved roads. Much of what you read in newspapers, magazines, textbooks, research reports, procedural manuals, and sales catalogs was produced to influence you to do something or believe something. You will have to evaluate all these uses of persuasion.

Because you have undoubtedly participated in your share of oral arguments, you are already familiar with a variety of persuasive strategies. You know, for example, that the context in which an argument takes place significantly determines which strategies are most successful. You know that you cannot yell at your boss at work or your instructor at school because this kind of inappropriate "persuasion" is more likely to result in your being dismissed or expelled. You have developed a finely tuned sense of when you should stand firm and defend a position, as well as when you should acknowledge the value of someone else's reasoning. Ideally, your experiences working with other people have given you a sense of *timing*—a sense of when it's a good time to challenge people about an issue. Your knowledge of how different contexts influence the shape and intensity of your arguments has taught you when to concede points and when to maintain and promote your position. As an author and speaker, you certainly want to draw on your experiences to avoid quibbling, to save your energies for circumstances that warrant serious consideration.

However, your participation in oral arguments has not necessarily prepared you for the rigors of written arguments. After all, written arguments are often more difficult to develop than oral arguments, especially in that you cannot see the people whom you are trying to persuade. Thus, you cannot modify the tone or force of your presentation in response to a nod of the head or shake of the fist. Your audience cannot interrupt you and ask for clarification of a point. You have no sense of whether anyone is agreeing or disagreeing with certain parts of your argument. Moreover, the run-of-the-mill arguments that you have with family, friends, and colleagues tend to be considerably less focused and less well developed than written academic arguments. Though an oral argument about the adequacy of our educational system may naturally flow into a discussion about a particular politician's stance or your experiences in fourth grade, a written academic argument would stress a single thesis. For example, most teachers would not encourage their students to take on the American educational system in one short essay, even though they might not overtly dissuade you from pursuing such a broad topic. Your teachers expect you to narrow your argument to one specific issue, such as "Students should write more theoretical, speculative, concise essays in high school" or "Parents can reinforce the importance of education by visiting their child's teachers and by helping their child complete homework" or "Industry and business need to play a more active role in the education of high school students." As these sample topics demonstrate, your teachers expect you to defend a single idea before a particular audience rather than present vague generalizations for no particular audience.

This chapter explores some of the intricacies and conventions of persuasion and argumentation by means of numerous writing samples, a review of the components of persuasion, and a variety of prewriting, drafting, revising, and editing strategies. By being more aware of various emotional, ethical, and logical appeals, you will be able to analyze other people's claims and enhance your own arguments.

The following chapter, Solving Problems by Negotiating Differences, discusses an alternative to traditional argumentative and persuasive strategies. You will want to refer to this next chapter when your subject is controversial or emotional or when your audience is highly unlikely to accept your ideas.

Writing Samples

Paul Ehrlich and Anne Ehrlich argue in the following essay that our world cannot support our burgeoning population. Now that there are more than five billion human beings on the planet, these authors believe that we need to curb our innate desire to reproduce or face dire consequences. This essay is excerpted from *The Population Explosion*, the Ehrlichs' second book on this problem.

Making the Population Connection*

Paul R. Ehrlich and Anne H. Ehrlich

Global warming, acid rain, depletion of the ozone layer, vulnerability to epi- 1
demics, and exhaustion of soils and groundwater are all, as we shall see,
related to population size. They are also clear and present dangers to the
persistence of civilization. Crop failures due to global warming alone might
result in the premature deaths of a billion or more people in the next few
decades, and the AIDS epidemic could slaughter hundreds of millions.
Together these would constitute a harsh "population control" program provided by nature in the face of humanity's refusal to put into place a gentler
program of its own.

We shouldn't delude ourselves: the population explosion will come to 2
an end before very long. The only remaining question is whether it will be
halted through the humane method of birth control, or by nature wiping out
the surplus. We realize that religious and cultural opposition to birth control
exists throughout the world; but we believe that people simply don't understand the choice that such opposition implies. Today, anyone opposing birth
control is unknowingly voting to have the human population size controlled
by a massive increase in early deaths.

Of course, the environmental crisis isn't caused just by expanding human 3
numbers. Burgeoning consumption among the rich and increasing dependence on ecologically unsound technologies to supply that consumption also
play major parts. This allows some environmentalists to dodge the population issue by emphasizing the problem of malign technologies. And social
commentators can avoid commenting on the problem of too many people by
focusing on the serious maldistribution of affluence.

But scientists studying humanity's deepening predicament recognize 4
that a major factor contributing to it is rapidly worsening overpopulation.
The Club of Earth, a group whose members all belong to both the U.S.
National Academy of Sciences and the American Academy of Arts and Sciences, released a statement in September 1988 that said in part:

> Arresting global population growth should be second in importance only to
> avoiding nuclear war on humanity's agenda. Overpopulation and rapid
> population growth are intimately connected with most aspects of the cur-
> rent human predicament, including rapid depletion of nonrenewable
> resources, deterioration of the environment (including rapid climate
> change), and increasing international tensions.[1]

When three prestigious scientific organizations cosponsored an interna- 5
tional scientific forum, "Global Change," in Washington in 1989, there
was general agreement among the speakers that population growth was a

---

substantial contributor toward prospective catastrophe. Newspaper coverage was limited, and while the population component was mentioned in *The New York Times's* article,[2] the point that population limitation will be essential to resolving the predicament was lost. The coverage of environmental issues in the media has been generally excellent in the last few years, but there is still a long way to go to get adequate coverage of the intimately connected population problem.

Even though the media occasionally give coverage to population issues, 6 some people never get the word. In November 1988, Pope John Paul II reaffirmed the Catholic Church's ban on contraception. The occasion was the twentieth anniversary of Pope Paul's anti-birth-control encyclical, *Humanae Vitae.*

Fortunately, the majority of Catholics in the industrial world pay little 7 attention to the encyclical or the Church's official ban on all practical means of birth control. One need only note that Catholic Italy at present has the smallest average completed family size (1.3 children per couple) of any nation. Until contraception and then abortion were legalized there in the 1970s, the Italian birth rate was kept low by an appalling rate of illegal abortion.

The bishops who assembled to celebrate the anniversary defended the 8 encyclical by announcing that "the world's food resources theoretically could feed 40 billion people."[3] In one sense they were right. It's "theoretically possible" to feed 40 billion people—in the same sense that it's theoretically possible for your favorite major-league baseball team to win every single game for fifty straight seasons, or for you to play Russian roulette ten thousand times in a row with five out of six chambers loaded without blowing your brains out.

One might also ask whether feeding 40 billion people is a worthwhile 9 goal for humanity, even if it could be reached. Is any purpose served in turning Earth, in essence, into a gigantic human feedlot? Putting aside the near-certainty that such a miracle couldn't be sustained, what would happen to the *quality* of life?

We wish to emphasize that the population problem is in no sense a 10 "Catholic problem," as some would claim. Around the world, Catholic reproductive performance is much the same as that of non-Catholics in similar cultures and with similar economic status. Nevertheless, the *political* position of the Vatican, traceable in no small part to the extreme conservatism of Pope John Paul II, is an important barrier to solving the population problem.[4] Non-Catholics should be very careful not to confuse Catholics or Catholicism with the Vatican—most American Catholics don't. Furthermore, the Church's position on contraception is distressing to many millions of Catholics, who feel it morally imperative to follow their own consciences in their personal lives and disregard the Vatican's teachings on this subject.

Nor is unwillingness to face the severity of the population problem 11 limited to the Vatican. It's built into our genes and our culture. That's one reason many otherwise bright and humane people behave like fools when confronted with demographic issues. Thus, an economist specializing in mail-order marketing can sell the thesis that the human population could increase essentially forever because people are the "ultimate resource,"[5] and a journalist can urge more population growth in the United States so that we can have a bigger army![6] Even some environmentalists are taken in by the frequent assertion that "there is no population problem, only a problem of distribution." The statement is usually made in context of a plan for conquering hunger, as if food shortage were the only consequence of overpopulation.

But even in that narrow context, the assertion is wrong. Suppose food 12 *were* distributed equally. If everyone in the world ate as Americans do, less than half the *present* world population could be fed on the record harvests of 1985 and 1986.[7] Of course, everyone doesn't have to eat like Americans. About a third of the world grain harvest—the staples of the human feeding base—is fed to animals to produce eggs, milk, and meat for American-style diets. Wouldn't feeding that grain directly to people solve the problem? If everyone were willing to eat an essentially vegetarian diet, that additional grain would allow perhaps a billion more people to be fed with 1986 production.

Would such radical changes solve the world food problem? Only in the 13 *very* short term. The additional billion people are slated to be with us by the end of the century. Moreover, by the late 1980s, humanity already seemed to be encountering trouble maintaining the production levels of the mid-1980s, let alone keeping up with population growth. The world grain harvest in 1988 was some 10 percent *below* that of 1986. And there is little sign that the rich are about to give up eating animal products.

So there is no reasonable way that the hunger problem can be called 14 "only" one of distribution, even though redistribution of food resources would greatly alleviate hunger today. Unfortunately, an important truth, that maldistribution is a cause of hunger now, has been used as a way to avoid a more important truth—that overpopulation is critical today and may well make the distribution question moot tomorrow.

The food problem, however, attracts little immediate concern among 15 well-fed Americans, who have no reason to be aware of its severity or extent. But other evidence that could make everyone face up to the seriousness of the population dilemma is now all around us, since problems to which overpopulation and population growth make major contributions are worsening at a rapid rate. They often appear on the evening news, although the population connection is almost never made.

Consider the television pictures of barges loaded with garbage wander- 16 ing like The Flying Dutchman across the seas, and news stories about "no room at the dump."[8] They are showing the results of the interaction between too many affluent people and the environmentally destructive technologies that support that affluence. Growing opportunities to swim in a mixture of sewage and medical debris off American beaches can be traced to the same source. Starving people in sub-Saharan Africa are victims of drought, defective agricultural policies, and an overpopulation of both people and domestic animals—with warfare often dealing the final blow. All of the above are symptoms of humanity's massive and growing negative impact on Earth's life-support systems.

Recognizing the Population Problem

The average person, even the average scientist, seldom makes the connection   17 between such seemingly disparate events and the population problem, and thus remains unworried. To a degree, this failure to put the pieces together is due to a taboo against frank discussion of the population crisis in many quarters, a taboo generated partly by pressures from the Catholic hierarchy and partly by other groups who are afraid that dealing with population issues will produce socially damaging results.

Many people on the political left are concerned that focusing on over-   18 population will divert attention from crucial problems of social justice (which certainly need to be addressed *in addition* to the population problem). Often those on the political right fear that dealing with overpopulation will encourage abortion (it need not) or that halting growth will severely damage the economy (it could, if not handled properly). And people of varied political persuasions who are unfamiliar with the magnitude of the population problem believe in a variety of farfetched technological fixes—such as colonizing outer space—that they think will allow the need for regulating the size of the human population to be avoided forever.[9]

Even the National Academy of Sciences avoided mentioning controlling   19 human numbers in its advice to President Bush on how to deal with global environmental change. Although Academy members who are familiar with the issue are well aware of the critical population component of that change, it was feared that all of the Academy's advice would be ignored if recommendations were included about a subject taboo in the Bush administration. That strategy might have been correct, considering Bush's expressed views on abortion and considering the administration's weak appointments in many environmentally sensitive positions. After all, the Office of Management and Budget even tried to suppress an expert evaluation of the potential seriousness of global warming by altering the congressional testimony of a top NASA scientist, James Hansen, to conform with the administration's less urgent view of the problem.[10]

All of us naturally lean toward the taboo against dealing with population   20 growth. The roots of our aversion to limiting the size of the human population are as deep and pervasive as the roots of human sexual behavior. Through billions of years of evolution, outreproducing other members of your population was the name of the game. It is the very basis of natural selection, the driving force of the evolutionary process.[11] Nonetheless, the taboo must be uprooted and discarded.

Overcoming the Taboo

There is no more time to waste; in fact, there wasn't in 1968 when *The Popu-* 21
lation Bomb was published. Human inaction has already condemned hundreds
of millions more people to premature deaths from hunger and disease. The
population connection must be made in the public mind. Action to end the
population explosion *humanely* and start a gradual population *decline* must
become a top item on the human agenda: the human birthrate must be lowered to slightly below the human death rate as soon as possible. There still
may be time to limit the scope of the impending catastrophe, but not *much*
time. Ending the population explosion by controlling births is necessarily a
slow process. Only nature's cruel way of solving the problem is likely to be
swift.

Of course, if we do wake up and succeed in controlling our population 22
size, that will still leave us with all the other thorny problems to solve. Limiting human numbers will not alone end warfare, environmental deterioration,
poverty, racism, religious prejudice, or sexism; it will just buy us the opportunity to do so. As the old saying goes, whatever your cause, it's a lost cause
without population control.[12]

America and other rich nations have a clear choice today. They can 23
continue to ignore the population problem and their own massive contributions to it. Then they will be trapped in a downward spiral that may well lead
to the end of civilization in a few decades. More frequent droughts, more
damaged crops and famines, more dying forests, more smog, more international conflicts, more epidemics, more gridlock, more drugs, more crime,
more sewage swimming, and other extreme unpleasantness will mark our
course. It is a route already traveled by too many of our less fortunate fellow
human beings.

Or we can change our collective minds and take the measures necessary 24
to lower global birthrates dramatically. People can learn to treat growth as
the cancerlike disease it is and move toward a sustainable society. The rich
can make helping the poor an urgent goal, instead of seeking more wealth
and useless military advantage over one another. Then humanity might have
a chance to manage all those other seemingly intractable problems. It is a
challenging prospect, but at least it will give our species a shot at creating a
decent future for itself. More immediately and concretely, taking action now
will give our children and their children the possibility of decent lives.

———————————————— **Notes** ————————————————

1. Statement released Sept. 3, 1988, at the Pugwash Conference on Global
   Problems and Common Security, at Dagomys, near Sochi, USSR.
   The signatories were Jared Diamond, UCLA; Paul Ehrlich, Stanford;
   Thomas Eisner, Cornell; G. Evelyn Hutchinson, Yale; Gene E. Likens,
   Institute of Ecosystem Studies; Ernst Mayr, Harvard; Charles D.
   Michener, University of Kansas; Harold A. Mooney, Stanford; Ruth

Patrick, Academy of Natural Sciences, Philadelphia; Peter H. Raven, Missouri Botanical Garden; and Edmund O. Wilson, Harvard.

The National Academy of Sciences and the American Academy of Arts and Sciences are the top honorary organizations for American scientists and scholars, respectively. Hutchinson, Patrick, and Wilson also are laureates of the Tyler Prize, the most distinguished international award in ecology.

2. May 4, 1989, by Philip Shabecoff, a fine environmental reporter. In general, the *Times* coverage of the environment is excellent. But even this best of American newspapers reflects the public's lack of understanding of the urgency of the population situation.

3. *Washington Post*, Nov. 19, 1988, p. C-15.

4. Italy is not a freak case. Catholic France has an average completed family size of 1.8 children, the same as Britain and Norway; Catholic Spain, with less than half the per-capita GNP of Protestant Denmark, has the same completed family size of 1.8 children. We are equating "completed family size" here with the *total fertility rate*, the average number of children a woman would bear in her lifetime, assuming that current age-specific birth and death rates remained unchanged during her childbearing years—roughly 15–49. In the United States, a Catholic woman is more likely to seek abortion than a non-Catholic woman (probably because she is likelier to use less-effective contraception). By 1980, Catholic and non-Catholic women in the U.S. (except Hispanic women, for whom cultural factors are strong) had virtually identical family sizes. (W. D. Mosher, "Fertility and Family Planning in the United States: Insights from the National Survey of Family Growth," *Family Planning Perspectives*, vol. 20, no. 5, pp. 202–217. Sept./Oct. 1988.) On the role of the Vatican, see, for instance, Stephen D. Mumford, "The Vatican and Population Growth Control: Why an American Confrontation?" *The Humanist*, September/October 1983, and Penny Lernoux, "The Papal Spiderweb," *The Nation*, April 10 and 17, 1989.

5. J. Simon, *The Ultimate Resource* (Princeton U P, Princeton, N.J., 1981).

6. B. Wattenberg, *The Birth Dearth* (Pharos Books, New York, 1987).

7. R. W. Kates, R. S. Chen, T. E. Downing, J. X. Kasperson, E. Messer, S. R. Millman, *The Hunger Report: 1988* (The Alan Shawn Feinstein World Hunger Program, Brown University, Providence, R.I., 1988). The data on distribution in this paragraph are from this source.

8. The name of a series of reports on KRON-TV's news programs, San Francisco, the week of May 8, 1989.

9. For an amusing analysis of the "outer-space" fairy tale, see Garrett Hardin's classic essay "Interstellar Migration and the Population Problem," *Journal of Heredity*, vol. 50, pp. 68–70 (1959), reprinted in G. Hardin, ed., *Stalking the Wild Taboo*, 2nd ed. (William Kaufmann,

Los Altos, Calif., 1978). Note that some things have changed; to keep the population of Earth from growing today, we would have to export to space 95 million people annually!

10. This story received broad coverage in both electronic and print media; for instance, *New York Times*, May 8, 1989.

11. For a discussion of natural selection and evolution written for nonspecialists, see P. R. Ehrlich, *The Machinery of Nature* (Simon and Schuster, New York, 1986).

12. "Population control" does not require coercion, only attention to the needs of society.

Critical Reading Questions

1. What purpose unifies this piece? What are the primary claims made by the Ehrlichs? Where in the essay do the Ehrlichs present their thesis?

2. Do you believe that American readers would be sympathetic to this essay? What assumptions about audience do these authors appear to be making? Why, for example, do the Ehrlichs compare the Catholic bishop's argument that it is theoretically possible for the world to feed 40 billion people to the theoretical possibility "for your favorite major-league baseball team to win every single game for fifty straight seasons"?

3. How did your opinion about overpopulation influence your reading? Which arguments did you find most (or least) persuasive?

4. What evidence do the Ehrlichs provide to support their assertions? Can you identify any points that need further development?

5. How would you describe the tone of this essay? Do you think the authors would be more successful if they adopted a different tone?

In the following essay, Sandra Serrano, a student writer, argues that the usage of "he or she" or "he/she" for "he" is cumbersome and unnecessary. Serrano intended this piece to be read by both men and women who are interested in language.

A View of the "Sex Bias" Pronoun in Writing

Sandra Serrano

As a little girl growing up in the 1950s, I learned the roles that were accept- 1
able for women to assume: homemaker, wife, mother. My mother frequently admonished me with, "When you grow up and have children of your own. . . ." She taught me to clean house, iron, and sew. She encouraged me to pursue my education so that I might become a teacher, an ideal profession for a woman with children. Somehow I never developed the desire to be what my mother thought I should become, yet I didn't consciously reject the

values that engendered her attitudes, either. I just thought I was different. Consequently, when I first became aware of the women's movement, termed feminism, in the late 1960s, I was surprised and pleased that there were other women like me—women who didn't just naturally love children, housework, and cooking. Gradually role alternatives to housewife and mother became acceptable; increasing numbers of women chose careers over families. Women assumed responsibility for directing their own lives. I identified with the movement.

The significant changes in social attitudes began to be reflected in writ- 2 ing styles. Writers substituted "he/she" or "he or she" for the personal pronoun "he" when the sex of the antecedent was uncertain. As awareness of women as equal members of society increased, this combined pronoun became fashionable and in some cases was considered mandatory. Writers who chose not to use it often felt obligated to explain their choice in a preface. Their explanations generally begged the readers' understanding and explained that the combined pronoun was just too cumbersome to use. It was, in effect, a disclaimer for the writer's use of "he."

I find it demeaning and a little silly that this use of a combined pronoun, 3 a change at a very superficial level, has come to characterize so much since the birth of the latest women's movement. The implication of this prevalent usage is that by altering a pronoun a writer can escape being labeled sexist. The necessity to avoid this label results in damage to clear, concise communication.

Proponents of the use of "he/she" believe that this combined pronoun 4 represents a neutral pronoun that is much needed in the English language. They further assert that the combined pronoun assists a reader by making clear something that was previously fuzzy. A writer who uses "he/she" proves that he is not a sexist. The prevalence of this usage is also supposed to indicate that social attitudes are truly changed in favor of equality for women. While it is true that the prevalence of the combined pronoun usage is indicative of the strength of the women's movement, the usage itself does lip service to the movement without contributing anything of substance. English already has a neutral personal pronoun; the language does not need another. The presence of a combined pronoun has little to do with sex bias in writing. And it actually hinders rather than helps the reader. After approximately twenty years and innumerable attitude adjustments, writers are moving away from the "he/she" bandwagon, perhaps for some of the reasons that I shall outline.

Several arguments exist for the use of the combined pronoun. One is 5 based on the assumption that the use of "he" indicates sex bias on the part of the writer. A writer who is so biased makes an incorrect and arrogant assumption that anyone he could possibly be referring to is male. For example, in the preceding sentence it would be assumed that my writer is a man because I referred to "him" as "he." Because I made that reference, I would be accused of being biased, sexist, or anti-feminist. In order to avoid similar accusations, many writers go to great lengths to use a combined pronoun, frequently at the price of a clear and concise style. Another assumption inherent in the use of "he/she" is that the English language possesses no neutral personal pronoun. It then follows that if an antecedent is not clearly male or female, there is no good choice except the use of "he/she." Therefore a writer who wishes to avoid being labeled sexist has no alternative but to use a combined pronoun. A third argument in favor of using a combined pronoun is that it helps a reader. A writer who uses "he/she" wishes to clarify something that could be construed as uncertain: the sex of the antecedent. When a reader encounters "he/she," he is enlightened and can continue reading, knowing that the writer is talking about someone who could be either sex. The reader knows that the writer knows that, too. Obviously communication between the writer and reader has been aided by this clever combined pronoun device.

On the surface, the statement that English possesses no neutral personal 6 pronoun appears to be true. Upon closer examination, however, one realizes that the language possesses no separate pronoun for neutral usage. Instead, "he" is neutral in certain contexts. It just happens that the same word is used for both masculine and neutral references. The evolution of "he" as the word of choice instead of "she" tells us something about the culture that developed beside the language: males dominated the culture and women were generally subordinate. But regardless of the problems with the culture, English's use of "he" in certain situations means either sex. This point of grammar is not a secret known only to the astute. Children learn to apply this lesson before their formal education begins. Clearly the use of the term "sex biased" to refer to any neutral use of "he" is a premise that cannot be accepted at face value.

Because the use of "he" depends on context, the reader must make a 7 judgment. But since such usage is learned early, the judgment is made quickly and unconsciously. Any native English speaker can discern the meaning of the pronoun "he." Consequently, the use of the combined pronoun to aid the reader in determining the sex of an antecedent is unnecessary. A combined pronoun can even be insulting by implying that the reader hasn't learned the basic use of his language: he cannot distinguish when "he" is masculine and when it is neutral.

The combined pronoun is a hindrance for other reasons. It's awkward. It 8 momentarily stops the reader. It interrupts the communication process. E. B. White wrote, in the introduction to *The Elements of Style*, ". . . the reader was in serious trouble most of the time, a man floundering in a swamp, and . . . it was the duty of anyone attempting to write English to drain this swamp quickly and get his man up on dry ground, or at least throw him a rope." A writer's commitment to the combined pronoun just continues to fill the swamp because it forces awkward constructions that alter the natural flow of words. The same commitment also alters the natural flow of thoughts. The reader, who normally addresses the content of a piece of writing, is suddenly hit with "he/she" and sex bias becomes an issue for no reason. The writer's ideas lose some of their force because the reader is forced to think of something besides the content of the writing. The writer has detracted from his purpose.

Actually, whether or not a writer is biased would be determined best by 9 addressing the content of his writing. Ideas are a more accurate communication of a writer's prejudices and positions than are his choices of pronouns. For example, in the E. B. White passage I quoted earlier, a reader was referred to not only as "he," but as a "man." This reference, however, does not render the analogy ineffective, nor does it indicate that E. B. White is a sexist. You need only to read the book to know that the content contains no sex bias. To test the idea that readers address content, I wrote a sentence using "he" and passed it to twenty friends—ten males and ten females. I requested them to assume that the statement was true and to indicate any reactions or opinions about the writer on the back of their sentences. Not one person failed to address the content of the sentence; all ignored the supposed sex bias of the pronoun. If a reader concentrates on the content, as he should, he will discover a writer's bias, irrespective of the writer's choice of pronouns. A writer's use of a combined pronoun will not disguise bias. Conversely, if the writer is not biased, the use of "he" should have no adverse effect on his reader.

Critical Reading Questions

1. What is Serrano's thesis? What are Serrano's primary arguments against the usage of "he/she"?

2. What information does Serrano provide to support her claim? Has she swayed your opinion? How?

3. Do you agree with Serrano that the pronoun "he" is already a neutral pronoun? What data does Serrano provide to support this assertion?

4. How would you describe Serrano's persona in this piece? What information does Serrano provide to make herself appear reasonable and logical?

5. How does Serrano consider the counterarguments of her opposition? Can you think of any other counterarguments?

6. What emotional appeals can you identify in this essay? Would additional emotional appeals strengthen or weaken it? Does the author's passion for her subject ever interfere with the development of her argument?

7. If Serrano were in your peer group, what goals for revision would you recommend?

Analyzing Pertinent Conventions

There is no single, ideal way to structure all of your persuasive documents. The best way to develop your work is to analyze the communication situation for each document that you write. One important aspect of this prewriting work is understanding the following conventions that academic readers expect you to follow when you write persuasive or argumentative essays.

Establish the Significance of Your Topic

Before attempting to convince readers to agree with your position on a subject, you may need to educate them about the topic. A declaration of the relevant issues and definition of terms can constitute a substantial part of your argument when you are writing for uninformed audiences, or it can constitute a minor part of your argument when you are writing for more informed audiences. Note, for example, how Serrano used the first two paragraphs of her essay to place the use of "he/she" in the context of the Women's Movement of the 1960s. Her introduction thus established her topic as both worthy of consideration and a point of conflict.

State Your Primary Claim

After educating readers about the complexity of the subject that you are addressing, you should establish your thesis—that is, your primary claim about the topic. For example, after reading the first two paragraphs of the Ehrlichs' essay, you know the problem they are addressing and their opinion on it:

> We realize that religious and cultural opposition to birth control exists throughout the world; but we believe that people simply don't understand the choice that such opposition implies. Today, anyone opposing birth control is unknowingly voting to have the human population size controlled by a massive increase in early deaths.

Of course, you do not always need to organize your arguments deductively—that is, by stating a general claim in the introduction and then marshalling examples to support it. If your audience is not likely to agree with you, you may want to wait as long as possible—perhaps even until the conclusion—before revealing your opinion. This alternative approach could be called an inductive organization because it moves from specific examples to a general conclusion. You should consider an inductive structure to your argument when your audience is likely to be threatened by your subject or your position on it. (See Chapter 7.)

Establish an Appropriate Tone and Persona

Your opening sentences generally establish the tone of your essay and present to the reader a sense of your persona, both of which play a tremendous role in the overall persuasiveness of your argument. When your readers are aware of your good reputation, they are more likely to give you the benefit of the doubt. For example, because of Ralph Nader's reliability in past crusades, we tend to believe him when he insists that a product is deficient. In contrast, when Saddam Hussein's troops invaded Kuwait in 1991 and the international community opposed him, Hussein tried to present himself as a warrior of Islam and defender of the Arab world against the West. In turn, United States President George Bush argued that the Arab world should distrust Hussein's persona as a savior and religious crusader. The president rallied American support by vowing that tyrants and bullies like Hussein needed to be overcome at whatever cost. Of course, as demonstrated by the opposition toward Hussein even in the Arab world, most people are unwilling to be swayed solely by a speaker's or writer's persona.

Your tone can play a fundamental role in the overall success of your argument. Most academic readers are put off by zealous, emotional, or angry arguments. No matter how well you fine-tune the substance of your document, the tone that readers detect significantly influences how the message is perceived. If readers dislike the manner of your presentation, they may reject your facts, too. If you do not sound confident, your readers may doubt you. If your paper is loaded with spelling errors, you look foolish. No matter how solid your evidence is for a particular claim, your readers may not agree with you if you sound sarcastic, condescending, or intolerant. For instance, can you see how the contentious tone in the following excerpt from Wilhelm Reich's *Listen, Little Man!* might actually interfere with the important message that Reich is attempting to convey?

> You could have become the master of your existence long ago if your thinking aimed at the truth. I'll give you an example of your thinking:
>
> "It's all the fault of the Jews," you say. "What's a Jew?" I ask. "People with Jewish blood," you say. "How do you distinguish Jewish blood from other blood?" The question baffles you. You hesitate. Then you say, "I meant the Jewish race." "What's race?" I ask. "Race? That's obvious. Just as there's a Germanic race, there's a Jewish race." "What are the characteristics of the Jewish race?" "A Jew has black hair, a long hooked nose, and sharp eyes. The Jews are greedy and capitalistic." "Have you ever seen a southern Frenchman or an Italian side by side with a Jew? Can you distinguish between them?" "No, not really . . ."
>
> "Then what's a Jew? His blood picture is the same as everyone else's. His appearance is no different from that of a Frenchman or an Italian. On the other hand, have you ever seen any German Jews?" "They look like Germans." "What's a German?" "A German is a member of the Nordic Aryan race." "Are the Indians Aryans?" "Yes." "Are they Nordic?" "No." "Are they blond?" "No." "See? You don't even know what a Jew or a German is." "But Jews do exist!" "Of course Jews exist. So do Christians and Mohammedans." "That's right. I meant the Jewish religion." "Was Roosevelt a Dutchman?" "No." "Why do you call a descendant of David a

Jew if you don't call Roosevelt a Dutchman?" "The Jews are different." "What's different?" "I don't know."

That's the kind of rubbish you talk, little man. And with such rubbish you set up and arm gangs that kill ten million people for being Jews, though you can't even tell me what a Jew is. That's why you're laughed at, why anybody with anything serious to do steers clear of you. That's why you're up to your neck in muck. It makes you feel superior to call someone a Jew. It makes you feel superior because you feel inferior. You feel inferior because you yourself are exactly what you want to kill off in the people you call Jews. That's just a sampling of the truth about you, little man.

Establish Appropriate Emotional Appeals

While appeals to emotions are generally frowned upon in traditional academic arguments, speakers and writers still use them because of their persuasive power. We all tend to perceive certain situations subjectively and passionately—particularly situations that involve us at a personal level. Even when we try to be objective, many of us still make decisions based on emotional impulses rather than sound reasoning. Those who recognize the power of emotional appeals sometimes twist them to sway others. Hitler is an obvious and extreme example. His *dichotomizing*—you're either for me or against me—and *bandwagon appeals*—"Everyone knows the Jews are inferior to true Germans"—helped instigate one of the darkest chapters in human history.

Additional emotional appeals include *appeals to authority* (According to the EPA, global warming will raise sea levels), *appeals to pity* (I should be allowed to take the test again because I had the flu the first time I took it), and *personal attacks* on the opposition, which rhetoricians call *ad hominem* attacks (I wouldn't vote for that man because he's a womanizer).

Like arguments based solely on the persona of the author, arguments based solely on appeals to emotions usually lack the strength to be totally persuasive. Most modern, well-educated readers are quick to see through such manipulative attempts. For example, after Americans and others in the international community established a blockade of Iraq during the 1991 Gulf War, Saddam Hussein tried to ignite religious fanaticism and class hatred. He called on the Arab countries to establish a Holy War to drive out the Americans. And he even called on Iranians, with whom his country had fought a bitter war for nearly ten years, to "deter all those fishing in dirty waters and cooperate to turn the [Persian] Gulf into a lake of peace free of foreign fleets." Describing the Americans as impure infidels tainting the Holy Lands and calling for Arabs to rally around a higher cause—the preservation of Mecca and the Arab way of life—was a purely emotional tactic. Fortunately, most of the Arab world turned their back to Hussein's emotional appeals because they remembered Hussein's cruelty to his Arab brothers and sisters, and they remembered that Hussein had led an anti-Moslem campaign when fighting Iran.

Of course, emotional appeals can be used to persuade readers of the rightness of good causes or imperative action. For example, if you were writing an essay advocating a school-wide recycling program, you might paint an emotional, bleak picture of what our world will look like in 50 years if we don't begin conserving now. Ultimately, however, emotional appeals by themselves lack persuasive force.

Present Substantive Evidence

Academic audiences expect authors to develop their claims thoroughly. By examining the point you want to argue and the needs of your audience, you can determine whether it will be acceptable to rely only on anecdotal information or whether you will also need to research facts and figures and include quotations from established sources. Personal observations have their place, say, in an argument about staying in athletic shape. But an anecdotal tone will leave an academic reader hungry for more information when you address touchy social issues such as gun control, pornography, drugs, or abortion. If you are addressing a complicated matter such as the need—or lack of need—for a "Star Wars" defense system, then your opinion alone will not be sufficient.

Despite the forcefulness of your emotional appeals, you need to appeal to logic if you hope to sway educated readers. Trained as critical readers, your teachers and college-educated peers expect you to provide evidence— that is, logical reasoning, personal observations, expert testimony, facts, and statistics. Like a judge who must decide a case based on the law rather than on intuition, your teachers want to see that you can analyze an issue as "objectively" as possible. As members of the academic community, they are usually more concerned with *how* you argue than with *what* you argue for or against. Regardless of your position on an issue, they want to see that you can defend your position logically and with evidence.

Unfortunately, it is not always easy to determine which ideas your readers will take for granted and which ones they are likely to question. Even professional writers have difficulty deciding which details they need to highlight and which they can assume the reader already knows. In fact, you may need to write several drafts before you can decide what information you can omit, what information you can leave as is, and what information you need to develop. In addition, you should fight the tendency to cling to evidence you discovered early in your investigation that has been contradicted or made obsolete by more comprehensive, updated research.

When you read or listen to an argument, remember to be skeptical about how the author knows what he or she knows. In our competitive world, you cannot take people or arguments at face value, even if it *feels* or *sounds* right. When reading, always take into account the credibility of the author's sources, the context in which the author is working, and the author's motives. For example, if you read in the *National Enquirer* that a space ship has been captured by farmers in Iowa and that the government is holding the crew, you consider the source and question the credibility of the reporter and the context. Yet if it is reported in the *Wall Street Journal*—and if the date isn't April 1—that the president of the United States has confirmed that aliens are being held captive, you might want to rush to the store to buy some new film for your VCR.

Present Counterarguments

At some point in your essay, you will probably present *counterarguments* to your claim. Essentially, whenever you think your readers are likely to disagree with you, you need to account for their concerns. Elaborating on counterarguments is particularly useful when you have an unusual claim or a skeptical audience. The strategy usually involves stating an opinion or argument that is contrary to your position, then proving to the best of your ability why your point of view still prevails.

When presenting and refuting counterarguments, remember that your readers do not expect your position to be valid 100 percent of the time. Few people think so simplistically. Despite the forced choices that clever rhetoricians present, few subjects that are worth arguing about can be reduced to *yes, always* or *no, never.* When it is pertinent, therefore, you should concede any instances in which your opponents' counterarguments have merit.

However, you will sabotage your hard-won persona as an informed and fair-minded thinker if you misrepresent your opponent's counterarguments. For example, one rhetorical tactic that academic readers typically dislike is the *straw man approach*, in which a weak aspect of the opponent's argument is equated with weakness of the argument as a whole. Unfortunately, American politicians tend to garner voter support by misrepresenting their opponent's background and position on the issues. Before taking a straw man approach in an academic essay, you should remember that misrepresenting or satirizing opposing thoughts and feelings about your subject will probably alienate thoughtful readers.

Speculate About Implications in Conclusions

Instead of merely repeating your original claim in the conclusion you should end by trying to motivate your audience. Do not go out with a whimper and a boring restatement of your introduction. Instead, elaborate on the significant and broad implications of your argument. Also, the wrap-up is an excellent place to utilize some emotional appeals. Note, for example, how the Ehrlichs conclude their essay on the population problem: they invoke the personal interests of their readers and compare the population explosion to a disease.

> People can learn to treat growth as the cancerlike disease it is and move toward a sustainable society. . . . It is a challenging prospect, but at least it

will give our species a shot at creating a decent future for itself. More immediately and concretely, taking action now will give our children and their children the possibility of decent lives.

In turn, the last paragraph of Richard Loudermilk's essay at the end of this chapter presents an excellent example of a "kicker conclusion." His revelation that Glen—the man who was unable to receive insurance coverage because of his Parkinson's Disease—is his father humanizes his call for medical reform.

Writing Assignments

1. Select an on-campus issue that requires attention. Freewrite in your journal about questions you have about your school and college life. For example, do you believe that students should be graded pass-fail rather than on an A, B, C, D, and F scale? Should all students be required to master a foreign language or be computer literate? What should the standards be for college admission? Given the AIDS epidemic, are college students too promiscuous? Should full-time students be prohibited from working full-time jobs?

2. Consider the recent debates that you have had with your friends and family, and write a persuasive document based on one of them. For example, you could persuade your parents that you would be happier pursuing a degree in X instead of in Y. You could write an argument against excessive drinking and share this with a friend who may be drinking too much. If you are curious about whether you are studying too hard, you could explore educators' ideas about the best ways to study and then advocate one particular approach.

3. Read the editorials and commentary section in your local newspaper or college newspaper for a two-week period. Then write a countereditorial to one of the columns. Do you think, for example, that it is appropriate for employers to require drug tests and polygraphs of job applicants? What limits should be placed on free speech, animal research, college sports? Or, visit the current periodical shelves at your library and skim through the tables of contents of journals and magazines that interest you. Select one of the debates that are occurring in these pages and then defend your own position.

Prewriting and Drafting Strategies

The prewriting strategies discussed below are specifically designed to help you start writing a persuasive essay.

Consider Your Communication Situation

You cannot write an effective persuasive essay or argument without a strong sense of your audience. To be successful, you need to analyze how different readers are likely to respond to your subject. Answering the following questions can help you develop your sense of audience:

1. Describe in one sentence the audience whom you are trying to sway. How knowledgeable is your audience about the subject? Are your readers willing to listen to reason?

2. What logical or emotional appeals can you make that will convince your audience to agree with your position?

3. What counterarguments would your audience be likely to pose? How can you respond to the counterarguments as you build your case?

Because your readers will be swayed by their perception of who you are, you must establish an effective tone in your introduction. In most academic situations, you will want to present yourself as knowledgeable, rational (as opposed to emotional), concerned, intelligent, and compassionate. Of course, it often takes considerable revision to "discover" and develop the exact tone that you wish to project.

As with all writing, your readers will make inferences about your personality based on the language that you use, the credibility of the data that you present, and the logic of your reasoning. If you are hot-headed about your claim, you may need to write several drafts before you can establish the calm, rational persona that your teachers and other academic readers expect and respect. Answering the following questions will help you choose the right voice:

1. Do you want to write in the first or third person? Why?

2. What feelings about the subject would you like to share with your readers? What is the most effective way to do that?

3. Given your audience, what persona should you establish? How can you win readers' trust?

Freewrite

For at least ten minutes, write without stopping in response to this prompt: "The problem with most people is that they don't understand. . ." Remember that when freewriting you should ignore critical, faultfinding thoughts. Instead of rereading passages or trying to get the words just right, let every thought, no matter how irrelevant it seems to be, spill out from your mind and fill the page. In the preliminary stages of freewriting, follow your impulses to develop a single argument or to brainstorm a range of subjects that you could argue.

Identify Primary Claims and Needed Evidence

After reviewing your freewriting, summarize in a sentence what your main argument is and then determine how you could limit its scope. Remember that you cannot take on a huge issue in three, five, or even fifteen pages. If you are writing about world hunger, for example, your instructor does not expect you to develop a comprehensive, country-by-country, food-by-food analysis of the problem. Instead, your instructor would probably prefer you to limit the scope of your subject so that you avoid overgeneralizations. For example, a well-reasoned account of the needs of the people in your community who live without proper food and shelter could be quite powerful.

To determine how to best develop your argument, ask yourself the following questions:

1. Can you prove your point with your own observations and memories or do you need to do some outside research? Can you get the necessary information from one or two references or will extensive research be necessary?

2. Where will you find the evidence to support your claim? What sources will your readers accept as credible?

3. Are there experts on your subject in your community whom you could interview?

4. Is your topic so contemporary that you will have difficulty finding material to support it?

As with other writing genres, you should also ask, "Where would my essay appear if it were published?" Editorials in a newspaper, for example, are shaped differently from traditional research papers for instructors in the sciences or social sciences. While authors of editorials may refer to sources in the text of their essays, authors of academic essays are expected to provide a "Works Cited" section at the end of the essay. In turn, if you were writing an argument with a friend in mind, the argument might be best placed in a letter format. Be sure to talk over with your instructors possible "real-world" outlets for your writing.

Draw an Issue Tree

To help give you a sense of how to best organize your report, you can draw an issue tree, which is a pictorial representation that highlights the major elements that you are addressing. As suggested by the diagrams on page 177, an issue tree allows you to check the logical connections between your ideas. In other words, each part of your argument must connect by way of a branch to the overall thesis of the report if coherence is to be established. If you find yourself unable to link an idea somehow to your major proposition, the information is probably tangential and does not contribute to your argument. Omit it.

Revising and Editing Strategies

As usual, give yourself as much time as possible between drafts. The following questions highlight special concerns that you will need to address when revising persuasive essays.

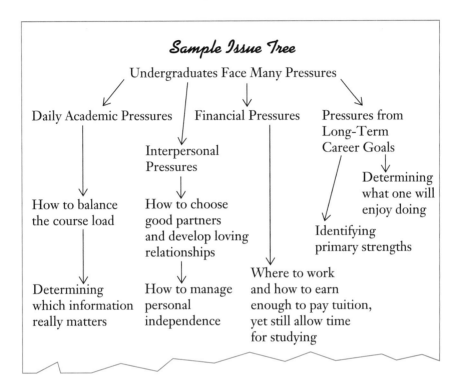

1. Have I successfully limited the scope of the argument? Have I presented my position clearly and accurately?

2. Have I presented sufficient data to support my claim? Do I need more facts and figures? Can I incorporate more quotations from authorities to substantiate my thoughts?

3. Do I treat opposing viewpoints clearly? Have I presented the opposition's most compelling arguments or passed off a weak counterargument as the opposition's strongest position?

4. What sort of emotional appeals have I made? Are they tasteful? relevant? effective? Have I established an appropriate tone and persona? Do I sound informed, intelligent, and compassionate? Have I overemphasized or overlooked any one of these strategies?

When revising your drafts, you may find it useful to pay special attention to your critics' evaluations of your past reports. Often, as your work in groups has probably demonstrated, it is easier for others than for you to identify problems with your work. Also, if you are having trouble drafting economical and emphatic sentences, use the guidelines presented in Chapters 11 and 12 to streamline your sentences so that they are precise and concise.

Change the Format of Your Text

To help yourself make the transition from writer to critic, place your text on the left side of the paper and comment on it in a column on the right. Sometimes changing the format of your work in this manner helps you view it objectively. In the following example, Sandra Grant has written criticisms of her second draft of *Dying with Dignity* on the right-hand side of the page. As you will see by reading her revision of this draft, printed below, evaluating her work in double-entry format helped Grant reconsider the organization of her essay.

Dying with Dignity (Third Draft)

Sandra Grant

Eventually each of us may be faced with (a) the difficult decision about death (and for no one is that an easy choice.) For some of us the only choice is to do everything possible to maintain a person's life no matter what the consequences. Personal beliefs and feelings in making a choice to resuscitate or not might make us feel like we were playing God. Unfortunately, we are faced with this moral dilemma in our society more and more as the number of elderly increases and technology improves.

> I am trying to present myself as a reasonable and sympathetic person here.

> I don't like how I have repeated the word "choice" here.

> This part seems wordy and clichéd. I guess I'm trying to dramatize the subject.

Everyone has heard stories of comatose patients with incurable diseases being kept alive, often at great cost in both money and suffering not only to the patient but to the patient's loved ones. Recently I remember an elderly man, in his 80s, who was admitted to I.C.U. because he appeared to have suffered a stroke that cut off oxygen to parts of his body, making him unresponsive to any type of stimuli. We obtained a lengthy medical history from his granddaughter who had been caring for him for the past two years at home. His diseases included cancer and Alzheimers, which kept him from doing activities of daily living on his own.

> Since my readers don't know me, I need to tell them that I work as a nurse. This should help me establish an ethical appeal, I think.

> I suppose I need to define "ICU" here.

After consulting with the physician and finding out that his overall prognosis and chance of recovery were poor and that he would have to be put on life support to be kept alive, the family had to decide: Was it time to make their loved one comfortable and let him die a natural death? Or should he be put on a ventilator which could lead to his being kept alive indefinitely, possibly in great discomfort yet without any real hope of recovery? A distraught family member came in from out of town and full of guilt for not being around for his father and not knowing what he would have wanted decided, "Do everything, we will spare no expense to keep my father alive."

> I know this section would be stronger if I could talk about this problem on a more national level. I need to be more specific about the incredible costs incurred trying to keep these patients alive.

> This first sentence is much too long.

> Ugh, I hate this sentence. It seems too wordy.

But who does bear the expense? Medicare bears most of the monetary expense if a patient is adequately covered but the cost to the family still can be financially devastating. One day in I.C.U. is approximately $1,000 and one day on a respirator is $824, plus lab, x-ray, and doctor fees all add up. A recent statistic showed that 65% of all medicare payments go toward patients who die within three to six months. Patients are receiving treatment that is of no benefit to them and indirectly depriving others of needed services because they are not communicating decisions about their medical treatment prior to getting ill.

> This paragraph now seems weak. I think I need to find what the real costs are.

> I know the teacher will want to know where I got the 65% figure from.

Obviously the decisions that must be made when an elderly patient faces a medical crisis are difficult ones for everyone—patient, loved ones, doctors, hospitals, and health care personnel alike. When a satisfying life is possible the decision is easy: You do everything you can. But when a terminally ill patient has had a medical crisis and is in failing health with little hope of recovery, then we need to let him or her die if that is what he or she wants.

> I guess that I'm finally getting around to my point here. I think my essay would be stronger if I focused more in the introduction about my purpose. What do I really want my readers to go away with—that they should have living wills? Maybe I can find a living will someplace so this piece would be less abstract.

> This draft seems to wander.

Dying with Dignity (Final Draft)
Sandra Grant

As a critical care nurse I often see patients with incurable diseases being kept 1
alive, often at great expense in both money and suffering not only to the
patient but to the patient's loved ones. I often ask myself, "Why is this being
done?" The answer is that family members just don't know what else to do. It
was never communicated to them how their family member felt about being
kept alive on life support or how they felt about dying. A Living Will is an
advance directive that can help alleviate this moral dilemma that our society
is faced with.

Recently I remember an 80-year-old man who was admitted to I.C.U. 2
(Intensive Care Unit) because he appeared to have suffered a stroke that cut
off oxygen to parts of his body, making him unresponsive to any type of stimuli. We obtained a lengthy medical history from his granddaughter who had
been caring for him for the past two years. His diseases included cancer and
Alzheimers, which made it impossible for him to care for himself.

After consulting with the physician and finding out that his overall prog- 3
nosis and chance of recovery were poor and that he would have to be put on
life support to be kept alive, the family had to decide: Was it time to make
their loved one comfortable and let him die a natural death? Or should he be
put on a ventilator which could lead to his being kept alive indefinitely, possibly in great discomfort yet without any real hope of recovery?

Obviously the decision that must be made by anyone involved is a diffi- 4
cult one. But when a satisfying life is possible the decision is easy: you do
everything you can. But when someone has had a medical crisis and there is
little hope of recovery, the decisions are more difficult. For some the only
choice is to do everything possible to maintain a person's life no matter what
the consequences. This choice may come from strong personal or religious
beliefs, but unfortunately sometimes it comes from a feeling of guilt as it did
with the case above. A distraught family member came in from out of town
and said, "Do everything; we will spare no expense." From other things he
said, it would obvious to all of us that he felt guilty for not being around his
father when he died.

But who does bear the expense? Medicare bears most of the monetary 5
expense if a patient is adequately covered, yet the cost to the family still can
be financially devastating. One day in I.C.U. is approximately $1,000 and one
day on a respirator is $824, plus all the lab, x-ray, and doctor fees. One of the
physicians whom I work with told me that 65% of all Medicare payments go
toward patients who die within three to six months.

Doctors and medical care personnel agree that every case is different; but 6
when faced with this difficult decision, advance directives often provide critical information about the patient's wishes. A living will is concerned with the
extent of treatment in the event a person is terminally ill, as illustrated by the
following two paragraphs:

Death is as much a reality as birth, growth, maturity, and old age—it is the one certainty of life. If the time comes when I can no longer take part in decisions for my own future, let this statement stand as an expression of my wishes, while I am still of sound mind.

If the situation should arise in which there is no reasonable expectation of my recovery from physical or mental disability, I request that I be allowed to die and not to be kept alive by artificial means or "heroic measures." I do not fear death itself as much as the indignities of deterioration, dependence, and hopeless pain.

Thirty-eight states have passed laws authorizing residents to provide instructions to family and physicians about what should be done, or not done, in the event they are unable to communicate a decision about their medical treatment. Most states require at least two people to witness the signing of a living will and some states require that it be notarized. It's recommended that you give copies to your physician, clergyman, lawyer and anyone to whom you give your power of attorney. Also, a living will can be revoked at any time if you ever change your mind.

A living will does not always provide the ultimate solution to this difficult problem, but it does help. None of us wants to think about death or even about physical or mental incapacity, and this is understandable. Yet each of us, at whatever age, should give some thought and talk about it with our families. A living will is just one alternative to making dying with dignity a little less traumatic.   7

Criteria-Based Evaluation

In addition to using the double-entry format for writing criticisms of your text and ideas for improving it, you may find the following checklist a useful way to identify strengths and weaknesses in your work. When reviewing with the following criteria in mind, however, do not assume that you need to record all 10s for your essay to be exemplary. There is, as was mentioned earlier, no single, ideal structure for all persuasive or argumentative essays. An article may score very low on emotional appeals, for instance, and yet still be thoroughly convincing because of its logic and organization.

	Low	Middle	High
I. Persuasive and Argumentative Appeals	1 2 3	4 5 6 7	8 9 10

Author presents an effective persona.

Author provides suitable logical appeals.

Author provides suitable emotional appeals.

Author introduces topic and clarifies its significance.

Author defines key terms and issues.

Author presents suitable evidence.

Author presents and refutes counter-arguments.

Author presents implications and conclusions.

	Low	Middle	High
II. Substantive Revisions	1 2 3	4 5 6 7	8 9 10

The significance of the subject is clarified.

The document is reader-based.

The tone is appropriate given the audience and purpose.

The document is organized effectively.

The document is formatted effectively.

The paragraphs are coherent and cohesive.

	Low	Middle	High
III. Edited Document	1 2 3	4 5 6 7	8 9 10

Unnecessary jargon and awkward abstractions have been edited.

The first person has been used, where appropriate.

To be verbs have been eliminated.

A high verb-to-noun ratio has been established.

Strings of prepositions have been avoided.

The document has been edited for economy.

The document has been copyedited for grammatical, mechanical, and formatting errors.

Collaborating Strategies

When you are responding to your peers' persuasive essays, you may become sidetracked by the issues that are addressed rather than focusing squarely on helping your classmates improve their work. It is especially important, therefore, to remember that your peers do not necessarily want to know your opinion on the subject. Although you certainly should feel free to share your honest responses to their ideas as written, this is not the time to argue with your peers, to show them the error of their thinking.

To make your critique as useful and realistic as possible, ask your peer who the primary audience is before critiquing an essay. You should then try to play the part of the intended audience. For example, if one of your peers is writing to members of the National Rifle Association about the need for gun control and you agree with him that semi-automatic weapons should be harder to buy, you should nonetheless attempt to read the manuscript as if you are a card-carrying member of the NRA.

PEER REVIEW WORKSHOP

The following questions are designed to help you adopt the critical stance necessary to help your peers improve their work. When offering your advice, remember that your purpose is not to rewrite your peers' drafts. Instead of assuming that you know the best way to improve their work and making vague statements like "Your primary problem is your tone and lack of focus," say: "I had difficulty following your discussion. In the first paragraph I thought you were going to discuss the problems with fraternities, so I was surprised in paragraph two when you compared them to Nazi youth camps."

1. Is the essay persuasive? What additional logical or emotional appeals would make the essay more convincing? Has the author provided suitable evidence to support claims? Are there any points in the discussion at which you are confused or you think additional evidence needs to be provided? What additional information do you believe the author should add before submitting the report for a grade?

2. Has the author made use of counterarguments effectively? Are any important counterarguments ignored?

3. Has the author provided the information the audience will need to understand the subject? Can any information be deleted because the audience is already likely to be familiar with it?

4. Do you think the report is well organized? Given the author's communication situation, do you believe the introduction should give readers more information about the report's content? Does the author actually accomplish what he or she promised to do in the introduction?

5. In what ways do you think the writer can revise the report to make it more interesting to readers?

Sample Peer Review Workshop

As you probably know by now, peer group work does not always go smoothly. It is understandably difficult to establish trust among group members so that people feel safe when functioning as critics. Also, reading is a subjective process, so writers can leave a peer group feeling confused and unsure about how to proceed. This is particularly true when students in a peer group disagree about how a particular manuscript can be improved. Nevertheless, imperfect as it must be, peer group work offers you the best opportunity available to see how your words and ideas influence others.

To help improve your ability to respond meaningfully to your peers, I have provided Emily Andre's newspaper editorial below in the left-hand column. On the right are a number of standard critical questions that you can use to evaluate her work. Take time to seriously consider these questions and add your own reactions. Then write a brief, 250-word, note to Emily outlining the two most important changes that you believe she needs to make to improve this document. Once you have completed this exercise, read her final product, which appears at the end of this chapter.

Dear Editor:

Hernando County is the fastest growing county in the State of Florida. The population has doubled in the last ten years. We have all benefited from this growth, but it has also brought us some problems. The price of growth has often been the loss of trees that have stood in one spot for well over a hundred years. A tree ordinance must be passed before our county is landscaped with cement blocks. We are rapidly running out of time! A tree ordinance must be passed before our county is landscaped with cement blocks.

Would readers who have not benefited from the county's growth be alienated by this introduction?

Many of us have become prosperous with the influx of people wanting to live in Hernando County. Our builders, merchants and professional people are thankful, I'm sure, for their prosperity. Isn't it time we repaid the cost of all this development?

Does this paragraph add in a meaningful way to the discussion begun in the opening paragraph? Does this paragraph seem audience-sensitive?

There are many fine people living and working here, people with integrity who are concerned about the ravaging of our country-side. The numerous Laurel Oaks growing in this area account for the attraction we have for newcomers. These trees, frequently draped with graceful Spanish moss, often grow to sixty feet in height. When they are gone there will no longer be anything special about Hernando County. We will look like every other county that has forgotten to watch its footsteps. We will have all the conveniences at our fingertips but

Could other reasons for the newcomers be equally as persuasive as the trees?

the price will be an environment that has turned ugly. The unnecessary removal of our trees is evident in many places. The reasons given for their removal seem weak.

How many trees have really been moved?

Not very long ago, I passed a lot that I pass every day when I leave my home. On this particular day there were thirteen tree stumps where the day before there had been thirteen mature oak trees. I know there were thirteen stumps because I stopped my car in outrage to count them. Eventually a new home was built and two or three little saplings were planted in the front yard and euphemistically called landscaping. Just in case my passions had taken over my reason, I discussed the need for this wholesale removal of trees with a friend, who is also one of the counties more ethical builders. He agreed; it was a needless travesty. In this case the owners went along with the builder's desire to easier and less costly construction. Before a tree is removed every effort should be made by the owner and the builder to try and incorporate the tree into the landscape. The excuse of over-cost can no longer be accepted. Some misguided souls remove trees to eliminate the bother of having to rake their yard of leaves.

How big were the stumps? Were these 200–300-year-old trees?

On Highway 50, a valuable piece of commercial property was home to several oak trees that saw union troops march toward Bayport in one of the few civil war skirmishes recorded in Florida. They are no longer there; they have been replaced by a parking lot that serves a strip shopping area. It only took one day to up-root them and they lay there for a few more days, like so many corpses, until they were eventually dismembered and all signs of them finally disappeared. The businesses there are

Does this image belong here? In what ways does this paragraph add to the discussion in the above paragraphs?

not doing too well. Tenants don't seem to stay very long, and the stores are often closed.

There is a feeling by many that people should be free to do what they want with their property, and not have to answer to anyone for their actions. If we try to curb their excesses we are accused of infringing on their rights. We are often at the mercy of power without a conscience. This is just as much tyranny as a government without a constitution. Laws are made to protect us from tyranny. A tree ordinance would protect us from the tyranny of people who put profit before conscience, who put themselves before their community. Property ownership should not be a license to arbitrarily destroy or damage our environment. An ordinance has to be severe enough and costly enough to discourage arbitrary tree removal. A system of reward to people who protect and respect their surroundings would encourage a sense of responsibility, rewards such as lower property taxes.

How would you describe the tone in this paragraph? How does the author's persona or tone shift in this paragraph from the above paragraphs?

A tree ordinance should give us a standard of expectation. We can work co-operatively with reasonable people but should penalize severely those unconscionable few who use freedom as an excuse for wantonness.

Write your response to Emily Andre's editorial here; then read her revision in your notebook.

Editorial

Emily Andre

You may remember several oak trees that had been growing on a valuable   1 piece of commercial property on Highway 50. What you may not know is that they had been there for over a hundred years and had seen union troops march toward Bayport in one of the few civil war skirmishes recorded in Florida. These trees were a part of the history of Hernando County, and indeed, the United States. They should have been a source of pride to everyone living here. Unfortunately, they are no longer there; they have been replaced by a parking lot that serves a largely unsuccessful strip shopping area. In one day, these magnificent trees, their crowns once seeming to touch the clouds while their lush branches dipped gracefully to the ground, were up-rooted, dismembered and left like corpses until, over time, all signs of them finally disappeared.

The reasons for the destruction of these trees and others like them are 2 varied, but all seem weak. Tree removal occurs most often for reasons of convenience and profit. Architects claim that buildings are easier to design without these living impediments, and when developers don't have to build around trees, they are able to offer properties at lower prices. Perhaps the weakest excuse comes from some misguided souls who remove trees to eliminate the bother of having to rake their yards of leaves. A third argument often used is the right of personal freedom; the right of the individual over the community. There is a feeling by many that people should be free to do what they want with their property and not have to answer to anyone for their actions.

The cost of all this destruction is enormous, and each of us will have to 3 pay eventually. The particular beauty of Hernando County accounts for the attraction we have for newcomers. Our numerous Laurel Oaks, often growing to sixty feet in height, and frequently draped with Spanish moss, are one of the features directly responsible for our growth. If we allow these oaks to be destroyed, our country will begin to look like every other area that has forgotten to watch its footsteps and has sacrificed its individual beauty to universal ugliness. If we allow this to happen we will pay not only in conformity to an undesirable norm, but in depletion of oxygen, change in climate, and the disappearance of our wildlife.

A tree ordinance must be passed before our county is landscaped beyond 4 repair. There are many fine people living and working here, people with integrity who are concerned about the ravaging of our countryside. We must work together to ensure that property ownership does not remain a license to arbitrarily destroy or damage our environment. Before a tree is removed every effort should be made by the owner and the builder to try to incorporate the tree into the landscape. Perhaps we can use incentives to encourage responsibility. We can lower the property taxes of people who protect and respect their surroundings, thereby financially penalizing those unconscionable few who use cost, convenience, and freedom as excuses for wantonness. As we discover more about our ecosystems, we must realize that the community suffers and benefits according to the actions of each of its inhabitants, and we must begin to act accordingly.

Hernando County is the fastest growing county in the State of Florida. 5 Our population has doubled in the last ten years. We have become prosperous with the influx of people attracted to the many benefits of our area. We would like the growth to continue, but it is up to us to see that this growth is controlled and responsible. It is up to us to develop a standard of expectation for the purpose of preserving the Hernando County that is now so attractive before we make the mistake of sacrificing our future for the fast buck. Let's work to incorporate a tree ordinance into our local laws for the benefit of all.

Additional Writing Sample

In the following selection, Richard Loudermilk, a student writer, argues that Americans should support a national health care system. Loudermilk intended this short essay to appear as an editorial in an urban newspaper.

America Could Use a National Health Care System

Richard Loudermilk

For some of us, the term "socialized medicine" conjures up images that are   1
certainly less than capitalistic. We're protective of America's democracy, and no one wants to endanger our way of life. However, our love for our country and distrust of socialism should still not keep us from thinking about the benefits of socialized medicine.

Glen found out almost two years ago that he had Parkinson's Disease.   2
The illness isn't fatal but does cause nerve damage; he's already losing some control of his left hand. He had to retire recently, at least 25 years before he normally would have. Glen's disability insurance will pay his living expenses from now on, but if he needs medical treatment, he's in trouble. Because of his Parkinson's Disease, his insurance company wouldn't renew his health insurance. No insurance company will give him medical insurance or even write him a policy covering everything *except* what Parkinson's Disease causes. Who knows how many of us have (or will have) the same problem of no health insurance?

Glen is a real person. If he were to have a heart attack tomorrow he   3
could not afford any major health care. If the United States adopted a national health care system, or socialized medicine, neither Glen, nor you, nor me, nor our families would ever fear the high cost of being sick.

One reason for rising health care costs could be the increasing trend in   4
patient-versus-doctor lawsuits. Under a national health care system, physicians would be employed by the government and would not have to worry about patients suing. Also, doctors would no longer be forced to charge all patients extra to make up for those who don't pay their bills.

Taxes might have to be raised to pay for a national health care system,   5
and we'd have to make sure that the increase wouldn't be more than we already spend on health care. Medical treatment and health insurance costs can add up to hundreds and thousands of dollars a year. If each American

added just over $16 a month to fund a national health care system, we would have $50 billion to work with annually (Walsh 241).

The United States is the world's only developed nation without a 6 government-sponsored health insurance or a health care guarantee for its citizens (Walsh 242). In Canada, a government-sponsored universal health insurance provides medical care for all residents. A national health insurance in West Germany furnishes almost the entire population with free health care. In Sweden, a combination of a government-funded national health insurance and socialized medicine give every person medical treatment.

In Great Britain, the 42-year-old National Health Service provides all 7 people with free medical attention. Most doctors have private practices but are paid by the government, so patients can choose their own physicians. Because British doctors don't fear lawsuits, they aren't forced to perform unnecessary tests just to cover themselves in case a patient sues. The British public is overwhelmingly in favor of the National Health Service (Walsh 239). Some *do* choose to pay for their medical care, but they make up less than ten percent of the population.

Statistics show little difference in the quality of health care in Britain and 8 in the United States, but the National Health Service is more economical and efficient (Walsh 240). Although Americans visit the doctor almost as often as British patients, our visits last two to three times as long (Walsh 240). Also, the United States spends almost three times as much per person for health care as Great Britain.

Twice as many surgeons are practicing in the United States today as were 9 ten years ago, which could create the possibility for unnecessary surgery. This likelihood is certainly reduced in Britain, because doctors aren't paid extra for performing operations. Surgery is part of their normal duties.

Insurance costs are going up, and simply having health insurance may 10 not be enough. Most insurance companies won't renew a policy if the holder gets a disease, such as Parkinson's Disease, cancer, or leukemia. This means no coverage, and hospitals don't readily admit patients who can't pay.

Before we see socialized medicine as a threat, let's consider our govern- 11 ment. We should remember that we don't even live in a "true" democracy. The government controls the postal system, regulates utilities, prints our money, influences interest rates and oversees immigration. A national health care system wouldn't be a step toward communism but instead a step toward taking better care of our citizens. We must realize the government already directly influences our lives in numerous ways, and we shouldn't fear government intervention.

What would happen if you, or your child, needed a heart transplant and 12 you couldn't afford it? Under a national health care system, you wouldn't be forced into bankruptcy: the government would pay for the treatment. A national health care system would also mean no more costly doctor bills. Instead of some times toughing it out when we're sick, we could see a doctor free of charge.

In the Declaration of Independence our forefathers wrote that we have 13 the right to life: "We hold these truths to be self-evident, that all men are created equal, that they are endowed by their Creator with certain unalienable Rights, that among these are Life, Liberty and the pursuit of Happiness." So doesn't it follow that we have the right to the medical care that would keep us alive?

So if you like the idea of a national health care system, drop a note to a 14 legislator. Get things started. The process will be gradual, and we might have to start with state health care systems. But we'd be on the road to better, less expensive health care for us all. A lot of us would like that. I know Glen would. He's my father.

Works Cited

Walsh, John. "Britain's National Health Service: It Works and They Like It, But—." *Science* 21 July 1988: 239–242.

Critical Reading Questions

1. In what ways do Loudermilk's introductory paragraphs represent an ethical appeal?
2. Where does Loudermilk establish his primary claim?
3. What data does Loudermilk provide to establish the logic of his claim? What additional sources could he provide to be more convincing?
4. What assumptions does Loudermilk appear to be making about his audience's attitude and knowledge of America's health care system?
5. How does this student handle the likely counterarguments of his opposition?
6. What emotional appeals can you identify in this article? Do you believe that this essay would be as successful without the final paragraph?

Evaluating Criticism

Below are some of the questions you have considered after concluding previous reports. Once again, take a few moments to analyze your strengths, weaknesses, and writing goals. By honestly considering the following questions, while recognizing that writing is a difficult art to master, you can chart your own personal growth, identify patterns in your critics' responses, and assure yourself that you are making progress.

1. Can you identify any mistakes that you have made in the past that you did *not* make when writing this current report? At the global level, for instance, did you establish a more effective tone or present more substantive information about your subject?

2. What have you learned about yourself as a writer as a result of the prewriting, drafting, revising, and collaborating techniques that you experimented with when writing your persuasive essay?

3. What similarities in your peers' and instructor's criticisms can you identify in this report that echo previous criticisms? What problems do you have writing or what weaknesses in your texts continue to interfere with your ability to successfully develop and communicate ideas?

4. Did you find that your peers' criticisms were more or less helpful than in past peer review workshops? What changes could you suggest to make the peer review workshops more productive?

5. What changes would you like to make in how you compose your next academic document? How, for example, will you manage your time differently in your next assignment?

Solving Problems by Negotiating Differences

How many times have you been in an argument that you knew you couldn't win? Are you reluctant to change your mind about certain social, political, or personal issues? Do you have an unshakable faith in a particular religion or philosophy? For example, are you absolutely certain that abortion is immoral under all circumstances? Are you categorically against animal experimentation for advancements in medicine? Do you believe that criminals who have tortured and killed people should receive the death penalty? Do you believe that parents should have no more than two children because of the world population problem? Do you believe it is your patriotic duty to buy solely American products?

Some of our beliefs and arguments are based on faith, some on emotion, and some on logic alone. We all hold different religious, political, and personal beliefs that largely define who we are and how we think. Within the past fifty years, as the size of our global village has appeared to shrink with the use of television, fax, and jets, we have become increasingly more sophisticated and knowledgable. As a result, most educated people now realize that few significant issues have simple solutions. Thanks to modern scholarship and research, we have come to realize that our personalities and thoughts are shaped to some degree by cultural expectations. Philosophers have challenged us to recognize that our worldviews—our assumptions about reality, what is good, what is possible—are influenced by our day-to-day experiences. We have realized that truth is not a fixed, static entity that can be carried into a battle like a banner.

One wonderful aspect of your college career is meeting different worldviews through books and through discussions with people whom you otherwise would not encounter. Indeed, many college campuses offer a wonderful glimpse of the diversity of modern-day life. A wide-eyed glance at students at the university center at my campus, for instance, will show you Chinese students working alongside students from Africa and South America. Young women dressed in their power suits mix freely with returning older adult students. Fraternity brothers rush from place to place, dressed in their blue blazers and short haircuts, while male musicians, dressed in the tie-dyed fashions of the 1960s and shoulder-length hair, play guitars and sing protest songs.

One result of our increasingly sophisticated world is that you cannot assume that your readers will believe or even understand everything you say. On the contrary, you need to assume that your readers will doubt you. They will question the validity of your evidence and test the logic of your conclusions. Modern readers tend to be particularly contentious when you insist on assertions that they find objectionable. Because of this shift in audience attitude, writers need to develop compelling ways of organizing and presenting arguments.

When you wish to address an emotional and controversial issue and when your audience is likely to be threatened by your ideas, you will probably not be successful if you make your claim in the introduction of your essay (or verbal argument). No matter how thoroughly you go on to support your ideas with careful reasoning and to refute other claims (such as those held by your audience) respectfully, your readers have already decided to ignore you. For example, can you imagine how your roommate would respond if you remark that he or she is a terrible slob? Even if you follow up your comment with photographs of the dirty dishes, cluttered rooms, and soiled carpet left in his or her wake, can you imagine that the final outcome of your detailed presentation might be resolution? More likely you will face anger, bitterness, and denial. Watch your introductory propositions!

Most of us tend to resist change and are threatened by ideas that challenge what we believe. Also, most of us dislike being told what to do and how to think, so even if our brains tell us to agree, our emotions (and egos) tell us to shut down and ignore what we are hearing. A male chauvinist who believes that women are intellectually inferior to men will be unlikely to listen to your argument that women are as intelligent as men. Your quotes from world-renowned educators and philosophers and your statistics from the Stanford-Binet or SAT, GRE, and MCAT scores would probably be dismissed as inaccurate because they threaten his assumptions. Of course, you could hope that the chauvinist would change his mind over time when he wasn't being pressed, yet you couldn't bet on this outcome.

Because conflict is inevitable, we need to seek creative ways to solve complicated problems and to negotiate differences between opposing parties. Although there are no simple formulas for bringing opposing factions together, we do have a relatively new form of communication founded on Carl Rogers's client-centered therapeutic approach to one-on-one and group counseling. Essentially, the Rogerian problem-solving approach reconceptualizes our goals when we argue. Instead of assuming that an author or speaker should hope to overcome an antagonistic audience with shrewd reasoning, the Rogerian approach would have the author or speaker attempt to reach some common ground with the audience. Thus, in a very real way, Rogerian "persuasion" is not a form of persuasion so much as it is a way of opening communication for negotiating common ground between divergent points of view. In terms of writing, we could say that the Rogerian approach melds the techniques of informative analyses with those of persuasive reports. Your goal when you employ the tactics of Rogerian problem-solving is not for you to win and for your opponent to lose, a scenario that more often results in both parties losing. Instead, you explore ways that will allow both you and your audience to win.

Writing Samples

In the following essay, Rachel Richardson Smith grapples with the abortion issue. Rather than arguing for or against, Smith analyzes the tactics of the pro-life and the pro-choice groups.

Abortion, Right and Wrong*

Rachel Richardson Smith

I cannot bring myself to say I am in favor of abortion. I don't want anyone 1 to have one. I want people to use contraceptives and for those contraceptives to be foolproof. I want people to be responsible for their actions; mature in their decisions. I want children to be loved, wanted, well cared for.

I cannot bring myself to say I am against choice. I want women who are 2 young, poor, single or all three to be able to direct the course of their lives. I want women who have had all the children they want or can afford or their bodies can withstand to be able to decide their future. I want women who are in bad marriages or destructive relationships to avoid being trapped by pregnancy.

So in these days when thousands rally in opposition to legalized abor- 3 tion, when facilities providing abortions are bombed, when the president speaks glowingly of the growing momentum behind the anti-abortion movement, I find myself increasingly alienated from the pro-life groups.

At the same time, I am overwhelmed with mail from pro-choice groups. 4 They, too, are mobilizing their forces, growing articulate in support of their cause, and they want my support. I am not sure I can give it.

I find myself in the awkward position of being both anti-abortion and 5 pro-choice. Neither group seems to be completely right—or wrong. It is not that I think abortion is wrong for me but acceptable for someone else. The question is far more complex than that.

Part of my problem is that what I think and how I feel about this issue 6 are two entirely different matters. I know that unwanted children are often neglected, even abandoned. I know that many of those seeking abortions are children themselves. I know that making abortion illegal will not stop all women from having them.

* From *Newsweek*, March 29, 1985.

I also know from experience the crisis an unplanned pregnancy can 7
cause. Yet I have felt the joy of giving birth, the delight that comes from feeling a baby's skin against my own. I know how hard it is to parent a child and how deeply satisfying it can be. My children sometimes provoke me and cause me endless frustration, but I can still look at them with tenderness and wonder at the miracle of it all. The lessons of my own experience produce conflicting emotions. Theory collides with reality.

It concerns me that both groups present themselves in absolutes. They 8
are committed and they want me to commit. They do not recognize the gray area where I seem to be languishing. Each group has the right answer—the only answer.

Yet I am uncomfortable in either camp. I have nothing in common with 9
the pro-lifers. I am horrified by their scare tactics, their pictures of well-formed fetuses tossed in a metal pan, their cruel slogans. I cannot condone their flagrant misuse of Scripture and unforgiving spirit. There is a meanness about their position that causes them to pass judgment on the lives of women in a way I could never do.

The pro-life groups, with their fundamentalist religious attitudes, have 10
a fear and an abhorrence of sex, especially premarital sex. In their view abortion only compounds the sexual sin. What I find incomprehensible is that even as they are opposed to abortion they are also opposed to alternative solutions. They are squeamish about sex education in the schools. They don't want teens to have contraceptives without parental consent. They offer little aid or sympathy to unwed mothers. They are the vigilant guardians of a narrow morality.

I wonder how abortion got to be the greatest of all sins? What about 11
poverty, ignorance, hunger, weaponry?

The only thing the anti-abortion groups seem to have right is that 12
abortion is indeed the taking of human life. I simply cannot escape this one glaring fact. Call it what you will—fertilized egg, embryo, fetus. What we have here is human life. If it were just a mass of tissue there would be no debate. So I agree that abortion ends a life. But the anti-abortionists are wrong to call it murder.

The sad truth is that homicide is not always against the law. Our society 13
does not categorically recognize the sanctity of human life. There are a number of legal and apparently socially acceptable ways to take human life. "Justifiable" homicide includes the death penalty, war, killing in self-defense. It seems to me that as a society we need to come to grips with our own ambiguity concerning the value of human life. If we are to value and protect unborn life so stringently, why do we not also value and protect life already born?

Why can't we see abortion for the human tragedy it is? No woman plans 14
for her life to turn out that way. Even the most effective contraceptives are no guarantee against pregnancy. Loneliness, ignorance, immaturity can lead to decisions (or lack of decisions) that may result in untimely pregnancy. People make mistakes.

What many people seem to misunderstand is that no woman wants to 15
have an abortion. Circumstances demand it; women do it. No woman reacts
to abortion with joy. Relief, yes. But also ambivalence, grief, despair, guilt.

The pro-choice groups do not seem to acknowledge that abortion is 16
not a perfect answer. What goes unsaid is that when a woman has an abortion
she loses more than an unwanted pregnancy. Often she loses her self-respect.
No woman can forget a pregnancy no matter how it ends.

Why can we not view abortion as one of those anguished decisions in 17
which human beings struggle to do the best they can in trying circumstances?
Why is abortion viewed so coldly and factually on the one hand and so judg-
mentally on the other? Why is it not akin to the same painful experience
families must sometimes make to allow a loved one to die?

I wonder how we can begin to change the context in which we think 18
about abortion. How can we begin to think about it redemptively? What is it
in the trauma of loss of life—be it loved or unloved, born or unborn—from
which we can learn? There is much I have yet to resolve. Even as I refuse to
pass judgment on other women's lives, I weep for the children who might
have been. I suspect I am not alone.

Critical Reading Questions

1. What information does Smith provide that shows she has thoroughly
   considered the positions of both the pro-life and the pro-choice
   groups? What additional facts or counterarguments do you believe
   could strengthen this piece?

2. Who is the primary audience for this essay? What makes you think so?

3. What sense of Smith's personality do you have after reading this essay?
   What is the tone of the piece? How do you believe the tone of this essay
   would be different if Smith eliminated paragraphs 9 and 10?

4. What appeals to emotion and to logic does Smith make in this essay?

5. If Smith were in your peer writing group and someone suggested taking
   the last sentence in paragraph 13 and moving it to the introductory paragraph, what would you say?

6. What consensus does Smith attempt to establish? Can you think of any
   additional information that Smith could add to help establish greater
   consensus?

In the following essay, Leslie Milne, a student writer, discusses the
advantages and disadvantages of remaining single. To help her focus on the
needs and concerns of her primary audience—that is, single women—Milne
completed an analysis of her communication situation.

Analysis of Communication Situation

Audience: Adults of prime marriage-potential age (22–35), whether
single or already married.

Purpose: I want people to appreciate both sides, but in the end to agree that marriage seems to offer more meaningful rewards.
Voice: Because this tends to be an emotional issue, I want to emphasize the humorous aspects involved.
Context: Periodicals aimed at young women, such as *Women* or *Self.*

To Be or Not to Be Single

Leslie Milne

Today's society presents a woman with the choice of whether to marry or 1
remain single. Such a choice was not a practical option for women even one
generation ago. It is worth examining the pros and cons of married versus
single life for the modern young women.

First impressions do much to recommend the single life. Freedom is, for 2
many, the most attractive feature of singlehood. Your time is your own. You
need answer to no one but yourself, in the form of your conscience. You are
at liberty to take full advantage of opportunities in both career and romance
when they arise. In addition, you may have as many sex partners as suits you
at any given time.

As an independent, self-reliant person, you are in charge of your own 3
life. You can be an assured, confident individual to whom others relate as
such, rather than as "his other half." You can be secure in your ability to
stand on your own two feet, rather than constantly worrying whether or not
you could ever really manage without him.

As a single woman, there is less pressure on you to adhere to the role 4
models ascribed by society. For instance, you don't have to cook, clean, have
babies, and generally evolve your lifestyle to cater to the needs and desires of
another. If you choose to live on pizza and TV dinners for a week, you can do
it without affecting anyone else.

The single lady often holds mystery and allure for the attached male. 5
Your friends' partners are apt to find you infinitely attractive and flirt outra-
geously with you. This is such a delightful ego-booster, and it tends to make
you glow all the more appealingly.

Even if heavily involved with someone, as a single woman you retain the 6
option of cutting loose, changing your mind, and resuming life on your own.
That important escape route is always clear. You can avoid the stigma of
divorce and all the damage which results from such a status move.

It certainly does seem that marriage would be rather a drag. Apart from 7
all the hassle of making a commitment, there is the inevitably dull routine of
it all. Also, for every one thing you adore about him, there are ten things that
drive you nuts. How much better to enjoy the fun side of a relationship, and
see a man on his best behavior, trying desperately to impress you on a date.

But wait! Is this a satisfactory way to live the rest of your life? Surely the 8
flip side of the coin merits at least some examination. It may require the
magical appearance in your life of the elusive Mr. Right, but somewhere

down the line you are going to be confronted with at least the idea of marriage. It may be a friend who is taking the plunge, or perhaps your current partner is popping *the* question. Suddenly, life as a single girl is put into a whole new perspective.

In the middle of celebrating your treasured freedom, you realize that you are often lonely. You are tired of friends and colleagues taking advantage of you because you have freedom from family responsibilities. Why would it matter if *you* worked later or over the weekend? Such experiences in the past have made you become quite selfish about your own time. Do others consider you promiscuous for having more than one boyfriend, or for dating lots of men over the course of the past year? Worse yet, are you in risk of being infected with the AIDS virus? 9

Far from being regarded as self-reliant and independent, you seem to be coming across as a threat to potential partners who can't see what they could possibly offer you. As time goes on and you remain single into your late thirties, men may regard you as unable or unwilling to commit to a serious relationship, or may even believe that you are gay. All this undermines your confidence and sparks feelings of paranoia: What is wrong with me? Why are men avoiding me like the plague? 10

Not having to cater for anyone else is all very well, but with only yourself to cook and clean for, it is easy to let everything slide until you are suddenly and painfully aware that you look like a slob and live like a pig. Far from seeming attractive to the husbands and partners of your friends, you may come to be regarded as a "third wheel," a real nuisance who is always tagging along. Women suspect you of flirting, while men resent you for cramping their style with their own partners. 11

Avoidance of intimacy can lead to a string of superficial, nonprogressive relationships which evaporate after the first flush of lust is over. Unwillingness to commit to anyone signals fear of taking risks to many potential marriage partners. 12

Even after divorce, a once-married person often holds a lot of appeal. At least he or she tried, even if it didn't work out. Surveys reveal that the majority of divorced people do remarry at some stage. Surely these people are not "lemmings," repeatedly hurling themselves over the cliff to certain death. Marriage really must have a lot going for it. 13

There is no doubt that getting close enough to someone to recognize him—"warts and all"—leads to a deeper, truer, more meaningful love relationship. Such a union holds satisfaction, many rewards, and the real promise of enduring happiness. Wouldn't it be cozier to share your pizza or TV dinner with some less-than-perfect, but eminently familiar person? Dates are fun, but the continuity, security, true intimacy, and closeness resulting from a marriage partnership deserve serious consideration as cause to rethink your attitude toward that widely debated status. 14

While the single life may be infinitely more appealing to some, the benefits and long-term rewards of marriage provide, on balance, the greatest satisfaction for the majority of people. 15

Critical Reading Questions

1. How would you describe Milne's voice in this essay? In what ways, for instance, does she seem to be either biased or objective? What passages do you find humorous? Why do you think Milne included such levity?

2. Were you surprised by Milne's conclusions, given the positive benefits she identifies with being single in the early part of the essay?

3. Do you believe Milne has fairly portrayed the advantages and disadvantages of single life? Can you identify any significant advantages or disadvantages that her discussion fails to address?

4. If Milne were in your peer review workshop, what goal for revising would you identify as most important?

Analyzing Pertinent Conventions

Below are some of the strategies that you can use to negotiate consensus between opposing parties. As usual, you should not consider the following to be a rigid formula. Instead, pick and choose from these strategies in light of your audience, purpose, and intended voice.

Present the Problem

In the introduction, identify the issue and clarify its significance. Because you need to adopt a nonthreatening persona throughout your essay, however, avoid dogmatically presenting your view as the best or only way to solve the problem. Unlike your strategy for shaping a conventional persuasive text (outlined in Chapter 6), at this point in your discussion you will not want to lay your cards on the table and summarize your presentation. Instead, explain the scope and complexity of the issue. You might want to mention the various approaches that people have taken to solve the problem and perhaps even suggest that the issue is so complicated that the best you and your readers can hope for is consensus—or agreement on some aspect of the matter.

In your introduction and throughout your essay, you will want to explain the problem in ways that will make your audience say, "Yes, this author understands my position." Because the people whom you are writing for may feel stress when you confront them with an emotionally charged issue and may already have made up their minds firmly on the subject, you should try to interest such reluctant readers by suggesting that you have an innovative way of viewing the problem. Of course, this tactic is effective only when you can indeed follow through and be as original as possible in your treatment of the subject. Otherwise, your readers may reject your ideas because they recognize that you have misrepresented yourself.

Challenge Yourself to Risk Change

Rather than masking your thoughts behind an "objective persona," the Rogerian approach allows you to express your true feelings. However, if you are to meet the ideals of Rogerian communication, you need to challenge your own beliefs; you must be so open-minded that you truly entertain the possibility that your ideas are wrong, or at least not absolutely right. According to Rogers, you must "run the risk of being changed yourself. You . . . might find yourself influenced in your attitudes or your personality."

Elaborate on the Value of Opposing Positions

In this part of your argument you will want to elaborate on which of your opponent's claims about the problem are correct. For example, if your roommate's messiness is driving you crazy but you still want to live with him or her, stress that cleanliness is not the be-all-and-end-all of human life. Commend your roommate for helping you focus on your studies and express appreciation for all of the times that he or she has pitched in to clean up. And, of course, you would also want to admit to a few annoying habits of your own, such as taking thirty-minute showers or forgetting to pay the phone bill. After viewing the problem from your roommate's perspective, you might even be willing to explore how your problem with compulsive neatness is itself a problem.

Show Instances When Your Assertions Are Valid

Once you have identified the problem in as nonthreatening a way as possible, established a fair-minded persona, and called for some level of consensus based on a "higher" interest, you have reached the most important stage in Rogerian negotiation: you can now present your position. At this point in your argument, you do not want to slap down a "But!" or "However!" and then come out of your corner punching. Remember the spirit of Rogerian problem solving: your ultimate goal is not to beat your audience, but to communicate with them and to promote a workable compromise. For example, in the sample argument with your roommate, rather than issuing an ultimatum such as "Unless you start picking up after yourself and doing your fair share of the housework, I'm moving out," you could say, "I realize that you view housekeeping as a less important activity than I do, but I need to let you know that I find your messiness to be highly stressful, and I'm wondering what kind of compromise we can make so we can continue living together." Yes, this statement carries an implied threat, but note how this sentence is framed positively and minimizes the emotional intensity inherent in the situation.

To achieve the nonthreatening tone needed to diffuse emotional situations, avoid exaggerating your claims or using biased, emotional language. Also, avoid attacking your audience's claims as exaggerated. Whenever you feel angry or defensive, take a deep breath and look for points in which you can agree with or understand your opponents. When you are really emotional about an issue, try to cool off enough to recognize where your language is loaded with explosive terms. To embrace the Rogerian approach, remember that you need to defuse your temper and set your pride and ego aside.

Present Your Claim in a Nonthreatening Way

Admittedly, it is difficult to substantiate an argument while acknowledging the value of competing positions. Yet if you have done an effective job in the early part of your essay, then your audience perceives you to be a reasonable person—someone worth listening to. Consequently, you should not sell yourself short when presenting your position.

Because of the emotionally charged context of your communication situation, you still need to maintain the same open-minded persona that you established in the introductory paragraphs. Although your main focus in this section is to develop the validity of your claim, you can maintain your fair-minded persona by recalling significant counterarguments and by elaborating on a few limitations of your claim. You can also remind your readers that you are not expecting them to accept your claim completely. Instead, you are merely attempting to show that under certain circumstances your position is valid.

Search for a Compromise and Call for a Higher Interest

Near the conclusion of your essay, you may find it useful to encourage your audience to seek a compromise with you under a call for a "higher interest." For example, if you were writing an editorial in an Israeli newspaper that called for setting aside some of the Gaza territory for an independent Palestinian state, your introduction might sympathetically explore all of the Israeli blood that has been lost since the Gaza was seized in the Seven Day War. Then you could address the "eye-for-an-eye" mentality that has characterized this problem. Perhaps you could soften your readers' thoughts about this problem by mentioning the number of Arabs who have died. Once you have developed your claim that some land should be set aside for the Palestinians, you might try to explore some of the "common ground" and call for Israelis and Arabs to seek out a higher goal expressed by both Jewish and Moslem peoples—that is, the desire for peace.

Writing Assignments

The Rogerian method of problem solving is designed for exploring controversial interpersonal, social, and political problems. You can use these techniques to help you begin or end a personal relationship or to help you raise your children. Knowledge of the Rogerian method can help you deal with instances of sexual discrimination in the workplace or help you encourage insecure authorities to take the action that you want. You could use Rogerian approaches to encourage your classmates and other students at your school to be more sympathetic about social problems such as poverty and ecological issues. To select a subject for a Rogerian analysis, try reviewing your journal and freewrite about significant interpersonal problems you have dealt with in your life. Below are a few questions that may help you identify a subject:

1. Do I want to write about an interpersonal issue? For example, am I having trouble communicating with someone? Could the breakdown be linked to my failure to employ Rogerian strategies? Are there any major differences in belief that I could bridge by communicating with him or her in a Rogerian way?

2. Do I want to write about a social or political problem? Are there any on-campus or work-related problems that I wish to explore? For example, am I worried by an important national issue such as the federal deficit? Or could I promote harmony in a local or campus conflict?

3. Are there any sports-related topics that I could tackle? For example, do I want to convince skiers that short skis have carved up the mountain in an ugly way? Do I want to persuade tennis players that we need to throw away the wide-body power rackets and go back to the days of wooden rackets because power tennis is killing finesse tennis?

4. Consider playing the role of a marketing executive. Find a new product that you believe is superior to an established product and then write some advertising copy that explains why people should shift their loyalty to the new product.

Prewriting and Drafting Strategies

Analyze Your Communication Situation

To help you get a handle on which claims you are willing to relinquish and which you wish to negotiate, write a profile of your anticipated audience. Because awareness of the opinions and fears of your audience is so crucial to successfully negotiating differences among competing positions, you need to try to "become" your audience. As usual, this process involves asking, "What do my readers believe and know about the subject? Why do they think and feel my position is wrong?" Ideally, this process extends beyond merely considering your audience's needs to setting aside your thoughts and feelings and embracing the opposition's notions about the subject.

After you have gotten "under the skin" of your audience, freewrite an essay about your subject from their perspective. Doing this in a Rogerian way means that you truly challenge your own beliefs and present your opponent's viewpoints as strongly as you would your own. If you find yourself unwilling to explore the strengths of your opponent's position, then you should select a new subject.

Write an Outline

After freewriting about your opponent's positions as if they were your own, you will probably have excellent ideas about how best to shape your essay. You may find it useful to jot down your objectives as suggested in the following outline. Remember, though, don't let the outline control your thoughts. If insights occur while you are writing, experiment with them.

I. Explain the issue's significance and scope.
   A.
   B.
   C.
II. In what ways are the major assumptions of the opposing position valid?
   A.
   B.
   C.
III. In what ways are your assumptions invalid and valid?
   A.
   B.
   C.
IV. What consensus can you establish?
   A.
   B.
   C.

Revising and Editing Strategies

As mentioned in past chapters, I strongly encourage you to refer to Chapters 11 and 12 when you are revising and editing drafts. Also, you should review your peers' and instructor's comments about earlier reports that you have written. By analyzing the strengths and weaknesses that your classmates and instructor have identified in past papers, you can know what special problems you should look for when evaluating your persuasive essay. As always, give yourself as much time as possible between drafts. Below I have listed some questions that highlight special concerns you will need to address when writing your Rogerian essay.

Is the Subject Appropriate for a Rogerian Approach?

A day or so after you have completed the first draft of your essay, reread it from the perspective of your intended audience. To conduct an honest self-evaluation, try to answer the following questions:

1. In the introduction have I truly been open-minded? Have I thoroughly reviewed the strengths of my opponent's counterarguments? Have I honestly challenged the weaknesses of my own position?

2. How could I change the essay to make it less emotionally charged?

3. Are the transitions from the opposing position to my position as smooth as possible?

4. When I present my claims, do I sound informed, intelligent, compassionate? What additional data would help my readers better understand my position? Do I need more facts and figures? Can I incorporate more outside quotations to substantiate my argument?

5. Have I successfully limited my analysis and elaborated on one specific, significant claim? Have I presented my position clearly and accurately?

6. Is the compromise I have suggested reasonable? Can I be more original in my call for a higher interest?

Read Your Work Aloud

Before submitting your essay to your peers or teacher, read it aloud to yourself several times. As you read, make a note of passages that seem difficult to read or sound awkward. Question whether the tone in the paragraphs is appropriate, given your audience and purpose. For example, can you find any passages that sound insincere or condescending?

Share Your Work with People Who Disagree with You

Ask people with different viewpoints from yours to critique your work. Let them know that you are attempting to seek a compromise between your position and theirs and that you welcome their suggestions.

Do a Criteria-Based Evaluation

In addition to making notes on criticisms of your text and ideas for improving it, you may find the following criteria-based format a useful way of identifying and correcting any weaknesses in your peers' drafts or your own.

I. Rogerian Appeals

                                                  Low   Middle   High

    Author establishes an empathic persona and   1 2 3 4 5 6 7 8 9 10
avoids threatening challenges.

    Author clarifies instances in which opposing assertions are valid.

    Author shows instances when assertions are valid.

Author develops claim in as nonthreatening way as possible.

Author seeks compromise and calls for an higher interest.

	Low	Middle	High
II. Substantive Revision	1 2 3 4	5 6 7	8 9 10

The document is reader-based.

The tone is appropriate given the audience and purpose.

The document is organized and formatted effectively.

The paragraphs are coherent and cohesive.

	Low	Middle	High
III. Edited Document	1 2 3 4	5 6 7	8 9 10

Unnecessary jargon and awkward abstractions have been edited.

To be verbs have been eliminated.

A high verb-to-noun ratio has been established.

Strings of prepositions have been avoided.

The document has been edited for economy.

The document has been copyedited for grammatical, mechanical, and formatting errors.

Collaborating Strategies

The following essay exemplifies the power of peer groups to help authors overcome problems with their work. Before reading the comments of Tracey Williams's peers in response to her fourth draft of "A Passive Habit," consider what you would tell the author if she were in your group. You can then compare your advice with the suggestions that her peers actually gave her.

Revising a Student Essay in a Peer Review Workshop

Analysis of Communication Situation

Audience: I'm writing to smokers who are tired of being criticized for their smoking.

Purpose: I want smokers to better understand the dangers of passive smoke.

> **Message:** Although smokers have a legal right to smoke, they do not
> have a legal write to injure non-smokers with their smoke.
> **Context:** My essay could appear as an editorial in a city or campus news-
> paper.

A Passive Habit (Fourth Draft)

Tracey Williams

I just returned from lunch with my father and grandmother. Emotionally, I 1
am happy. Physically, I feel lousy. My eyes sting and feel dry and so do my
sinuses. I greet my fiance who kisses me and then quickly pulls away, wrin-
kling his nose in distaste. "You smell awful!" he complains. I sigh and hurry
off to the shower. I took one only three hours ago, but my fiance is right: I
smell as if I have attended a bonfire rather than a family lunch. This scene
isn't new to me. My father and grandmother are chain smokers.

Most smokers are probably as sick of hearing complaints about their 2
smoking as the non-smokers are about the smoke. But a fact is a fact. Smoking is the leading cause of preventable illness and death in this country. Each
year there are almost a million smoking-related deaths. Cigarette smoke is a
killer because it is a poison. According to Watson, cigarettes contain almost
five thousand chemicals. Tar and nicotine are commonly known, but how
many smokers are aware that cigarettes also contain formaldehyde, radon
gas, and carbon monoxide? Heavy smokers are often pale and have dark cir-
cles under their eyes. They're being poisoned and they look it. They are also
slowly suffocating themselves since smoke causes the lungs to operate at a
very low capacity.

It is unfortunate that smokers are addicted to nicotine and must acquire 3
it through the harmful medium of smoking. More unfortunate is the fact
that those of us who do not smoke must also suffer from the very side effects
that the smokers have brought upon themselves. Second-hand smoke is
annoying as well as dangerous. Not only does it cling to everything it touches
(hair, clothes, curtains, lung cilia), but it also threatens passive smokers'
health. Because non-smokers don't have the "benefit" of being used to the
smoke, it affects them in ways not obvious to the smoker. How many smokers (and non-smokers) can remember the first time they tried smoking and
how it affected them physically? Did they feel nauseous? Lightheaded? Many
people cough and choke the first time that they inhale from a cigarette. The
passive smoker often deals with these "first experiences" again and again.
The smoker, used to the smoke, may not realize the consequences of his
habit on others.

I've always accepted smoking as part of my family's lifestyle. Although I 4
felt bad physically after being around the smoke that day, I reminded myself
it would pass. But the smoke was especially bad that day because we were

in a poorly ventilated area. After I came home, my sinuses started closing up. I have allergies, so I didn't worry about it at first. But, a few hours later the glands in my throat were swollen and by bed time I was sneezing my head off. I couldn't breathe and I had a sore throat. These symptoms were identical to the ones I had two weeks ago when I had a bad cold. I had just recovered a few days before my family arrived in town. But here was my cold, back in full force only because I spent two hours breathing second-hand smoke. I know that my cold returned as a result of passive smoking because this is not the first time it's happened to me.

I'm not the only one in my family suffering from the side effects of passive smoke. My sister and her husband smoke around their three small children. They live in a northern state and their house is often tightly closed for economical heating. One of my nephews has chronic asthma and another was recently hospitalized with pneumonia. At any given time of the year, one of the three kids has a cold. One of the worst facts about passive smoke is that much of it is unfiltered. Those who don't smoke still breathe the emission from the lit end of the cigarette. This smoke is unfiltered and is actually more poisonous than the smoke going through the filter into the smoker's lungs. Not only will my nephews grow up in a smoky environment that poisons them, but they will also have an increased chance of becoming smoking adults. Smoking parents may one day find themselves facing the same charges of child abuse as the mothers who drink and take drugs during their pregnancies. 5

Another personal effect of the smoke concerns my exercise program. Jogging has become a habit for me. It makes me feel great and I enjoy it immensely. But, I can't jog if I can't breathe. As I write this I am angry that I may not be able to run for a few days because of this cold. I'm angry because the air I had to breathe around my family is always full of smoke and caused me not only to have a cold relapse, but to sacrifice my exercise program as well. The average smoker is not able to endure cardiovascular stress. Passive smoking lessens the endurance of the non-smoker as well. 6

The issue of passive smoking has recently become a national concern. Surgeon General Koop dedicated much of his term to the pursuit of informing the public about the dangers of second-hand smoke. According to one spokesperson from the American Cancer Society whom I spoke with the other day, 35 percent of all women who died of lung cancer in 1988 were the non-smoking spouses of smokers. Other non-smoking spouses have a two to three times higher risk of lung cancer than in couples who don't smoke. General Koop also led a study on illness in the children of smokers. These youngsters have a higher incidence of colds, bronchial pneumonia, chronic asthma, and ear infections than the children of non-smokers. 7

Don't get me wrong; I'm not a prima donna who holds her nose each time someone lights up or who has "no smoking" signs posted everywhere. And I don't insist on sitting in the non-smoking section of a restaurant when I know someone in my party smokes. I don't ever pester the members of 8 my family to quit. In fact, I just quit myself. I stopped smoking only last year. After many years of smoking a pack a day, I think I'm qualified to present an argument about the disadvantages of smoking, the primary disadvantages being to the non-smoker. I have a strong objection to passive smoking because I chose to give up smoking and thus remove myself from the side effects. When I'm around smokers I end up feeling as I did when I smoked: tired, congested, and poisoned. I battled the habit successfully and I resent being exposed to the very thing I've struggled to stay away from.

Before I quit smoking I used to tell myself, "After I quit, I'll never be like   9 those prissy non-smokers who get on their soap box about how their rights are being violated." And I still won't do that. But as a non-smoker my point of view has changed slightly about the subject of rights. Smokers have the right to smoke just as non-smokers have the right to not smoke. But when second-hand smoke subjects the non-smokers to the same health risks associated with cigarette use, something must be said. Smoking in closed unventilated areas such as airplanes, trains, public restrooms, and offices should not be allowed unless there is a totally smoke-free area available for non-smokers. Smokers should carefully use discretion about where and when they smoke in public. If smokers expect their right to smoke to be protected, they must respect the rights of non-smokers.

--------------------------------- **Works Cited** ---------------------------------

American Cancer Society. Telephone interview. 5 Feb. 1990.
C. E. Mendez Foundation. Telephone interview. 5 Feb. 1990.
Watson, Tom. "The Filthy Habit: 40 Million Have Given Up Smoking." *Creative Loafing* 17 Feb. 1990: 10, 19.

Writers at Work: Round 1   Tracey began the peer-group conference by explaining that her purpose for writing the essay was to inform smokers about the dangers of their habit. Although the following is not a word-by-word transcription, it is fairly representative of the discussion that she had with her peers about revising her draft.

> "Look, guys," Tracey said, "I really want you to tear this piece apart. Last time I felt you all were too easy on me. But listen, I can take criticism. I know this piece needs it. I really want you to tear this essay apart, okay?"
>
> "Well, okay," Robert said. "So what's bothering you so much about it?"
>
> "I guess my biggest concern, I mean the thing I'd like you to look at most is whether or not I'm being as informative as I need to be. I guess I'm also worried about the tone. I mean, do I sound too angry?"
>
> "Well," Sarah said, "you've certainly given me the sense that you feel strongly about this issue, that you're committed to your subject and well informed."

"Thanks, I enjoyed writing this essay. Believe it or not, I used to smoke two packs a day."

"Yeah," Nancy added, "I found your piece to be informative and interesting. I never knew there were so many chemicals in cigarettes."

"Yeah, I thought it was really informative," Robert said, "but I'm not so sure that you're as focused as you need to be. In the beginning of your essay I thought you wanted smokers to quit and then by about page three I thought that you were mostly concerned with passive smoke. I don't think you should be so strong in the introduction if you only want smokers to be more sensitive about the dangers of passive smoking. I mean, if I were a smoker, I think I'd have a hard time swallowing all of the facts that you give in that second paragraph."

Larry rolled his eyes as if he thought Robert was crazy and said, "Hey, I think this paper is really a killer. I don't think it can be improved."

Tracey vigorously shook her head from side to side. "Well thanks, Larry," she said, "but I know it's still pretty rough. I really want you guys' criticism."

"Well, if you really want to know," said Sarah, "I think you sound too angry in this piece. Like in the eighth paragraph you say you're not a 'prima donna who holds her nose each time someone lights up,' but later in that same paragraph you say that you have 'a strong objection' to being exposed to passive smoke." Sarah pointed her finger at her copy of Tracey's essay and said, "In paragraph six, you certainly don't need to say that you're angry. That's obvious in the first paragraph when you say that you smell awful, like you've been around a bonfire."

"Wow, that helps. Now that you point it out, it's obvious to me."

Sarah said, "Well, maybe you shouldn't be writing a Rogerian paper. Maybe this subject makes you too angry for you to be sympathetic about your audience."

"Yeah, you might be right."

"Nah, I think this is a great topic for a Rogerian essay," Robert said. "The subject is controversial. And sometimes you do a good job at talking to your audience. Like I think it's real good when you say, 'Most smokers are probably sick of hearing complaints.' I just think you need more statements like that."

"Yeah, I think you're right. I don't know how I could have missed all this."

Robert drew a big box around the third paragraph and said, "You should probably take out this sentence that says, 'Second-hand smoke is annoying as well as dangerous.' I mean, I think it's good to be informative and all, but if I were a smoker I know I wouldn't want to hear in the second paragraph that a million people died last year from smoking. Anyway, I find that number hard to believe. Where did you get that statistic from?"

"I got that out of *Creative Loafing* magazine. Those statistics are just for the U.S."

"Well, you'd better document that source."

"Yeah, you're right. I've got to do that still."

In response to her peer-group conference, Tracey produced the following revised draft.

Passive Smoke (Final Draft)
Tracey Williams

As a cigarette smoker in America, do you think the world has gone mad? 1
Your once acceptable habit has become a social faux pas equivalent to belching loudly at your mother-in-law's dinner table. Our role models no longer smoke. Twenty years have passed since we've had a president and first lady who indulged in this habit. John Wayne, Bette Davis, Rod Serling, Kirk Douglas, Sean Connery, and countless others once freely imbibed without self-consciousness and guilt, on screen and off. Yet those days are gone for celebrities and common people alike.

The social acceptance of smoking has been in decline ever since the 2
Surgeon General announced that it was unhealthy. The American Heart and Lung Association and the American Cancer Society began a campaign against smoking. It's easy to understand and appreciate the concern of these organizations, but there has to be a limit to their "help." They sponsor tacky commercials that attempt to "guilt" the smoker into quitting. It is humiliating for a smoker to listen to a famous person declare that only losers smoke—particularly in the presence of family and friends. These ads are unfair and a violation to the smoker. If you can't smoke in your own home without being harassed, then where can you smoke? For the many smokers who are considerate and limit the amount they smoke in their households, these invasions of privacy are especially unjust.

The point often missed by anti-smoking activists is that smokers already 3
know the risks involved in their habit and don't need to be reminded via television commercials and various messages on cigarette packages. Many smokers who are cautious about their habit purposely smoke only at certain times. They use the habit as it was originally intended, as an occasional treat. These smokers limit themselves to one cigarette after a meal or perhaps when they come home from work. Is it fair to target them along with the inconsiderate chain-smoker? "Soap Box" non-smokers often see only the Big Picture—that is, in their view one smoker is as bad as another and smoking in public should be completely banned. These non-smokers can be adamant to the point that their self-righteousness seems more offensive than the smoke. Why did smoking suddenly become so unacceptable? How did smokers become the pariahs of the 90s?

The following facts, taken from an article by Tom Watson, may clarify 4
the reasons non-smokers are often adamant about controlling smoking ("The Filthy Habit: 40 Million Have Given Up Smoking," *Creative Loafing* 17 February 1990: 10, 19). Watson based the facts of his article on the findings from studies conducted at the University of Georgia and by the

Department of Agriculture. The studies revealed that passive smoke (the smoke from the lit cigarette) is much more harmful than previously believed. The most significant finding was that passive smoke is actually more poisonous than the smoke inhaled by the smoker. One of the worst things about passive smoke is that it is unfiltered and non-smokers breathe the emission from the lit end of the cigarette. Collectively, cigarette smoke contains formaldehyde, radon gas, and carbon monoxide, and the concentrations of carbon monoxide and nicotine in second-hand smoke are two to three times higher than in the smoke directly taken from the cigarette. Who can blame the non-smokers for not wanting to breathe smoky air in light of these facts?

There are other statistics that support the non-smoker's desire to not 5 breathe passive smoke. When I interviewed a volunteer at the C. E. Mendez Foundation (an organization similar to the American Cancer Society), I learned that 35 percent of all women who died of lung cancer in 1988 were the non-smoking spouses of smokers, and that 75 percent of all lung cancer deaths in women were smoke-related. The C. E. Mendez Foundation obtained these facts from studies led by former Surgeon General Koop. Also disclosed was the fact that non-smoking spouses have a two-to-three-times higher risk of lung cancer than in couples who don't smoke. The American Cancer Society has published a collection of literature also based on General Koop's findings. One of the subjects included in its work is a study on illness in the children of smokers. These youngsters have an increased incidence of colds, bronchial pneumonia, chronic asthma, and ear infections over the children of non-smokers.

I am a former smoker who held onto that habit for fourteen years. I aver- 6 aged at least a pack a day during that time. Since I have quit, I can attest to the effects of passive smoke. As a non-smoker, I no longer have the "benefit" of being used to the smoke. When I'm in a smoky room, I can tell right away that the smoke's affecting me. It's not a pleasant feeling. How many smokers (and non-smokers) can remember the first time they tried smoking and how it affected them physically? Did they feel nauseous? Lightheaded? Many people coughed and choked the first time they inhaled from a cigarette. The passive smoker (former smokers included) often has to deal with these "first experiences" again and again. The smoker, being used to the smoke, may not realize the consequences of his habit on others.

While it isn't fair that smokers are unmercifully harassed about a habit 7 that they should have the freedom to practice, it is equally unfair for non-smokers to suffer because of that habit. There's no reason why a compromise can't be reached. Non-smokers should limit their anti-smoking campaigns and smokers should be more considerate about where, when, and how often they imbibe. Smokers have the right to smoke and non-smokers have the right to not smoke. But when passive smoke subjects the non-smoker to the same health risks associated with cigarette use, can the non-smoker be blamed for protesting? Perhaps if smokers accept legislation against smoking in closed, unventilated areas such as airplanes, trains, public restrooms and offices, the non-smokers will back off. In return, harassing ads portraying smokers as less than socially acceptable can cease.

Works Cited

American Cancer Society. Telephone interview. 5 Feb. 1990.
C. E. Mendez Foundation. Telephone interview. 5 Feb. 1990.
Watson, Tom. "The Filthy Habit: 40 Million Have Given Up Smoking." *Creative Loafing* 17 Feb. 1990: 10, 19.

PEER REVIEW WORKSHOP

1. Has the author selected a topic that can be dealt with in a Rogerian way? What passages indicate sensitivity to opposing points of view? Can you identify any passages where the author appears to be coming on too strong, or does a spirit of fairness and a willingness to negotiate pervade the piece?

2. Do the introductory paragraphs introduce in a nonthreatening way the problem that needs to be solved?

3. What kind of persona do you perceive when you read the work? Does the author appear to be sensible, believable, benevolent? Does he or she seem to understand the complexity of the problem at hand?

4. What can the author do to improve the transitions between discussion of the readers' ideas and his or her own ideas?

5. When encouraging readers to move toward a compromise, does the author establish a higher goal or interest that can help unite the opposing factions and promote unity? Does the author provide a true compromise?

Additional Writing Sample

Martin Luther King, Jr., wrote the following letter to eight black Alabama clergymen in response to a letter they had written condemning his involvement in civil rights demonstrations in Birmingham. As this excerpt from their public letter suggests, the clergymen conceded that race relations needed to be improved in Birmingham, yet they considered the demonstrations to be "extreme measures" and asked King to work at ending the riots.

> We further strongly urge our own Negro community to withdraw support from these demonstrations, and to unite locally in working peacefully for a better Birmingham. When rights are constantly denied, a cause should be pressed in the courts and in negotiations among local leaders, and not in the streets. We appeal to both our white and Negro citizenry to observe the principles of law and order and common sense.

On April 12, 1963, King was arrested and jailed for his involvement in the nonviolent demonstrations. He wrote the following letter from his cell in the Birmingham jail.

Letter from Birmingham Jail*
Martin Luther King, Jr.

My Dear Fellow Clergymen,

While confined here in the Birmingham City Jail, I came across your recent   1 statement calling our present activities "unwise and untimely." Seldom, if ever, do I pause to answer criticism of my work and ideas. If I sought to answer all of the criticisms that cross my desk, my secretaries would be engaged in little else in the course of the day and I would have no time for constructive work. But since I feel that you are men of genuine good will and your criticisms are sincerely set forth, I would like to answer your statement in what I hope will be patient and reasonable terms.

I think I should give the reason for my being in Birmingham, since you   2 have been influenced by the argument of "outsiders coming in." I have the honor of serving as president of the Southern Christian Leadership Conference, an organization operating in every Southern state with headquarters in Atlanta, Georgia. We have some eighty-five affiliate organizations all across the South—one being the Alabama Christian Movement for Human Rights. Whenever necessary and possible we share staff, educational, and financial resources with our affiliates. Several months ago our local affiliate here in Birmingham invited us to be on call to engage in a nonviolent direct action program if such were deemed necessary. We readily consented and when the hour came we lived up to our promises. So I am here, along with several members of my staff, because we were invited here. I am here because I have basic organizational ties here. Beyond this, I am in Birmingham because injustice is here. Just as the eighth-century prophets left their little villages and carried their "thus saith the Lord" far beyond the boundaries of their home town, and just as the Apostle Paul left his little village of Tarsus and carried the gospel of Jesus Christ to practically every hamlet and city of the Graeco-Roman world, I too am compelled to carry the gospel of freedom beyond my particular home town. Like Paul, I must constantly respond to the Macedonian call for aid.

Moreover, I am cognizant of the interrelatedness of all communities and   3 states. I cannot sit idly by in Atlanta and not be concerned about what happens in Birmingham. Injustice anywhere is a threat to justice everywhere. We are caught in an inescapable network of mutuality tied in a single garment of destiny. Whatever affects one directly affects all indirectly. Never again can we afford to live with the narrow, provincial "outside agitator" idea. Anyone who lives inside the United States can never be considered an outsider anywhere in this country.

You deplore the demonstrations that are presently taking place in Birm- 4 ingham. But I am sorry that your statement did not express a similar concern for the conditions that brought the demonstrations into being. I am sure that each of you would want to go beyond the superficial social analyst who looks merely at effects, and does not grapple with underlying causes. I would not hesitate to say that it is unfortunate that so-called demonstrations are taking place in Birmingham at this time, but I would say in more emphatic terms that it is even more unfortunate that the white power structure of this city left the Negro community with no other alternative.

In any nonviolent campaign there are four basic steps: (1) collection of 5 the facts to determine whether injustices are alive; (2) negotiation; (3) self-purification; and (4) direct action. We have gone through all of these steps in Birmingham. There can be no gainsaying of the fact that racial injustice engulfs this community. Birmingham is probably the most thoroughly segregated city in the United States. Its ugly record of police brutality is known in every section of this country. Its unjust treatment of Negroes in the courts is a notorious reality. There have been more unsolved bombings of Negro homes and churches in Birmingham than any city in this nation. These are the hard, brutal, and unbelievable facts. On the basis of these conditions Negro leaders sought to negotiate with the city fathers. But the political leaders consistently refused to engage in good faith negotiation.

Then came the opportunity last September to talk with some of the lead- 6 ers of the economic community. In these negotiating sessions certain promises were made by the merchants—such as the promise to remove the humiliating racial signs from the stores. On the basis of these promises Reverend Shuttlesworth and the leaders of the Alabama Christian Movement for Human Rights agreed to call a moratorium on any type of demonstrations. As the weeks and months unfolded we realized that we were the victims of a broken promise. The signs remained. As in so many experiences of the past, we were confronted with blasted hopes, and the dark shadow of a deep disappointment settled upon us. So we had no alternative except that of preparing for direct action, whereby we would present our very bodies as a means of laying our case before the conscience of the local and national community. We were not unmindful of the difficulties involved. So we decided to go through a process of self-purification. We started having workshops on nonviolence and repeatedly asked ourselves the questions, "Are you able to accept blows without retaliating?" "Are you able to endure the ordeals of jail?"

We decided to set our direct action program around the Easter season, 7 realizing that, with the exception of Christmas, this was the largest shopping period of the year. Knowing that a strong economic withdrawal program would be the by-product of direct action, we felt that this was the best time to bring pressure on the merchants for the needed changes. Then it occurred to us that the March election was ahead, and so we speedily decided to postpone action until after election day. When we discovered that Mr. [Eugene "Bull"] Connor was in the run-off, we decided again to postpone action so that the demonstrations could not be used to cloud the issues. At this time we agreed to begin our nonviolent witness the day after the run-off.

This reveals that we did not move irresponsibly into direct action. We 8 too wanted to see Mr. Connor defeated; so we went through postponement after postponement to aid in this community need. After this we felt that direct action could be delayed no longer.

You may well ask, "Why direct action? Why sit-ins, marches, etc.? Isn't 9 negotiation a better path?" You are exactly right in your call for negotiation. Indeed, this is the purpose of direct action. Nonviolent direct action seeks to create such a crisis and establish such creative tension that a community that has constantly refused to negotiate is forced to confront the issue. It seeks so to dramatize the issue that it can no longer be ignored.

I just referred to the creation of tension as a part of the work of the 10 nonviolent resister. This may sound rather shocking. But I must confess that I am not afraid of the word tension. I have earnestly worked and preached against violent tension, but there is a type of constructive nonviolent tension that is necessary for growth. Just as Socrates felt that it was necessary to create a tension in the mind so that individuals could rise from the bondage of myths and half-truths to the unfettered realm of creative analysis and objective appraisal, we must see the need of having nonviolent gadflies to create the kind of tension in society that will help men rise from the dark depths of prejudice and racism to the majestic heights of understanding and brotherhood. So the purpose of the direct action is to create a situation so crisis-packed that it will inevitably open the door to negotiation. We, therefore, concur with you in your call for negotiation. Too long has our beloved Southland been bogged down in the tragic attempt to live in monologue rather than dialogue.

One of the basic points in your statement is that our acts are untimely. 11 Some have asked, "Why didn't you give the new administration time to act?" The only answer that I can give to this inquiry is that the new administration must be prodded about as much as the outgoing one before it acts. We will be sadly mistaken if we feel that the election of Mr. [Albert] Boutwell will bring the millennium to Birmingham. While Mr. Boutwell is much more articulate and gentle than Mr. Connor, they are both segregationists dedicated to the task of maintaining the status quo. The hope I see in Mr. Boutwell is that he will be reasonable enough to see the futility of massive resistance to desegregation. But he will not see this without pressure from the devotees of civil rights.

My friends, I must say to you that we have not made a single gain in civil 12 rights without determined legal and nonviolent pressure. History is the long and tragic story of the fact that privileged groups seldom give up their privileges voluntarily. Individuals may see the moral light and voluntarily give up their unjust posture; but as Reinhold Niebuhr has reminded us, groups are more immoral than individuals.

We know through painful experience that freedom is never voluntarily 13 given by the oppressor; it must be demanded by the oppressed. Frankly I have never yet engaged in a direct action movement that was "well timed," according to the timetable of those who have not suffered unduly from the disease of segregation. For years now I have heard the word "Wait!" It rings in the ear of every Negro with a piercing familiarity. This "wait" has almost always meant "never." It has been a tranquilizing Thalidomide, relieving the emotional stress for a moment, only to give birth to an ill-formed infant of frustration. We must come to see with the distinguished jurist of yesterday that "justice too long delayed is justice denied." We have waited for more than 340 years for our constitutional and God-given rights. The nations of Asia and Africa are moving with jet-like speed toward the goal of political independence, and we still creep at horse and buggy pace toward the gaining of a cup of coffee at a lunch counter.

I guess it is easy for those who have never felt the stinging darts of segre- 14 gation to say wait. But when you have seen vicious mobs lynch your mothers and fathers at will and drown your sisters and brothers at whim; when you have seen hate-filled policemen curse, kick, brutalize, and even kill your black brothers and sisters with impunity; when you see the vast majority of your twenty million Negro brothers smothering in an air-tight cage of poverty in the midst of an affluent society; when you suddenly find your tongue twisted and your speech stammering as you seek to explain to your six-year-old daughter why she can't go to the public amusement park that has just been advertised on television, and see tears welling up in her little eyes when she is told that Funtown is closed to colored children, and see the depressing clouds of inferiority begin to form in her little mental sky, and see her begin to distort her little personality by unconsciously developing a bitterness toward white people; when you have to concoct an answer for a five-year-old son asking in agonizing pathos: "Daddy, why do white people treat colored people so mean?"; when you take a cross country drive and find it necessary to sleep night after night in the uncomfortable corners of your automobile because no motel will accept you; when you are humiliated day in and day out by nagging signs reading "white" men and "colored"; when your first name becomes "nigger" and your middle name becomes "boy" (however old you are) and your last name becomes "John" and when your wife and mother are never given the respected title "Mrs."; when you are harried by day and haunted by night by the fact that you are a Negro, living constantly at tip-toe stance never quite knowing what to expect next, and plagued with inner fears and outer resentments; when you are forever fighting a degenerating sense of "nobodiness"—then you will understand why we find it difficult to wait. There comes a time when the cup of endurance runs over, and men are no longer willing to be plunged into an abyss of injustice where they experience the bleakness of corroding despair. I hope, sirs, you can understand our legitimate and unavoidable impatience.

You express a great deal of anxiety over our willingness to break laws. 15 This is certainly a legitimate concern. Since we so diligently urge people to obey the Supreme Court's decision of 1954 outlawing segregation in the public schools, it is rather strange and paradoxical to find us consciously breaking laws. One may well ask, "How can you advocate breaking some laws and obeying others?" The answer is found in the fact that there are two types of laws: There are *just* laws and there are *unjust* laws. I would be the first to advocate obeying just laws. One has not only a legal but a moral responsibility to obey just laws. Conversely, one has a moral responsibility to disobey unjust laws. I would agree with Saint Augustine that "An unjust law is no law at all."

Now what is the difference between the two? How does one determine 16 when a law is just or unjust? A just law is a man-made code that squares with the moral law or the law of God. An unjust law is a mode that is out of harmony with the moral law. To put it in the terms of Saint Thomas Aquinas, an unjust law is a human law that is not rooted in eternal and natural law. Any law that uplifts human personality is just. Any law that degrades human personality is unjust.

All segregation statutes are unjust because segregation distorts the soul 17 and damages the personality. It gives the segregator a false sense of superiority and the segregated a false sense of inferiority. To use the words of Martin Buber, the great Jewish philosopher, segregation substitutes an "I-it" relationship for the "I-thou" relationship, and ends up relegating persons to the status of things. So segregation is not only politically, economically, and sociologically unsound, but it is morally wrong and sinful. Paul Tillich has said that sin is separation. Isn't segregation an existential expression of man's tragic separation, an expression of his awful estrangement, his terrible sinfulness? So I can urge men to obey the 1954 decision of the Supreme Court because it is morally right, and I can urge them to disobey segregation ordinances because they are morally wrong.

Let us turn to a more concrete example of just and unjust laws. An unjust 18 law is a code that a majority inflicts on a minority that is not binding on itself. This is *difference* made legal. On the other hand a just law is a code that a majority compels a minority to follow that it is willing to follow itself. This is *sameness* made legal.

Let me give another explanation. An unjust law is a code inflicted upon a 19 minority which that minority had no part in enacting or creating because they did not have the unhampered right to vote. Who can say the legislature of Alabama which set up the segregation laws was democratically elected? Throughout the state of Alabama all types of conniving methods are used to prevent Negroes from becoming registered voters and there are some counties without a single Negro registered to vote despite the fact that the Negro constitutes a majority of the population. Can any law set up in such a state be considered democratically structured?

These are just a few examples of unjust and just laws. There are some 20
instances when a law is just on its face but unjust in its application. For
instance, I was arrested Friday on a charge of parading without a permit.
Now there is nothing wrong with an ordinance which requires a permit for a
parade, but when the ordinance is used to preserve segregation and to deny
citizens the First Amendment privilege of peaceful assembly and peaceful
protest, then it becomes unjust.

I hope you can see the distinction I am trying to point out. In no sense 21
do I advocate evading or defying the law as the rabid segregationist would do.
This would lead to anarchy. One who breaks an unjust law must do it *openly*,
lovingly (not hatefully as the white mothers did in New Orleans when they
were seen on television screaming "nigger, nigger, nigger") and with a willingness to accept the penalty. I submit that an individual who breaks a law
that conscience tells him is unjust, and willingly accepts the penalty by staying in jail to arouse the conscience of the community over its injustice, is in
reality expressing the very highest respect for law.

Of course there is nothing new about this kind of civil disobedience. It 22
was seen sublimely in the refusal of Shadrach, Meshach, and Abednego to
obey the laws of Nebuchadnezzar because a higher moral law was involved. It
was practiced superbly by the early Christians who were willing to face hungry lions and the excruciating pain of chopping blocks before submitting to
certain unjust laws of the Roman Empire. To a degree academic freedom is a
reality today because Socrates practiced civil disobedience.

We can never forget that everything Hitler did in Germany was "legal" 23
and everything the Hungarian freedom fighters did in Hungary was "illegal."
It was "illegal" to aid and comfort a Jew in Hitler's Germany. But I am
sure that, if I had lived in Germany during that time, I would have aided and
comforted my Jewish brothers even though it was illegal. If I lived in a
Communist country today where certain principles dear to the Christian
faith are suppressed, I believe I would openly advocate disobeying these
antireligious laws.

I must make two honest confessions to you, my Christian and Jewish 24
brothers. First I must confess that over the last few years I have been gravely
disappointed with the white moderate. I have almost reached the regrettable
conclusion that the Negroes' great stumbling block in the stride toward freedom is not the White Citizens' "Counciler" or the Ku Klux Klanner, but the
white moderate who is more devoted to "order" than to justice; who prefers a
negative peace which is the absence of tension to a positive peace which is the
presence of justice; who constantly says "I agree with you in the goal you
seek, but I can't agree with your methods of direct action"; who paternalisti-
cally feels that he can set the timetable for another man's freedom; who lives
by the myth of time and who constantly advises the Negro to wait until a
"more convenient season." Shallow understanding from people of good
will is more frustrating than absolute misunderstanding from people of ill
will. Lukewarm acceptance is much more bewildering than outright rejection.

I had hoped that the white moderate would understand that law and 25 order exist for the purpose of establishing justice, and that when they fail to do this they become the dangerously structured dams that block the flow of social progress. I had hoped that the white moderate would understand that the present tension in the South is merely a necessary phase of the transition from an obnoxious negative peace, where the Negro passively accepted his unjust plight, to a substance-filled positive peace, where all men will respect the dignity and worth of human personality.

Actually, we who engage in nonviolent direct action are not the creators 26 of tension. We merely bring to the surface the hidden tension that is already alive. We bring it out in the open where it can be seen and dealt with. Like a boil that can never be cured as long as it is covered up but must be opened with all its pus-flowing ugliness to the natural medicines of air and light, injustice must likewise be exposed, with all of the tension its exposing creates, to the light of human conscience and the air of national opinion before it can be cured.

In your statement you asserted that our actions, even though peaceful, 27 must be condemned because they precipitate violence. But can this assertion be logically made? Isn't this like condemning the robbed man because his possession of money precipitated the evil act of robbery? Isn't this like condemning Socrates because his unswerving commitment to truth and his philosophical delvings precipitated the misguided popular mind to make him drink the hemlock? Isn't this like condemning Jesus because His unique God consciousness and never-ceasing devotion to His will precipitated the evil act of crucifixion? We must come to see, as Federal courts have consistently affirmed, that it is immoral to urge an individual to withdraw his efforts to gain his basic constitutional rights because the quest precipitates violence. Society must protect the robbed and punish the robber.

I had also hoped that the white moderate would reject the myth of time. 28 I received a letter this morning from a white brother in Texas which said: "All Christians know that the colored people will receive equal rights eventually, but is it possible that you are in too great of a religious hurry? It has taken Christianity almost two thousand years to accomplish what it has. The teachings of Christ take time to come to earth." All that is said here grows out of a tragic misconception of time. It is the strangely irrational notion that there is something in the very flow of time that will inevitably cure all ills. Actually time is neutral. It can be used either destructively or constructively. I am coming to feel that the people of ill will have used time much more effectively than the people of good will.

We will have to repent in this generation not merely for the vitriolic 29 words and actions of the bad people, but for the appalling silence of the good people. We must come to see that human progress never rolls in on wheels of inevitability. It comes through the tireless efforts and persistent work of men willing to be co-workers with God, and without this hard work time itself becomes an ally of the forces of social stagnation.

We must use time creatively, and forever realize that the time is always 30
ripe to do right. Now is the time to make real the promise of democracy, and
transform our pending national elegy into a creative psalm of brotherhood.
Now is the time to lift our national policy from the quicksand of racial injustice to the solid rock of human dignity.

You spoke of our activity in Birmingham as extreme. At first I was rather 31
disappointed that fellow clergymen would see my nonviolent efforts as those
of the extremist. I started thinking about the fact that I stand in the middle of
two opposing forces in the Negro community. One is a force of complacency
made up of Negroes who, as a result of long years of oppression, have been
so completely drained of self-respect and a sense of "somebodiness" that they
have adjusted to segregation, and of a few Negroes in the middle class who,
because of a degree of academic and economic security, and because at points
they profit by segregation, have unconsciously become insensitive to the
problems of the masses. The other force is one of bitterness and hatred and
comes perilously close to advocating violence. It is expressed in the various
black nationalist groups that are springing up over the nation, the largest and
best known being Elijah Muhammad's Muslim movement. This movement is
nourished by the contemporary frustration over the continued existence of
racial discrimination. It is made up of people who have lost faith in America,
who have absolutely repudiated Christianity, and who have concluded that
the white man is an incurable "devil."

I have tried to stand between these two forces saying that we need not 32
follow the "do-nothingism" of the complacent or the hatred and despair of
the black nationalist. There is the more excellent way of love and nonviolent
protest. I'm grateful to God that, through the Negro church, the dimension
of nonviolence entered our struggle. If this philosophy had not emerged I am
convinced that by now many streets of the South would be flowing with
floods of blood. And I am further convinced that if our white brothers dismiss us as "rabble rousers" and "outside agitators"—those of us who are
working through the channels of nonviolent direct action—and refuse to
support our nonviolent efforts, millions of Negroes, out of frustration and
despair, will seek solace and security in black nationalist ideologies, a development that will lead inevitably to a frightening racial nightmare.

Oppressed people cannot remain oppressed forever. The urge for free- 33
dom will eventually come. This is what has happened to the American
Negro. Something within has reminded him of his birthright of freedom;
something without has reminded him that he can gain it. Consciously and
unconsciously, he has been swept in by what the Germans call the *Zeitgeist*,
and with his black brothers of Africa, and his brown and yellow brothers of
Asia, South America, and the Caribbean, he is moving with a sense of cosmic
urgency toward the promised land of racial justice. Recognizing this vital
urge that has engulfed the Negro community, one should readily understand public demonstrations.

The Negro has many pent-up resentments and latent frustrations. He ³⁴ has to get them out. So let him march sometime; let him have his prayer pilgrimages to the city hall; understand why he must have sit-ins and freedom rides. If his repressed emotions do not come out in these nonviolent ways, they will come out in ominous expressions of violence. This is not a threat; it is a fact of history. So I have not said to my people, "Get rid of your discontent." But I have tried to say that this normal and healthy discontent can be channeled through the creative outlet of nonviolent direct action. Now this approach is being dismissed as extremist. I must admit that I was initially disappointed in being so categorized.

But as I continued to think about the matter I gradually gained a bit of ³⁵ satisfaction from being considered an extremist. Was not Jesus an extremist in love? "Love your enemies, bless them that curse you, pray for them that despitefully use you." Was not Amos an extremist for justice—"Let justice roll down like waters and righteousness like a mighty stream." Was not Paul an extremist for the gospel of Jesus Christ—"I bear in my body the marks of the Lord Jesus." Was not Martin Luther an extremist—"Here I stand; I can do none other so help me God." Was not John Bunyan an extremist—"I will stay in jail to the end of my days before I make a butchery of my conscience." Was not Abraham Lincoln an extremist—"This nation cannot survive half slave and half free." Was not Thomas Jefferson an extremist—"We hold these truths to be self-evident that all men are created equal."

So the question is not whether we will be extremist but what kind of ³⁶ extremist will we be. Will we be extremists for hate or will we be extremists for love? Will we be extremists for the preservation of injustice—or will we be extremists for the cause of justice? In that dramatic scene on Calvary's hill three men were crucified. We must never forget that all three were crucified for the same crime—the crime of extremism. Two were extremists for immorality, and thus fell below their environment. The other, Jesus Christ, was an extremist for love, truth, and goodness, and thereby rose above His environment. So, after all, maybe the South, the nation, and the world are in dire need of creative extremists.

I had hoped that the white moderate would see this. Maybe I was too ³⁷ optimistic. Maybe I expected too much. I guess I should have realized that few members of a race that has oppressed another race can understand or appreciate the deep groans and passionate yearnings of those that have been oppressed, and still fewer have the vision to see that injustice must be rooted out by strong, persistent, and determined action. I am thankful, however, that some of our white brothers have grasped the meaning of this social revolution and committed themselves to it. They are still all too small in quantity, but they are big in quality. Some like Ralph McGill, Lillian Smith, Harry Golden, and James Dabbs have written about our struggle in eloquent, prophetic, and understanding terms. Others have marched with us down nameless streets of the South. They have languished in filthy, roach-infested jails, suffering the abuse and brutality of angry policemen who see them as "dirty nigger lovers." They, unlike so many of their moderate brothers and sisters, have recognized the urgency of the moment and sensed the need for powerful "action" antidotes to combat the disease of segregation. . . .

. . . I have no fear about the outcome of our struggle in Birmingham, 38 even if our motives are presently misunderstood. We will reach the goal of freedom in Birmingham and all over the nation, because the goal of America is freedom. Abused and scorned though we may be, our destiny is tied up with the destiny of America.

Before the pilgrims landed at Plymouth, we were here. Before the pen 39 of Jefferson etched across the pages of history the majestic words of the Declaration of Independence, we were here. For more than two centuries our foreparents labored in this country without wages; they made cotton "king"; and they built the homes of their masters in the midst of brutal injustice and shameful humiliation—and yet out of a bottomless vitality they continued to thrive and develop. If the inexpressible cruelties of slavery could not stop us, the opposition we now face will surely fail. We will win our freedom because the sacred heritage of our nation and the eternal will of God are embodied in our echoing demands.

I must close now. But before closing I am impelled to mention one other 40 point in your statement that troubled me profoundly. You warmly commended the Birmingham police force for keeping "order" and "preventing violence." I don't believe you would have so warmly commended the police force if you had seen its angry violent dogs literally biting six unarmed, nonviolent Negroes. I don't believe you would so quickly commend the policemen if you would observe their ugly and inhuman treatment of Negroes here in the city jail; if you would watch them push and curse old Negro women and young Negro girls; if you would see them slap and kick old Negro men and young Negro boys; if you will observe them, as they did on two occasions, refuse to give us food because we wanted to sing our grace together. I'm sorry that I can't join you in your praise for the police department.

It is true that they have been rather disciplined in their public handling 41 of the demonstrators. In this sense they have been rather publicly "nonviolent." But for what purpose? To preserve the evil system of segregation. Over the last few years I have consistently preached that nonviolence demands that the means we use must be as pure as the ends we seek. So I have tried to make it clear that it is wrong to use immoral means to attain moral ends. But now I must affirm that it is just as wrong, or even more so, to use moral means to preserve immoral ends. Maybe Mr. Connor and his policemen have been rather publicly nonviolent, as Chief Prichett was in Albany, Georgia, but they have used the moral means of nonviolence to maintain the immoral end of flagrant racial injustice. T. S. Eliot has said that there is no greater treason than to do the right deed for the wrong reason.

I wish you had commended the Negro sit-inners and demonstrators of 42 Birmingham for their sublime courage, their willingness to suffer, and their amazing discipline in the midst of the most inhuman provocation. One day the South will recognize its real heroes. They will be the James Merediths, courageously and with a majestic sense of purpose, facing jeering and hostile mobs and the agonizing loneliness that characterizes the life of the pioneer. They will be old, oppressed, battered Negro women, symbolized in a 72-year-old woman of Montgomery, Alabama, who rose up with a sense of dignity and with her people decided not to ride the segregated buses, and responded to one who inquired about her tiredness with ungrammatical profundity: "My feets is tired, but my soul is rested." They will be young high school and college students, young ministers of the gospel and a host of the elders, courageously and nonviolently sitting in at lunch counters and willingly going to jail for conscience sake. One day the South will know that when these disinherited children of God sat down at lunch counters they were in reality standing up for the best in the American dream and the most sacred values in our Judeo-Christian heritage, and thus carrying our whole nation back to great wells of democracy which were dug deep by the founding fathers in the formulation of the Constitution and the Declaration of Independence.

Never before have I written a letter this long (or should I say a book?). 43 I'm afraid that it is much too long to take your precious time. I can assure you that it would have been much shorter if I had been writing from a comfortable desk, but what else is there to do when you are alone for days in the dull monotony of a narrow jail cell other than write long letters, think strange thoughts, and pray long prayers?

If I have said anything in this letter that is an overstatement of the truth 44 and is indicative of an unreasonable impatience, I beg you to forgive me. If I have said anything in this letter that is an understatement of the truth and is indicative of my having a patience that makes me patient with anything less than brotherhood, I beg God to forgive me.

I hope this letter finds you strong in the faith. I also hope that circum- 45 stances will soon make it possible for me to meet each of you, not as an integrationist or a civil rights leader, but as a fellow clergyman and a Christian brother. Let us all hope that the dark clouds of racial prejudice will soon pass away and the deep fog of misunderstanding will be lifted from our fear-drenched communities and in some not too distant tomorrow the radiant stars of love and brotherhood will shine over our great nation with all of their scintillating beauty.

Yours for the cause of
Peace and Brotherhood,

—M. L. KING, JR.

Critical Reading Questions

1. In what ways does King respond to the egos, beliefs, educational background, assumptions, and opinions of his audience?

2. How does the tone of this letter shift from the introduction to the conclusion? What examples, images, or words does King use to establish his tone?

3. What consensus and common ground does King appear to be arguing for in his letter? What specific passages call for consensus?

4. What distinction does King make between "just" and "unjust" laws?

5. How has King organized his introductory and concluding paragraphs to account for his readers' emotions? How do you suspect this letter would challenge and perhaps change the minds of King's readers regarding racial discrimination and nonviolent protest?

Evaluating Criticism

Reflect for a few moments on your growth as a writer when your teacher returns your Rogerian report to you. To help put your role as apprentice in perspective, you may find it useful to consider the following questions in your Writing and Research Notebook:

1. What have you learned about yourself as a writer as a result of writing your Rogerian essay?

2. In what ways has your knowledge of Rogerian negotiation and problem solving influenced how you will make oral and written arguments in the future? When writing this report, did you find your original point of view softening?

3. Based on your peers' and teacher's responses to your work, what goals will you set for your next writing assignment?

Writing Reports Based on Library Research

Even students who say they detest research assignments often conduct research on a daily basis without calling it such. Imagine, for example, the steps a man goes through when he sees a woman he would like to meet at a party. Even though he may associate the term "research" with the boring pursuit of intricate information, his desire to meet the woman may transform him into a superb researcher. Rather than immediately approaching the woman and running the risk of being shot down, he may run reconnaissance. In other words, he may ask his friends, "Who's that woman? What's her name, her major? Where does she work? Where is she from? Is she dating anyone?"

Whenever you ask questions, you are conducting research. For instance, an intelligent consumer doesn't buy a car simply because she loves the paint job. Instead, she talks with her friends who have purchased the same car or who know people who own one. She studies recent copies of *Consumer Reports, Car and Driver,* or similar periodicals, to check on repair records and driver satisfaction. To ensure that she gets the best price, she visits dealerships to compare figures, option packages, and service. She test drives different models. This is all research.

In this chapter, I explore how to develop a research question; how to organize documents based on research; how to quote, paraphrase, and summarize secondary sources; and how to format research reports. If you are unfamiliar with how to use general reference encyclopedias, the library card catalog, periodical indexes, or on-line and CD-ROM databases, you should consult the latter half of Chapter 2. (Chapter 2 also reviews the Modern Language Association guidelines for citing sources.)

Writing Samples

The following essay, "Formal Equal Opportunity," is the first chapter of Roy L. Brooks' thought-provoking book, *Understanding the American Race Problem.* Like most other introductory chapters, the intention of this opening is to introduce the book's subject and to engage readers' interests. As you review this sample, consider how Brooks' use of secondary sources contributes to his tone.

Incidentally, because this book was published by the University of California Press, which requires the Chicago Style of Documentation, the sources cited are not listed in accordance with the MLA guidelines discussed in Chapter 2. While the Chicago style differs from the MLA style in that footnote numbers are used instead of parenthetical citations, it is similar to the MLA in that it provides all of the information readers need to track down original sources—that is, the author's name, the title of the publication, the place of publication, and the date of publication. As mentioned in Chapter 2, the MLA, APA, and Chicago styles are the most common, yet there are more than 350 other style guidelines used in various academic disciplines.

Formal Equal Opportunity*

Roy L. Brooks

Formal equal opportunity is the nation's fundamental public policy on civil 1 rights. Like its predecessor, the separate-but-equal policy under Jim Crow,[1] formal equal opportunity seeks to regulate in rather broad terms the treatment that government and, to a lesser extent, private individuals accord to society's racial groups in relation to one another. Formal equal opportunity, in other words, determines the direction and tone of interracial relations in our society today.

Clearly, the past holds the key to understanding formal equal opportu- 2 nity. The meaning and significance of this civil rights policy are rooted in the community attitudes and beliefs that fueled Jim Crow's separate-but-equal policy, for formal equal opportunity is intended to run counter to Jim Crow and all that it represents.[2]

Those historical attitudes and beliefs, which helped to shape the devel- 3 opment of formal equal opportunity later on, are unmistakable. African Americans were regarded as an alien breed, lower than the entire community of whites. They were stereotyped as bestial, unteachable, uncouth, odious, and inferior to whites in every essential respect. In 1896 the Supreme Court in *Plessy v. Ferguson* determined that these community attitudes and beliefs had gelled into a strong community expectation concerning interracial relations: that the races were to be held separate but equal—meaning, of course, unequal.[3] The separate-but-equal policy, in which at least one prominent African American, Booker T. Washington, acquiesced, was thereby born; and a parade of laws designed to enforce it soon followed.[4] These laws, which condoned ubiquitous discrimination against African Americans and mandated "colored" and white public accommodations, schools, libraries, restrooms, drinking fountains, and so forth endured until formal equal opportunity became public policy in the 1950s and 1960s.[5]

* From *Rethinking the American Race Problem*, pp. 25–33. Copyright © 1990 The Regents of the University of California. Used with permission.

Formal equal opportunity is a first-time blend of African American and 4 white community expectations regarding interracial relations having the force of law. At its most basic level, formal equal opportunity can be defined as a civil rights policy in which African Americans and whites are held to be of equal legal status. The races are deemed to differ in no legally material way and are therefore entitled to equal legal treatment. Racism and its humiliating effects—segregation and discrimination—are no longer the official policies of or condoned by the government.[6]

Formal equal opportunity has certainly not reversed all the negative atti- 5 tudes that whites held toward African Americans during the Jim Crow era. Racism and stereotyping continue to thrive in our society. The survival of these racial attitudes does not, however, call into question the legitimacy of formal equal opportunity as our current public policy. So many social institutions and conventions have been built around formal equal opportunity that community expectations favoring this policy are clearly stronger and more consistent with our liberal democratic society than those favoring separate-but-equal treatment.

In *The Structure of Scientific Revolutions,* Thomas Kuhn demonstrates that 6 new paradigms often have a long and uncertain gestation period.[7] In the case of formal equal opportunity, the first serious indication that it might replace separate-but-equal as the nation's civil rights policy came during World War II. President Franklin D. Roosevelt issued Executive Order 8802 on June 25, 1941, which (in what has become standard legal jargon for creating formal equal opportunity rules of law) "prohibited discrimination on the basis of race, creed, [or] color" in certain areas of federal employment, vocational training programs administered by federal agencies, and the national defense industry. Executive Order 8802 also created a federal agency, called the Fair Employment Practices Committee, that was authorized to receive and investigate charges of employment discrimination, redress proven grievances, and make recommendations to carry out the purposes of the executive order.[8]

Further indications of the advent of formal equal opportunity appeared 7 in the military itself during the Second World War. Before the war, African Americans in the armed services had been confined to segregated units and assigned to noncombat, low status jobs, usually in labor details. African American soldiers during World War I, for example, were often trained in the United States using broomsticks as weapons; they fought gallantly in Europe, but as part of the French, not the American, armed forces. The experiences of these soldiers, in other words, reflected the overall experience of African Americans under Jim Crow. By the end of World War II, however, the army had desegregated most of its officer candidate schools, although Army Air Corps training was still segregated; the navy had its first African American commissioned officer, although African American sailors generally were permitted to serve on ships only as mess stewards; and the Marine Corps, which had been exclusively white since the late eighteenth century, enlisted African Americans but assigned them to segregated units.[9]

Although racial progress in the military during World War II was minor, 8
matters were greatly improved by the time of the Korean War, when African
Americans fought in desegregated units in all branches of the service. This
turn of events was the direct result of Executive Order 9981, signed by President Harry Truman on July 26, 1948, which required "equality of treatment
and opportunity for all persons in the armed services without regard to race,
color, religion, or national origin." A companion order, Executive Order
9980, signed on the same day, brought formal equal opportunity to most
areas within the federal government's civilian departments.[10]

In bringing about these early promulgations of formal equal opportu- 9
nity, however, the confluence of several domestic and international conditions was more important than the altruism of lawmakers. Demographic
changes in the industrialized North were crucial. Between 1940 and 1944,
470,000 African Americans moved from the rural regions of the South to the
urban areas of the North looking for better jobs and better racial relations.
For the first time, most African Americans lived in cities rather than in the
rural South. This massive migration placed desegregative pressures on
employment markets in the cities and, most important, provided a welcome
supply of labor for hungry civilian industries supporting the war effort.[11]

The war itself was an important motivation for the executive orders 10
issued by Roosevelt and Truman. Fighting for democracy abroad made it
increasingly difficult to defend racial oppression at home. African Americans,
who felt the contradiction intensely, applied increasing pressure on government officials through demonstrations, marches, and other forms of protests.
Union leader A. Philip Randolph's threatened march on Washington in
1940, which helped to persuade Roosevelt to issue Executive Order 8802, is
an example of the new activism that took hold of African Americans. The
success of this activism also served to convince the followers of Booker T.
Washington, who died in 1915, that it was time to jettison their support for
separate-but-equal and to embrace the more assertive civil rights policy, formal equal opportunity, advocated by such leaders as W. E. B. DuBois and
Randolph.[12]

Finally, the rise of Keynesian economics and the decline of laissez-faire 11
economics in the United States during the 1930s made government intervention schemes, such as formal equal opportunity, seem proper. Indeed, the
failure of laissez-faire government to prevent or to extricate the nation from
severe economic depression made government regulation of institutional
behavior seem not only legitimate but also necessary.[13]

Formal equal opportunity during the war years was but a community 12
impulse struggling to become a public policy, however. Separate-but-equal
was still the dominant community value—it was still "law"—although it had
been significantly vitiated.

On May 17, 1954, formal equal opportunity came of age when the 13
Supreme Court handed down its momentous decision in the cases consolidated under *Brown v. Board of Education*.[14] Against the backdrop of all the

pressures that had caused Roosevelt and Truman to establish pockets of formal equal opportunity in selected areas of American life, and with the momentum of a line of its own cases chipping away at separate-but-equal,[15] the Supreme Court in *Brown I* took a decisive turn for the better in the government's approach to race relations. *Brown I* was the first act of government to make the ideal of racial equality—the push for racial inclusiveness—a constitutional imperative and, hence, unequivocally the official civil rights policy of the United States. In *Brown I*, a unanimous Supreme Court promulgated, as the Court itself would later say, "the fundamental [policy] that racial discrimination in public education is unconstitutional" and declared that "[a]ll provisions of federal, state, or local law requiring or permitting such discrimination must yield to this [policy]."[16]

Although *Brown I* dealt solely with the issue of public education, the fact that for the first time the Supreme Court had construed the Constitution, the nation's legal infrastructure, to require nonracial access to such an essential societal resource would inevitably project a towering shadow over virtually every aspect of interracial relations in this country. Indeed, *Brown I* has been credited with engendering "a social upheaval the extent and consequences of which cannot even now be measured with certainty" and with changing the *legal* status of African Americans from mere supplicants "seeking, pleading, begging to be treated as full-fledged members of the human race" to persons entitled to equal treatment under the law.[17] 14

In the years following *Brown I*, courts and legislatures identified and accentuated two major operational tenets derived from formal equal opportunity. These tenets have guided the way legal institutions and the community at large have applied this policy since *Brown I*. Today, formal equal opportunity is often defined in terms of these operational tenets. 15

The first is racial omission, what some might call color blindness or a race-neutral approach. Racial omission may be seen, in some respects, as a restatement of the fundamental meaning of formal equal opportunity, discussed earlier in this chapter—equal legal status and treatment. Racial omission is the belief that racial differences should be ignored and omitted from legal consideration. Rules of law and practices regulating access to education, employment, housing, and other social resources must be formulated without regard to race or racial dynamics. Members of all racial groups are entitled to be treated the same in all essential respects by the government. Accordingly, white Americans may not receive any opportunities not also available to racial minorities, and vice versa. 16

Racial integration is the sibling tenet of racial omission. Racial integration is racial mixing. It is simply any governmental policy that mandates or encourages a physical merger or juxtaposition of various racial groups. If the government favors racial integration, it necessarily must disfavor racial separation. Both policies cannot be promoted simultaneously. 17

Racial integration should be contrasted with desegregation. Desegregation is the removal of legal restraints on one's actions or designations placed 18 on one's status that were intended to stigmatize. The removal of these government-imposed conditions permits a group or its members to choose to go their separate or integrated ways. In this sense, it can be said that racial integration presupposes desegregation.

There is also a sense in which racial omission presupposes desegregation. No government could logically or successfully operate a public policy that mandates the omission of race from legal considerations without first (or at least simultaneously) removing legal designations designed to exclude and stigmatize. The failure to do so would at worst create governmental dysfunction and at best engender cognitive dissonance among the public. 19

The ultimate purpose of formal equal opportunity is to change our society from one marked by racial exclusivity to one characterized by racial inclusion. This fundamental civil rights policy seeks to bring African Americans into the mainstream of American society, to make them first-class citizens. Racial omission and racial integration are simply specific strategies or vehicles for engendering real opportunities for racial inclusion.[18] 20

The Civil Rights Act of 1964, the Voting Rights Act of 1965, and the Fair Housing Act of 1968 are the most significant federal rules of law implementing these two strategies.[19] More sweeping than any other piece of civil rights legislation in American history, the 1964 Civil Rights Act has eleven titles, each of which prohibits discrimination "on the basis of race or color" in a major sector of American life: voting (Title I), public accommodations (Title II), public education (Title IV), and employment (Title VII), among others. The 1965 Voting Rights Act vastly improves the voting protections offered by Title I of the 1964 Civil Rights Act (which mainly establishes standards applicable to voter registration) by banning all forms of racial discrimination in voting, from literacy tests to complex schemes of vote dilution, and by enforcing these rights with powerful remedies. Finally, the 1968 Fair Housing Act makes it illegal for certain property owners, real estate agencies, and lenders to discriminate "on the basis of race or color" in the sale or rental of housing. 21

But after all the civil rights laws and passions promoting formal equal opportunity since *Brown I*, it is nevertheless true that millions of African Americans are still living a life that in many ways reflects second-class citizenship, a life that in many respects is Jim Crow in all but name. Class by class, African Americans continue to shoulder more than their fair share of societal hardships such as racial discrimination, poor public schooling, and poverty. Why? 22

My answer to that question targets formal equal opportunity itself. I argue that there is a relationship between formal equal opportunity and intra-class racial disparity, the American race problem. Specifically, I argue that there is something dreadfully wrong about the way our fundamental civil rights policy has been *applied* since *Brown I*. 23

Some legal instrumentalists, particularly legal realists, would argue that formalism is what is wrong with formal equal opportunity, that this policy has not been grounded in the social reality it seeks to regulate. For example, 24 the late Judge Skelly Wright, one of the most influential modern legal realists, faulted those who would apply our civil rights law and policy in a way that is too concerned with abstractionism, deductive logic, and internal consistency.[20] Wright would advise judicial decision makers implementing formal equal opportunity to proceed from the Holmesian maxim concerning the content and growth of law—"The life of the law has not been logic; it has been experience"—rather than from the Langdellian syllogism:

> All P are M [principle of law from formal equal opportunity]
> No S are M [crucial facts of problem]
> Ergo, No S are P [authoritative decision][21]

Although decision makers, both judicial and nonjudicial, have not always 25 been attentive to socioeconomic reality when implementing formal equal opportunity, many of these decision makers, especially judges, do attempt to ground their decisions in that reality. And many of these individuals are generally supportive of civil rights. For example, the Supreme Court in *Bakke* sincerely tried to devise a remedy that could deal with the real-life obstacles that African American students continued to face in college admissions.[22]

The real problem with the application of formal equal opportunity has 26 less to do with formalism than with the degree of deference given to African Americans' view of reality. It is the lack of priority given to African American civil rights interests in the implementation of formal equal opportunity that is most at fault. Formal equal opportunity (through its operational tenets of racial omission and racial integration) gives low priority, little weight to African American rights interests at critical times, despite the fact that civil rights would seem to be the one arena in American society in which these interests, damaged for so long by earlier policies, should receive top priority.

With the increased class stratification in African American society since 27 the 1960s, various African American civil rights interests occasionally conflict. This, of course, can make it more difficult to emphasize or promote a particular interest. Yet in most instances, these civil rights interests are not contraposed, and the conundrum of which interest to promote does not usually present itself.

At this point, some may argue that formal equal opportunity never 28 sought to ensure equality of results, only equality of treatment by government.[23] My initial response to this argument is to recognize that formal equal opportunity has had a greater impact on African Americans at the normative level than at the ground level. In many respects, African Americans and whites are accorded equal treatment by government more in theory than in the reality of daily life. African Americans have certainly received a legalistic, formalistic type of equality. But that is a poor proxy for the real thing—an equal chance to improve or protect one's chances for worldly success and personal happiness.

This leads to a more substantial response to the argument. I fault formal 29 equal opportunity (or, more precisely, its implementation through racial omission and racial integration) for its inability to deliver equal opportunity for the races, not equal results. Coming out of the Jim Crow era, the government essentially had two choices concerning how to redress the racial disparity set in motion by centuries of unequal status and treatment. The first and more direct was simply to upgrade the living conditions of African Americans by, for example, providing housing or jobs in proportion to the racial group's percentage of the population. Although some deemed this tactic, equality of results, immoral because it undermined the principle of desert (for instance, qualified workers could be denied jobs because their employment would upset an employer's racially balanced work force), recent scholarship has demonstrated how some forms of equality of results might be morally defensible.[24]

Formal equal opportunity did not, in any event, represent this approach to the problem. Rather, it meant choosing a second, indirect strategy that focused on racial starting positions, attempting to provide African Americans with the opportunities necessary to gain parity with whites by such actions as proscribing employment discrimination and making available the means to enforce that prohibition—not a bad plan if properly implemented. 30

I contend, however, that formal equal opportunity is operationally flawed, even though it is conceptually sound; that although it was designed to level the playing field for African Americans and whites, too often it has done this only within the rarefied pages of the law books, not within the mundane living conditions of American society. To claim that the playing field should be level—that African Americans should have roughly the same opportunities as whites, in reality, to augment or preserve their socioeconomic position in society—is quite different from claiming that the results or the achievements of the competition should be equal. I make the former, not the latter, claim. 31

--------------------------------- Notes ---------------------------------

1. The origin of the term *Jim Crow* is lost in obscurity, as C. Vann Woodward points out in his book *The Strange Career of Jim Crow* (2d rev. ed. [New York: Oxford University Press, 1966], p. 7n). The words were first used in a song-and-dance score written in 1832. The term, however, is most often used to refer to the segregation statutes that began to appear in the South before the turn of the twentieth century. The large number, great detail, and effective enforcement of these statutes distinguish them from the black codes that followed the withdrawal of federal troops from the South in 1877, ending the Reconstruction era, and from the ubiquitous slave codes that regulated not only race relations inside the peculiar institution but also relations between whites and free or quasi-free African Americans in the North and South from the inception of American slavery. In the generic sense, Jim Crow refers to the system of discrimination and segregation laws born in the North, developed contemporaneously with slavery, and passed down in a variety of forms intergenerationally through the 1960s.

In this book, the term *Jim Crow* is used in a somewhat more specific sense. Most important, it does not encompass the separate-and-unequal policy that governed interracial relations prior to the "equality" amendments to the Constitution (the Thirteenth, Fourteenth, and Fifteenth amendments) and the "equality" laws enacted by Congress during Reconstruction. Rather, I use the term as coextensive with the separate-but-equal policy brought alive by the Supreme Court's interpretation of the Reconstruction amendments and statutes in the final decades of the nineteenth century. For this reason, *Plessy v. Ferguson* (163 U.S. 537 [1896]), which, more than any other Supreme Court case, institutionalized the separate-but-equal policy, is an appropriate historical "starting date" for Jim Crow.

See Woodward, *Strange Career of Jim Crow*, chaps. 1–3; Franklin, *From Slavery to Freedom*, chaps. 6–19; Derrick A. Bell, Jr., *Race, Racism, and American Law*, 2d ed. (Boston: Little, Brown, 1980), pp. 364–379; Roy L. Brooks, "Use of the Civil Rights Acts of 1866 and 1871 to Redress Employment Discrimination," *Cornell Law Review* 62 (1977): 258, 261–266. On the subject of Reconstruction, see, e.g., Eric Foner, *Reconstruction: America's Unfinished Revolution, 1863–1877* (New York: Harper and Row, 1988).

2. For extensive discussions of the transition from a separate-but-equal public policy to one of formal equal opportunity, see Williams, *Eyes on the Prize*; Richard Kluger, *Simple Justice* (New York: Alfred A. Knopf, 1976); Woodward, *Strange Career of Jim Crow*.

As used in this chapter, the term *community* means more than just a neighborhood or a physical locality; it refers to a society or body of people. For further discussion of this concept, see, e.g., *In re Huss*, 126 N.Y. 537, 27 N.E. 784 (1891).

3. *Plessy v. Ferguson*, 163 U.S. 537 (1896).

4. For further discussion of Washington's philosophy, see the Introduction, above, note 22.

5. See, e.g., Williams, *Eyes on the Prize*, pp. 237–257; Kluger, *Simple Justice*, pp. 1–256; Woodward, *Strange Career of Jim Crow*, pp. 67–110.

6. See *Brown v. Board of Education*, 347 U.S. 483 (1954).

7. Thomas S. Kuhn, *The Structure of Scientific Revolutions*, 2d ed. (Chicago: University of Chicago Press, 1970).

8. Exec. Order No. 8802, 3 C.F.R. 957 (1941).

9. See, e.g., Charles C. Moskos, "Blacks in the Army: Success Story," *Current*, September 1986, pp. 10–17; Philip McGuire, "Desegregation of the Armed Forces: Black Leadership, Protest, and World War II," *Journal of Negro History* 63 (Spring 1983): 147–158; Daniel L. Schaefer, "Freedom Was as Close as the River: The Blacks of Northeast Florida and the Civil War," *Escribano* 23 (1986): 91–116; Saralee R. Howard-Filler, "Two Different Battles," *Michigan History* 71 (January/February 1987): 30–33; Gregory Evans Dowd, "Declarations of Dependence: War and Inequality in Revolutionary New Jersey, 1776–1815," *New Jersey History* 103 (1985): 47–67. One

of the best books on African Americans in the military is Richard O. Hope, *Racial Strife in the U.S. Military: Toward the Elimination of Discrimination* (New York: Praeger, 1979).

10. Exec. Order No. 9981, 3 C.F.R. 722 (1948); Exec. Order No. 9980, 3 C.F.R. 720 (1948).

11. See Franklin, *From Slavery to Freedom*, pp. 523–545.

12. See, e.g., Edwin Dorn, "Truman and the Desegregation of the Military," *Focus*, May 1988, pp. 3–4, 12.

13. See, e.g., Franklin, *From Slavery to Freedom*, pp. 546–611.

14. *Brown v. Board of Education [Brown I]*, 347 U.S. 483 (1954). Lawyers often refer to this decision as *Brown I* to distinguish it from the second Supreme Court decision in the case, rendered in 1955. The second decision, called *Brown II* (cited as 349 U.S. 294 [1955]), deferred implementation of constitutional rights granted in *Brown I* by allowing school desegregation to proceed with "all deliberate speed" rather than immediately.

15. See, e.g., *Shelley v. Kraemer*, 334 U.S. 1 (1948) (Fourteenth Amendment's equal protection clause prohibits state enforcement of racially restrictive covenants in housing); *Sweatt v. Painter*, 339 U.S. 629 (1950) (African American law students ordered admitted to the all-white University of Texas Law School on the ground that the state law school established for African Americans failed to offer equal educational opportunity); *McLaurin v. Oklahoma State Regents for Higher Education*, 339 U.S. 637 (1950) (state-imposed restrictions placed on African American graduate students attending an otherwise all-white university produced such inequalities as to offend the equal protection clause); *Henderson v. United States*, 339 U.S. 816 (1950) (Southern Railway's discriminatory dining-car regulations violated the equal protection clause). For the best account of the legal history leading up to *Brown I*, see Kluger, *Simple Justice*.

16. *Brown v. Board of Education [Brown I]*, 349 U.S. 294, 297 (1955).

17. Robert Carter, "The Warren Court and Desegregation," *Michigan Law Review* 67 (1968): 247.

18. See, e.g., Thomas R. Frazier, ed., *Afro-American History: Primary Sources* (New York: Harcourt Brace and World, 1970), p. 368 (quoting from the NAACP Legal Defense and Education Fund's summary argument in *Brown I*).

19. Civil Rights Act of 1964, Pub. L. No. 88–352, 78 Stat. 241 (1964) (codified as amended at 42 U.S.C. §§ 1971–2000h-6 [1982]); Voting Rights Act of 1965, Pub. L. No. 89–110, 79 Stat. 445 (1965) (codified as amended at 42 U.S.C. § 1971 [1982]); Fair Housing Act of 1968 (Title VIII), Pub. L. No. 90–284, 82 Stat. 81 (1968) (codified as amended at 42 U.S.C. §§ 3601–3619 [1982 and Supp. 1987]).

20. Skelly Wright, "Professor Bickel, the Scholarly Tradition, and the Supreme Court," *Harvard Law Review* 84 (1971): 769–805.

21. Holmes's maxim is quoted from Oliver Wendell Holmes, Jr., *The Common Law*, ed. Mark Howe (Cambridge, Mass.: Harvard University Press, Belknap Press, 1963), p. 5. This expression appears in a somewhat different form in an unsigned review of Langdell's Contracts book; see Book Note, *American Law Review* 14 (1880): 233–236.

The Langdellian syllogism refers to the legal formalism promoted by the famous Harvard Law School dean, Christopher C. Langdell; see Langdell, *A Selection of Cases on the Law of Contracts* (Boston: Little, Brown, 1871). Not surprisingly, this book received a negative review from Holmes, who was an instrumentalist.

Legal realism, a form of instrumentalism, purports to be a realistic and scientific view of the law, meaning that it: (a) focuses on what judges do rather than on what judges say; (b) is cognizant of the consequences judicial decisions have on the community; and (c) believes all legal institutions operate pursuant to a pleasure-pain calculus in which they attempt to maximize the welfare of the greatest number of individuals within the community. See, e.g., Jerome Frank, *Law and the Modern Mind* (New York: Tudor, 1930); Karl N. Llewellyn, *Jurisprudence: Realism in Theory and Practice* (Chicago: University of Chicago Press, 1962). In contrast, legal formalism is primarily concerned with the internal order of law, deductive logic, or what Roberto Unger has called "a restrained, relatively apolitical method of analysis" ("The Critical Legal Studies Movement," *Harvard Law Review* 96 [1983]: 565).

Various scholars have provided a detailed analysis of legal realism and legal formalism. See Oliver Wendell Holmes, "The Path of the Law," *Harvard Law Review* 10 (1897): 457–478; this is a restatement and refinement of conclusions worked out by Holmes in *The Common Law* (originally published in 1881). See also Benjamin N. Cardozo, *The Nature of the Judicial Process* (New Haven, Conn.: Yale University Press, 1921). Two other books by Cardozo may provide a more definitive statement of his views on legal process and the social end of the law: *The Growth of the Law* (New Haven, Conn.: Yale University Press, 1924); and *The Paradoxes of Legal Science* (New York: Columbia University Press, 1928). Holmes was a utilitarian; see H. L. Pholman, *Justice Oliver Wendell Holmes and Utilitarian Jurisprudence* (Cambridge, Mass.: Harvard University Press, 1984). To the extent that Cardozo appeals to considerations of what he calls "social welfare" for guidance in deciding cases, he too can be classified as a utilitarian. In his later books, however, Cardozo seems more metaphysical, perhaps a neonatural law jurisprudent, undertaking a search for generalized principles of law. On utilitarianism, see, e.g., Jeremy Bentham, *An Introduction to the Principles of Morals and Legislation* (New York: Hafner, 1948); Gerald J. Postema, *Bentham and the Common Law Tradition* (Oxford: Clarendon Press, 1986). For a recent defense of legal formalism, see Ernest J. Weinrib, "Legal Formalism: On the Immanent Rationality of Law," *Yale Law Journal* 97 (1988): 949–1016.

22. *Regents of the University of California v. Bakke*, 438 U.S. 265 (1978).

23. For further discussion of this argument, see, e.g., Owen Fiss, "A Theory of Fair Employment Laws," *University of Chicago Law Review* 38 (1971): 235–341.

24. See, e.g., Joel J. Kupperman, "Relations Between the Sexes: Timely vs. Timeliness Principles," *University of San Diego Law Review* 25 (1988): 1027–1041; Roy L. Brooks, "The Affirmative Action Issue: Law, Policy, and Morality," *University of Connecticut Law Review* 22 (1990): 323–372.

Critical Reading Questions

1. According to Brooks, what were some of the demographic, social, and economic factors that led to the development of formal equal opportunity?

2. In what ways does Brooks distinguish racial integration and racial omission from racial segregation? How did these tenets evolve under *Brown v. Board of Education*?

3. What faults does Brooks find with how American decision makers have applied formal equal opportunity policies? In particular, what does Brooks mean when he mentions that legal realists, such as Judge Skelly Wright, fault decision makers for formalist thinking? Also, what does Brooks mean when he says, "It is the lack of priority given to African American civil rights interests in the implementation of formal equal opportunity that is most at fault"?

4. How would you describe the tone of this introductory chapter? Does this brief introduction educate you about the evolution of formal equal opportunity? Does it pique your interest sufficiently so that you want to read the rest of Brooks' book? What evidence do you suspect Brooks will provide to substantiate some of the claims made in this opening chapter?

5. Why does Brooks use so many footnotes to qualify passages in the text? What would happen if these explanatory statements were integrated into the body of the text?

In the following brief report, Beverly Naminsky, a student writer, analyzes the effects of pesticides on crop production, pests, and beneficial insects. Naminsky argues that pesticides are overused and sometimes do more harm than good. When Naminsky shared her first draft with her peer writing group, she said that she was writing for growers with the hope of encouraging them not to use pesticides. When the people in her group told her that they believed growers would be insulted by the opening paragraph and unlikely to read further, she decided that the piece should be targeted for a more general audience.

To provide you with a sense of the critical questions that experienced readers ask when critiquing essays based on library research, I have provided Naminsky's second draft (left column) and the commentaries that her peers and instructor offered her (right column). I have also presented Naminsky's final draft to show how an author can use critics' feedback to improve a report.

Who Is Winning in the Battle with the Bugs? (Second Draft)

Beverly Naminsky

Imagine being exposed to a nerve poison that should short-circuit the signals to your brain and cause respiratory collapse, but, instead of dying, you just get sick. Inside your body, a gene mutates in response to this assault. The next time you are exposed to the poison, you do not get sick at all. The mutated gene passes on to your offspring, and now they are immune to this poison, too. Generations later, your offspring are immune not only to this poison but many others as well. This unlikely scenario of resistance development is exactly what is happening in greenhouses, nurseries, and fields around the world. Growers must be aware of pest biology, resistance development, and alternative control strategies to prevent the loss of chemical controls before viable alternatives have been formulated.

> Would this introduction anger as opposed to persuade your secondary audience—that is, growers?

> What do you mean by viable alternatives?

Over the last 40 years, the number of pests resistant to one or more chemical controls rose from approximately 50 to over 500. New formulations cannot be developed fast enough to keep up with the rate of mutation in the pest population. Because of insufficient research and by the injudicious use of pesticides, growers have vaccinated pests against the poisons intended to kill them. Research shows that pests adapt to chemical controls in a variety of ways.

> Where do these statistics come from? Review the conventions for documenting sources.

> When you say "Research shows," what research are you talking about?

They detect treated areas and avoid them. Their shells harden so that poisons cannot enter their bodies as easily. Their internal systems mutate to metabolize the poison into a harmless waste product. Gene mutations change the way their nervous systems respond, rendering the poisons ineffective. Many pests that were once secondary pests, such as scale and aphids, are primary pests simply because chemical controls eradicated their natural predators. Perversely, predators have not exhibited the same ability to develop resistance as the pests have.

Does your audience know what distinguishes pests from predators? Can you provide more background information here?

While the grower has some alternative methods of control available, the methods are not without risk or considerable effort. He or she can stop using synthetic chemicals and try organics. Unfortunately, pests show resistance to at least two organic compounds, including pyrethrum and Bacillus thuringiensis. Many organics, thought to be safe as they are derived naturally, are more dangerous then some of the synthetics in use. (Nicotine sulfate is listed by the EPA as a dangerous poison and rotenone is highly toxic to fish and reptiles.) Reliance on natural predators is difficult as nurseries and greenhouses are sterile from the use of chemicals. These predators could take years to re-establish at an effective level.

How does this paragraph relate to the previous one?

Are you providing your opinion here or can you provide sources here to substantiate these claims?

Is nicotine sulfate an organic chemical?

What does "sterile" mean in this context? If the chemicals are stopped, will the nurseries and greenhouses remain sterile?

Research data on pest population genetics shows that it may be possible to avert the loss of chemical controls if these chemicals are applied under an Integrated Pest Management program. The program would include proper timing of application, certain dosage rates, and rotation of the chemicals being used. However, chemicals would be used only when the infestation has reached the level where economic

What research are you talking about here?

damage is likely. Treating for pests by the traditional method of spraying, without assessing the pest infestation, will only hasten the resistance process.

As it is unlikely that the resistance process can be stopped, growers need to be aware of how the process occurs to prevent its acceleration. At this time, it is impossible to know if growers could produce the quality of crops that most consumers demand without using chemical controls. For now, growers have a choice but, as resistance continues to develop, that choice will be lost.

Given the importance of your argument, would it make sense to develop a stronger conclusion? Do you, for example, want to call for laws against pesticide use?

Who Is Winning in the Battle with the Bugs? (Final Draft)

Beverly Naminsky

Imagine being exposed to a nerve poison that should short-circuit the signals 1 to your brain and cause respiratory collapse. But, instead of dying, you just get sick. Inside your body, a gene mutates in response to this assault so the next time you are exposed to the poison, you do not get sick at all. This mutated gene is passed on to your offspring, and now they too are immune to this poison. Generations later, your offspring are immune not only to this poison but to many others as well.

This unlikely scenario of resistance development is exactly what is hap- 2 pening in greenhouses, nurseries, and croplands around the world. Because of insufficient research and by the injudicious use of pesticides, growers have unknowingly vaccinated insect pests against the poisons that should kill them. In his article "The Evolution of Insecticide Resistance: Have the Insects Won?" James Mallet cites several research studies that show that pests have made adaptations in response to chemical controls in a variety of ways (337). They have learned to detect treated areas and avoid them. Their shells have hardened so that poisons cannot enter their bodies as easily. Their internal systems have changed, allowing them to metabolize the poison into a harmless waste product. Gene mutations have changed the way their nervous systems respond, rendering the poisons ineffective. Many insects, such as scale and aphids, became pests simply because chemical controls eradicated their natural enemies, the beneficial insects that parasitize or prey on them. For a given pest population, many beneficials and pests are killed by the chemicals, but the survivors respond quite differently. Pests increase in number due to the decline in predatory beneficials, developing resistance rapidly. Surviving beneficials have less pests to prey on initially and respond by slowing their rate of reproduction, which slows their resistance development. Each time a population is treated, more pests and fewer beneficials will survive (Mallet 337).

Pesticides are no longer the panacea they were meant to be. Over the last 3 40 years, the number of pests resistant to one or more chemical controls rose from 14 in 1946 to almost 500 by 1984 (Mallet 336). In spite of that, about 850 million pounds of pesticides and herbicides were applied to crops in 1989, compared to 40 million pounds in the 1920s (Rhetts). While use has increased and efficiency decreased, humans remain guinea pigs for the long-term effects of these poisons as less than 20 percent of the compounds have been tested for their ability to cause cancer or genetic damage (NCAMP).

The damage to the environment is better documented. According to the 4 *Tampa Tribune*, the E.P.A. has verified ground water contamination in 38 states. Toxic waste sites are found throughout the nation. Pesticides kill or sicken birds, mammals, bees, and even the microbes essential to soil health. Nothing seems to be escaping destruction except the pests. Both growers and consumers need to be aware of this complex problem. Immediate abandonment of all pesticides is not likely to work as growers need to be educated in alternative controls, and beneficial insect populations need to increase. Yet, traditional methods of pest control must be modified, both to preserve the interim usefulness of these controls and to prevent further damage to our health and the environment.

Growers are fearful of relinquishing synthetic controls for a variety of 5 reasons. According to an editorial in *Greenhouse Manager* (34), opponents of the California Environmental Protection Act in 1990 known as "Big Green" claimed that if the chemicals were banned as proposed, growers would experience crop losses of 40 percent. Many researchers continue to tell growers that pest control of less than 100 percent is inadequate (Parella 139). Consumer attitudes also influence growers as most consumers still demand unblemished produce and perfect plants. Though the grower has alternative methods of pest control available, they are not without risk, effort, or increased cost. Some organic controls are just as dangerous as the synthetics in use. Though natural derivatives, nicotine sulfate is listed by the E.P.A. as a "dangerous" poison and rotenone is highly toxic to fish and reptiles. In addition, pests have shown resistance to at least two organic compounds, including pyrethrum and Bacillus thuringiensis (Mallet 336). However, no resistance to insecticidal soaps has been documented (Parella 158). These soaps have no toxicity to mammals or the environment and spare many beneficial insects, yet they are costly to use and require repeated applications (Parella 156). Reliance on biological controls is difficult because fields, nurseries, and greenhouses are sterile from the use of chemicals. They have neither pests nor beneficial insects, which are necessary for this strategy to work. It could take years for beneficials to re-establish themselves at an effective level, as they return to these levels much more slowly than the pests do (Mallet 338). However, many beneficials can be bought and artificially introduced into the growing environment. Ladybugs and certain species of mites, wasps, and beetles have shown good results in the control of aphids, mites, and scale insects ("Good Bugs").

The most comprehensive and perhaps most sensible approach at this 6 point is the concept of Integrated Pest Management. The program includes monitoring for infestation levels, implementing biological controls, considering various treatment options, proper timing of any chemical application, certain dosage rates, and rotation of the chemicals that are used. However, chemicals would be used only when biological or cultural controls have failed, and the infestation has reached the level where economic damage is likely.

The development of pesticide resistance cannot be stopped, and both 7 growers and consumers should be willing to make some concessions. Growers cannot continue to use chemicals freely or they will only accelerate the resistance process, add to the environmental damage, and increase everyone's health risks. Consumers must be willing to accept plants and produce that look like they were created by Mother Nature, not Disney World. By working together and understanding the concerns on both sides of this issue, perhaps we can wean ourselves of these poisons and live in a world where nature is once again in balance and able to provide for our needs and desires.

Works Cited

"EPA Finds Water Pollution from Pesticides in 38 States." *Tampa Tribune* 14 Dec. 1988.

"Good Bugs." *Greenhouse Manager* June 1990: 44–49.

Mallet, James. "The Evolution of Insecticide Resistance: Have the Insects Won?" *Trends in Ecology and Evolution* Nov. 1989: 336–340.

Parella, Michael. "Soap Kills Insects, Offers Advantages." *Greenhouse Manager* Aug. 1987:155–158.

Pesticide Safety: Myths and Facts. National Coalition Against the Misuse of Pesticides, 1991.

Rhetts, Joan. "Pesticide Use Raises Questions." *Tampa Tribune* 2 Mar. 1989.

Critical Reading Questions

1. For what primary and secondary audiences is Naminsky writing in this report—growers, environmentalists, the general public?

2. How would you describe Naminsky's tone in this piece? What specific passages enhance or interfere with the tone she is attempting to present? Did Naminsky's tone shift in a significant way in her final revision?

3. Does Naminsky appear to be well informed about the problems related to pesticide use? Can you think of any information that she could have added to strengthen her report? Were you confused at any point in the report by the information that she presented?

4. If Naminsky were in your peer writing workshop, what specific advice would you give her to help make her work more interesting to readers?

5. What was the most significant improvement Naminsky made in her final draft?

6. How did her essay reflect effective library research?

Analyzing Pertinent Conventions

The conventions for shaping research reports differ from discipline to discipline and in accordance with one's communication situation. To determine the best way to proceed, you should analyze the conventions for presenting and evaluating evidence, for organizing information, and for establishing an appropriate tone. As always, you need to pay particular attention to your instructor's assignment. Determine whether your instructor wants you to take a stand on an issue and argue persuasively, whether you are expected to propose a solution to a problem, or whether your report is to be an objective analysis.

Abstracts, tables of contents, tables of figures, headings and subheadings, reviews of literature, and substantive content—these features, discussed at length below, tend to distinguish formal academic research writing from less formal writing genres. Learning how to shape your ideas and adopt an academic voice is critical to succeeding in college and university settings.

Provide an Abstract

In some academic and professional situations, your readers will expect you to provide an informative *abstract*, which briefly summarizes the essential information in your report. Although abstracts vary in length from 30 to 500 words, they rarely extend beyond 250 words. As you may know from your experience doing other library-based research projects, abstracts for articles and scientific reports published in scholarly periodicals are often reprinted in computerized databases and printed indexes (such as *Chemical Abstracts* and *Dissertation Abstracts*). Because they need to make sense by themselves, abstracts should not contain any footnotes, tables, graphs, obscure abbreviations, or jargon.

Readers scan an abstract to determine whether it is worth their time to read the full report. Your instructors, for instance, may be wondering whether the topic is interesting and significant. They may be curious about the primary focus of your report, and the informative abstract helps them understand how you have organized your ideas, which, in turn, can help them better understand your message.

Although you may find it impossible to write your abstract (or the introduction of your essay) until you have nearly completed the final draft of your report, this does not mean that you should forget about the abstract until

Sample Abstract

Tropical rain forests benefit us in many ways but are being rapidly destroyed by their overpopulated Third World owners. At present rates of destruction, we will lose our rain forests by the year 2050, and then we will face serious consequences: global warming, climate changes, and mass extinctions. Fortunately, there are helpful measures we can take to stop deforestation, such as letter writing and boycotting certain items.

your report is done. Instead, writing drafts of your abstract and introduction while you work on the body of the report will help you structure your presentation sensibly.

Provide Headings and a Table of Contents

When writing a long, technical report, consider breaking up the prose into sections and using headings and subheadings to cue your reader to your organization. If your essay is over ten pages, consider providing a table of contents that lists those headings and subheadings. Like the abstract, a table of contents gives readers a sense of the focus and flow of ideas, which in turn helps them identify what they should pay most attention to when reading. If the subject is complicated and can be separated into logical sequences, you may wish to number the sections, as the writer has in the sample on page 244. Readers in scientific fields—particularly engineering and computer science—tend to use numbered headings whereas readers in the humanities and arts may find such enumeration cumbersome.

Introduce the Topic in an Engaging Way

Readers always want to know that you are addressing a significant subject before they commit to reading your research essay. Rather than testing the patience of your audience, quickly clarify the focus of your investigation. If you reached an interesting, significant interpretation as a result of conducting your research, say so in the introduction. Unlike a short story or a novel in which you may save the best for last, a report should usually be straightforward and state its importance at the start. By opening your report with an original insight or some intriguing results, you can engage your readers' interest in your subject and increase the likelihood of their reading your complete report.

The following excerpt by the editors of *MS* magazine is the introduction to a series of articles on male-female relationships. Note the editors' attempt

Sample Table of Contents

INTRODUCTION

1. TROPICAL RAIN FORESTS: FACT AND FICTION
    1.1 Differences Between North American Forests and South
         American Rain Forests
    1.2 Our Everyday Debt to the Tropical Rain Forest

2. DEFORESTATION: HOW MUCH WE'RE LOSING

3. DEFORESTATION: LACK OF DATA

4. CAUSES OF DEFORESTATION
    4.1 Native Citizens
         4.1.1 Slash-and-Burn Agriculture
         4.1.2 Fuel and Wood Gathering
    4.2 Commercial Loggers
    4.3 Cattle Ranchers

5. RAMIFICATIONS
    5.1 Harm to Developing Countries
    5.2 The Greenhouse Effect
    5.3 Mass Extinctions

6. SOLUTIONS
    6.1 Past Actions
    6.2 How We Can Help

7. CONCLUSION

8. FIGURE 1: MAP OF TROPICAL RAIN FORESTS

9. WORKS CITED

to interest and tantalize us with the possibility of new contemporary insights. Then, in the concluding two sentences, note how the editors lead into and summarize the upcoming articles:

> When it comes to sex, things are rarely simple. There are rules, rituals, codes, taboos, fears, feelings. We seek definition, and ways to express its meaning. We agonize and moralize about how much importance sex should have in our lives. We talk endlessly, drawing on experience and desire, searching for the words and phrases that will capture our need. We debate who with, when, and how. One minute the cry is for sexual liberation, and sex without guilt, doubt, commitment, or penalty becomes the goal. Next we want sex that is safe. Often that means simply safe from the threat of disease, most especially AIDS, unwanted pregnancy, or social censure. But when our emotions are involved, risk will always be a factor. How then are we finding our way as we play this most intimate game? The following reports and personal essays explore the ever-shifting sexual terrain.

Review Relevant Literature

As Mike Rose poignantly explains in *Lives on the Boundary*, scholarship is built on the shoulders of other academic writers. In other words, your instructors do not expect you to come up with original insights. Instead, they expect you to listen in on the conversation that is occurring about your topic, synthesize what is known, and then extend it or reformulate it for a different audience. Because of this tendency to perceive scholarship as an ongoing dialogue among interested professionals, most academic disciplines require authors to acknowledge the writers and researchers that have informed their thinking. Thus you need to document your sources thoroughly. Moreover, even as a student writer, your library-based research will make you an insider, expert, or authority writing to others who are less informed. Naturally you need to educate your readers about the scholarship that exists on your topic. Depending on their familiarity with your topic, you may need to educate them about its significance and scope as well.

As with other genres, it generally makes sense in research writing to proceed from given information—what the reader knows—to new information. The length of your review of pertinent literature (that is, secondary sources) will be determined by the sophistication of your readers. Because people are quickly bored by lengthy discussions of the obvious, you will want to succinctly explain how your ideas or findings contribute to or refute existing assumptions. As you become more aware of the important ideas, methods, and scholars in your field throughout your education, you will become more adept at summarizing complex ideas simply.

Of course, even if you have a special section in the introduction for reviewing literature related to your subject, this does not mean that you will link your work to the work of others in this one section alone. Instead, academic readers expect you to refer to relevant studies throughout your report.

Adopt an Appropriate Voice

Although the conventions for formatting long, academic documents tend to be similar across disciplines—that is, writers in most disciplines use abstracts, introductions, body, results, discussion, recommendations—disciplines differ regarding what constitutes an appropriate voice. Many academicians in the sciences and social sciences, for example, eschew the first person. (Even though the American Medical Association and the American Psychological Association journals encourage authors to write in the first person and to avoid confusing passive sentence constructions, some academicians erroneously assume that their research seems more objective if they write, "Thirty subjects were examined over a two-year period" rather than "I studied thirty subjects over a two-year period.")

When writing research reports, you should not assume that instructors expect you to avoid the first person or narrative voice. You may not even be expected to provide a traditional introduction or establish an objective voice. Instead, examine the models of writing in your discipline that your instructors offer and discuss with them how authors should present themselves in relation to the subject matter.

Present Substantive Evidence and Cite Sources

One of the primary skills you learn in college is to avoid making unsupported generalizations. Regardless of your opinion on a subject, your teachers expect you to be able to set aside your emotions and to analyze a subject in a rational way. You can state your opinion as an opinion, but beware of assuming your opinions are facts. As illustrated by the following excerpt taken from John Handy's essay, a writer's feelings about an issue can taint his or her ability to reason effectively:

Women who have abortions routinely walk away from their experience with feelings of depression and guilt but these feelings are eventually replaced with feelings of positive life changes and relief. Also, most of these women are now educated about contraception and they can carry on with a fulfilling, productive life, perhaps bearing children later in life when they are psychologically and financially stable.

On what evidence does the author believe that all women have these feelings?

On what evidence are these assumptions being based? Why assume these women are now educated about contraception?

Why assume that psychological or financial limitations are responsible for most abortions?

Of course, Handy's assertions may be true. Yet educated readers—particularly ones who disagree with him—are unlikely to believe these generalizations because he has supplied no evidence to back them up. If Handy does not wish to support his assertions by consulting printed sources, then he could present them as personal opinions. Unless Handy is a well-known and respected person, however, his unsupported opinions are unlikely to impress his readers. If he hopes to educate or persuade his audience, then he could relate personal experiences to support his opinions. If he wishes to avoid autobiographical disclosure, then he could talk with women who have had abortions or seek out secondary sources in the library—and be sure to document them.

When Do You Need to Document Sources? While you may be an unusually bright, innovative thinker, your instructors still expect your research reports to link *your* insights with those of other scholars. Research involves "listening in" on a scholarly discussion in professional periodicals, books, and reference volumes, and then synthesizing or extending what you discover.

The conventions for acknowledging sources are the cornerstone of academic research. Therefore, you need to acknowledge your indebtedness to other authors throughout your report by following an established method for documenting sources. Each discipline has its own procedures for citing material, which you will need to familiarize yourself with if you hope to be accepted as knowledgeable and competent in your chosen field. Although style guides differ in regard to where the author's name or publishing source is listed, they are all designed to ensure that proper credit is given to authors. As you know from your experience as a writer, developing insights and conducting original research are difficult and time-consuming, so you can understand why people want to receive proper credit for their original ideas. In addition, when you are conducting your research, you can review other authors' Works Cited sections to generate ideas about useful reference materials.

Use the following questions to ascertain whether you need to cite sources of information written up in your report:

1. Is the information taken directly from another source? Is this information not generally well known?
2. Am I paraphrasing or summarizing someone else's original thoughts?
3. Is the information controversial? Is my audience likely to question it?

Whenever you answer yes to any of these questions, then you need to document the source.

When Should You Quote, Paraphrase, or Summarize Sources? Your instructors do not want to read miscellaneous quotations that are thrown together one after another. The problem with essays that use extensive direct quotations is that they tend to lack voice, continuity, or authority. If you offer quotations every few lines, your ideas become subordinate to other people's ideas and voices, which often contradicts your instructor's reasons for assigning research papers—that is, to learn what *you* think about a subject. Therefore, you are generally better off paraphrasing and summarizing material, and using direct quotations sparingly.

When is it appropriate to rely on a direct quote? You might want to provide one if the quoted material goes to the heart of your discussion or argument; if it is so well written that it cannot be condensed further; if it contains a dramatic eyewitness account of an event; if it is written by a prestigious author or philosopher; or if it contains relevant statistics. For example, if you were writing an essay about corporate crime, you would probably be hard-pressed to summarize or paraphrase the following paragraph from Russell Mokhiber's "Crime in the Suites," which appeared in *Greenpeace*.

> The financial cost [of corporate crime] to society is staggering. The National Association of Attorneys General reports that fraud costs the nation's businesses and individuals upwards of $100 billion each year. The Senate Judiciary Committee has estimated that faulty goods, monopolistic practices and other such violations annually cost consumers $174 to $231 billion. Added to this is the $10 to $20 billion a year the Justice Department says taxpayers lose when corporations violate federal regulations. As a rule of thumb, the Bureau of National Affairs estimates that the dollar cost of corporate crime in the United States is more than 10 times greater than the combined total from larcenies, robberies, burglaries and auto thefts committed by individuals.

This paragraph, for many of the reasons mentioned above, is eminently "quotable."

Paraphrasing, on the other hand, involves recasting someone else's ideas into your own language. As a student, you routinely paraphrase your instructors' lectures and the contents of textbooks. Exams, in one sense, are one large paraphrase in that they require you to review and restate material from assigned reading and lectures. Of course, when you paraphrase, you want to be careful that you do not alter the author's original message, eliminate any significant background information, misrepresent the author's intentions, or copy too closely the original wording. To help you distinguish effective paraphrases from faulty paraphrases, consider how the following paragraph from Russell Mokhiber's "Crime in the Suites" is handled:

Original Passage: The full extent of the corporate crime wave is hidden. Although the federal government tracks street crime month by month, city by city through the FBI's Uniform Crime Reports, it does not track corporate crime. So the government can tell the public whether burglary is up or down in Los Angeles for any given month, but it cannot say the same about insider trading or illegal polluting.

Faulty Paraphrase: In "Crime in the Suites" Mokhiber has noted that the full extent of the corporate crime wave is hidden. The federal government does not track corporate crime, yet it does track street crime month by month, city by city through the FBI's Uniform Crime Reports. So the government can tell the public whether burglary is up or down in San Francisco for any given month, but it cannot say the same about insider trading or illegal polluting.

Rather than being an accurate paraphrase, this passage is a good example of academic dishonesty—that is, *plagiarism.* While a few words have been changed and the structure of the second sentence has been changed, this passage as a whole has not been revised in the "paraphraser's" own words.

> *Effective Paraphrase:* In "Crime in the Suites" Mokhiber has noted that we lack information about the prevalence of corporate crime. While the FBI monitors crime statistics for the federal government on a monthly basis, it fails to do so for corporate crime. Consequently, we may know that violent crime is up by 10 percent in Manhattan, but we can't be sure that less insider trading is occurring this year on Wall Street.

As with most other skills, *practice* is the best way to become effective at paraphrasing. Also, you may need to write several drafts before developing one that accurately reports the author's intentions *in your own words.* Note also that if you cite three or more words from the original or even one word that was coined by the author, you should acknowledge your indebtedness by placing quotation marks around the borrowed terms.

To give you a sample of how writers mix direct quotes with paraphrase, I have provided a short excerpt from Stephen North's influential book, *The Making of Knowledge in Composition.* As you read the passage, note how North intermixes his own opinions about ethnography along with an occasional direct quote from the work of Clifford Geertz. Note also that North is careful to show readers how Geertz quoted from the work of Paul Ricouer. Finally, North cues readers that he has not emphasized Geertz's words by italicizing them by writing "his emphasis" in parentheses; when he felt the need to clarify Ricouer's terms, he placed his clarification in brackets.

> Ethnographic inquiry produces stories, fictions. Ethnographic investigators go into a community, observe (by whatever variety of means) what happens there, and then produce an account—which they will try to verify or ground in a variety of ways—of what happened. The phenomena observed are gone, will not occur again, and therefore cannot be investigated again. What remains, then, is whatever the investigators have managed to turn into words. Clifford Geertz perhaps put it best in Chapter 1 of his *The Interpretation of Cultures:* "Thick Description: Toward an Interpretive Theory of Culture": "The ethnographer 'inscribes' social discourse, *he writes it down.* In so doing, he turns it from a passing event, which exists only in its own moment of occurrence into an account, which exists in its inscription and can be reconsulted" (p. 19, his emphasis). This is not to say, as Geertz is careful to explain, that the Ethnographer transcribes, literally, all of what a community's members say. Rather, the inscribing is an effort to capture what he calls, borrowing from Paul Ricouer, the "said": "'the *noema*

["thought," "content," "gist"] of the speaking. It is the meaning of the speech event, not the event as event.'" (p. 19)

Like paraphrasing, summarizing involves reporting someone else's ideas in your own language. Unlike paraphrasing, however, summaries allow you to sort through the information in the secondary source and report only what you consider to be essential. A summary is therefore much shorter than the original, whereas a paraphrase may be the same length. Below is a sample summary of the passage paraphrased in the above example:

> *Summarized Version:* In "Crime in the Suites" Mokhiber has noted that we are unsure about the prevalence of corporate crime because the federal government does not compile crime statistics for white collar crime.

While the above passage overlooks the comparison between corporate crime versus street crime, it does not misconstrue the author's original meaning, so it meets the standards of academic fairness. In contrast, a revised summary such as the following would be considered ineffective because it changes the author's meaning:

> *Ineffective Summary:* In "Crime in the Suites" Mokhiber argues that the federal government does not track corporate crime as thoroughly as it does street crime.

To fall within the purview of academic fairness, a simple change could transform the above into an effective summary:

> *Effective Summary:* In "Crime in the Suites" Mokhiber implies that the federal government does not track corporate crime as thoroughly as it does street crime.

Establish the Credibility of Your Sources. By definition, critical readers are skeptical. They do not take the results of research as the final word on the subject, but instead look for flaws in the reasoning, or if it is an empirical study, flaws in the research design. As an author you may need to calm the critical faculties of your readers by offering background information about where the research you are citing was published and how the research was designed. When reading the following excerpt on the greenhouse effect, what questions do you believe a skilled reader would raise?

The greenhouse effect is likely to change rainfall patterns, raise sea levels 4 to 7 feet by the year 2100, and increase the world's mean temperature 2.7 to 8 degrees Fahrenheit by the year 2050 (Brown & Flavin 6, 16). Everyone will suffer as irrigation and drainage systems become useless and agriculture faces its first changes in a "global climatic regime" that has changed little since

On what evidence is this information based?

According to the Works Cited section, this information appears in the following source: Brown, Lester R., and Christopher Flavin. "The Earth's Vital Signs." *State of the World* (1988): 5–7, 16–17. Critical readers would probably question the reliability of this source farming began (Brown & Flavin 16). Some places will cease to be productive such as the North American heartland, and the Soviet Union's grainbelt (Brown & Flavin 17). Although some areas, previously unproductive, will suddenly become good farmland, scientists say these climate shifts could occur so abruptly that agricultural losses would be hard to readily adjust for (Brown & Flavin 16).

because the claims are so controversial and because they are not familiar with the journal.

The credibility of this information could be significantly improved by "power quoting" (see Chapter 2).

Brown and Flavin may be correct in their dire predictions. However, chances are that critical readers such as your instructors would be more likely to believe these predictions if additional information about the authors and their research were provided or if the author could "power quote"—that is, cite numerous other studies that reached similar conclusions.

Below is a student paper that contains several interesting but controversial statements. As you read the two paragraphs, what critical questions do you have about the research that is cited?

It is imperative to realize that protecting dolphins should be a priority because they are gentle animals which possess many human-like qualities. Did you know, for instance, that dolphins, like humans, live in communities where mothers work cooperatively, protecting their young from predators, and that they "baby-sit" for one another if a mother must temporarily leave the school (Booth 57)? These communities are stable systems that exist for long periods of time; they exist within certain territorial ranges; and they are composed of dolphin peer groups and families (Booth 57). Also, like humans, dolphins assist one another when ill or in danger; they have social norms for attending to deceased members of their community, and they have even been known to assist mariners who are in danger at sea (Booth 57).

But the most notable fact is that dolphins are capable of communicating and comprehending language symbols such as the ones with which we communicate (Chollar 52). The ability to interact with others using language is an accomplishment that only human beings have been associated with performing, and it is certainly far beyond the capabilities of other ordinary land or sea creatures. As consumers, we must therefore ask ourselves if we are willing to tolerate the needless slaughter of these unique, gentle animals just for the sake of having tuna fish on our tables or as a filler for pet food.

By turning to the Works Cited section, an academic reader's critical faculties would be soothed by the following references:

Booth, William. "The Joy of a Big Brain." *Psychology Today* 23 (Apr. 1989): 57.
Chollar, Susan. "Conversations with Dolphins." *Psychology Today* 23 (Apr. 1989): 52–56

Clearly, the imprimatur of *Psychology Today* is nothing to scoff at. Nevertheless, for readers to entertain the possibility that dolphins have such human
qualities, more background information about these scholars' studies should
be provided in the text of the student's paper. Without more background
information about the research, critical readers would remain skeptical about
dolphins' ability to communicate via oral language.

Here are some of the standard questions that academic readers ask when
reviewing research reports:

1. Is the source a first-hand or second-hand account? That is, are the
   authors reporting results of their own research or reviewing someone
   else's work?

2. Is the source of publication credible? (For example, an essay in the *New
   England Journal of Medicine* would influence most physicians' opinions
   about a surgical procedure far more easily than an essay in a biweekly
   community newspaper.)

3. Do the authors work for research institutes, publications, private companies, or universities? Are they well-known authorities? Do the authors
   seem biased or can you identify any hidden agendas?

4. Have the authors followed traditional research methods?

The following annotated passages demonstrate how questions like these
can help you improve the way you integrate secondary sources into your discussion.

In the United States today, a teenager is diagnosed with having sexually trans-mitted disease every 30 seconds. This constitutes approximately 3 million infected teenagers each year. These statis-tics prove that sex in today's society has become more than just a moral or reli-gious issue; it has also become a major health issue that must be dealt with quickly, seriously, and responsibly.

> Where does this figure come from? How reliable is it? What sort of sexually transmitted diseases are we talking about?

Studies show that men and women report similar stress levels in many areas, but female college students reported greater stress regarding family relation-ships and their own mental health (Zuckerman 429). According to Zucker-man, writer for the journal *Sex Roles*, low self-esteem and a lack of confidence in interpersonal skills causes an individual to be more prone to stress. According to

> How many people did Zuckerman study before reaching these conclusions? How reliable did his method appear to be? How did Zuckerman define stress?

> What are some of the factors that lead to stress in interpersonal situations?

Zuckerman's study of gender as related to stress, women on the whole possessed lower self-esteem, which led to depression and anxiety suffered due to stress. Zuckerman also noted that stress from intimate relationships produced lower self-esteem in women, but not in men. Female college students also reported a higher level of school-related stress as opposed to men (Zuckerman 438).

What was the percentage breakdown? How was it measured?

Do any other contemporary studies substantiate Zuckerman's findings?

According to Zuckerman's study, schoolwork and intimate relationships caused the most stress among college students of both genders. Men, however, did not register as high a level of stress as women. As far as reasons for low self-esteem, which Zuckerman established as interrelated with stress, male students listed financial stress and health-related stress, as well as low self-confidence in math and science skills, as causing low self-esteem.

What levels of stress are we talking about?

When researchers produce results in line with what you perceive to be the truth, it can be especially difficult to critique the researcher's reasoning or methodology. Nevertheless, if you expect others to trust the research findings, then you should provide a few statements about the researcher's background and methods.

Another powerful way to convince readers about controversial points is to *appeal to authorities*. In research reports, appeals to authority appear as "power quotes." In other words, if a point is extremely important to your argument, you can emphasize it and establish its authenticity by listing numerous sources that support it, as illustrated in the following examples:

> A number of researchers (Bellack et al.; Cazden, John & Hymes; Barnes; Flanders; Sinclair & Coulthard) have analyzed the gender-based language in math classrooms and textbooks. These researchers have come to the common conclusion: women are trained to fail in mathematics education.

> Our world began with 4.3 billion acres of lush, green tropical rainforest (Stone; Anderson; Wilcox and Murcay). According to most recent figures, we've already deforested 1.9 billion acres and we continue to strip 27 million acres a year (Brown & Flavin; Watson; Lewis; Steinburg). That's an area the size of Tennessee. In the ten minutes it may take to read this report, 500 acres of tropical rainforest will be destroyed (Lewis; Stone; Anderson; Wilcox and Murcay). At these rates of destruction, *U.S.A. Today*

calculates, "only small patches of the world's tropical forests, even in remote [areas], will last beyond the year 2050" (Stone 74).

Unfortunately, these are conservative estimates. The Rainforest Action Network cites 50 million acres deforested every year and the Florida Rainforest Alliance predicts the loss of most rainforests by the year 2000. When the Brazilian Space Institute released satellite images of the Amazon Basin in 1987, 20 million acres were found to have been deforested that year, a figure that exceeded some estimates for worldwide deforestation (Booth 1428).

Inform Your Reader When You Are Citing, Paraphrasing, or Summarizing

While documentation styles differ in their formats and procedures, they all agree on one point: you must ensure that your readers know when you are borrowing from secondary sources. Remember, in particular, that readers read from left to right. They should not—and truly cannot—be expected to read backwards to determine just how much of a paragraph or section is borrowed from a secondary source. For example, note the confusion a reader would have in evaluating Theresa Lovins's interesting essay, "Objectionable Rock Lyrics":

Many Americans fear government intervention when it comes to human rights. They fear that government censorship of rock lyrics might lead to other restrictions. Then too, what would the guidelines be, who would make these decisions, and how might it affect our cherished constitutional rights? Questions like these should always be approached with serious consideration. We have obligations as parents to protect our children and as Americans to uphold and protect our rights. Therefore, it's important to ask what effects proposals like Tipper Gore's, president of PMRC, might have on our freedoms in the future. She recommends that the record companies utilize a rating system: X would stand for profane or sexually explicit lyrics, V for violence, O for occultism, and D/A for drugs/alcohol. The PMRC also suggests that the lyrics be displayed on the outside cover along with a general warning sticker which perhaps might read "Parental Guidance:

Although Lovins provides complete documentation for Morthland—the source that she is citing in this paragraph—she does not clarify for the reader exactly what she is borrowing from Morthland. As a result, the reader cannot know if the author is indebted to Morthland for all of the thoughts in this paragraph or merely the section on PMRC's proposal. This problem could be easily rectified by including a transitional sentence that distinguished her thoughts from those of other authors whom she is citing. For example, Lovins could write, "According to John Morthland's recent essay in *High Fidelity*, Tipper Gore has recommended that record companies do such and such." If Lovins did not want to call so much attention to Morthland, she could merely put Morthland's name in parentheses after the word "future" in the sixth sentence of this paragraph.

Explicit Lyrics." To date, record companies have not agreed to all these demands but some have decided to put warning labels on certain questionable albums (Morthland).

While the PMRC's request needs to be studied, perhaps they have merit. Rating systems could actually serve to alert the public, similar to how movie ratings have helped motion picture audiences choose the types of movies they wish to view. A committee could be appointed by a reputable party such as the Federal Communications Commission (FCC). The group would perform its duties in a manner similar to that used by the Academy of Motion Pictures. This type of system has not hurt the movie industry, but has actually aided in promoting some movies. For instance, "The Black Hole" by Walt Disney Productions was given a PG rating. Disney was trying to reach a broader audience and by receiving this kind of rating they did just that. It told the adult audience that it wasn't along the same lines as a Mary Poppins film, and perhaps it contained material which they could enjoy but was too sophisticated for a 4–6 year old to grasp. Movie rating is a good example, proving that rating systems can and do, in fact, work (Wilson).

Lovins runs into the same problem in this paragraph as she did in the previous one. Because she doesn't inform the reader about exactly when she is referring to Connie Wilson's *Time* essay, "A Life in the Movies," readers cannot be sure whether it is Lovins's idea or Wilson's that "a committee could be appointed" to evaluate the lyrics of rock music. If this idea was originally propounded by Wilson, then Lovins could be considered guilty of plagiarism, yet most people would merely describe this to be sloppy scholarship.

Critical Reading Exercise

As you critique the following nine excerpts from student papers, play the role of a skeptical reader. What kind of documentation would you expect? Is it provided? Have the writers clearly distinguished their feelings and opinions from the facts? Do they provide sufficient data for their claims? When the content appears to be underdeveloped, what kind of background information do you think the authors should add?

1. Over 100,000 women have suffered bloody, brutal deaths at the hands of money-hungry back-alley strangers who call themselves "pregnancy terminators."

2. Did you know that television is in more than 95 percent of all American households, and more common than telephones and toilets? Most

homes have more than one operating television set and in an average residence a set is turned on about seven hours a day. The average child devotes two and one-half to five hours a day to viewing television programs. By the time children reach high school graduation, they will have spent more time in front of the television set than in a classroom.

Did you realize that television has become more violent than ever? In fact, children's shows have been rated as being three times more violent than prime-time programs. Cartoons such as Woody Woodpecker and Tom and Jerry averaged approximately twenty violent acts per half-hour. Today, the most popular war cartoons average forty-eight violent acts per half-hour.

4. People are dying. Over 20,000 murders were committed last year, and that number is expected to grow even higher this year.

5. The U.S. Justice Department reports that over 27,000 children aged 12 to 15 were victims of handguns last year and the numbers are steadily increasing. Children in New York City can acquire a handgun on the street, and some dealers will rent a youth a pistol over night until he or she can acquire the money by mugging or robbing someone. Children of poverty see a gun as an opportunity to gain power. They see the gun as a status symbol to help them climb the ranks of crime.

6. A less obvious problem is overpopulation. Advanced technology and medicine enable people to live longer, but with fewer people dying and more being born, we're crowding ourselves out of our own world. Every generation is afraid to bring children into this world for fear of war, illness, crime, and pollution. Today, that same fear exists in a greater magnitude, yet surprisingly, the birth rate has not dropped.

7. The spread of venereal diseases and AIDS does not seem to be improving either. At the University of California, they took a survey of San Francisco. The survey showed that of all of the people anonymously tested for AIDS, a quarter of them said that they did not intend to tell their partner of a positive result.

8. An international study of 13-year-old kids shows U.S. students ranked last in math proficiency, but first in calculator usage. What does this mean for the U.S. in the growing globalized society?

9. The MADD organization has predicted that two of every five people from every political and social level will be affected by an alcohol-impaired driver in their lifetime. For example, Norma Phillips (the current president of MADD) and her husband are extremely wealthy people, have a 52-room, custom-designed home, two Mercedes-Benz automobiles, a Rolls Royce, and a Jaguar, but all of these possessions did not save their son from being killed by a drunk driver.

MADD members feel that they were instrumental in lobbying the legislature and getting the drinking age raised to 21. They also believe judges are handing down stiffer sentences as a result of their campaign, as evidenced by the Bruce Kimball case in the Brandon, Florida, area. Other advancements credited to MADD are prosecutors are less willing to plea bargain, teenagers are receiving anti–drunk driving messages, and victims of impaired drivers are receiving counseling and support.

Writing Assignments

If you are given the opportunity to select your own topic for a research report or if the teacher's guidelines are broad and open-ended, then the first question for you to consider is, "What do I care about?" When your teacher challenges you to develop your own research topic, you are limited only by your imagination and level of commitment. You can identify a topic to research by considering subjects that you have written about in the past that have absorbed your interest, by considering problems your world or society is confronting, by skimming through your favorite periodicals and identifying topics of interest to you, or by brainstorming ideas with classmates.

1. *Review past writing projects.* Professional writers are seldom without ideas because the writing process itself engenders thinking. Many times authors build on their past works by conducting more research and extending their knowledge on a specific subject. Rather than beginning a totally new project, consider revising and expanding an earlier report.

2. *Take a survey of your concerns and interests.* You might also find it useful to consider this assignment a challenge to explore a personally meaningful issue. For example, are you trying to decide on a career? If so, perhaps you can research the various options open to you. Or perhaps you are shy and you have often wondered how other people managed to overcome their shyness. You could research techniques psychologists have developed to help the afflicted overcome shyness. If you are interested in developing your spiritual side, you could study the tenets of a religion, yoga, or philosophy.

3. *Consider writing about important social issues.* What have you heard on the news or read in a newspaper or magazine that intrigues you? What social issues do you generally look for when scanning through the newspaper? For example, are you interested in a particular environmental or economic issue? Are you interested in some sort of psychological concept, such as Maslow's model of self-actualization? Is there some subject that you have always wanted to learn more about, such as how to become an entrepreneur or how to build a log cabin? Have you ever wondered who invented glass or when it was first used in homes? Have you had a discussion or argument recently in which you wished you had more facts to drive home your point?

4. *Collaborate with your classmates.* Talk with some of your friends and classmates who have lots of good ideas. Ask them what they find odd or mysterious. What subjects would they write about if permitted to pursue any subject?

Prewriting and Drafting Strategies

The following prewriting strategies can help you develop innovative topics and use your time wisely. If you have not undertaken extensive library research in the past, you will probably also need to review the guidelines for developing a library search strategy, as discussed in Chapter 2.

Consult Pertinent Reference Material

To use your time most effectively, try experimenting with the following research strategies.

1. Review *Encyclopedia Britannica*, *Encyclopedia Americana*, or *Collier's Encyclopedia* to gather background information about your specific research problem. Review the *Statistical Abstract of the United States* or *The World Almanac* to determine whether these sources can provide you with helpful facts and figures.

2. Review *Bibliographic Index* to see if any bibliographies have been published on your topic.

3. Review pertinent CD-ROM or on-line computer databases, such as *ERIC*, *The MLA International Bibliography*, or the *Social Science Citation Index*. When possible, print the abstracts of related studies and consult the one or two that seem most effective.

4. Check *Ulrich's International Periodicals Directory*, Sheehy's *Guide to Reference Books*, Katz's *Magazines for Libraries*, or McCormick's *The New York Times Guide to Reference Materials* to see what periodicals may supply useful articles.

Identify Your Communication Situation

As always, you need to question what audience you are writing for, what your purpose is (which determines what to include and exclude), and what voice would be appropriate in light of your audience and purpose. Unfortunately, many students freeze up when beginning to write a research report. They are afraid to express themselves and believe that they must adopt a totally objective persona when writing a research report. Rather than assuming that is the case, review your instructor's assignment. Given your audience and purpose, question whether you should argue persuasively or adopt a Rogerian approach to work out a negotiation.

Identify a Specific Research Question

Experienced researchers often contend that their work begins in earnest once they can express their intention in a single sentence. Of course, because of the generative nature of language, experienced researchers are also wary of deciding too soon exactly what they will research. They are usually willing to jettison an idea if a better one comes along during the research process.

Because of the added burden of needing secondary sources to support your ideas, you should work especially hard in the early stages of writing to identify a specific research question. You may not always know exactly what your purpose is or even exactly for whom you are writing. Sometimes you will need to work with the material—that is, do some reading and writing—before you can narrow the focus of your essay. For example, after hearing a televised news report that personal computers may cause cancer, you might begin researching the dangers of VDTs (video display terminals) on computers. Then after gathering reliable information and learning that credible scientific evidence suggests that VDTs emit extra low frequency (ELF) electric and magnetic fields that cause cancer (perhaps by impairing the ability of t-lymphocyte cells), your purpose of analyzing the dangers of VDTs changes into a persuasive one: you decide to encourage consumers to purchase LCD (liquid crystal displays) monitors instead of traditional VDTs because the LCD monitors do not give off potentially hazardous magnetic fields. Or, your audience could be a governmental agency and your purpose is to argue that the government should develop regulations for limiting the non-ionizing electromagnetic radiation that is emitted by personal computers with VDTs, as well as other sources such as power lines, radio and television transmitters, microwave ovens, electric blankets, and electrically heated waterbeds.

Organize a Research Notebook

As mentioned in Chapter 1, maintaining a Writing and Research Notebook can help you identify a specific research question, organize reading notes, draw inferences from what you read, and construct a Works Cited section for your report. In addition, maintaining a log and a list of goals can help you maneuver your way toward meaning by giving you greater control over the thinking and writing process.

Establish a Schedule. If you tend to procrastinate, you should draft a tentative schedule for completing the various stages of your research. Nothing can make the research process more dreadful than putting off the work until the last minute. You should therefore plan your work so that it is completed a week before the due date. Of course, because conducting research is typically not a step-by-step process, you will need to routinely reevaluate your reasons for writing and subsequently revise your goals for research and interim completion dates. To help develop a realistic schedule, you may find it useful to answer the following questions:

1. How much time will I spend finding a topic?
2. When will I have reviewed enough sources to begin writing a solid draft? What sources and information are likely to be difficult to obtain? How will I get them? For example, do I need to write a letter to an expert on my topic? Will I need to drive to a different library if my campus library lacks the resources I need? Will I need to order material through interlibrary loan?

3. At what point can I develop a tentative description of my communication situation? In other words, when will I have a good idea of my audience, purpose, and voice for the research project? If published, where would the research be likely to appear—in a professional magazine, a student newspaper, a corporate newsletter?

4. Will it be possible for me to run "a research proposal" by my classmates and instructor? (A research proposal contains the description of your communication situation, a statement of your research question, a brief overview of the problem, and a bibliography of potential sources.)

5. When will I have a draft that is solid enough to show my peers for their responses?

6. When will I have a second and third draft completed? How much time can I devote to revising and editing?

Sample Schedule for a Research Paper

Week 1

1. Begin work on narrowing the topic.
2. Check available information in library.
3. Preliminary reading—begin research.
4. Narrow focus of topic.
5. Jot notes on ideas, thoughts in research notebook.

Week 2

1. Select sources for paper; copy ones to use.
2. Analyze sources.
3. Conduct interview(s) if needed.
4. Organize/sort information in notebook.
5. Draft Works Cited.
6. Outline and freewrite on topic.
7. Make notes on ideas, thoughts.

Week 3

1. Complete several drafts of paper.
2. Revise draft—add, delete, redo as necessary.
3. Peer review—further revision.

Week 4

1. Final revision.
2. Edit for grammar, spelling, etc.
3. Submit on Thursday.

Revising and Editing Strategies

As usual, you can best improve your manuscript by attacking it as if it were written by an enemy. Prior to submitting your work to classmates and your instructor, you will want to make it as strong as possible. Because your current draft is likely to exhibit a few of the same problems as your other writing projects in the class, you may want to review your instructor's and peers' criticisms once again. By identifying the problems that you commonly make, you can focus more specifically on these issues.

Ask Critical Questions

The special concerns you will need to consider when revising research reports are featured in the checklist below.

1. Have I provided the background information that will enable readers to understand the significance of my subject?

2. Will readers understand my purpose for writing the report?

3. Have I provided enough evidence for all of the claims that I have made in the essay? Does each of my quotations clearly relate to my purpose?

4. Have I established the credibility of the sources I have cited?

5. Have I used so many block quotations or outside sources that my voice and purpose seem vague, soft, underdeveloped?

6. Can any of the direct quotations be paraphrased?

7. Are my paraphrases and summaries accurate representations of the original material?

8. Is the report well organized? Would a different ordering of points be more forceful? Has the order in which I found the information determined the way I organized the final document? Is this the best way to organize it?

9. Is my language straightforward and clear? Have I avoided excessive abstract words and jargon? Can I use more concrete and sensory words?

10. Is my writing economical? Can I combine and edit some of the sentences to make them more vigorous?

11. Is the essay grammatically and mechanically correct? Are there any specific errors I tend to make that I still need to check for?

While you may understandably become discouraged when you identify flaws in your writing, remember that even experienced writers feel moments of despair and frustration when they perceive gaps between what they said and what they intended to say.

Do a Criteria-Based Evaluation

No simple set of standards can be used to evaluate the effectiveness of all reports based on library research. Nevertheless, you may find the following criteria to be useful as you critique your own and your peers' research papers.

I. Format

Low   Middle   High

1 2 3 4 5 6 7 8 9 10

The report contains the necessary sections and has an effective format.

Title Page

Abstract

Table of Contents

List of figures and illustrations

Introduction

Body

Conclusion

Works Cited

Appendixes

II. Secondary Sources

Low   Middle   High

1 2 3 4 5 6 7 8 9 10

Sufficient secondary sources are provided for factual information, controversial statements, and emphasis.

It is clear when outside sources are being cited.

The credibility of secondary sources has been established.

The proper form of documentation is used.

III. Edited Document

Low   Middle   High

1 2 3 4 5 6 7 8 9 10

The significance of the subject is clear.

The document is reader-based; the tone is appropriate given the audience and purpose.

The document is organized and formatted effectively.

Unnecessary jargon and awkward abstractions have been edited.

The first person has been used, where appropriate.

A high verb-to-noun ratio has been established.

	Low	Middle	High
Strings of prepositions have been avoided.	1 2 3 4 5 6 7 8 9 10		

The document has been edited for economy.

The document has been copyedited for grammatical, mechanical, and formatting errors.

Collaborating Strategies

When your manuscripts are short, you may be wise to defer having others evaluate them until you have polished them to the best of your ability. However, such shyness—or patience, depending on how you look at it—could get you in deep water when you are writing a research report. Narrowing your topic, finding suitable reference material, organizing your work, finding a voice—these are admittedly difficult activities. Your determination to get the job done, although praiseworthy, may actually interfere with your success. In short, you need to avoid "tunnel vision"—that is, concentrating so thoroughly on a single aspect of your work that you lose sight of the overall picture. Whenever possible, therefore, you should share your work with your peers and instructor. Give them an outline of your research project and ask for their criticisms. As usual, you would be wise to inform your critics that you truly want to hear their suggestions, that you recognize that accepting criticism is one way you can improve as a writer.

PEER REVIEW WORKSHOP

1. How would you define your peers' audience, voice, and purpose in this research report? What changes or additions can the author make to create a more persuasive or informative report?

2. Are there any points in the discussion at which you are confused or where you think additional evidence needs to be provided? What additional information do you believe the author should add before submitting the report for a grade? Do you believe that the author has provided sufficient evidence to support claims? Are any important counterarguments ignored? Has the author provided the information the audience will need to understand the subject? Can any information be deleted because the audience is already likely to be familiar with it?

3. Are you ever unsure about whether the author is paraphrasing, quoting, or summarizing sources?

4. Do you believe the author needs to cite more sources? Would you prefer the author to summarize and paraphrase more instead of quoting so much?

5. Has the author established the credibility of the sources and research that he or she has reviewed? What additional information do you need the author to present for you to believe in the authenticity and authority of the quoted, paraphrased, or summarized material?

6. Has the author followed the expected conventions for documenting sources?

Additional Writing Sample

In the following report, Tracey Williams, a student writer, evaluates the nutritional value of fast foods. To help her determine what to say and how to say it, she established a specific communication situation. As you read her essay, consider how Williams has tried to make her piece speak directly to her primary audience, young women on the go.

Analysis of Communication Situation

Audience: I'm writing for married and single women in their 20s and 30s. They lead busy lives, and eating fast foods and snacks when they are in a hurry or don't feel like cooking is very much a part of their routine. But, these women also have concerns about their weight and are not very well informed about nutrition.

Purpose: To inform the audience that fast food and snacks tend to have a great amount of fat and calories, even when eaten in seemingly insignificant quantities. The audience can keep their routine of eating fast foods, and also keep their figures, if they make a small effort to carefully choose only fast foods and snacks that are low in fat and calories.

Voice: I hope to appear objective, yet persuasive.

Context: I believe my essay could appear in a woman's magazine or in the food section of a newspaper.

The Fast Food Diet

Tracey Williams

It's a typical day for the typical woman. She gets out of bed, showers, dresses, and goes into the kitchen. Pressed for time, she grabs a jelly donut to eat on the way to work. When lunchtime arrives, she and her friends rush off to Burger Chef where she orders a Chicken Club sandwich. After work she rents a movie and goes home. At 8:00 she throws a turkey pot pie in the microwave. What would she think if she knew that during the course of the day she consumed over 1300 calories and 70 grams of fat? As far as she's concerned, she ate only a jelly donut, a club sandwich, and a small pot pie. It doesn't sound like much, but here's the breakdown:

Table 1		
	Calories	Fat (grams)
Jelly Donut	253	14.3
Chicken Club	521	25.1
Turkey Pot Pie	538	30.6

Source: *Jean Carper's Total Nutrition Guide,* by Jean Carper. Copyright © 1987 by Jean Carper. Used by permission of Bantam Books, a division of Bantam Doubleday Dell Publishing Group, Inc.

Nutritious dining sometimes seems impossible in this rush hour society. 2 The June Cleavers of the world have disappeared and left us to fend for ourselves. Many women juggle school with work and family. We don't have the time to plan and prepare three square meals a day. Luckily, our high-speed society is also high tech. We can choose from a variety of prepared foods and use microwave ovens to cook them. There are countless fast food restaurants and pizza delivery shops. And if we're *really* in a hurry, there's always snack food. Vending machines and convenience stores offer a sizable variety of foods to eat on the run.

Many fast foods and snacks are no longer loaded down with questionable 3 chemicals and dangerous preservatives. In response to a health-conscious public, food manufacturers now limit the use of msg and artificial flavors and colors. The packaging makes it obvious by stating, in bold letters, "LOOK! NATURALLY FLAVORED!" or "NO PRESERVATIVES!" The FDA also requires companies to print accurate content listing on product labels. It takes only a quick glance to tell if you're about to eat something that could double as hair coloring.

There are those, of course, who wouldn't dream of eating at a Wendy's 4 or of dining on a Swanson's fresh from the microwave. Those people probably have the money to eat out, the time to cook, or are concentrating on a special diet. Those of us who are on the run often have no alternative but to eat quickly, and our choices are somewhat limited.

A concern with eating on the run is lack of nutrition. Most of us are 5 aware that a donut for breakfast, a chicken sandwich for lunch, and a pot pie for dinner don't exactly provide a complete RDA. But our high-tech world has rescued us with multiple vitamins to help replace the minerals that fast foods and snacks lack.

However, the major problem with eating on the run doesn't concern 6 RDA requirements or harmful chemical intakes. The problem lies within the calorie and fat content of fast foods and snacks. Like the "typical woman," what we don't know may make us fat. Consider that the average woman burns about 1200 calories during a normal day, and that the maximum recommended fat intake is 40 grams a day (Carper 35). As you can see, the "typical woman" in my example didn't fare so well in the battle of the bulge. Her consumption of 1300 calories wasn't significant, but the 70 grams of fat will give her trouble if she wants to watch her weight.

Although weight gain is the least desirable side effect of fat consumption, 7 excess fat intake poses other problems for the individual. Dr. Clifford Grobstein, chairman of the National Academy of Sciences' Committee on Diet, Nutrition, and Cancer, has stated, "Among the dietary factors we examined, a linkage between total fat consumption and colon, breast, and prostate cancer stands out most prominently" (Carper 38). Although cancer is a real and dangerous risk of high fat diets, the immediate concern is the damage to the cardiovascular system. In 1953, Dr. Ancel Keys of the University of Minnesota found that a diet high in saturated fat was connected with high rates of atherosclerosis (the hardening of the arteries) in humans (Carper 39).

Fortunately, there are fast foods and snacks available that are not high in 8 calories and fat. Consider the following fast food meals:

A) A Filet O' Fish sandwich from McDonald's and a pair of Reese's Peanut Butter Cups.

B) A Hot Stuffed Baked Potato topped with Chicken a la King from Wendy's and a 3 Musketeers bar.

It seems that these meals would be close in calories and fat content, doesn't it? But, there is a difference of 228 calories and 30.6 grams of fat between the two. Below is the analysis:

Table 2		
	Calories	Fat (grams)
McDonald's Filet O' Fish	435	25.7
Reese's Cups	243	13.9
Meal A Total	**678**	**39.6**
Wendy's Stuffed Potato	350	6.0
3 Musketeers bar	100	3.0
Meal B Total	**450**	**9.0**

Source: *Jean Carper's Total Nutrition Guide*, by Jean Carper. Copyright © 1987 by Jean Carper. Used by permission of Bantam Books, a division of Bantam Doubleday Dell Publishing Group, Inc.

As Table 2 illustrates, it pays to know the calorie and fat content of fast food. Subsequently, you may wish to purchase one of the inexpensive books that contain calorie and fat counts, such as *Jean Carper's Total Nutrition Guide*. Using a book like Carper's can help you decide which foods you should avoid. Another helpful bit of information contained in a book like this is the comparison of similar foods from different fast food chains. For example, a chicken sandwich from Wendy's has only 366 calories and 11.9 grams of fat, while the Hardee's chicken sandwich has 510 calories and 26 grams of fat

(Carper 300). As for snacks like candy and cookies, a quick glance at the wrapper will often reveal the calorie and fat content of these foods.

There are many snacks available besides candy and cookies that are con- 9 venient, low calorie and low in fat. Fruit Roll-ups are sweet as well as low-fat (82 calories, .6 grams fat) and Sunkist Fun Fruits (104 calories, 1 gram fat) are also convenient and tasty (264). Many food manufacturers now package individual servings of foods that could be eaten as low-fat snacks. Mixed fruit cups, low-fat yogurt, frozen fruit bars, trail mixes, flavored rice cakes, and most hard candies are a few examples. Beware of snacks that appear to be low in fat by virtue of having a nutritious name. For example, the healthy-sounding Carob and Granola bar has 143 calories and 9.0 grams of fat (Carper 266) and the seemingly harmless yogurt peanuts have 8.7 grams of fat in a 1 oz. serving (Carper 286).

It is not necessary that we resign ourselves to being overweight and at a 10 health risk just because we want to eat fast foods and snacks. Many of us are not aware that there is a choice between fattening and non-fattening fast foods and that a wide variety of low-fat snacks are available. Through the purchase of an inexpensive calorie/fat counter book and by paying a little more attention to the nutritional information provided on food packages, we can continue to practice the time-saving habit of eating fast foods and snacks while remaining slim and healthy.

Works Cited

Carper, Jean. *Jean Carper's Total Nutrition Guide*. New York: Bantam, 1987.

Critical Reading Questions

1. What passages make you believe that Williams is sympathetic to the problems her primary audience faces?
2. What is your impression of a research report based exclusively on one resource? What additional information or counterarguments might Williams have addressed to substantiate her claims?
3. What did you learn as a result of reading this piece?
4. If Williams were in your peer review workshop, what specific advice would you give her for improving this draft?

Evaluating Criticism

Before rushing on to tackle your next writing assignment, it makes sense to pause and reflect on your growth as a writer. Draw a line down the center of one of your Writing and Research Notebook pages and on the left-hand side note all of the weaknesses that became apparent while writing this assignment. Then, on the right-hand side, reflect on what you have learned and what goals you want to set for your next assignment.

Focusing on strengths and weaknesses can be a humbling experience, but this process can also help you grow as a writer. Remember that writing is a lifelong experience: the more you write, the better you'll write.

1. What have you learned about yourself as a writer as a result of the prewriting, drafting, revising, or collaborating techniques that you experimented with when writing your research report?

2. Did your perception of yourself as a writer or person change as a result of this assignment? How?

3. In what ways has writing your research report changed your understanding of the research process?

4. If you exchanged papers and critiqued some of your peers' work, what did you learn as a result of these experiences?

5. If you were to begin this process again, what would you do differently?

6. In what ways have your thoughts about your subject changed as a result of the research that you completed?

7. How was your peers' and teacher's evaluation of your research report similar to and different from their evaluation of past writing projects?

8. What additional feedback do you feel you need from your instructor or peers in order to improve as a writer?

Writing Reports Based on Interviews and Questionnaires

Conducting research based on interviews and questionnaires requires many of the same skills as library-based reports (see Chapter 8). For instance, researchers still need to focus on one specific purpose; they must refer to previous scholarship to support controversial claims; they must follow an accepted form of documentation to acknowledge the scholars and researchers who have informed their work; and they must establish the credibility of the references that they cite. Because authors of reports based on interviews or questionnaires often cite the ideas of other scholars and the results of other researchers, they also need to be familiar with how to research information in a library.

Yet there are a few substantial and exciting differences between reports based solely on secondary sources and reports based on original research. First and most importantly, authors of essays based on interviews or questionnaires have the satisfaction of knowing that they are doing original work. Instead of merely summarizing the opinions and research of others or making an argument and supporting it by referring to secondary sources, field researchers are adding to the literature on a subject. Second, these authors are responsible for shaping a research method that will uncover the information they need and at the same time minimize distortion by eliminating inadequate or unnecessarily biased data. Authors of reports based on interviews need to listen to hours of recorded interviews or, preferably, sift through pages of transcripts to discover significant information. Authors of reports based on questionnaires must be careful to prepare crucial questions, and then analyze results to identify themes and patterns in the data.

This chapter explains techniques to interview people productively and to develop questionnaires that solicit needed information. I explain the conventions for shaping field-based reports and offer step-by-step guidelines for prewriting, writing, and revising reports based on interviews and questionnaires. The chapter provides a variety of writing assignments—such as conducting a family history or surveying classmates to uncover their attitudes about campus issues. Samples of student reports based on interviews and questionnaires are presented throughout the chapter so that you can have a sense of the range of voices and purposes possible and an appreciation of the problems that researchers face.

Writing Sample

In the following essay, Joseph Scaglione, a student writer, analyzes the horror awaiting anyone who is victimized by a criminal. During the course of his investigation, Scaglione conducted some library research and interviewed three families who had lost loved ones. Because of the emotionally painful and potentially litigious nature of his subject, Scaglione gave fictitious names to the people he interviewed; some requested complete anonymity. Scaglione also drew on his own experience as a victim, yet he decided not to specifically discuss his own loss because he believed readers would prefer, and benefit by, a more detached tone.

> ### Analysis of Communication Situation
>
> **Subject:** The treatment of crime victims by the officials of the criminal justice system.
>
> **Audience:** The general public, uninformed lawmakers, and new crime victims.
>
> **Voice:** The voice of this piece attempts to be both compassionate and bold, told in third person.
>
> **Purpose:** To inform the audience of the fragile nature of the relationship between crime victims and the criminal justice system; to inform the audience of the many forces faced by crime victims; to inform the audience that crime victims do have rights and can exercise them.
>
> **Context:** Local, statewide, and national victims' rights organizations, popular magazines, and literary publications.

Into the Wilderness—Victimization and the Criminal Justice System

Joseph Scaglione

The Wilderness Awaits

A wilderness awaits each American at work, at play and at sleep. This is a wilderness of violent crime and of a justice system which protects the rights of the accused rather than those of the victimized, a wilderness for which no special qualifications are required to enter, and a wilderness in which the victim feels alone, betrayed, and cast out. 1

The back alleys, the main streets, even the once secure homes of America are the playgrounds of those who, as of 1990, have turned the United States into the number one rated nation in the world in violent crimes 2 (murders, rapes and robberies). In 1988 the United States Department of Justice listed a total of 35,795,840 victimizations in all categories. This number reflects, of course, only those crimes actually reported to law enforcement agencies. Of these, 127,370 attempted rapes were reported; 65,550 rapes were carried out. The number of robberies totalled 1,048,000 and the number of thefts was 14,056,390 (*Criminal Victimization* 14). The U.S. Department of Commerce also provides additional statistics: for every one thousand citizens, there were sixteen homicide arrests (*Statistical Abstracts* 168).

As a result of these excessive crime rates, both the individual and society 3 become victims. Higher crime rates lead to escalating insurance costs, increased security costs, and increased taxation to support the legal infrastructure created to deal with crime. But a much higher price is extracted from the individual who has been victimized: first by the criminal who commits the assault, then by the justice system which abuses the victim by ignoring his or her rights.

Naive misconceptions concerning the process of justice are held by the 4 everyday citizen. The police know the truth; the court officials know the truth; the defense attorneys know the truth. And, the criminals know the truth.

For the victim, the truth comes in many forms. The following accounts, 5 which are based on true stories told to me by victims, forcefully illustrate the terror that awaits each of us around every corner. To protect the privacy of those involved, I have fictionalized some of the names of the people whom I interviewed during this investigation.

The Edge of Wilderness

"Your son has been killed. Call Police." So read the yellow Post-It note on the front door of Mary Wilson's home. As she arrived from shopping, she stood, arms full of grocery bags, fumbling for her keys. As she lifted her head, her eyes suddenly focused on the small yellow note; she dropped all her groceries. Mary Wilson had FOUR sons.

The telephone ring pierced the night in the downtown New Orleans hotel room. This was Sugar Bowl weekend, 1990, and the Simpson family had just been asleep a short while following a night of revelry. Bill Simpson groped for the phone, still half-asleep.

"Hello."

"Mr. Simpson?"

"Yes, who is this? What time is it?"

"Sorry, Mr. Simpson; it's 2:15, and I'm Sergeant Nelson of the Tampa Police Department. I'm calling to inform you . . ." Sergeant Nelson paused for a moment, swallowing a deep breath, "to inform you that your daughter Cindy has been killed in an automobile accident here in Tampa."

"What? I don't understand."

"Your girl was killed tonight in a car wreck. That's all the information I have at this time."

The conversation ended abruptly, and the Simpsons were left with a long car ride home.

Ann Williams reached to the night stand and lifted the telephone to her ear.

"Is this Ann Williams?"

"Yes, may I help you?"

"Do you have a daughter named Missy, Mrs. Williams?"

"Yes, I do. Who is this? What's the problem?"

"This is Sergeant Jackson of the Tampa Police Department. I'm sorry to have to tell you. Your daughter has been a fatality in a three-car crash."

She slowly absorbed these words; her body rose to a defensive position as she sat upright in her bed. The muscles in the small of her back became taut and began to throb as a strong feeling of nausea overcame her. The sweaty palm of her left hand covered her mouth gently in disbelief as she thought to herself that this must be some cruel hoax.

"Who is this again?" She caught her breath between words.

"Sergeant Jackson. I'm sorry. If you have any more questions, please call Detective Mason of the Vehicular Homicide Division on Tuesday after the holiday." (This was Saturday morning, two days before the 1990 New Year.) Mrs. Williams' eighteen-year-old daughter had been killed 1.6 miles from their home over two and one-half hours before.

Examples such as these display the insensitivity of members of the law en- 6 forcement community toward surviving victims. This treatment violates the basic principles of human compassion by ignoring the right of crime victims to be treated with dignity.

The first reaction upon reading such accounts as these is that they can- 7 not be true. Tragically, all the accounts described here are true.

The second reaction is a strong sense that "this won't happen to me." 8 The harsh reality is that this very well could. Crime is spreading throughout every segment of society and is touching the young and old, the rich and poor, the strong and defenseless. The effects of each crime extend far beyond the individual victim, much like a web, a web of victimization.

The Web of Victimization

The nature of crime is such that for each crime committed there is at least 9 one victim. This equation does not change. Whether a murder, a rape, or a robbery, the effects of the violent criminal act immediately impact the victim and subsequently affect the victim's "support network": mothers and fathers, wives and husbands, sisters and brothers, as well as other family members and friends who try to help the victim rebuild his or her life. These are the "secondary victims" of crime, who share the agony, the sorrow, and even the guilt that the victim experiences. They too ponder the many "what ifs" that people normally engage in when tragedy strikes. And, many times, even close friends and family abandon the victim, because they just do not know what to say or how to help.

In some cases, the secondary victims are the survivors of the deceased. In 10
homicide cases, these survivors then become the only ones who represent the case of the victim. This also applies to victims who are physically or mentally incapacitated as a result of a criminal act. In an attempt to seek justice, secondary victims become entangled in a web of victimization by the legal system. This leads to frustration due in great part to the lack of concern, commitment, or care by police, district attorneys, judges, pre-sentencing investigators, probation officials, and others.

The Wilderness of the System

As victims are exposed to the realities of the criminal justice system, they dis- 11
cover a slow process which may take years. This process includes pre-trial hearings, motion hearings, delays for evidence to be obtained and analyzed, more motion hearings, seemingly endless subpoenas issued, more motion hearings, postponements, attempted plea bargain arrangements, and then possibly a trial. The trial itself can be delayed by more motion hearings, jury selection, appeals, and even overturned verdicts. This provides a view of what the victim faces: a system which serves the convenience of the perpetrator; a system which hears the voice of the criminal clearly but has muted the victim's cry for justice.

The size and complexity of the system overwhelms most victims and 12
exacts additional tolls: constant reliving and retelling of the criminal act, dehumanizing discourses by defense attorneys who attempt to shift blame from the client to the victim, lost wages and even lost jobs resulting from unaccommodating employers who do not understand the legal needs of the victim. In many cases continual visits with mental health professionals are necessary to help the victim maintain a sense of balance in his or her life. This is only a small glimpse into the long-term price of proclaiming to police that you have been victimized. No wonder so many crimes go unreported.

Fighting Back

While the exhaustion that results from dealing with this process is heavy, 13
some victims choose to fight back. Bob Preston is one who did. He founded Justice For Surviving Victims after his daughter Wendy was murdered in his home in 1977. The murder suspect was quickly apprehended and pleaded guilty to second-degree murder. The legal process took six years before a trial was held. Mr. Preston was appalled (Weinstein).

Working with other state victims' rights groups, he led an eleven-year 14
battle to place a constitutional amendment for victims' rights on a statewide ballot in Florida. Amendment Two, the victims' rights amendment, was

ratified by the November 8, 1988, statewide ballot. The voters of the State of Florida agreed with Mr. Preston that this was an idea whose time had come. Now operating under the jurisdiction of the State Attorney's office, victims have direct access to rights during the legal process such as the right to be informed, the right to be present, and the right to be heard. This is accomplished through the Victims' Advocate Office, an agency which meets the victim's needs by providing an avenue to the legal system. The personnel of this agency act as a buffer zone between the system and the victim. While this is one example of a step toward a greater voice for the victim, there is a long way to go. While laws set the framework for proper societal behavior, the success or failure of our laws will always rely on the most uncertain of factors: the human element, the PEOPLE.

The Human Failure

A victim's problem should be handled with the utmost compassion and dig- 15 nity. Because law enforcement officials deal daily on an individual level with the must rudimentary problem of survival, they must not succumb to the urge of just doing their job or worse, passing the buck.

The system does place undue pressure upon criminal justice officials: 16 law officers are understaffed and undertrained; prosecuting attorneys have heavy caseloads; and judges have dockets that overflow. These are valid reasons for the slowness of the system, but there is no excuse for the mistreatment of victims. A very strong need exists for the training of officials in the proper handling of victims. But a lack of training does not justify abuse. The Harmon family experienced this abuse first-hand and shared their story with me.

Into the Wilderness

The Harmon family entered the wilderness of the criminal justice system 17 when Lisa Harmon, 19, was murdered in their home. Administrators at the Methodist college Lisa had been attending were stunned. Some offered that "everyone knew" Lisa and that "her death would be a personal loss" (Knight).

Sam and Carla Harmon had two beautiful daughters, Lisa and Carol, 17, 18 and a son Billy, 22, who was serving in the Army. This July morning, Sam had left for work. Mom and her two girls had piled into Lisa's bedroom and acted as three teenagers at a slumber party. They laughed and giggled, sharing secrets and dreams only best friends would dare to reveal.

At ten o'clock Carla and Carol left together. Lisa, now all alone, donned 19 a new green and white, two piece bathing suit and laid down on the chaise lounge outside on the deck to improve her tan. She was napping as the blue Ford Bronco was driven quietly into the driveway.

At 12:30, Carla arrived home from shopping to the sound of a ringing 20 telephone. She hurriedly entered. Reaching the phone, one of Lisa's friends was calling her. "Just one minute please, I'll get her," responded Carla.

As she left the kitchen and gazed out to the deck, no Lisa. Carla then 21 entered the family room and, finding it empty, proceeded into the den. There Lisa sat upright in a big brown lounge chair. Her bathing suit top was off. Her arms rested upon the arm rests. "Lisa," called her mom, as she knelt down in front of her.

Lisa did not answer. The huge frame of the lounge chair embraced Lisa's 22 still body. Her right eye was bloody from a deep wound which her mother thought at first had been inflicted by the family dog, a chow. "Lisa, I told you that dog was going to bite you if you kept bothering him." First denial, and then reality struck: Lisa was dead.

Carla rose slowly, mechanically. A few seconds became a lifetime as she 23 edged back toward the telephone. "I'm sorry . . . Lisa can't come to the phone right now." Amazing calmness swept over her. Carla realized she must do something. But what?

As Lisa's friend hung up the phone, Carla dialed 911 and explained 24 clearly to the operator what she had found. The operator assured her that someone would be out immediately. Then, calling Sam at work, Carla calmly asked him to return home quickly. She went to her bedroom closet to find a shirt or jacket with which she could cover Lisa's body. She knew how modest Lisa was.

She examined the first jacket. No, she thought; Sam would be mad if she 25 got blood on his nice blue blazer. No, not her dark green blouse, she would wear that to church Sunday. Finally, she settled on a soft brown flannel shirt.

Returning to Lisa, Carla covered her eldest daughter's nude torso with 26 the shirt and spoke gently, "It's ok, honey." Caressing Lisa's soft brown hair with the tips of her fingers, Carla promised Lisa that all would be okay. She waited 45 minutes before the first authorities arrived.

As deputy sheriffs and detectives arrived, they took Carla into another 27 room. Convinced that Lisa had committed suicide, the detectives had one problem: no weapon.

"You can't have a suicide without a weapon," they said. 28

The interrogation that ensued was unrelenting. Convinced that Carla 29 had disposed of the revolver that Lisa had used, investigators insisted that she produce it. At Carla's insistence they searched the premises; they dragged the pond behind the house; they questioned Carla again and again. No weapon was found. No APB was issued concerning the blue Bronco neighbors had seen speeding down the street.

As Carla relates here, "They were convinced that Lisa had committed 30 suicide and that I had hidden the gun. The detective told me that the Medical Examiner had come out and claimed it was a suicide, too. They wanted me to show them where I had put the gun; otherwise, they would have to consider this a murder. They made a mess of things. So many people were here touching everything. They found the sheets dragged off her bed upstairs. Yet, they still claimed it had to be a suicide."

Sam had waited patiently, comforting his younger daughter. Now he 31 intervened. He took Carla and his younger daughter to his mother's house. When the detectives were finished, the family returned. The detectives left, still convinced this was a suicide, nothing more. The Harmons returned to their fractured home and cleaned Lisa's blood from the floor of the den; they slept in the house that night.

Three days later, the Crime Investigation Squad returned. The Medical 32 Examiner had found a second bullet lodged inside Lisa's throat. This was now officially a murder. But fingerprints had been cleansed from the scene; the whole house had been scoured clean room by room. As Sam now reflects, "They didn't treat this like a murder. That first day they didn't even rope off the area. They really botched this investigation, and they know it. All they could think was that my wife covered up a suicide."

Over two years later, no suspect has been apprehended. But the scars of 33 this investigation continue to haunt the Harmon family. Several weeks later, another detective came to the Harmon's home while only Carla and Carol were there. When Sam came home later, both women were visibly distraught. The detective had described how the murderer had mentally and physically tortured Lisa, based on a reconstruction of her wounds.

The long term emotional impact experienced by the Harmons can never 34 be measured and will never disappear. They can only hope that their strong Christian faith and professional help will cause the events of that July day to dim. But they will never leave completely.

Out From the Wilderness

Crime is no respecter of persons. Becoming a victim can be as arbitrary as 35 taking a stroll after dinner. All the best security measures cannot completely shield an individual from a criminal act. But the way officials handle fragile human beings in their most vulnerable state (grief and violation) must be improved. Crime victims are thrust into the wilderness of crime; they must not be left there, alone and abandoned, sensing betrayal from the justice system sworn to protect their rights.

The scenarios that have been portrayed here need not repeat themselves. 36 Surely Mary Wilson, Bill Simpson, Ann Williams, and the Harmons do not wish for others to receive the treatment they experienced. Amendment Two has made it law that victims are now part of the process. Victims' advocates now make it possible that victims no longer need experience the criminal justice system without guidance. Bob Preston and other victims have created organizations to which new victims can turn. And training of law enforcement and victim advocate professionals is beginning to be performed by trained counselors.

Victims' rights is one of the hottest issues of the 1990s. As well it should 37 be, to which the stories related here attest. Trained, compassionate, involved public officials, willing and capable of leading crime victims out from the wilderness, are vital. This will only come about by first informing the public and governmental officials that this is a real life problem, and, secondly, by convincing them to enact laws and to allocate funds to assure that victims are properly cared for throughout the legal process.

Then the savagery of the wilderness will have been blunted, not 38 destroyed, merely blunted. Law enforcement officials will then know the type of abuse described here will no longer be tolerated by victims, victims' advocates, nor by the system itself. Hopefully, that day is nearing.

Works Cited

Knight, Ken. "Slain Woman Remembered as Christian, Fun Loving." *Tampa Tribune* 7 July 1988: 1/East Hillsborough.

United States Department of Commerce. *Statistical Abstract of the United States, 1990.* Bureau of the Census. Washington: GPO, 168.

United States Department of Justice. *Criminal Victimization in the United States, 1988.* Bureau of Justice Statistics.

Weinstein, Joshua. "Amendment 2 Underscores Victims' Rights." *St. Petersburg Times* 18 Oct. 1988: 1B.

Critical Reading Questions

1. How would you describe the tone of this piece? What specific passages encourage you to assess his tone as you do? Are there any instances when Scaglione's tone seems distracting or ineffective? Where and why do you find this to be so?

2. What are some of the details that Scaglione provides to help readers understand the brutality yet commonplace nature of violent crime? How does Scaglione use sensory and concrete language to help readers understand his position?

3. Rather than presenting his interview findings in a question/answer format, Scaglione attempts to recreate the victim's experience. In what ways is this strategy successful or unsuccessful?

4. Do you believe that this report would be stronger if Scaglione had provided additional information about the interviews he conducted or do you prefer his current focus on violent crime and faults within the criminal justice system?

The following survey is the result of a semester-long research project in an advanced writing course at the University of South Florida. This project was conceived by all the members of the course and was administered by

James Clark and Patrick Poff. The results were written by Todd W. Taylor and Charles Oldham. Our intention was to gather general information about students' life-styles, with the hope that this survey would be useful to members in the class.

View from the Bread Box: Race Issues on Campus

Todd W. Taylor and Charles Oldham

A recent survey of 258 students at the University of South Florida found 1 almost exactly what you might expect statistically: they're perfectly normal. If this population was a family unit, then they would have 2.5 children and 1.2 pets. The group was split evenly between males and females, most of them single, junior college graduates who commute to campus and have a G.P.A. between 2.8 and 3.7. As an amalgamation, these eighteen- to twenty-five-year-olds get drunk about once a week, aren't learning disabled, handicapped, bulimic or in need of help from the counseling center. While 85 percent of the students believe in God and 57 percent of them claim to pray weekly, less than a quarter of them regularly attend religious services. They're also 84 percent white. They have changed their major a couple of times and have to change schedules because of full classrooms. Only 20 percent of them hold Greek affiliations. Only 13 percent feel they have been discriminated against on campus because of gender. In other words, our survey represents the perspective of the average, white-bread American college student—a view from the bread box.

Yet this campus, like many others, exhibits tension over issues of race, 2 particularly affirmative action admission policies. The editors of *The New Republic* in a recent special issue titled *Race on Campus* write:

> On America's campuses today the issue of race is unavoidable. The impact of affirmative action upon the tenor of even the simplest class discussion is profound. Resentful whites tussle uncomfortably with suspicious minority students struggling with situations they find personally overwhelming. (Derisory Tower 5)

Dinesh D'Souza's article in the same issue further acknowledges this tension as he summarizes reports from *The Chronicle of Higher Education* by stating, ". . . many white students who are generally sympathetic to the minority cause become weary and irritated by the extent of preferential treatment and double standards" (D'Souza 33).

Our survey supports these conclusions. For example, the respondents 3 displayed some "politically correct" views on race: 84 percent felt interracial dating was acceptable; 75 percent said they were not "biased toward another race." The students were also very divided over perceived institutional policies. In response to the question, "Do you believe the university adequately addresses racial issues?" 49 percent answered "yes" while 32 percent answered "no" and a significant 19 percent were "unsure."

Reverse discrimination seems to be a particular problem—a vast majority 4
feel that reverse discrimination exists. One-third of the students think they
have been victim of reverse discrimination. Likewise, our campus was very
divided over the issue of affirmative action. Almost exactly one-third favors
that policy while one-third opposes it with the other third unsure. Less than
10 percent believe affirmative action has helped them, which may be
expected in a population that is so predominantly white. A similar survey
published in March of 1992 in *The Chronicle* made it clear that a student's
race is very likely to influence his or her view of affirmative action.

According to that source, only 26 percent of the white students favor 5
preferential treatment for college minorities while 52 percent of the black
students favor such assistance (Collison 1). This situation might seem obvious; who wouldn't want an advantage for themselves and not for someone
else? Not so obvious, however, are the effects of policies like affirmative
action. A significant effect, according to our survey and others, emerges from
the divisions created between college students over issues of race. In response
to an incident of racial hate mail involving Yale law students, Jeff Rosen, a
student himself, writes:

> . . . most students expected the racist letters to unite the campus in appalled
> condemnation. Instead, the frenzied reaction to the letters has divided the
> campus bitterly, demonstrating how difficult it has become for Yale stu-
> dents to distinguish between imagined racism and the real thing. (Rosen 19)

As we see it, our university, like many other campuses in America, is having a
hard time resolving race issues. On the surface it seems easy to support the
idea of racial equality; yet beneath the surface lies something else. For example, only 18 percent felt they were "biased toward another race" while an
overwhelming 88 percent answered "yes" to the question, "Do you think
someone could be racist and not know it?" Here lies an interesting contradiction: if only one-fifth of the students believe they are biased but believe that
nearly 90 percent of the population is racist and does not know it, just who
are these nine out of ten who are harboring prejudices? As Shelby Steele
wrote in the June 1988 issue of *Harper's*, "As a black person you always hear
about racists but never meet any" (Steele 48).

The *Chronicle* finds "that American youths are generally pessimistic 6
about race relations in the United States" (Collison 1). Their survey highlights a big difference in student perceptions toward minority enrollment
policies. Forty-eight percent of the 1,170 students polled felt "special consideration" for minorities was appropriate; but only 34 percent favored "special
preference." How can someone receive "special consideration" without, at
the same time, receiving "special preference"? Again, on the surface the
"politically correct" view toward race is maintainable. But, the application in
the real world is quite a contrast.

Our research indicates the following about mainstream, white college 7
students: they claim to want to eliminate racial biases but are suspect of

even themselves; however, tangible policies, such as affirmative action, are hard to accept. And maybe the divisive nature of such policies as they are currently employed should carry the blame. After all, if the goals of affirmative action are unity, equality, and acceptance among different races, then the suspicions and separations it causes inside student populations are antagonistic to its purposes. William Hussey, a professional advisor at Brooklyn College, was recently demoted for pointing out how the idiosyncrasies of affirmative action "show how difficult it is to have 'perfectly reasonable' discrimination" (Hussey 23). If students, such as the ones we studied, are ever going to be able to connect their perceived lack of prejudice with campus policies toward minorities then maybe some progressive policy changes need to be made. Dinesh D'Souza promotes such an idea in his article "Sins of Admission: Affirmative Action on Campus":

> If universities want to eliminate race as a factor in their students' decision-making, they might consider eliminating it as a factor in their own. It may be time for college leaders to consider basing affirmative action programs on socioeconomic disadvantage rather than ethnicity. This strategy would help reach those disadvantaged blacks who desperately need the education our colleges provide, but without the deleterious effect of racial head-counting. And it would set a color-blind standard of civilized behavior, which inspired the civil rights movement in the first place. (D'Souza 33)

Works Cited

Collison, Michelle N-K. "Young People Found Pessimistic about Relations Between the Races." *The Chronicle of Higher Education* 25 Mar. 1992: 1, 32.

"Derisory Tower." Editorial. *The New Republic* 18 Feb. 1991: 5–8.

D'Souza, Dinesh. "Sins of Admission: Affirmative Action on Campus." *The New Republic* 18 Feb. 1991: 30–33.

Hussey, William W. Letter. *The New Republic* 15 Apr. 1991: 23.

Rosen, Jeff. "Hate Mail." *The New Republic* 18 Feb. 1991: 19–22.

Steele, Shelby. "I'm Black, You're White, Who's Innocent?: Race and Power in an Era of Blame." *Harper's.* June 1988: 45–53.

Appendix

Please take a moment to complete the following questionnaire. This is an anonymous questionnaire, so please provide honest answers. We hope to use your opinions in a study of student life at USF. Select the answer you feel most appropriate and fill in the corresponding oval on the Scantron sheet.

Thank you for your time.

Demographic Questions

1. Year in school:

    a. Freshman   (10%)

    b. Sophomore   (12%)

    c.   Junior   (31%)

    d.   Senior   (43%)

    e.   Graduate   (4%)

2. Age:

    a.   18–21   (43%)

    b.   22–25   (35%)

    c.   26–29   (7%)

    d.   30–34   (10%)

    e.   36 or higher   (5%)

3. Gender:

    a.   Male   (51%)

    b.   Female   (49%)

4. Ethnic origin:

    a.   White (non-Hispanic)   (84%)

    b.   Black (non-Hispanic)   (8%)

    c.   Hispanic   (5%)

    d.   Asian/Pacific Islander   (3%)

    e.   Other   (0%)

5. Are you a:

    a.   Commuter Student   (77%)

    b.   Non-Commuter Student   (23%)

6. Marital status:

    a.   Married   (20%)

    b.   Single   (76%)

    c.   Divorced   (3%)

    d.   Widowed   (0%)

7. Are you:

    a.   Not disabled   (92%)

    b.   Learning disabled   (5%)

    c.   Physically disabled   (2%)

8. Cumulative G.P.A.

    a.   0–2.0   (0%)

    b.   2.01–2.8   (24%)

    c.   2.81–3.0   (35%)

    d.   3.01–3.7   (30%)

    e.   3.71–4.0   (11%)

9. How many times have you changed your major?

   a. 0 (36%)

   b. 1 (34%)

   c. 2 (24%)

   d. 3–4 (5%)

   e. 5 or more (0%)

10. In the past year, how often have you had to change your schedule because a class was full?

    a. 0 (26%)

    b. 1 (32%)

    c. 2 (21%)

    d. 3–4 (11%)

    e. 5 or more (10%)

11. Are you a member of a fraternity or sorority?

    a. Yes (20%)

    b. No (80%)

    c. I plan to join (0%)

12. How many times a week do you get drunk?

    a. 0 (51%)

    b. 1 (24%)

    c. 2 (16%)

    d. 3–4 (7%)

    e. 5 or more (2%)

13. How often have you used the USF counseling center?

    a. 0 (79%)

    b. 1 (11%)

    c. 2 (5%)

    d. 3–4 (0%)

    e. 5 or more (4%)

14. How often have you purged a meal in an effort to control weight?

    a. 0 (93%)

    b. 1 (2%)

    c. 2 (2%)

    d. 3–4 (0%)

    e. 5 or more (2%)

15. At USF, how many times have you felt treated unfairly because of your gender?

    a. 0   (87%)

    b. 1   (9%)

    c. 2   (2%)

    d. 3–4   (2%)

    e. 5 or more   (0%)

16. Do you believe inter-racial dating is acceptable?

    a. Yes   (84%)

    b. No   (12%)

    c. Unsure (4%)

17. Do you believe the university adequately addresses racial issues?

    a. Yes   (49%)

    b. No   (32%)

    c. Unsure (19%)

18. Do you know what is meant by reverse discrimination?

    a. Yes   (84%)

    b. No   (12%)

    c. Unsure (4%)

19. Do you think reverse discrimination exists?

    a. Yes   (84%)

    b. No   (3%)

    c. Unsure (13%)

20. Have you been a victim of reverse discrimination?

    a. Yes   (33%)

    b. No   (45%)

    c. Unsure (22%)

21. Do you know what affirmative action is?

    a. Yes   (76%)

    b. No   (10%)

    c. Unsure (14%)

22. Do you support affirmative action?

    a. Yes   (35%)

    b. No   (35%)

    c. Unsure (30%)

23. Has affirmative action helped you?
    a. Yes   (9%)
    b. No   (58%)
    c. Unsure   (33%)

24. Are you biased toward another race?
    a. Yes   (18%)
    b. No   (75%)
    c. Unsure   (8%)

25. Do you think that someone can be racist and not realize it?
    a. Yes   (88%)
    b. No   (10%)
    c. Unsure   (2%)

26. Do you feel that your race has affected your grades in any way?
    a. Yes   (11%)
    b. No   (82%)
    c. Unsure   (7%)

27. Do you believe in the existence of God?
    a. Yes   (85%)
    b. No   (5%)
    c. Unsure   (10%)

28. How many times a week do you pray?
    a. 0   (43%)
    b. 1–2   (34%)
    c. 3–4   (9%)
    d. 5–6   (8%)
    e. 7 or more   (7%)

29. When you were a child, how often did your family attend religious services?
    a. Weekly   (69%)
    b. Monthly   (5%)
    c. Holidays   (14%)
    d. Never   (8%)
    e. Other   (3%)

30. How often do you attend religious services now?
    a. Weekly   (24%)
    b. Monthly   (5%)

    c. Holidays   (31%)

    d. Never   (33%)

    e. Other   (7%)

Critical Reading Questions

1. How would you define Taylor and Oldham's tone in this study? Are there places where their tone is inconsistent?

2. Do you question any of Taylor and Oldham's conclusions based on the survey they provide in the appendix? In other words, do their data support their conclusions?

3. How does your experience relate to the issue of affirmative action and ethnicity as reported in this study?

4. In what ways did Taylor and Oldham refer to secondary sources to help interpret their results?

5. What changes would you make to the questionnaire to make it more authentic, revealing, or useful?

Analyzing Pertinent Conventions

As with other writing projects, you can determine the best way to shape your writing by identifying a specific audience, voice, and purpose. For example, several of the essay components discussed below—particularly the abstract, the statement of research question, the review of relevant literature, and the method, results, and discussion sections—would be especially appropriate if you were writing a report for a sociology, psychology, or education class. Although essays in the humanities and fine arts are likely to include some of these sections, they might be arranged in a different order, and they probably would feature more engaging headings than Results or Discussion. The method section that appears in the body of a social scientist's report is likely to be relegated to an appendix in a humanist's report. Argumentative essays and speculative reports are much more likely to emphasize the importance of a researcher's results and minimize or exclude discussions of any methods. For example, Scaglione's essay on victims' rights never mentions the exact questions he asks the victims, nor does Scaglione elaborate on where he interviewed the victims or how he set up the appointments. Instead, Scaglione keeps the focus exactly where his audience expects him to—on the subject of victims' vulnerability under current laws.

    Because no ideal format for a field-based research essay can be provided, you will not be able to use the following strategies as absolute blueprints.

Provide an Abstract

As mentioned in the chapter on library-based research reports, abstracts should provide readers with a sound idea about the focus and importance of your work. Abstracts summarize the significance of the subject and your method of analyzing the topic, results, discussion of results, and recommendations. Abstracts contain as little jargon as possible and no references. In general, the voice of your abstract—as reflected, for example, by your use of active or passive voice in sentences and by your level of diction—should be similar to that used in the body of the report. After all, abstracts serve as a "sample" of the report, so you would not write a formal-sounding abstract to introduce an informal-sounding report. You probably won't be able to complete your abstract until the report is finished, yet you should try to write tentative drafts of the abstract as you write the report because this drafting will help clarify the constraints placed on your writing by your communication situation.

Identify Your Primary Research Question

If you are writing the results of a questionnaire-based study, you should probably identify your primary goals for conducting the study in the introduction. Yet if you are simply reporting the results of interviews, this may not be necessary. In general, though, readers want to know whether you are addressing a significant subject that interests them. As a result, you may need to clarify the focus of your investigation by identifying your research question in the opening paragraphs of your report.

Incidentally, don't be concerned about expressing your research question the same way it was phrased in the abstract. Although you are wise to avoid redundancy, academic readers expect some repetition from the abstract to the introduction.

Hook Your Reader with Interesting Results and Intriguing Ideas

Some authors of academic and technical prose assume that they do not need to make their work interesting. And, of course, in some business and professional settings readers *must* read and study the material, interesting or not. Yet even if you have a "captive audience," you would be foolish to assume that you shouldn't try to make your work enjoyable to read. After all, even readers steeped in technical training are people with passions and a desire to be treated as such, so you should try to simplify and humanize your presentation of material as much as possible. Even when addressing highly technical subjects, you would be wise to remember that readers are more likely to enjoy and remember your work when you draw on their natural curiosity.

Did someone you interviewed say something shocking or comical? Did your survey reveal an unexpected attitude on the part of your respondents? Highlighting surprises in your introduction can hook your readers' interests. Although some academic readers dislike this practice of placing results in the introduction, you may still want to do this in a succinct way. Your introduction, then, should be a short paragraph that piques the readers' interest and helps them comprehend the substance of your report by clarifying the information to pay attention to.

Given the avalanche of printed material in our information age, it is understandable that experienced readers have become adept at scanning introductions to determine whether documents are worth reading. Readers may give the report a careful reading if the abstract or introduction seems intelligently composed and if the subject matter seems truly significant. In contrast, readers are less likely to study—or even read—a report if the introduction seems unduly technical, if the focus seems cloudy, if the conclusions appear spurious in light of the methodology employed, or if the recommendations appear to exceed the findings.

Review Relevant Literature

While your energies are primarily focused on answering a research problem that you want answers to, you should not assume that others have failed to examine your subject. In fact, when prewriting, as discussed earlier, you will want to identify whether others have developed a questionnaire or set of interview questions that you can use. And even if you cannot find examples of others who have gone into the field and conducted similar research, you can still use library research techniques to help develop a solid methodology and to interpret results. For example, if you wanted to explore the elements of a successful marriage, you might examine existing literature to determine the frequency of divorce; theories of positive interpersonal communication skills; the influence of class, education, and religious background; and so forth.

You may sometimes have a separate section that essentially evaluates the scholarship related to your topic. It is, in fact, quite common for authors to review current thinking on a subject in the introduction of their report. As you can understand, this review of literature can help clarify the significance of the author's report and help hook the reader's interest.

Provide a Method Section

Particular disciplines—such as psychology, sociology, anthropology, journalism, or literary criticism—have very specific expectations about how to conduct field research. Certain professions stick to established procedures for conducting research so that other experts in the discipline can conduct follow-up studies and better evaluate the validity of results. Part of your apprenticeship in a discipline involves becoming sensitized to what constitutes an acceptable methodology. Whenever you are writing for specialized audiences, you will need to account for their expectations if you hope to have them take you seriously.

In a writing class, however, your instructor is primarily concerned with how your research is written. Because this may well be one of your first opportunities to conduct an interview or draft a questionnaire, and because the rules on original research differ from discipline to discipline, your English teacher will be sympathetic to problems with your method. As mentioned throughout this chapter, you should view this current writing project as an open-ended challenge to your imagination. However, even though you are not bound by any rigid methodological guidelines and even though you will not be generalizing from your sample to a larger population, you should still try to develop a solid methodology. Below are some guidelines that can help you achieve this goal.

Report the Methodology for Interviews. Occasionally, you may wish to elaborate on the setting in which you conducted an interview and on the specific questions that you asked. Consider, for example, the following excerpt from Paul Reith's study of below-knee amputees. Reith, a student writer, presents background information about his research questions in this report because he thought it would help him establish a more credible tone.

> Fitting of a prosthesis—that is, an artificial replacement for a missing limb—is one of the most emotionally laden events to an amputee, second only to amputation. Except for the small amount of time that medical treatment is involved, hospital personnel—in particular physicians and nurses—have little to do with the psychological rehabilitation of the amputee. Instead, psychotherapeutics is performed by the other members of the "health team"—the prosthetist, the physical therapist, and the occupational therapist. This is unfortunate because treating an amputee's psychological problems often has more significance on his life than how well surgery was performed (location of suture lines, endpad thickness) or the type of prosthetic device used.
>
> As a prosthetist, I wondered what I can do to psychologically facilitate the rapid recovery of Below-Knee (BK) male amputees—amputees that historically compose the majority of the amputee population. To gain some insight into what I can say or what information I can provide to reduce the BK amputee's level of anxiety, fear, frustration, and anger, I interviewed ten amputees about their problems before amputation, after amputation, and during office visits. Each of the ten amputees that I interviewed were two-year veterans—that is, at least two years had passed since their BK amputation. Over a two-hour interviewing period with each of the ten amputees, I asked questions about the following subjects:
>
> 1. Feelings about loss of limb before amputation, after amputation, and during office visits.
> 2. Rapport with vascular surgeon, hospital staff, and prosthetist.
> 3. Feelings about prosthetic fittings.
> 4. Comfort, cosmesis, and control of prosthesis.
> 5. Acceptance by others after loss of limb.

Reports of how you conducted interviews are often unnecessary, however, and they can even be counterproductive. For example, if Joseph Scaglione had incorporated a discussion of where he interviewed the victims and presented the results in a question and answer format, he would have been less successful creating the persuasive tone and narrative voice that he ultimately established.

Report the Methodology for a Questionnaire. Reporting your method for a questionnaire is more difficult than reporting your method for an interview. When you survey people, you should provide a copy of the questionnaire, either within the report or attached as an appendix. Moreover, before readers can understand the significance of your work, you will need to inform them about how you developed the survey, whom you submitted it to, how many people responded to it, and—as much as possible—the characteristics of the respondents. Below is the description of the method I followed to survey teachers' goals and methods of responding to student writing:

> I pretested the survey by submitting it to twenty graduate teaching students at my institution and to ten professors who teach writing at both private and state universities and colleges throughout the country. During pretesting, I asked all participants to complete the survey and write criticisms of the questions and suggest questions that I had omitted or overlooked. Meeting with these participants or speaking with them over the phone to evaluate their interpretation of the survey questions enabled me to omit, revise, and add additional questions; in addition, this process helped me recognize that some of the survey questions created awkward forced choices. For example, some of the teachers whom I interviewed during pretesting remarked that they were uncomfortable about question 3. Although I recognized that teachers typically serve as judges and coaches, I decided not to provide a "both coach and judge" response, because I wanted to uncover teachers' primary allegiance.
>
> Because of financial limitations, I settled on a sample size of 800, which would roughly account for 25 percent of the nation's 3,587 two-year and four-year colleges (*Statistical Abstract* 153). However, based on my past experience with national surveys and because of the traditionally low response rate attributed to surveys of this sort, I expected to receive about 35 percent to 50 percent of the surveys back. To account for differences in the number of four-year and two-year colleges—that is, 2,135 four-year colleges and 1,452 two-year colleges (*Statistical Abstract* 153)—I used a table of random numbers to randomly select 320 two-year colleges and 480 four-year colleges and universities. So that I would be able to distinguish responses from instructors at four-year colleges from teachers at two-year colleges, I color-coded the questionnaires. A self-addressed, stamped envelope was enclosed with each survey.
>
> After an eight-week waiting period, I had received back 168 responses from two-year colleges and 294 responses from four-year colleges and universities. By analyzing the data, I could detect few distinctions between the responses of two-year and four-year college teachers. Nevertheless, to

account for the difference between the number of two-year and four-year colleges, I randomly discarded 43 of the four-year college teachers' responses so that I could write about the teachers' responses as a single group. This left me with a sample size of 419 teachers, which represents about 12 percent of the nation's two-year and four-year colleges and universities.

The 419 teachers who responded to the questionnaire were seasoned professionals; 16 percent had been in the profession for 8–11 years; 18 percent, 12–16 years; 26 percent, 17–23 years; 18 percent, 24 or more. Twenty-five percent of the respondents teach 1–2 writing courses per year, 33 percent teach 3–4 writing courses per year, and 18 percent teach 5–6 writing courses. Below is a complete review of their answers to the survey questions.

Report Methodological Limitations. Skilled academic readers—particularly those who write—understand that criticizing ideas and research methods is far easier than creating them. Indeed, most research methods are open to criticism. Few questionnaires—or, for that matter, few research designs—are totally solid. Even professionals who routinely conduct field-based research make methodological errors, so you shouldn't be terribly upset if there are flaws in your early studies. Sympathetic readers tend to be lenient when you make methodological errors. And although they may be understandably skeptical about your method, they will still be curious about your results and interpretations if you have selected an important subject to examine. To show that you are aware of the methodological problems and to warn future researchers away from the errors or deadends that you experienced, you may want to compile a separate section called "Limitations with this Study."

Report Results and Discuss Their Significance

The heart of a successful field report, of course, is the results. Many readers, in fact, will skim over the earlier sections of your report and concentrate on studying the outcome. Skilled academic and professional readers will be particularly curious about how your results refute or support earlier studies of a similar research question (if, of course, such scholarship is available). Thus, if your research findings bear on those of other researchers, you should mention this.

In the sciences and social sciences, authors are encouraged to separate reporting the results—for example, the statistical findings—from a broader discussion of their implications. Regardless of whether you develop a separate discussion section to elaborate on the significance of the investigation, however, you will need to analyze and organize the data for your reader. This rigorous process involves throwing out whatever data simply aren't helpful. To determine what material to omit or emphasize, you need to determine whether any common *themes* or major *points of disagreement* can be found in the data. You can do this by seeing what your subjects agree or disagree about. For example, if you interviewed business people to determine what attributes they look for in successful executives and most of them agreed that qualities A, B, and C are essential to effective leadership, you certainly want to tell your readers about this.

In addition, you will also want to mention whether the interviewees or respondents to the questionnaire express any unusual, contentious, or contradictory attitudes. For example, in a questionnaire-based study that I conducted with a colleague, we wanted to determine if English department chairs at American universities were working with freshman English directors to institutionalize modern rhetoric in their freshman writing programs. Much to our surprise, however, we discovered that many of the chairs held the freshman English director and the field of Composition Studies in low regard.* We had gone fishing for tuna, so to speak, but we ended up with carp. Making the best of a bad situation, we quoted a few of the English department chairs whose hostile attitudes and low regard for Composition Studies might create interest in our subject.

Reports of surveys invariably have fewer direct quotations from respondents than research based on interviews. However, to breathe life into your statistics when reporting the results of questionnaires, you would be wise to excerpt some quotations from any open-ended questions you asked. (See Prewriting and Drafting Strategies below for a discussion of open-ended questions.)

Carefully selected quotations from your questionnaire can establish your credibility and drive home the important points. For example, in Reith's interviews with BK (below-knee) amputees about how medical personnel can soften the psychological blow caused by loss of a limb, he reported the following conclusions:

> All interviewees reported shock when seeing their stump for the first time. Anxiety about the future and depression were common. I have found these emotional reactions to be intense the first few weeks after surgery, then slowly receding thereafter. Half of my interviewees felt a discussion with a BK amputee prior to the operation would have been useful for alleviating fear and anxiety. The others reported that they were probably too emotionally unstable to talk with an amputee or to see his or her artificial leg.

Although Reith's primary readers—that is, people in the medical community who work with amputees—are well aware of the pain and fear involved, his recommendation that patients should have the opportunity to meet with other amputees before their operations might be more forceful if he had quoted a few of his interviewees directly. Perhaps the following example could help break through the emotional barriers that hospital personnel construct when working with such cases:

---

* See Olson, Gary, and Joseph M. Moxley. "Directing Freshman Composition: The Limits of Authority." *College Composition and Communication* Feb. 1989: 51–60.

> My God, I wanted to die. I didn't want to talk to anyone or even look at it. I kept thinking that there was something they could have done, that they didn't have to amputate my leg. It was really touch and go. I hated everyone for a while because they could walk. Then when I got the prosthesis I was shocked. I could walk again after a little practice. And now I'm back at work and really feeling pretty good, all things considered.

The following discussion, extracted from an investigation of how graduate students respond to the stress created by working full-time while going to school full-time and raising children full-time, offers another example of how much stronger a results section can be if quotations back up the statistical trends:

> Ms. Wikon, one of the students I interviewed for this research study, reported experiencing headaches, insomnia, weight gain, and indigestion when she returned to school. Because she did not know how to handle the new stress she was under, she ignored all of these physical signs of stress until one morning she woke up numb on the whole left side of her body; only then did she pay attention to what her body was telling her. It said, "Your stress is handling you, and you better learn to handle it."
>
> Another student I interviewed said that he is on prescription drugs for the pain in his stomach which is severe during periods of heightened stress. This same person suffers from insomnia, weight gain, and backache. During stressful times, these physical problems cause him to be depressed and tired; he wants to quit the career he loves.

Follow the Conventions for Citing Sources

Throughout your report, you will need to acknowledge your indebtedness to other authors by adhering to the conventions for citing sources. If you interviewed people during the course of your investigation and they have not requested anonymity, then you should also acknowledge their contributions in the text and the Works Cited section. Citing sources involves considerable attention to detail, both while you conduct research and while you prepare your final draft. Be exceedingly careful that you properly follow the conventions for giving credit properly; always provide references for facts and ideas that are not part of the "general domain."

See Chapter 8 for a more complete discussion of how to avoid plagiarism and cite correctly. You can review Chapter 2 for a reminder of when to provide direct quotations, when and how to paraphrase and summarize, and of the Modern Language Association's guidelines for documenting sources.

Writing Assignments

If you are given the opportunity to select your own research question or if the teacher's guidelines are broad and open-ended, ask yourself, first of all, "What do I care about?" Then, as with library research, you should narrow the subject to one that you can realistically explore in the amount of time available to you. And finally, because your work must ultimately communicate to others, you need to ask, "Who cares? What audience am I targeting?"

The key to being a successful researcher is identifying a meaningful question. You can pretty much assume that if you are fascinated by a subject, other readers will be also. For example, students in my classes have surveyed other students' knowledge and feelings about nuclear arms, local environmental issues, and on-campus issues, such as whether students believe the four-year engineering program should be turned into a five-year program; whether students should be required to purchase personal computers and be computer literate; whether students are taking necessary precautions to avoid AIDS and other sexually transmitted diseases.

If a topic doesn't immediately occur to you, then you should freewrite on possible subjects, skim through current periodicals that you subscribe to or come across in your daily life, and talk over possibilities with friends and students in your writing class. To prime the pump of your imagination, you may find it useful to freewrite in response to the following "topic prompts."

1. How aware are you of your family history? If you would like to learn more, consider interviewing your older relatives. For instance, you could interview one of your grandparents to learn more about his or her life. Where were your grandparents born, what were their life's goals, what major obstacles did they face?

2. If you are unsure about what academic major or career you would like to pursue, perhaps you could meet with an adviser at your school's academic counseling center and gather information about possible alternatives. To gain some insight into your interests, you may also find it useful to take the General Aptitude Test Battery, the Edwards Personal Preference Schedule, the Strong-Campbell Interest Inventory, the Kuder Occupational Interest Survey, or the Myers-Briggs Personality Inventory. You could then use the insights these tests provide, along with your interview with a career counselor, to evaluate the suitability of various academic majors and professions.

3. If you already know what career you wish to pursue but are unsure about the day-to-day responsibilities that such a position involves, then you could interview professionals in the field to discover more about their responsibilities, financial rewards, and job satisfaction.

4. What unusual people do you know whom you would like to interview? Who are these people and what makes them so interesting to you?

5. Are there any practices or policies on your campus that you and other students you know find particularly annoying? For example, are there too many students in each class, too many speed bumps and not enough lights in the parking lot, or insufficient athletic facilities? Once you identify an issue, decide what survey questions would enable you to prove that other students are equally concerned.

6. Have you ever wondered what women on your campus really want from men or vice versa? Draft a survey to analyze the desires, ambitions, problems, and concerns of your classmates.

7. What opinions in your community do politicians appear to be blind to? For example, do the roads in your community need to be improved? Do trees and shrubs need to be planted? Do better restaurants need to be opened? Review your local newspaper and freewrite about the issues that local politicians appear to be unaware of which you might remedy by producing a survey of attitudes.

8. What have you heard on the news or read in a newspaper or magazine that intrigues you? What social issues do you generally look for when scanning through the newspaper? For example, are you interested in the plight of the homeless? Would it interest you to go to a shelter in your city and interview its director, other social workers, and clients?

9. Is there some subject that you have always wanted to learn more about, such as how to become an entrepreneur? Would it be interesting for you to interview several prominent business owners and try to analyze their work habits, experiences, and skills that have made them successful?

10. Have you written an essay earlier in this course that could be improved by incorporating interviews or surveys?

11. Interview one of your classmates or a writer on campus. Often professors, English department teaching assistants, and journalists who write for the school paper are eager to talk about their writing. Inquire about the writer's positive and negative writing experiences. Where does this writer typically write—a student cafeteria? a classroom? a library? a private office? What audiences, purposes, and aims does the author typically address? What important experiences have contributed to the author's goals? to his or her identity as a writer?

Prewriting and Drafting Strategies

Consult Pertinent Reference Material in the Library

Interviews and questionnaires do not necessarily need to lean on previous research for credibility. The advantage of consulting library sources, however, is that you can learn from previous researchers and scholars. First, you can learn more about your subject by studying what others have written about it. Second, you can often improve your methodology by observing how others have studied your topic. For example, if other researchers have used questionnaires to analyze your subject, you can use their questionnaires, or a variation of them, rather than drafting your own. (Of course, if you adopt or adapt someone else's method, you need to acknowledge their contribution.)

The following research strategies, which were presented in the previous chapter, are equally helpful as you support and develop an effective questionnaire or interviewing strategy:

1. Gather general background information about your topic. Review *Encyclopedia Britannica, Encyclopedia Americana,* or *Collier's Encyclopedia* to gather background information about your specific research problem. Review the *Statistical Abstract of the United States* or *The World Almanac* to determine whether these sources can provide you with helpful facts and figures.

2. Review pertinent CD-ROM or on-line computer databases, such as *ERIC, The MLA International Bibliography,* or the *Social Science Citation Index.* Print the abstracts of related studies and consult those that seem most on target.

3. Check *Ulrich's International Periodicals Directory,* Sheehy's *Guide to Reference Books,* Katz's *Magazines for Libraries,* or McCormick's *The New York Times Guide to Reference Materials* to see what periodicals may contain useful articles.

4. Check your student and local papers for essays related to your topic.

If you are unfamiliar with how to gather information in the library, and your teacher wants you to relate your interview or questionnaire to previous scholarship, you may find it useful to consult the latter half of Chapter 2. This discussion explains how to use reference encyclopedias, the card catalog, periodical indexes, and CD-ROM and on-line databases.

Develop a Research Notebook

As discussed in the previous chapter, the increased intellectual challenge and scheduling demands placed on you by the research process can be effectively managed by maintaining a research notebook. Essentially this notebook is different from a traditional writer's journal in that it is structured to help identify a specific research question, organize reading notes, draw inferences from reading, and construct a bibliography. Listed below are a few of the notebook strategies that will help you identify a topic, narrow the presentation, and polish the writing.

Set a Schedule. Research projects offer ample opportunities to procrastinate. It is therefore especially important that you establish daily priorities and due dates for your research project. You can avoid the urge to procrastinate by breaking the research project down into meaningful parts and then establishing deadlines for conducting the work. For example, you might plan six hours on reviewing literature, eight hours on interviewing authorities and analyzing their ideas, and four hours on revising and editing the report.

Incidentally, studies based on questionnaires and interviews tend to be top-heavy; in other words, much of the work comes during the beginning stages. It will probably take you at least a week to review literature about the topic, and, if pertinent, to develop good interview questions as well as schedule interviews.

Freewrite Your Introduction. Even though the bulk of your study cannot be written until you have gathered all of the questionnaires or completed all of your interviews, you can best find your focus by constantly revising your introduction and asking yourself, "What have I discovered that is unique, interesting, or significant?"

Keep a Record of Pilot-Testing and Critical Comments. Experienced researchers know that little is as important as preparation. The best way to know if your questionnaire includes the important questions is to have a broad range of people fill it out and critique it. In turn, ask your instructor and classmates to evaluate your interview questions to ensure that you are asking the right sorts of questions for your purpose. Below are some guidelines you can follow to develop a successful methodology.

Develop an Effective Research Methodology

Being unprepared for an interview or distributing a shoddy questionnaire are surefire ways of committing intellectual suicide. For instance, if you are surveying students' attitudes, morals, and behaviors and you neglect to have respondents record their gender on the questionnaire, then your results will be severely flawed. Preparation is essential if you hope to gather worthwhile results. As explored in greater detail below, you need to carefully consider where you will conduct an interview, how you will take notes, and what sort of questions you will ask to elicit the information you need. In turn, extensive field-testing of a questionnaire is required if you hope to do anything more than waste paper and earn a C grade.

Below are a few recommendations for drafting effective interviews and questionnaires. By accounting for these conventions, you can ensure that your methodology is as sound as possible. I also caution you at this point to spend some time limiting the focus of your research. At the beginning of a research project, you need to work to keep your project in perspective. If you were attempting to earn a Ph.D. or publish your report, then you might be expected to interview thirty or more people or conduct a survey of hundreds. Your writing teacher does not expect this sort of rigorous research methodology. Instead, you should view this project as practice, or as a *pilot study*, not as the last word on the topic. Later in your academic career you may be introduced to sophisticated sampling and statistical procedures, but these disciplinary conventions need not presently concern you in your English class.

How to Prepare an Interview Strategy

You informally interview people on a daily basis. Asking your friends and people you meet about their ideas and day-to-day experiences has sensitized you to how people respond to questions—sometimes opening up, sometimes clamming up. And while you should naturally rely on your innate people skills, as a researcher you also need to develop a strategy to ensure that you get the information you need to write your report. By using the term "strategy," I do not wish to imply that you should attempt to manipulate interviewees in order to force a particular outcome. Indeed, effective research interviewers set their biases aside and remain quiet during interviews so that the interviewees can feel free to express themselves.

When I suggest that you need a strategy, I mean that you need to take appropriate steps to make the interview environment conducive to self-expression; to clarify your purpose for the interview; to devise appropriate questions to solicit the desired information; to maintain sufficient flexibility so you can respond to new issues as they develop during the interview. Below is a more complete account of interviewing strategies.

Create an Effective Ambience. Since the interviewee is being kind enough to set some time aside to meet with you, you in turn need to be flexible about where and for how long you meet and whether or not it is acceptable for you to tape-record the session. In general, you should try to conduct the interview away from as many distractions as possible. Establishing a climate of trust and support is difficult when the interviewee is bombarded with the daily distractions of professional life—such as phone calls, piles of messages, and pages of "to-do" lists. Also, recognize that when people are "put on the spot," many tend to freeze up. When they realize that their words are being put down "on the record," even talkative people may tend to tighten up and withhold information. As a result, you need to be calm and relaxed and do more listening than talking. Remember, also, that your body invariably sends clear messages about whether you are bored or frustrated or annoyed by the interviewee's comments. Rather than being quick to judge the interviewee's comments and their usefulness to your report, try to focus your energy on being a receptive listener. Show tact in your responses and interject humor to put the interviewee at ease.

If the interviewee doesn't mind having the session taped, then you would be wise to pretest your recorder and insert fresh batteries. (Incidentally, some interviewers use two recorders to avoid the embarrassment of discovering too late that one didn't work.) A second useful tip is to use microrecorders—that is, small recorders that use minicassettes—rather than obtrusive "boom boxes." Finally, try to place the recorder out of the interviewee's eyesight and avoid looking at, discussing it, or checking to see whether or not it is working, so that it is forgotten as soon as possible. If you notice the interviewee appears distracted by the recorder even though he or she has said it's okay, you would be wise to stop using it and take careful notes instead.

When you begin the interview, it is important to shake the interviewee's hand and greet him or her warmly. Smile and thank the person for his or her time and clarify the focus of the interview:

It's a pleasure to meet you, Dr. Wilson. I appreciate your willingness to spend some time with me so that I can learn more about a career in mass communications.

Hi, John, it's really good to see you again. Listen, I appreciate your help on this report I'm doing for English. Anyway, as I told you on the phone, I'm writing the report on how to select growth stocks, and since you're an expert in money management, I was hoping that you could give some advice on handling money. Say, do you mind if I tape this session? If it bothers you, we don't need to tape it, but it would help me write the report. In any case, if you like I don't have to use your name.

Ask Open, Closed, Hypothetical, and Mirror Questions. The questions you will ask are determined by the purpose of your research. As a result, you need to be very clear in your own mind about what you hope to discover as a result of conducting the interview. The best way to develop solid questions is to freewrite as many as possible. By refining the purpose of your research and by sharing your questions with other people, you will be able to identify the ones that are most apt to uncover the information you need. You may also find it useful to categorize the questions that you have freewritten according to the sort of information that the questions are likely to elicit. There are three major types of questions, each of which is suited to a particular part of the interview: open questions, closed questions, and hypothetical questions.

At the beginning of the interview, you may wish to establish rapport by asking *open-ended questions.* Essentially open questions allow an interviewee to say just about anything, thereby revealing his or her general attitudes and beliefs. For example, if you asked an accomplished business leader, "What skills does a college graduate need to succeed in business?" he or she might talk for a half-hour about leadership capabilities, writing skills, and a can-do attitude.

When you wish to limit an interviewee's range of responses or pin him or her down to one answer, you should ask *closed questions.* "Do you believe that the university should require all students to be computer literate?" is an example of a closed question because it forces a "No," "Yes," "I don't know," or perhaps a "Well, yes, under these conditions . . ." sort of answer. Because people don't like being interrogated, however, you would be wise to limit the frequency of closed questions that you ask during an interview. As a result, you need to be selective about which closed questions you really need to ask.

Finally, before conducting an interview, you may also wish to consider developing a few *hypothetical questions.* Although these sorts of questions are more commonly used in employment interviews, they also can be used profitably in a research interview. For example, if you were trying to evaluate the circumstances under which students cheat on a test, you could ask, "If you were sure that you wouldn't get caught and you needed a high score on a final exam to earn a passing grade, would you cheat?"

Here are the strategies for developing useful interviewing questions:

- *Closed Questions:* What specific information do you need that can best be attained by the pinning down of a closed question?
- *Open Questions:* What philosophical issues underlie your research? What two or three major questions do you need to ask to open up your interviewee to really communicate?
- *Hypothetical Questions:* What creative situations can you devise to determine an interviewee's true feelings and likely responses to various circumstances?

There are, of course, other kinds of questions appropriate to interviews. You will find it useful, for example, to ask *mirror questions*. Essentially, mirror questions restate the interviewee's last statement in question form. Because you want to keep the interviewee talking, these questions can be essential to illustrating your interest and attentiveness to his or her ideas. Here are a few examples:

> *Interviewee:* So anyway, I think the old-boy network is the biggest problem this hospital faces. These administrators are so entrenched that they cover each other's tracks and hire incompetent technicians who won't intimidate or rat on them for cheating on their vacation time.
> *Interviewer:* So you think the biggest problem this hospital faces is the old-boy network?
>
> *Interviewee:* All of my friends cheat on tests, so I don't see why I shouldn't. I've plagiarized at least a half-dozen essays this year alone. We've got quite a selection at the fraternity house.
> *Interviewer:* Just a minute, John, I'm not sure I'm following you here. Are you saying that the fraternity house has copies of essays on file that you can use?

Finally, you should try to present your questions in a relaxed, conversational way. You can also show the interviewee that you are carefully listening by responding spontaneously to his or her remarks. Asking *spontaneous questions*—that is, questions that occur to you on the spot in response to the interviewee's comments—allows you to demonstrate that you are curious about what the interviewee has to say. When you let go a little in your interview and give it the feeling of a discussion, the interviewee will probably be more willing to share.

How to Design Effective Questionnaires

At first glance, constructing a questionnaire seems fairly simple. All you need to do, it seems, is identify the open, closed, and hypothetical questions that you would normally ask in an interview, type them up, and then distribute them. However, unlike the situation in a face-to-face interview, you cannot rephrase an awkward or imprecise question in response to a puzzled look on your respondent's face. Moreover, unless you ask in your questionnaire, you won't know if your respondent is a ninety-year-old or twenty-year-old man or woman.

To construct precise and comprehensive surveys, therefore, you would be wise to "pilot" the survey by giving drafts of it to friends and classmates. Ask these people to record their answers and to let you know if any of the questions seem confusing or inappropriate.

To give you an example of how important this review process is and how damaging an incomplete questionnaire can be, let me share with you a few problems with several questions that I once constructed to measure teachers' goals and methods of responding to student writing.

When first developing the questionnaire, I read all of the published essays that were then available on responding to student writing, noting common concerns and problems. Next, I devised a 40-item questionnaire and submitted it to 30 writing instructors, asking them to fill out the questionnaire and write their criticisms of any questions that seemed inappropriate or imprecise. As result of this process, I was able to delete ten questions and revise many of the others. For example, rather than asking,

11. Do students

    a. think seriously about your comments and try to apply them to their next writing assignment?

    b. think seriously about your comments but prove unable to apply them to later assignments?

    c. essentially ignore your comments and focus primarily on the grade you assign?

    d. n/r

I rephrased the beginning of this question to "Do you believe students . . ." because the instructors pointed out that they couldn't ever know for sure their students' intentions. After making numerous similar revisions to the questionnaire, I believed it would provide the information I needed. As a result, I went ahead and mailed it to 800, randomly selected, writing program administrators throughout the United States. At the time, I hoped that the following two questions would give me enough information to determine how often teachers asked students to revise essays with their comments in mind. As you read over these questions, can you identify any information that they will fail to capture?

21. How often do you review drafts of your students' essays in a one-to-one conference with students **before** students submit a final draft for a grade?

a. never   (16%)

b. 1 time   (48%)

c. 2 times   (20%)

d. 3 times   (7%)

e. 4 times   (1%)

f. 5 or more times   (4%)

g. n/r   (4%)

25. How many papers during the semester do you allow students to revise for a higher grade **after** you have evaluated them once?

a. 0   (23%)

b. 1   (19%)

c. 2   (12%)

d. 3   (11%)

e. 4   (8%)

f. 5 or more   (26%)

g. n/r   (1%)

The problem with the above questions, as you may have already surmised, is that they fail to account for those circumstances in which teachers collect drafts of students' essays and read them by themselves and make written commentaries. Given the focus of the questionnaire, this was a serious omission, one which was very difficult to write around. Of course, errors such as this one are fairly routine even for seasoned survey-researchers, so you shouldn't feel overly concerned if you make similar oversights. Nevertheless, when planning the survey, you can make it as solid as possible by considering the following features of effective surveys: forced-choice questions, demographic questions, rank-ordered questions, and open-ended questions.

Forced-choice Questions. When constructing closed questions, you need to provide choices that will allow you to make meaningful interpretations. For example, in a survey of accounting students to determine whether they needed more career information, student researcher Frank Werner asked the following questions:

1. Do you know what field of accounting you want to go into?

   Yes   No

2. Do you know the job description of the fields you are interested in?

   Yes   No

3. Is there enough information at our school to answer your questions concerning a career in accounting?

    Yes   No

4. Would you like more information about the various fields of accounting?

    Yes   No

5. If a list of local accounting firms who would allow you to observe them were available, would you consider going to a firm to observe someone working in your field of interest?

    Yes   No

Of course the problem with Frank's questions is that they cannot provide much meaningful information. Because Frank's survey is so vague, it may provide more insights into how curious his respondents are than how knowledgeable they are about the accounting field or how much information they need about the accounting profession. After all, who wouldn't find more information about a field useful in choosing a career? Who wouldn't consider going to a firm and observing professionals at work? To provide truly meaningful results—that is, to determine whether more information should be provided by the career counseling center or the accounting department— Frank would need to revise these questions to measure students' knowledge of the accounting field.

Demographic Questions. Because your English teachers are not expecting you to generalize from a small sample to a larger population, your sample does not need to reflect characteristics in the overall population. Nevertheless, so that you can talk meaningfully about your sample, you still want to describe the characteristics of your respondents as specifically as possible. Of course the kinds of characteristics you should identify are determined largely by the purpose of your research. Gender, income, age, and level of education are examples of the sort of demographic characteristics that you may want to account for in your survey. For example, in my study of writing teachers' goals and methods of responding to student writing, I asked the following demographic questions:

2. Did you **primarily** learn how to evaluate student papers from

    a. personal experience?   (68%)

    b. academic training?   (18%)

    c. recommendations published in professional
        journals or discussed at conferences?   (7%)

    d. co-worker's(s') advice?   (6%)

    e. n/r   (1%)

17. How many writing courses do you teach **each year**?
    a. 1–2   (25%)
    b. 3–4   (33%)
    c. 5–6   (18%)
    d. 7–8   (11%)
    e. 9–10   (7%)
    f. 11–12 (4%)
    g. n/r   (2%)

26. How many students are in each writing course that you teach?
    a. 10–15   (5%)
    b. 16–20   (22%)
    c. 21–25   (53%)
    d. 26 or more (18%)
    e. n/r   (2%)

27. How many years have you taught writing?
    a. 10–15   (5%)
    b. 3–4   (7%)
    c. 5–7   (9%)
    d. 8–11   (16%)
    e. 12–16   (18%)
    f. 17–23   (26%)
    g. 24 or more (18%)
    h. n/r   (1%)

Rank-ordered Questions. When your library research has informed you that your audience is likely to be concerned about several issues, you can determine which concern is most troubling by asking a rank-ordered question. Essentially, as illustrated by the following example, the rank-ordered question presents respondents with several alternatives and requests that they rank them according to priority:

> Please rank your five most important reasons for not contributing to our company's blood drives. Put a #1 by your most important concern, a #2 by your second most important concern, and so forth.
>
> ——— Lack of time
> ——— Lack of awareness of former blood drives
> ——— Perception that the blood bank has plenty of blood

—— Concern about possible pain

—— Concern about infection

—— Concern about fainting

—— Concern about vomiting

—— Concern about bruising

—— Concern about being infected with AIDS

—— Belief that the company should provide some compensation

Open-ended Questions. Although they are impossible to quantify, open-ended questions are often invaluable. For example, in Jane Demkovich's study of ways to improve her company's blood drives, she determined that 38 percent of her sample reported having "a negative experience resulting from a blood donation" and that 70 percent of these people had not donated blood since that negative experience. These are certainly intriguing statistics that require further analysis and study if Demkovich is to succeed in increasing the number of participants in the blood drives. Fortunately, at the end of her survey, she asked two open-ended questions: "What other incentives (excluding cash) would you like the company to offer for your blood donation?" and "What general comments do you have about the possibility of donating blood?" Because several of the respondents elaborated on their negative experiences donating blood, Demkovich was able to use these commentaries to develop some recommendations for the technicians who worked for the blood bank. Of course, it would have been even better if Demkovich had done some pre-survey research on the negative consequences that sometimes occur when people donate blood. If she had done so, then she could have offered a greater range of response in the questionnaire on side effects such as dizziness, flu feelings, headache, or pain from the needle prick.

While the percentage of responses to the closed questions offers evidence of specific beliefs and actions, responses to open-ended questions can help you identify the surrounding attitudes and assumptions. Consequently, Demkovich could have improved her questionnaire even more by providing open-ended follow-ups after certain questions:

3. Have you ever had a negative experience resulting from blood donation?

( ) No

( ) Yes. Please describe. ————————————

————————————————————

————————————————————

Because open-ended commentaries can enrich your interpretation of the statistics, you would be wise to include a few such questions in all surveys that you conduct. One generic question that you might find useful is, "What important item(s) has/have been left out of this survey?" However, because they are difficult to tabulate and because they require time on the part of your respondents, be sure to limit the number of open-ended questions you ask.

How Many Questions?

Of course, when you are freewriting possible questions, you should attempt to generate as many questions as possible. You might also ask friends and colleagues what questions they would ask if pursuing your topic. Consider using questions that other researchers have asked, and base additional questions on the sources you have consulted to develop an informed survey. Ultimately, however, you will need to limit the questions so that you have a better chance of getting the surveys back. Before submitting your survey to your targeted sample, ask a few people to take it and time how long it takes them to complete it. Many people are willing to give 15 minutes to a survey, yet find a survey that takes more than 30 minutes intolerable.

Revising and Editing Strategies

Because of the more extended nature of reports of questionnaires and interviews, you cannot wait until the last minute to get the work done. To keep a fresh perspective on what you're doing, you may find it useful to work on your project a little each day as opposed to binge writing. Yet even if your project feels as fresh as three-day old fish, you still must re-see it through your readers' eyes. As you critique your work, pay special attention to how you have established credibility as a researcher. Remember that your readers do not have the benefit of your notes. Before accepting your conclusions, they want to see and understand your evidence.

Ask Critical Questions

Below I have listed a few of the special concerns that you will need to consider when revising reports based on interviews or questionnaires. While you may understandably become discouraged when you identify flaws in your research design, remember that even experienced researchers feel moments of despair and frustration when discovering weaknesses in their methods. Remember, also, that you are conducting a pilot study and that you are permitted to have a section in your report that admits to the weaknesses with your method. If things go totally awry, you may even have a lengthy appendix that tells future researchers what not to do! Throughout the planning, revising, and editing stages, however, you should attempt to construct as sound a study as possible. Considering the following questions can help you develop solid results:

1. Have I provided the background information that will enable my readers to understand the significance of my subject? Will my readers understand my purpose for writing the report?

2. Have I provided sufficient information about the method I used to conduct the study so that interested readers could replicate it if they so desired?

3. Have I thoroughly explained the credentials of those whom I interviewed or provided background information about the people who responded to my survey?

4. Can my readers tell when I am quoting from the interview, the questionnaire, or outside sources? Are my paraphrases and summaries accurate representations of the original material?

5. Is my interpretation of the survey responses or interviews logical? Have I thoroughly explained for the reader the logic behind my commentaries?

6. Would my report be stronger if I related the findings of my research to that of other researchers, or, given my communication situation, is this unnecessary or impossible?

7. Is the report well organized? Would a different ordering of sections be more forceful?

8. Is my language straightforward and clear? Have I avoided excessive abstract words? Can I use more concrete words?

Do a Criteria-Based Evaluation

No single standard can be used to evaluate the effectiveness of all research reports. Nevertheless, you may find the following criteria useful in critiquing your own and your peers' research papers.

	Low	Middle	High
	1 2 3	4 5 6 7	8 9 10

I. Format

Distinctive cover

Title page

Abstract

Table of contents

List of figures and illustrations

Introduction

Methods

Results

Discussion

Conclusions

Works Cited

Appendixes

	Low	Middle	High
	1 2 3 4 5 6 7 8 9 10		

II. Methodology

    A. Interviews

    Extensive original research was completed.

    Interview questions probe pertinent subjects.

    Background of interviewees is provided.

    Selected dialogue from interviewees is effective.

    B. Questionnaires

    Questionnaire appears comprehensive.

    Background of respondents is provided.

    The complete questionnaire appears in the body or appendix of the report.

Low   Middle   High
1 2 3 4 5 6 7 8 9 10

III. Secondary Sources

    Sufficient secondary sources are provided for factual information, controversial statements, and emphasis.

    It is clear when outside sources are being cited.

    The credibility of secondary sources has been established.

    The proper form of documentation is used.

Low   Middle   High
1 2 3 4 5 6 7 8 9 10

IV. Substantive Revision

    The significance of the subject is clarified.

    The document is reader-based.

    The tone is appropriate given the audience and purpose.

    The document is organized and formatted effectively.

    The paragraphs are coherent and cohesive.

Low   Middle   High
1 2 3 4 5 6 7 8 9 10

V. Edited Document

    Unnecessary jargon and awkward abstractions have been edited.

    The first person has been used, where appropriate.

    To be verbs have been eliminated.

    A high verb-to-noun ratio has been established.

	Low	Middle	High
Strings of prepositions have been avoided.		1 2 3 4 5 6 7 8 9 10	

The document has been edited for economy.

The document has been copyedited for grammatical, mechanical, and formatting errors.

Collaborating Strategies

As usual, you should share your work with critical readers. Once you have worked on a research project for several weeks, you will inevitably have difficulty seeing weaknesses in your interpretation or methodology. Even though you see your survey as absolutely rock solid, a more objective peer may spot shortcomings in the way you phrased your questions or drew conclusions. Seek the advice of others, therefore, throughout the research process. The following questions can help you focus your discussions and make your group time as productive as possible.

PEER REVIEW WORKSHOP

1. How would you define your peers' audience, voice, and purpose?
2. Are there any points in the discussion at which you are confused or where you think additional evidence needs to be provided? What additional information do you believe the author should seek before submitting the report for a grade? Do you believe that the author has provided sufficient evidence to support claims? Has the author provided the information the audience will need to understand the subject? Can any information be deleted because the audience is already likely to be familiar with it?
3. Are you ever unsure about whether the author is quoting, citing, or paraphrasing sources? Are there any passages in which you sense the author is falsely interpreting the source's ideas?
4. When presenting interviews, has the author clarified the background and authority of the interviewee(s)? Are you ever unsure about the interviewee's opinions about a subject?
5. When reviewing the results of a survey, has the author clarified who completed it or how it was distributed? Has the author presented the complete survey in an appendix? Are there any instances in which the author seems to be incorrectly interpreting the survey results?
6. In what ways do you think the writer can revise the report to make it more interesting, informative, or persuasive?

Evaluating Criticism

1. What have you learned about yourself as a writer as a result of the prewriting, drafting, collaborating, or revising techniques that you experimented with when writing your research report?

2. Did your perception of yourself as a writer or person change as a result of this assignment?

3. In what ways has writing your research report changed your perception of the research process?

4. If you exchanged criticisms of your peers' work, what did you learn as a result of these experiences?

5. If you could begin this report again, what would you do differently?

6. In what ways have your thoughts about your subject changed as a result of the research you completed?

7. How were your peers' and teacher's evaluations of your field research similar to and different from their evaluation of past writing projects? What can you learn from these differences or similarities?

Writing Reports Based on Ethnographic Methods

Chapter 8 explained the conventions for writing a report based on library research; Chapter 9 showed how to extend knowledge about a subject by interviewing authorities or surveying beliefs and habits with questionnaires. This final chapter of the writing portfolio explains how to conduct research based on ethnographic methods. As you will see, this chapter draws on the previous two chapters because ethnographers need to be familiar with both library research and survey and interview techniques.

Essentially, ethnography involves studying a specific culture or community. By living among the members of a culture and playing the role of *participant-observer*, ethnographers attempt to define the beliefs, rituals, symbols, problems, and patterns of behavior that distinguish this culture from other dominant cultures. For example, ethnographers have attended Alcoholics Anonymous meetings and written about the culture of alcoholics. Ethnographers have studied the community of prostitutes, pimps, and drug dealers on inner-city streets and in housing projects. Researchers have used ethnographic techniques to study classrooms in colleges, high schools, and middle schools.

The purpose of ethnography is *not* to generalize from a smaller population to a larger one. Instead, ethnographies are conducted to better understand specific groups and to understand how people are influenced by their environment. While ethnographers typically interview *key informants* in the culture, their emphasis in writing an ethnography is *not* to tell discrete life stories. Instead, ethnographers use their observations, conclusions from informal and formal interviews, results of psychological tests, and interpretations of insider-written documents to weave together an account of key people in the community and to explicate the community's values, ceremonies, problems, and prospects.

In a variety of college classes, your instructors may challenge you to play the exciting role of a field researcher. For example, in a sociology class you may be asked to observe and analyze behavior in a college dormitory. For an education class you may need to analyze how different sociological backgrounds or teaching techniques affect learning. Instructors in business management or communication classes might ask you to study the interpersonal factors that influence how decisions are made or how different people respond to certain leadership and management styles.

Thick description, triangulation, counting—these and other ethnographic techniques will be explained in this chapter so that you can use them to conduct your own study based on ethnographic methods. Ethnographies written by college students and professional ethnographers are presented throughout the chapter so that you can have a sense of the range of communities, research techniques, and voices available to you. As usual, I have also presented prewriting, drafting, revising, and editing strategies as well as ideas for ethnographies.

Writing Samples

The following ethnographic sample is the prologue to Douglas Harper's book *Good Company*. Harper rode the rails with tramps for several years as part of his research, and the first 138 pages of his book read more like an adventure novel than a traditional academic research report. In fact, it isn't until the final chapter of his book that Harper steps back from his role as participant and speaks with the voice of a researcher analyzing the meaning of his experience.

Good Company*

Douglas Harper

I was drinking beer with some tramps one night in the fall of 1973. Jack and 1 Eddie had buddied up when Jack picked Eddie "out of the gutter" in Wenatchee, and he'd taken him along to a job he'd arranged picking apples. Jack had an old car and called himself a rubber tramp. Eddie didn't say much and he didn't work very hard. He looked old and worn out but Jack had an interest in him for some reason and was always saying things like: "Now Eddie, you aren't going off to drink that old wine no more, now are you?" And Eddie would shake his head back and forth—he wasn't going back; he wasn't going back.

I didn't know how they'd ended up together, but I thought that they 2 must have known each other someplace down the road. Jack was talking about the times he'd had: jobs, cars, drunks, bad rides, when Eddie interrupted: "Last job *I* had was making brooms for fourteen cents an hour—made two-hundred-forty dollars in sixteen months."

Jack banged his beer down on the table and stared at the other tramp: 3 "Two-hundred-forty in sixteen months? You been on the *inside?*"

---

* From *Good Company*, 1982. Used by permission of the University of Chicago Press.

The tramp looked like he'd wished he'd kept his mouth shut. He finally 4
nodded and started telling us about twenty years behind the bars of San
Quentin, Alcatraz, and other prisons I'd never heard of. Jack kept looking at
him like he couldn't believe his ears, and I was a little surprised the subject
hadn't come up in the month they'd been together. Jack finally asked him
what he'd done to get himself in so much trouble and the tramp said: "It's
checks—always little chickenshit checks. My problem is my education—I
know how to write my name. Did you ever think of it? Just sign your name
and they give you money. It never fails to amaze me to find out my name's
still good after all the trouble I've been in."

Jack shook his head and looked away: "You must have liked it in there to 5
keep going back."

"You don't know what you're talking about," Eddie shot back.   6

"If you didn't like it, why did you keep going back?"   7

"I ain't been in for two years, and I ain't going back," Eddie said.   8

Then Jack cooled off and told Eddie he thought he'd turned a corner. 9
"You know what your problem is? You got to choose the right company.
You got to choose the right company for a change—you gotta stay away
from those goddam *skid* rows. How many times you been rolled on *skid*
row?"   10

"Pretty near every time."   11

"You got to learn to choose your company better," Jack repeated slowly. 12

Eddie took a long pull from his beer, looked hard around the room and
said: "That's something I been thinking about one hell of a lot these past
twenty-three years—just who *is* good company?"

Critical Reading Questions

1. How would you describe Harper's voice in this prologue?

2. What does Harper's purpose appear to be?

3. What details does Harper provide to help you imagine his experience?
   Can you identify any particularly vivid sensory images?

4. What do you learn about the life of tramps here? How does the
   researcher seem to feel about these people and their life-style?

In the following ethnography, Suzanne Faber drew on her experience as a cocktail waitress in a bar to analyze the relationship between
customers' tipping behaviors and their social class. To determine whether
tipping behaviors were correlated with income level, Faber used participant observation as well as formal interviews. This ethnography was
published in *Researching American Culture*, a collection of ethnographies
written by professional anthropologists and students at the University of
Michigan.

Social Class, Tipping, and Alcohol Consumption in an Ann Arbor Cocktail Lounge*

Suzanne Faber

American culture is marked by diversity based on differential access to strate- 1
gic resources. Various attempts have been made to prove that behavioral
differences between representatives of the many social strata are observable.
Speech patterns, style of dress, mannerisms, and so forth, have been analyzed
as indicative of a particular background, a particular class. While class differences are indeed evident in many areas of behavior, questions nevertheless
remain as to the specific circumstances in which differences may be dis-
cerned. Are class-based differences manifest in even the most commonplace,
routine activities? The focus of my research is an attempt to answer precisely
this question.

Through observation of individual behavior in a bar situation, based on 2
examination of drinking and tipping habits, I have attempted to determine
whether or not class-based behavioral differences in such routinized circumstances are apparent. Being employed as a waitress at a local bar has afforded
me the opportunity to compile the necessary data.

Both the location and the atmosphere of this tavern proved conducive to 3
comparative analysis of class. The fact that it is situated in a hotel implies that
its patronage is not limited to local customers. It is located near an express-
way off-ramp but still close to many large and small businesses. It is large,
clean, and tastefully decorated. There is a dance floor and live entertainment,
usually including the kind of pop and soft rock music that appeals to a variety
of age groups. Compared to other bars in the area, it attracts customers from
a fairly broad range of income groups, as will be demonstrated further on.

The data were compiled over four weeks, during which I worked ten 4
shifts. I approached more than 150 people in order to recruit 100 participants. Due to the nature of my research, I did not wish to alter their normal
behavior patterns. I explained that I was a student doing anthropological
research involving income distribution of people who patronize local bars.
They were unaware that I would be taking note of particular aspects of their
behavior.

I needed to obtain three different types of information. Obviously I had 5
to determine the individual informant's social class. Realizing that most people would respond to a direct inquiry about their social position by affirming
their membership in the middle class, and recognizing the social unaccept-
ability of asking such a question, I decided to use a less conspicuous approach. After showing them a card I had previously prepared, which listed
five gross income groups, I asked them to write down on the back of their

* From *Researching American Culture*, 1982, pp. 157–163. Reprinted with permission of the
University of Michigan Press.

check the letter which corresponded to their own approximate gross income. The choices were as follows:

A. $0.00–$10,999

B. $11,999–$19,999

C. $20,000–$35,999

D. $36,000–$59,999

E. $60,000 and above

I chose to use such wide income margins primarily because I felt that if the list had been more specific or if I had asked the participants to write down their exact income, many would have felt the invasion of privacy too great and might have withdrawn their offer to participate. It is true that income level alone does not necessarily determine social class. However, since class is the sum total of a number of interrelated variables, including income, certain generalizations may be drawn. Usually someone who draws a relatively large income has better access to strategic resources and thus is in a higher class than someone who earns substantially less. Upper, middle, and lower classes, then, are not absolute concepts, but merely ways in which the sum of personal variables may be understood relatively. Accepting this as a prem-ise, I divided the participants, on the basis of income, into the following categories:

A. Lower class

B. Lower middle class

C. Middle class

D. Upper middle class

E. Upper class

The second category of information needed for the study was alcohol 6 consumption patterns. On the back of each participant's check I noted the number of drinks ordered and the frequency with which they were ordered. I discarded the information taken from participants who stayed for less than two hours. Classification of the participants with regard to consumption habits was as follows:

Four or more drinks per two hours = excessive
Three drinks per two hours = heavy
Two drinks per two hours = average
One drink or less per two hours = low

The third area of concern was tipping behavior. After the participants 7 had left I made note on their check of the amount left as gratuity. The basis for classification here was as follows:

20 percent or more = excessive
15–20 percent = high

10–15 percent = average
10 percent or less = low

Upon completion of the data-gathering process I was able to correlate 8
the results in an effort to determine whether or not class-based differences
were indeed manifest in drinking or tipping behavior. The findings are documented in tables 1 and 2.

Examination of the data reveals some definite trends. Most striking are 9
the class-based differences with regard to tipping. The pattern is that persons
of the lower to lower middle class tipped more generously than individuals
of the middle to upper classes. Excessive tipping is apparent among only 3
percent of the higher income groups, while among those with lesser means,
about 30 percent left tips upward of 20 percent. (I should point out that one
man who claimed to be in the bottom income category left a tip of $20.00 for
a bill that totaled only $8.50.)

There are a few possible explanations for this. It may be that lower class 10
people, who are less confident about their social status than wealthier individuals, feel a need to overcompensate by tipping excessively. They may also
feel a certain loyalty to their class and identify with their waitress, whom they
see as another member of their own working class. Generous or excessive
tipping may thus express a certain class "camaraderie." Conversely, high-
income people, secure in their social and economic positions, are less likely

Table 1 Alcohol Consumption by Social Class

Social Class	Drinks Consumed per Two Hours				Total People
	4	3	2	1	
Upper class	2	3	2	3	10
Upper middle class	4	8	9	7	28
Middle class	4	10	11	8	33
Lower middle class	4	6	8	5	23
Lower class	0	2	3	1	6
Total	14	29	33	24	100

Table 2 Tipping Behavior by Social Class

Social Class	Percent Tip			
	20	15–20	10–15	10
Upper class	0	30	70	0
Upper middle class	4	18	71	7
Middle class	3	18	61	18
Lower middle class	26	39	22	13
Lower class	33	33	33	0
All social classes	10	25	54	11

to overcompensate. Most of them were cautious to leave a tip close to the traditional 15 percent. Though it is difficult to pinpoint a specific cause for class-based differences with regard to tipping behavior, the trend is significant. The variation in the percentage of the bill left for the waitress implies that a number of other factors also dictate tipping behavior. These will be discussed further on.

The data fail to reveal any marked trend that might support the hypothe- 11 sis that variations in alcohol consumption are class-based. Among all classes, between one-third and one-half drank at least three drinks per two hours, but most people consumed one drink per hour or less. It becomes clear that drinking is a cross-class phenomenon and that level of income has little to do with amount or frequency of consumption. (More significant, though not related to the current hypothesis, however, are the obvious implications of such enormous liquor consumption to American culture in general. The data support the notion that alcohol is the most widely abused drug in this country.)

The data seem to indicate that class-based differences are indeed mani- 12 fest in such routinized behavior as tipping. Yet, after completion of the data-gathering process, I must express my own skepticism about the validity of its results. The conditions under which information was taken were not conducive to either my own nor my informants' objectivity. My appearance, sadly enough, was a factor. The uniform I must wear for work is a lowcut black leotard and a slinky slit skirt. It certainly did not enhance my credibility as an anthropologist. Moreover, my dual role as waitress and researcher often conflicted, as customers who felt they had to wait too long for service subsequently did not cooperate. In addition, although I tried to be inconspicuous in determining participants' class, the fact that at least some of them were interested in making a positive impression (with others at the table and myself, too) makes me hesitant to accept their claims. For example, one of the men who claimed to earn over $60,000 per year left his room key on the table with a note that said he would be interested in discussing the results of my research.

More generally, too many variables could have affected both tipping and 13 consumption data for me to be certain of their validity. Frame of mind, and desire to impress a member of the opposite sex, or a superior, are some of the many variables that operate in bar situations. My own frame of mind must also be considered. Those people who seemed anxious to cooperate in my research were naturally treated better than those who were reluctant. Tipping behavior therefore was not accurately or objectively expressed. In addition, although I tried to carefully monitor the consumption patterns of the participants, my personal dislike of overt drunkenness, along with my responsibility as a waitress, might have caused me to avoid tables where I felt the customer had drunk too much. It is for these reasons that I feel that a repetition of the experiment using a different researcher might not result in similar findings.

Although I am skeptical about the validity of the data, I am certain of 14 other (nonquantitative) trends that became evident during data gathering. I noticed significant behavioral differences along class lines in both my approach to the customers and their reaction to me. Many of the better dressed, more sophisticated individuals I approached took great offense to my efforts to recruit them. I received many threats that the manager would be told of my behavior, and one gentleman went so far as to remind me of my "place." The vast majority of the overtly less sophisticated customers I approached greeted me with a great deal of warmth and enthusiasm. Recognition of the social boundaries reinforced by class differences was thus at least tacitly expressed.

Another phenomenon also became clear in my research. Many of the 15
participants expressed difficulty in accepting the fact that I am both a student and a waitress. A waitress is seen as a lower middle class worker, socially stagnant, while students are perceived as being upwardly mobile, the inheritors of high social positions. My dual role was thus somewhat incongruous in the minds of many, and in almost every case, the customers expressed their great surprise.

It becomes difficult to draw any conclusions, based on either my statisti- 16
cal or qualitative findings. In the first case, I doubt the accuracy of the data (for the reasons stated previously), and the degree of subjectivity involved in the second case would make conclusions suspect. Nevertheless, after having done the field research, I must affirm my belief that class differences do indeed exist, even in the most routinized, commonplace activities. Perhaps, given more objective and scientific circumstances, this hypothesis may yet be proven.

Self-Evaluation

I began the project with the best of intentions. I later realized that my 17
approach and methodology were naive. I was not fully aware of the complexities involved in any field research project and I am sure that is evident in the paper. I did, however, learn a great deal. I have begun to be much more aware of subtle class-based behavioral differences among people in all situations, not just in the bar. Yet I am disappointed by the fact that I spent a great deal of time and suffered a lot of aggravation for what turned out to be inconclusive. Some of the things that happened were, in hindsight, somewhat humorous. Some of the "regulars" who found out that I was doing research now refer to me as "Professor," and leave larger tips in an effort to help me with my tuition. One gentleman offered to fly me to the Caribbean with him so that I could research the natives there; his wife tipped me twenty dollars after I told him off.

Critical Reading Questions

1. What research question does Faber present in the opening paragraph? How does this introduction establish the significance of her research?
2. What effect in terms of tone and credibility is achieved by Faber's use of tables?

3. Does Faber make any interpretations that seem unfair based on the information that she has gathered, or does she effectively qualify her conclusions and clarify limitations?

4. How would you define Faber's tone in this report?

In the following ethnography, Todd Taylor, an English graduate student, narrates his observations of an American Studies class. To gather the information for this study, Taylor observed the class for an entire semester, interviewed 17 students before and after a major writing assignment was evaluated, and interviewed the instructor who presented the assignment. Taylor also reviewed a number of secondary sources to help him organize and reflect on his observations.

What Happened on the Way to Grandma's House

Todd W. Taylor

August 27. The syllabus, seating, orientation. Late students try to negotiate 1 around thirty-nine desks and a cart full of audio-visual equipment. The institutional, windowless, cement-block room holds the last chance to obtain a full schedule for many of these students. The university experiences a budget crisis and everyone scrambles for available seats.

The professors scramble too. That's right *professors*, plural. A trio serves 2 as our academic guide into American culture from post–World War II until Viet Nam. They overtly admit that their course is designed to attract sophomores and juniors toward majoring in their department. And so the entertainment begins.

Today's presentation features a black and white civil defense video called 3 "Duck and Cover." It's easy to laugh at the McCarthy-era antics, "Remember kids, if you see the flash from an atomic bomb, DUCK AND COVER!"

A lecture on "the Age of Anxiety" follows; the audience tend to their 4 notebooks dutifully. If you peak over their shoulders you might get a better idea of what's going on here.

"Anxiety," Dr. Barthe, one of the two female teachers, says, "is defined 5 by the dictionary as a feeling of uneasiness."

"Anxiety—a feeling of uneasiness," the notebooks produce simulta- 6 neously. And then the students wait for the next cue.

Dr. Barthe writes on the chalkboard, "Modern Examples: terminal ill- 7 ness, war . . ."

"Terminal illness, war," are inscribed now. If you use your hand to cover 8 your spying eyes, no one will know that you know that after twenty minutes all notes are basically identical. Hey, it's just the first day though. And maybe notetaking won't really reflect the nature of writing in this course. Duck and cover.

In My Tribe: Familiar and Unfamiliar Places

September 17. At half past the hour a small herd of students wanders 9
nervously through the media center trying to find UMC 221. Exploring the
innards of the library is no fun when you're late—especially when you keep
disturbing the mole-like creatures who inhabit these catacombs. Our class,
"American Culture from 1945–1963," meets today in some difficult to find
audio-visual room. Three separate authorities failed to give us successful directions to our destination—"Now, go down that way, and it's just a
little jog and the first right after that. . . ." Maybe that's how writing is
for these students. Wandering around, thinking you're gonna arrive, finding
out you're lost, following others who seem to know where they're going,
receiving advice from those who know the territory but can't exactly express
the route. The analogy also applies to this author and the research you currently read.

Throughout my participation in the sophomore class I have questioned 10
the depth of my immersion into their culture. On one hand, a definite division lies between the culture and the researcher. They participate in AMS
3930 for credit and a grade. I participate to learn from them. On the other
hand, we are the same. "You blew off the last two classes too," John says as
we continue lost in the media center. "I hate not knowing what's going on in
class. We aren't having a quiz today are we? I think there's one coming up."
John thinks I belong to his tribe and he's right. I emerged from this culture,
his anxiety recreates all too familiar feelings in my stomach, and the only real
difference is eight years.

So, here I am, trying to observe this culture as much as possible from the 11
inside. What am I trying to learn? As Stephen North says in *The Making of
Knowledge in Composition*, "If the Ethnographer's object is to investigate an
'imaginative universe' other than his own, it makes little sense for him to for-
mulate, in advance of such investigation, hypotheses about how things mean
in that universe . . ." (285). In other words, I won't know my purpose until I
am finished. This is not to say I have no focus. My interest is writing. Fortunately, this culture concerns itself a great deal with writing. All grades in this
American Studies class result from writing tasks beyond sentence length. In
fact, half of their grade depends directly on two 2,500 word papers. In my
study, I will investigate the students' perspective on one of these writing
assignments through two interviews, one before and one after the paper's
due date.

State of the Student: Goatees and Soccer Shorts

November 7. Our class seems representative of the student culture outside 12
in the hallways and on the sidewalks. Current fashion reaches conspicuously
toward appearing non-fashionable. Loose, beaten clothing highlights the
fabric of those who stand out. Both sexes like triple-oversized soccer shorts—
impenetrable to poor laundering. A couple of nonthreatening guys bare fresh

tattoos high on their shoulders. Semimisanthropic bohemianism is popular—antagonizing haircuts, tie-dye, goatees, and vintage clothing color the more overstated. Yet, a mainstream still dominates. Guys wear the logo of the most recent athletic champion or a fraternity emblem. The gals have sorority stuff or comfortable Florida fashion. T-shirts rule.

What do the appearances represent? The mainstream, according to Dr. 13
Miller, "attends college in order to enhance [their] ability to get a good paying job, unfortunately."

Alan, a shaved-head-goatee guy, displays genuine interest in a writing 14
assignment on car culture: "You know how the assignment says to start out with fifteen sources," he says proudly. "I started out with *twenty-eight*." Alan focuses expressly on individuality, "I hope [the teachers] don't close [the assignment] off and that's it. In my papers I try to at least shed light on something rather than take ideas everyone else has had." He's concerned because his research explores "business aspects" of car culture instead of the "themes we've talked about in class." I wonder what my second interview will reveal beneath Alan's appearances.

Research: Mine and Theirs

September 22. The folk decorations in Dr. Barthe's office lose the struggle 15
with the same cold, institutional walls as in the classroom. Our conversation moves casually, lulling me slightly with its lack of emotional infusion.

Until, "I have a problem," she says, "with the way composition is taught 16
to freshmen [at this university]."

"HEY! Don't talk about MY department like that," I think at first. But 17
I'm suppose to be a semi-undercover observer, so, I act emotionless and nudge her toward elaboration.

She continues cautiously, "When I taught English as a graduate student, 18
we used a panel to grade student papers. I have seen some unfair things happen to students here."

I agree with her. I think committee grading is a superior way to grade 19
papers. And then I find myself adding the exception: *if your department has the means.* This really bothers me, for I know our composition program holds the best intentions and aspires toward progressive and educated philosophies of writing. Yet, classroom reality falls short of scholarly ideals. As Jane Tompkins says in her essay "Pedagogy of the Distressed," "our practice in the classroom doesn't often come very close to instantiating the values we preach." Tompkins's "our" refers specifically to teachers of English. For the purposes of my study, however, I would like to expand her "our" to include the student, reflecting more the idea that "we should remember that the class belongs to the students and that it is to their benefit as well as ours that they take their rightful share of responsibility for its procedures and its general direction" (Carroll). As I said before, I am searching for the students' vision in my study. So, even though Dr. Barthe brought up an interesting point concerning teachers and composition, I am going to appeal to the third-base

umpire, the student, to see just how much they actually "share in the responsibility" of the writing classroom.

Patterns of Composition: Six Students and Their Teacher

November 18. As of today, I have completed 17 interviews with eight 20 students and their teacher, Dr. Miller, the other female professor besides Dr. Barthe, who delivered their writing assignment. In the first eight student interviews, I solicited declarations about individual writing processes with a bent toward trying to get them to predict what would happen on the car paper. These interviews lasted about a half an hour each. One took over an hour. Another used three locations—an office, a hallway, and a street-side cafe in Tampa's historic cigar manufacturing district. I listened to the recordings of these interviews over and over, looking for patterns, preparing myself for angles into follow-up interviews with each student. The second interviews averaged about fifteen minutes; they focused on what occurred tangibly with this assignment—how much time did they spend researching their topic, when and how did they physically compose the paper, what grade did they receive, how much revision and collaboration was involved, where did their intentions fall short and why, what role did their perception of Dr. Miller and her assignment play, how fair was all this stuff?

Some very definite patterns emerged. What struck me was the gap 21 between student expectations of their own writing and how they actually performed. The difference between what they actually did was not so much denial or delusion—they usually weren't unaware of the distance—the difference was mostly between what they knew they should do and what they ended up doing. As recent graduates of modern composition classrooms, they were knowledgeable of recommended practices such as prewriting, revising, collaboration, and a deemphasis on mechanics and products. And, indeed, these ideas were employed to varying degrees by each individual writer. And, in fact, there was a positive correlation between these ideas and success and the assignment, gradewise. Yet, something funny happened; every student admitted that a great deal of their knowledge about ideal composition didn't get put into practice. Why? What happened on the way to grandma's house?

Well, we may never know exactly what the wolf looked like. After all, 22 Red was all alone in those deep dark woods. She didn't carry a video camera for us (see Flower and Hayes). The best I can do is to extrapolate the experience. For there seems to be a consistency to their descriptions of this wolf, or whatever it was that bushwhacked them on their way to writing the paper they wanted. I have consolidated my data according to some features which all eight students identified; they are fear, problems with collaboration, procrastination, delusion, and mechanics. While I have selected five out of the eight individual voices to tell the story of these five topics, I would like to emphasize the fact that these traits were common to most of the students in the study.

Amy: Fear

October 1. "You've got to help me. I hate writing," she says frenetically. "I 23 get physically ill, sick to my stomach. Really," she laughs.

Composition Theory's cumulative efforts over the past twenty years aim 24 at the Amys of the world. In twenty minutes she identified every classic symptom of the unsuccessful writer as perfectly descriptive of herself. She opens with knowledge of her most basic problem and reels off from there:

> "I have no confidence. Zero. I have this paranoia. I took 'average curriculum' in high school, we read stories and took spelling tests. I have trouble with usage. I can't make arguments because I'm a feeler, not a thinker. I can't produce creative ideas because I wasn't born with the talent. I hated to read in high school. It snowballs, if you don't practice reading, you don't learn vocab, you get frustrated, I have terrible comprehension skills. I got A's in 9th grade because we kept journals—I can do that—I write great letters, people love to read my letters, but in school, AH! My parents didn't go to college, but my fiance's parents. . . ."

And, fortunately, Amy, conscious of all these barriers, works really hard 25 at overcoming. "I am not a quitter. It began in junior college. I had this great teacher, she motivated me, and I wanted to do well for her as well as myself. But that was tear time, that's when I realized I had a problem with my writing. . . . It's a challenge for me now, I want to do well." And she will. Amy's advantage is herself. I watched her all semester aggressively seek help from Dr. Miller, Dr. Barthe, and myself, not to mention her fiance who she constantly brings into her discussion on writing. Currently, however, her writing lags behind her peers. She clings desperately to safe constructions claiming "the five paragraph formula saves me" and righteously defends the use of third person only. I spent a couple of hours on two separate occasions trying to build her confidence for this paper. She really wants a B, and I feel a personal stake in her getting it.

November 12. Amy's paper, not unlike every other car culture paper in 26 this class, returns bright red. "How's your fear of writing after this paper?" I ask, scared.

"There's more red ink than black ink; I'm afraid of the next paper." And 27 rightly so. Most of the students seem surprised by the extent of Dr. Miller's commentary. "Everybody always writes negative comments. I need positive feedback if I'm ever going to get some confidence." And, yet Amy got a B minus—pretty good considering the highest two grades were A minuses.

An abundance of wolves stalk Amy's forest. Slash-and-burn editors are 28 one. Don't-be-bothered-by-artificial-convention optimists such as myself can be another. And, admittedly, Amy has waylaid herself by avoiding academics until she is twenty-something. Yet, she identifies explicit hope: "This semester I realized that there are lots of people who can help me: Dr. Miller, Dr. Barthe, and you have really helped." And we all know how important a visit to the teacher's office can be.

Jessica: Problems with Collaboration

October 7. Jessica notices the two books by bell hooks in my briefcase. 29
She gets enthusiastic about the topics of counter-culturalism and feminism. I
don't think Jessica's a radical; in fact, she seems kind of mellow but intellectual. After that, we talked at length about her experiences in the freshman
writing program at USF. She mentions offhandedly a number of composition topics such as revision and mechanics with which she has little concern.
The most exciting aspect of her experience in writing class, however, was the
encouragement to develop an individual "voice." And, in relation to voice,
she mentioned a sincere dislike for peer editing; in fact, "I hated it," she said
unequivocally. Every student who I interviewed disliked the presence of for-
eigners in their private editorial forests; but Jessica was the most adamant.

"Hated it," she continued thoughtfully. "I don't like other people to cri- 30
tique my work . . . because everyone's writing style is different. I know when
I try to critique someone else's work, I try to make it my own. I got put with
this girl, I couldn't stand the way she wrote, there were a million things
wrong with it. But it's not MY paper. And then I would have the same girl
whose paper I hate criticizing my paper, so I got nothing out of it at all."

The October 1992 of *College Composition and Communication* featured 31
four articles arranged in a special "*In Focus* Collaboration and Composition."
As I read these articles I kept seeing an image described by my interviewees—sad guinea pigs, coerced into a failing, progressive exercise. Why
collaborative learning did not work for these students specifically would
require a comprehensive study, different from the one at hand. My point,
here, is that Composition might need to look at what is actually happening
with some of its experiments before moving on to more sophisticated collaborative pedagogies such as the combinations suggested in Mara Holt's "The
Value of Peer Criticism." The title of Felicia Mitchell's following article,
"Balancing Individual Projects and Collaborative Learning in an Advanced
Writing Class," suggests awareness of a tension in the collaborative classroom but does little to solve rudimentary problems such as Jessica's. While
Anne Greenhalgh's words, "we need to help our students hear modulations
in voice so that they, in turn, can better negotiate the balance of power, the
asymmetrical relationship, etched in teacher responses," may be true—her
musings are stratospheric in comparison to Jessica's voice which says, "I hate
peer evaluation."

October 15. Meanwhile, Jessica takes peer review in stride along with 32
the rest of her college experience. Her writing reflects a good deal of confidence and supports her emphasis on individual voice. Dr. Miller writes "nice
touch" in the margin next to Jessica's closing lines, " . . . in the context of
post–WWII suburbia, when women were not kings of the open road, but
more likely queens of the open stove." I feel she could have done better than
a B, although that's exactly what she predicted. I think Jessica's probably content in herself. I don't think she's too concerned with external input; in fact,
I'm pretty sure she would rather be smoking pot and listening to The Dead.

Alan: Procrastination

October 7. The paper is due in twenty-six hours. Alan, the goatee-guy from 33
earlier, tells me a story of self-ambush as we search for a room to conduct an
interview. "When I was five," he explains of the scar on his nearly bare scalp,
"I wanted to see if I could throw this brick over the clothesline. Before I
threw it I thought for just a split second that I had better be careful so that I
didn't hit myself with it. As soon as it left my hand I got scared, closed my
eyes, and ended up running right underneath it. The stupidest thing I've ever
heard of anyone doing." As of today, Alan admits he "has a ways to go as far
as direction" on his car culture paper. He emphasizes research as the most
important aspect to writing papers and even though he has collected a lot of
material, he doesn't seem to have made much sense out of his work so far.
Surprisingly, though, he describes himself as a successful college writer,
receiving mostly A's with an occasional B.

"I like writing papers. I think that the format for writing papers makes a 34
lot of people nervous. But not me."

"What is the format?" I reply. 35

"To get it done early, and to keep going over it." 36

Just like the brick scenario, Alan has found that he has set himself 37
up for exactly the danger he sought to avoid. "I don't know if I follow that
format, though," he grudgingly admits, not having written word one for
tomorrow.

November 12. The only hair on Alan's head today is around his eyes. 38
He got a B plus on his paper; but failed to get any sleep. After our last meeting Alan went to the library and "ended up scrapping everything." He tells
me of a horrific night and a sleep deprived morning of neighbor's typewriters
and trucks with transmission problems. According to Dr. Miller, his paper's
success came from its use of advertisements as support for his argument—a
global change made at the last minute. Alan's use of peer editing and revision
also seemed to have helped.

"Some neighbors who were up studying all night read my rough draft. 39
They didn't give grammatical advice, more like areas where it was fuzzy or I
didn't explain myself." So, in spite of procrastination, he achieved a good
paper.

"I got A's in English by staying up all night," he says. 40

"There's no reason to change, is there?" I offer. 41

"There IS a reason," he emphasizes. "I don't like staying up all night. I 42
was stressed all day. I was typing while class was going on. I'd rather not be
that way, it's hard—you've really got to learn your lesson hard before you
start to change."

All but one of the eight students wrote the paper the night before, none 43
as dramatically as Alan. Yet, I think he lost so much sleep because he wanted
to write a really good paper. Maybe his brand of conscientious sleep deprivation is better than someone who finishes papers according to her bedtime.

Barbara: Delusions

November 6. When I ask Barbara about her writing, she turns the discussion to her difficult adjustment to a big university. Overcoming confusion dominates her concerns with this paper—confusion over the library and in particular, confusion over her instructor's expectations ("I used to get A's, but since coming to this campus I've gotten straight B minuses; I can't seem to figure out what they want"). Yet, a great deal of Barbara's problems arise from unrealistic and undisciplined approaches to her writing. 44

Barbara began our first interview with a nearly arrogant tone. She described herself as an Advanced Placement student. She talks about how she likes to write and thought of herself, at one point, as a potential novelist. "You can't teach someone creativity," she asserts later. And I get the feeling by the way she says, "my aunt is an author, as a matter of fact," that she is implying a similar genetic make-up. Barbara politely disdains most of her external writing instructions since high school; she feels she can generate an A whenever an assignment is sufficiently interesting. Yet, inconsistencies begin to pop up all over her self-portrait. 45

For example, she claims to NOT like to have to express her own opinion; she would rather argue a specific topic provided by the teacher. This idea contradicts her earlier claim toward excelling when allowed the opportunity to generate a paper through personal interest. She talks about how badly she wants an A and how important it is to not procrastinate; but, by my estimation, she is going to spend only about fifteen hours on this entire project. I am beginning to get the feeling that the culprit is not the library, the teacher, or the long bridge between her house and the campus. 46

November 12. Barbara seems to be hearing Alan's observation on maturity from earlier today: "You've really got to learn your lesson hard before you start to change." The abundant criticisms frighten her. The sudden contrast between her former A's and her current B minuses starts to strike her as she begins to realize that Dr. Miller doesn't know anything about her family tree. As I write this, I am wondering if I'm too hard on Barbara and if maybe Dr. Miller is too hard also. A detail which I discovered after listening closely to the recordings of the interviews with Barbara ended up supporting my view. Barbara had previously turned in papers to Dr. Miller, in another class, with the identical results. "I thought she wouldn't grade so much on grammar in this class," Barbara explains of her disappointing grade. She guessed wrong, ignoring previous contrary evidence. Barbara's grandma is gonna get lonely if her offspring doesn't begin to recognize the difference between the daydream of rationalization and the reality of genuine effort. The wolf likes easy prey. 47

Debby: Mechanics and Content

October 3. Perfectly normal from about ten feet away. However, the outside corners of her eyes bare extended, painted-on mascara eyelashes like a 48 stage actor might use. Her clothes spin slightly off center too, not *out* of fashion, but definitely not *in* either. In addition, she is a painter and extends some of the best qualities from that medium into written composition. In opposition to Amy in most areas except motivation, Debby is the ideal writing student. She takes intellectual and artistic pride in her work, is deeply motivated by knowledge and expression, and is creative and humble at the same time. We had a long discussion of the benefits of criticism and collaboration in both writing and painting. Firmly confident in the process of peer review, she says, "I would rather someone look at my work and say it's shit than just go 'oh, wonderful.'"

Five days before the due date, she ricochets through three or four sound 49 directions for her research. Today, negotiating the "ton of ideas" forms her biggest problem. Later this afternoon, not knowing of Debby's involvement in my study, Dr. Miller raves about this student's imagination: "She was in my office, going on and on for a half an hour—she had ideas flooding all over my floor. She eventually came up with this idea of androgyny in car ads. We'll just have to see how it comes out."

October 15. "She is the hardest grader I have ever seen," says Debby, 50 upset with a B plus. Of all the students in my study, Debby worked the hardest on the assignment and produced the most original paper. By her estimates, she spent about fifty hours over two weeks on her project. Debby's paper "Opposites Attract" successfully identifies the androgynous nature of car advertisements in 1958, revealing a singular marketing scheme aimed at dual stereotypes of American women and men. Dr. Miller shares enthusiasm for the paper's originality; it didn't get an A because of mechanical errors. Yet, of the ten car culture papers I possess, Debby's has the fewest serious errors.

"I couldn't believe it. When she gave the papers back, she started writing 51 all of these codes for editorial corrections she made—she went from one end of the board to the other—I've never seen anything like it." Debby needs to break up her paragraphs and she mismanages some tenses and some verb agreements; but, she feels her content should have mattered more. Debby's case, however, is different from the other five students in my study. To some degree, the others were mostly victims of their own espionage; Debby, on the other hand, seems to arrived at grandma's house only to find she moved away. Unfortunately, this experience will probably discourage Debby's writing. Yet, there's a certain toughness about her situation. It's as if, as I quoted earlier, "the students . . . take their rightful share of responsibility for [the class's] procedures and its general direction." Different values toward content and mechanics are part of the territory—part of the nature of the forest.

The Researcher: His Two Cents

November 27. Rather than declare some discovery or perform acrobatic 52 connections of the myriad of ideas in the previous pages, I would like to provoke you with something that is still floating around in my head at the end of the study. I must confess that I avoided, until now, one significant pattern which emerged from the interviews. I asked each writer a series of hypothetical questions which sounded like this, "Say you worked for the Department of the Interior, and you had to present a paper to your boss. How would you go about writing THAT paper?" In their incredibly consistent answers may lie the key description of the wolf in American Studies 3930. Debby, the most successful writer in my study, replies, "Well, if I were writing FOR REAL. . . ."

Works Cited

Greenhalgh, Anne M. "Voices in Response: A Postmodern Reading of Teacher Response." *College Composition and Communication* 43 (1992): 401–410.

Harris, Muriel. "Collaboration Is Not Collaboration Is Not Collaboration: Writing Center Tutorials vs. Peer Response Groups." *College Composition and Communication* 43 (1992): 369–383.

Holt, Mara. "The Value of Written Peer Criticism." *College Composition and Communication* 43 (1992): 384–392.

Mitchell, Felicia. "Balancing Individual Projects and Collaborative Learning in an Advanced Writing Class." *College Composition and Communication* 43 (1992): 393–400.

North, Stephen M. *The Making of Knowledge in Composition: Portrait of an Emerging Field.* Portsmouth: Boynton/Cook, 1987.

Tompkins, Jane. "Pedagogy of the Distressed." *College English* 52 (1990): 653–660.

Critical Reading Questions

1. How does Taylor use dialogue to give readers a sense of the classes he observed and the people he interviewed?

2. How would you describe Taylor's tone in this piece? Given that he is writing for other English teachers, does his tone seem appropriate?

3. What does Taylor achieve by integrating so many secondary texts? Should any of these references be deleted?

Analyzing Pertinent Conventions

Experts strongly disagree about what constitutes an effective ethnography. For example, how active a role should researchers play in the community that they are studying? While some ethnographers formally interview respondents, give them psychological tests, and inform community members about their role, others are less candid. Instead of revealing their status as observers, these ethnographers prefer to enter the community as silent detectives. Although this secrecy about their goals can result in an ethical quandary, some professional anthropologists prefer this approach, believing it results in better data collection. This is particularly true when the experimenter will not visit the culture long enough for participants to forget their "company behavior" and act as they would if an observer were not present.

Ethnographers also differ in how they write the results of their research. Some ethnographers, as illustrated by the excerpt from Douglas Harper's study of tramps, shape their ethnographies like stories. They depict the people that they are studying in a realistic way and expect readers to draw their own conclusions about the way in which the participants' environment shapes behavior. In contrast, other ethnographers adopt a more scholarly and analytical tone. Consider, for example, Suzanne Faber's study of tipping behaviors in a small bar.

Because of the many differences among experts about how to conduct ethnographies and how to write ethnographic studies, the following guidelines probably wouldn't please all specialists. Do your best to construct the tightest possible methodology, and recognize that our current goal is to give you an opportunity to experiment with ethnographic methods. Rather than expecting yourself to produce a flawless study, consider your current attempt to be a *pilot study*—a best effort attempt.

Establish a Narrative or Analytical Voice

Ethnographies often possess two different voices. The first and often most powerful voice is that of a narrator who is telling a story. In fact, many ethnographic studies appear to be more like short stories or novels than formal research papers. When ethnographies rely heavily on the narrative form, they take on a different look from the analytical structure of the traditional research paper. Rather than bundling up the results of research into a concise paragraph near the introduction, an ethnographer may wish to *show* what he or she witnessed so that readers can draw their own inferences about the values and behaviors of individuals in the community and of the community at large. Rather than talking abstractly about the community's values, ethnographers will try to show these values by offering samples of conversations or behavior.

The second voice that often appears in ethnographies is that of the scholar or researcher who interprets observations, identifies themes (that is, patterns of behaviors and beliefs), and compares them with those observations made by previous ethnographers and field-based researchers. The degree to which researchers express this voice varies from one ethnography to another. Some integrate this second voice into the study as a whole, as Taylor did in his study of students in an American Studies class. Others, like Douglas Harper, present the more academic voice in an appendix. For example, compare Harper's voice in the following passage, excerpted from the appendix, to the prologue of *Good Company*, which was printed at the beginning of this chapter:

I have mentioned certain expectations tramps have of their work experiences as common throughout their history, and that a certain view of independence remains at the basis of nearly all the tramp does. There are, however, several tramp voices to consider beyond these I've reported.

The dominant theme in tramp tales is that of the tramp as trickster. The tramp invariably gets his last laugh, his free ride after the train crews and police grow weary of the chase, or his free food after the successful hustle. The tramp takes none but his own rules seriously and even those are negotiable.

Strawberry, in my reports, even manipulated the local police to take him to and from his jungle for daily supplies of wine and beer. The tramp remains free of and unrepentant to a society which he perceives as a set of pressures to conform, to take orders, and to be unadventuresome. These messages run throughout early biographies (Flynt 1899; Tully 1924; London 1907; Kemp 1920, 1922); they appear in the memoirs of those who lived the tramp life in the thirties (as cited earlier, the work of Guthrie, Foster and Eiseley); they appear as qualities of the hobos encountered in the beat writers Kerouac (1955, 1960), and Cassady (1971); and they permeate nearly everything Carl said to me. The tramp is a trickster both because he is colorful and arrogant, and because he has, compared to what most people naturally expect from the material world, little to lose. When jobs are intermittent and easily replaced, even a jail term for loitering, for a public drunk or for an illegal ride is a temporary stall along the road, and one with regular food.

Because academic readers expect researchers to link their ideas to those propounded by other researchers and scholars, ethnographers usually work toward this connection when writing for academic audiences. Check your instructor's assignment to determine how much emphasis you should give to presenting an analytical, academic voice. You may find it necessary to write several drafts of your ethnography before deciding whether you want to separate the voices of scholar and storyteller or if you want to interweave them.

Provide an Overview of the Culture and Purpose

Some ethnographers explain the purpose and the organization of their work in the introduction of their report. As with other genres, thesis and forecasting statements enhance reader comprehension of difficult material.

While thesis and forecasting statements can aid readability, you do not necessarily need to provide them. As illustrated in Harper's prologue some researchers prefer not to be explicit about their purpose and organization. Instead, they assume the persona of a novelist and emphasize *showing* the results of their research rather than *telling* readers what the experience meant.

Provide a Credible Account of the Culture

As discussed in previous chapters, college-educated readers tend to be critical readers. Rather than accepting a researcher's findings at face value, they question, for example, whether the researcher spent enough time in the field, or whether the researcher is basing conclusions on too few informants to represent the opinions of a whole community.

Given the subjective nature of interpretation, it would be unrealistic to expect ethnographers to develop an account of the community that *all* members would agree is valid. However, ethnographers do have several ways to ensure that their descriptions of a culture are as objective as possible.

Adopt an Appropriate Persona. Most ethnographers would be quick to dispute the assumption that any kind of research can be totally objective. Yet this does not mean that ethnographers do not struggle to be as objective as possible. After all, ethnography is intended to be a research technique and not a means to prove one's opinions.

Because college-educated readers are trained to look for flaws in reasoning or methodology, you cannot afford to ignore considering how your personality, gender, and socioeconomic experiences have influenced your perceptions of the community you have studied. To be an effective ethnographer, you need to be passive and receptive, yet discerning. Instead of imposing your own values and expectations, you need to be receptive to those expressed by the members of the community. If you tend to be a "strong personality," you may find it especially challenging to avoid the urge to control your environment and to have an influence in shaping positive change. You need to sit back and watch how others react to stressful situations. Of course, this does not mean that you should not help put out a fire in a burning building, but it does mean that you should have one eye on the fire and one eye on observing how the participants in the community respond to the crisis.

Provide Extensive Thick Description. "Thick description" is concrete and sensory language that describes what the community and participants look like. Because you are exploring how a particular context influences behavior, you must pay attention to describing the setting in which the ethnography takes place. If your readers are to understand your behavior and the behavior of your subjects, then you must clarify the *context* in which you are experiencing the actions that are being discussed. If your readers are to live vicariously by imagining themselves in your shoes, then you need to provide descriptive and sensory language. Some ethnographers also include photographs or VCR recordings of members of the community and environment.

Provide Sample Dialogues. In addition to thick description, ethnographers provide extensive quotations so that readers can have a sense of the texture and flow of conversation. However, because they hope to tell stories and allow readers to form their own judgments about what the stories mean, many ethnographers present fictionalized dialogues rather than question-and-answer format interviews.

Practice Triangulation. To ensure that they are not ignoring contrary evidence and focusing only on information that confirms their preliminary hunches, ethnographers practice "triangulation," which essentially means that they verify the authenticity of information and interpretation by checking it against other sources. If an ethnographer were studying the lives of campus police, for instance, the ethnographer would not believe one police officer's opinions about the morale of the squad if it conflicted with the opinions of the other officers.

Try Counting to Identify Patterns. Some academicians accuse ethnographers of putting on airs when they incorporate statistics into their work. However, ethnographers can often produce more reliable data by incorporating a few statistical procedures. For example, an ethnographer who was studying gender relations in a college mathematics course could record the number of times males and females asked questions of the instructor. The ethnographer could also time the length of time the instructor takes to answer the questions from males and females, or could record how many times the teacher deferred the male and female students' questions to an upcoming lecture or out-of-class meeting. After tallying these response patterns over a period of months, the ethnographer could be more confident in reporting, for instance, that females asked more questions but that the males' questions were treated more seriously.

Spend Sufficient Time in the Field. Ethnographers disagree enormously about how much time needs to be spent in the field. Some researchers claim that at least one year of data collection is necessary before a study can qualify as an ethnographic study; others believe three or four hours over a week or two is sufficient time to conduct an ethnographic study. Some researchers claim that the experimenter must live full-time with the members of the culture; others believe it is acceptable to spend slices of time with the culture over a few months.

We can assume with some certainty that the longer you spend working as a member of the culture, the stronger the credibility of your report will be. Therefore, always inform readers about the length of time you spent in the field. You can temper the forcefulness of your interpretations by providing qualifiers that acknowledge limitations caused by insufficient field time.

Don't Generalize to a Larger Population. The most divisive debate among ethnographers is whether a small sample can be generalized to a large population. Based on a classroom of twenty students, for instance, some ethnographers would make observations that they contend are valid for all college students. However, this tendency to generalize from a small sample to a larger population is indefensible and contrary to the primary goals of ethnography—that is, to understand specific communities. Human lives and problems are far too complicated to be understood based on observations of a small group of people. Skilled academicians such as your instructors are curious about your observations and how your thoughts on the culture have changed as a result of doing the research. They do not expect you to wax philosophically about the human condition based on a small study.

Follow the Conventions for Citing Sources

As with other academic reports, you should be sure to provide correct documentation for sources and authorities you have cited. Also, unless they request anonymity, be sure to give credit to the people you interviewed or observed.

Writing Assignments

Obviously, your instructor does not expect you to take a few years off from school so that you can immerse yourself in a community. Unlike Douglas Harper, we can't give you several years to ride the rails in order to write an ethnography, nor do we expect you to conduct a semester-long ethnography like Todd Taylor's. Instead, your task is to experiment with the ethnographic methods discussed in this chapter. Rather than spending six months observing the community, spend as much time as you can given the overall time allotted. You may need to base your observations on only two visits, as Diane Cabrero does in her study of Overeaters Anonymous, which appears later in this chapter. Or, you may wish to describe to outsiders a culture of which you are already a member, as Russell Boyce does in his study of working conditions at a packaging company. (Boyce's study also appears later in this chapter.)

1. Freewrite a list of all of the different cultures that you have participated in over the last year and then question whether or not any of these groups are worth studying in detail. For example, can you write about the classroom dynamics of an unusual class? Do you work with an interesting group of people? Are you a member of a fraternity or sorority?

2. What communities have you ever considered joining or simply been interested in? For example, are you curious about car salespeople on the showroom floor, about politicians on a student government committee, about an on-campus environmental concerns group, about writers at a writers' group sponsored by your college or university? Think about places where cultures are likely to congregate. For example, is there a local hot spot where your peers go to dance? Is there a local church that has intrigued you? Perhaps there is an on-campus group like a philosophy club, a history club, a debating club, or a skiing club that will allow you to sit in on a few meetings.

3. Have you ever wondered how local government works? If so, you can attend a few city council meetings. If you are curious about the judicial process, you can sit in on a few court cases.

4. Do you have any homeless people living in your city whom you could observe? Do you think it would be interesting to go to a shelter in your city and interview its director and community social workers?

Prewriting and Drafting Strategies

Select a Culture to Study

The athlete's gym, the women's club, the student government committee, the hair salon, the transcendental meditation circle, the children's play group, the news room—all of these unique communities could provide fascinating sites for ethnographic analysis. Of course, you want to exercise caution when selecting a community to study. Neither I nor your English teacher would ever want you to enter a potentially dangerous community. It certainly wouldn't be wise, for example, to enter a community of drug-users or "skin heads."

Experts disagree about how involved you can be in a community before studying it by means of ethnographic methods. Because you are experimenting for the first time with these methods, your instructor may allow you to study a community to which you already belong. The problem, however, with studying such a community is that you are less able to be passive and objective when you gather data. In a sense, what you think about the community and the people in it may control what you perceive. Rather than trying to discover why and how people behave as they do, your membership and history with the culture may blind you to new insights. Instead of going into a community with an open mind and systematically examining behavior, you may end up merely writing what you already believe, which undercuts our current goal—that is, to conduct research. If time limitations prohibit you from studying a new community, therefore, you will need to pay special attention to triangulating your data, as discussed below.

Learn Everything You Can about the Culture

Ethnographers disagree vehemently about the degree to which library research must support field study. Many well-respected anthropologists have written ethnographies that contain few if any references to secondary sources. The job of entering a culture, living as an insider, and then writing to outsiders, they claim, is already so demanding that they do not have the time, energy, or zeal to connect their work to the work of others. In addition, because ethnography is a fairly new technique, many ethnographers are truly breaking new ground and other scholarly references may simply be unavailable. If permitted by your instructor, you may want to focus on the story-telling aspects of ethnography and model your report on an ethnography like Douglas Harper's, which appears in the beginning of this chapter.

Of course, it is possible to use the narrative voice and still integrate outside sources into your story. Note, for example, how Diane Cabrera introduces her ethnography of Overeaters Anonymous with statistics regarding dieting behavior of high school and college-age females. In fact, even if you decide to emphasize the voice of the storyteller and downplay the voice of the academic researcher, I strongly recommend conducting some library research of your culture *before* beginning your field research. Familiarizing yourself with the culture before entering it can provide you with the information you need to know to participate without being too obtrusive. For example, if you are going to study the local chess club, you need to learn the rules of chess and play a few games. If you want to study an engineering fraternity, you need to learn the engineering terms that people in the community will use. By learning the language and by knowing what other ethnographers and researchers have had to say about the culture, you will know what questions to ask, what behaviors to look for, and even how to dress. For example, if you wanted to research how cancer patients interact with each other in a support group, you would be wise to spend some time in the library reading about how people typically respond to potentially terminal diseases. You would be wise to see if any case studies or ethnographies have already been done with cancer patients. Adequate preparation for your entrance into the community is crucial if you are to blend into the background and subsequently understand the values, expectations, roles, and ceremonies of the community. Conducting extensive library research before entering the community will help you understand the subjects' thoughts, feelings, and actions.

To see whether any ethnographies have been done on the culture you have selected to study and to find some useful background information about its history and the problems it now faces, you may find it useful to survey pertinent CD-ROM or on-line computer databases, such as *ERIC*, the *MLA International Bibliography*, or the *Social Science Citation Index*. You might also check out *Sociological Abstracts* or *Abstracts in Anthropology*.

Develop a Field Notebook

In past chapters I have argued that the increased intellectual challenge placed on you by the research process can be managed effectively by maintaining a research notebook. This advice is even more important when you are conducting an ethnographic study. For while it is possible (although not recommended) to put off the writing until the last minute when writing a report based on library research, questionnaire, or even interviews, such a strategy is nearly impossible when writing an ethnography.

Ethnographers are constantly writing. In the preliminary stages, they are writing about how they choose the community, synthesizing in writing the literature that exists about the community, writing thick description about what the culture and members look like, and recording dialogues and insights. Ethnographers rely extensively on their field notes to determine what attributes define members in the community, what common problems community members face, and what power relations or rituals exist. In short, ethnographers rely on their field notes to make preliminary interpretations. Rather than waiting until it's time to leave the community, they are constantly writing up their observations and results, drawing tentative conclusions.

As with a research notebook, you are free to generate any categories you find useful when developing your field notebook. These are the categories that students in my writing and research courses have developed:

Set a Schedule. As usual, you are wise to take a look at the time you have available to gather data and write your ethnography. If you tend to procrastinate, you should probably set a due date well in advance of your instructor's.

Log Work Completed. Maintaining a record of your work completed will give your instructor a good sense of your efforts. More importantly, this tactic may challenge you to make use of small segments of time as opposed to binge writing. As discussed in the opening chapter to this book, writing a little each day is likely to result in higher grades, more substantive work, and less stress.

Maintain a Chronological Record of Field Notes. The heart of your field notebook, this is where you record conversations, the results of interviews with key informants, and descriptions of people and places that you have observed. If possible, take notes while you are in the field instead of trying to construct later what people said or did. To help recreate your ethnography for readers, you might even want to take pictures of key participants and people.

Identify Key Patterns and Themes. You can best begin analyzing and organizing your final report by rereading your chronological record of field notes. As you review, look for recurring behaviors, attitudes, and themes. For example, if you were conducting an ethnography that examines students' attitudes regarding a large lecture course and you heard several students make similar comments—such as, "I have no idea what the professor is talking about, but there's no way I'm going to ask any questions. I don't want to look stupid"—then you might posit a *theme:* that is, students are afraid of looking silly by asking questions in large groups. Over time, you could check the validity of this theme against what other people in the community say or suggest by their actions. In addition, other themes would emerge which you could then compare with the first. For example, when you discuss the course with several students, they tell you they have heard that the teacher has been using the same lecture notes for years and that it's best to study the course text carefully and mostly ignore the lectures—all but the last three before each test—in order to get good grades. The ethnographer could then take these two themes and posit a *pattern:* that is, students' drive to earn a good grade encourages them to be quiet and ignore most of the professor's lectures.

When you are attempting to make sense of your observations, you will need to guard against the human tendency to form patterns too quickly and then look for confirming evidence while ignoring disconfirming evidence. Of course, you ultimately cannot escape your own selective and subjective perception of reality, yet you can try to be as objective as possible by checking your version of reality against what other people in the community have to say.

Drafts, Works in Progress.   Rather than waiting to write your results until you leave the field, try drafting your ethnography while you are in the field. In this way you can take advantage of the meaning-making nature of language.

Develop a Research Proposal

Because getting started can be more than half the battle, you may find it useful to challenge yourself to write a proposal for your study and share it with your classmates and instructor. While true ethnographers have the luxury of spending large chunks of time in the field and can discover their purpose after lengthy observations, you may find it necessary to focus on a more clearly defined purpose early in your research. Note, for example, how Faber focused on tipping patterns while Taylor focused on writing strategies and response to teacher criticism. Asking the following questions can help you narrow the scope of your research.

1. What specific culture or community will you study? Why is the culture worth studying? What religious, economic, or political forces define the culture? How would you describe the environment of the culture? What relationship can you define between the culture you are studying and the dominant culture?

2. What literature about the culture is available? Do you know any people who used to be members of the culture whom you could interview to help develop a sense of what to look for once you enter the community?

3. Do you have a viable way of entering the culture?

4. Do you have access to inside written documents—such as interoffice memoranda, research studies, or general essays—that can provide you with information about program goals, problems, and power relations?

5. What methods will you use to gather data? Will you, for example, use any questionnaires, interviews, psychological tests?

6. What schedule do you plan to follow? How much time do you allow for data collection or for data interpretation? When will you have a rough draft completed?

Arrange for Access to the Community

Experts typically agree that how you are introduced into the community plays a crucial role in the overall success of your study. If the people in charge introduce you to the community and ask participants to do what they can to help you, you may be perceived as a spy or enemy. It is, therefore, often better to enter a community less obtrusively. Because being introduced to the community by someone in power or by someone considered to be a member of an "opposing faction" can irreparably taint your results, you may have to reject the role implied by your introduction or withdraw from the community and select another site to conduct the research.

In addition, you should try to be positioned in a spot that will enhance your data collection and ability to make observations. For example, one student whom I worked with was intrigued by what she heard at the teachers' lounge when she was undergoing her training to be teacher. After extensive reading about the concerns of high school teachers, she conducted an ethnography of the teachers' lounge at the school where she was assigned to intern for her teacher training. The result of her study was a sometimes inspiring and sometimes depressing account of ten teachers' struggles, ideas, and ambitions.

Ask the Journalist's 5 W's

In order to avoid overlooking important material, you should keep the journalist's 5 W's and H in mind:

1. *Who* are key actors in the culture?
2. *What* happens? What key events can you describe to give us a heightened impression about values, rituals, and problems?
3. *Where* is the culture located? What does the environment look like?
4. *When* did the events happen in time? Do any events or statements routinely seem to follow each other, suggesting a pattern?
5. *Why* did the events happen?
6. *How* did the events happen?

By asking the journalistic questions when making field notes, you can ensure that you do not neglect any important observations.

Experiment with Kenneth Burke's Pentad

In *A Grammar of Motives,* philosopher and critic Kenneth Burke presents the *pentad* as a model for understanding and even predicting human behavior. Burke suggests that we ask the following five questions:

1. What are people doing "in thought or deed"?
2. Where does the act take place?

3. What person or kind of person performed the act?
4. What "means or instruments" did the person use?
5. What is the purpose of the act?

By asking these fundamental questions, Burke proposes that we can generate insights about the factors that led up to the action. In particular, these questions will offer us insights into the following five components of a situation:

1. The Act
2. The Scene
3. The Agent
4. The Agency
5. The Purpose

While analyzing specific acts or scenes can obviously lead us to some understanding about what motivated someone to do something, what really makes Burke's pentad useful is his emphasis on the relationships among the terms. Burke is especially interested in the ratios that occur when the following terms are compared:

actor to act	act to agency
actor to scene	act to purpose
actor to agency	scene to agency
actor to purpose	scene to purpose
act to scene	agency to purpose

For example, by analyzing an *act to scene ratio*, we can gain information about how the scene, or social context, influenced the act. More specifically, as an ethnographer you might try to understand how criminal behavior is expressed in the inner city. If violence is an everyday part of the scene in a housing project in the inner city, then we can understand why residents might express a lot of fear about being a victim of violence. If we interviewed people in the community who acted violently (i.e., agents), then we might have a better sense of how they commit the violence (scene to agency) or why they believe they commit the violence (act to scene).

Revising and Editing Strategies

Ask Critical Questions

The following assessment questions can help you revise your report at the content level. Because several of them highlight common problems that authors face when writing ethnographic reports, you will want to consider them carefully, in addition to the readability and editing guidelines discussed in Part III.

1. Have I provided the thick description of my culture and people that will enable my readers to understand the makeup of the community that I have studied? Have I provided enough details about why the people I am writing about respond as they do to the circumstances I am describing?

2. Have I clarified how I entered the community? Have I accounted for how my presence may have influenced behavior? Will readers understand how I made my observations?

3. Have I effectively triangulated my data? In what ways have my personal values influenced my observations?

4. Have I ignored the diversity of the culture?

5. Is the ethnography well organized? Would a different ordering of events be more forceful?

6. Is my language straightforward and clear? Have I avoided excessive abstract words? Can I use more concrete words? Have I attempted to appeal to my readers' senses?

7. Is my writing economical? Can I combine and edit some of the sentences to make them more vigorous?

8. Is the essay grammatically and mechanically correct? Are there any specific errors I tend to make that I haven't yet checked for?

Share Your Report with Members of the Community

Another way to check whether your observations are as objective as possible is to share the results of your work with a few of your key informants. Although you should not necessarily expect informants to agree with your interpretations, you can be satisfied that you have rendered the events accurately if they agree with the bulk of your presentation. Some distinguished anthropologists, in fact, suggest that all ethnographers should share their work with informants and not rest until the informants agree that the researcher has adequately described the community setting and key actors. As you can well imagine, this sort of commitment can result in some fairly sticky complications. What, for example, would you do if your interpretation of events cast the key participants in a negative light? As a result, I recommend that you do not promise beforehand to share your final results with community members. Instead, you can make this option available if you feel it is appropriate once you have completed a few drafts.

Do a Criteria-Based Feedback

Using pre-established criteria to evaluate writing is always problematical given that serious writing cannot be reduced to simple formulas. Because ethnographic research is still in its infancy as a research method, it is impossible to present standardized criteria that you must follow. Instead, you should look at the following criteria as possible ways to judge your ethnographic account.

	Low	Middle	High
I. Voice	1 2 3 4 5 6 7 8 9 10		

The voice of the storyteller is distinctive and credible.

The voice of the scholar is effective and credible.

The voices of scholar and storyteller work effectively as developed.

	Low	Middle	High
II. Methodology	1 2 3 4 5 6 7 8 9 10		

Extensive original research was completed.

A description of the community is provided.

The researcher's entrance into the community is described.

Thick description is provided.

Sample dialogues are provided.

Triangulation of information has been conducted.

Counting was attempted where appropriate.

The researcher spent sufficient time in the community.

Problems with the methodology are acknowledged.

	Low	Middle	High
III. Outside References	1 2 3 4 5 6 7 8 9 10		

The proper form of documentation is used.

It is clear when outside sources are being cited.

Sufficient outside sources are provided for factual information, controversial statements, and emphasis.

	Low	Middle	High
IV. Substantive Revision	1 2 3 4 5 6 7 8 9 10		

The significance of the subject is clarified.

The document is reader-based.

The tone is appropriate given the audience and purpose.

The document is organized and formatted effectively.

The paragraphs are coherent and cohesive.

	Low	Middle	High
	1 2 3	4 5 6 7	8 9 10

V. Edited Document

Unnecessary jargon and awkward abstractions have been edited.

The first person has been used, where appropriate.

To be verbs have been avoided.

A high verb-to-noun ratio has been established.

Strings of prepositions have been avoided.

The document has been edited for economy.

The document has been copyedited for grammatical, mechanical, and formatting errors.

Collaborating Strategies

As you share your work with critical readers, ask people who are unfamiliar with the culture that you have studied to read your ethnography and answer the following questions.

PEER REVIEW WORKSHOP

1. How would you define your peer's audience, voice, and purpose? What changes or additions can the author make to create a more persuasive or informative report? Can you visualize the people whom the author is describing?

2. Is enough information given about the setting for the ethnography?

3. Has the author clarified his or her interpretations? Do these interpretations seem valid?

4. What aspects of the author's account remain confusing? What additional information could the author provide that would help you better understand the community that has been analyzed?

5. Do you think the report is well organized? Has the author effectively presented the voice both of storyteller and researcher? Can you suggest any changes that would make the presentation of either voice more effective?

6. How could the author appeal more to the interests of readers?

Additional Writing Samples

Because of her concern for a good friend's eating disorder, student writer Diane Cabrera decided to use ethnographic methods to study the local chapter of Overeaters Anonymous. Cabrera chose to be covert about her role as a researcher because she feared informing authorities at Overeaters Anonymous that she was conducting an ethnography would result in her study being prohibited.

An Ethnography of Overeaters Anonymous

Diane Cabrera

Many college students, especially women, are obsessed with their weight; 1 some of my friends have tried drastic liquid diets, expensive weight programs, and vigorous exercise to lose weight. I recently learned that my friends' behavior may have started earlier than college age. Dr. Pauline Powers and Dr. Robert C. Fernandez state in their book, *Current Treatment of Anorexia Nervosa and Bulimia,* "There is an alarming tendency for concerns about size and dieting behavior that occurs in young age groups: 52 percent of high school girls are dieting, and 14 percent are already chronic dieters" (11).

Some people are so concerned about their weight that they develop 2 eating disorders such as anorexia or bulimia. Anorexia is an obsession with weight loss, and bulimia is overeating which is followed by self-induced vomiting. Both of these eating disorders are more common than we think among college students, especially females. Here is an example of one college student.

> A 22-year-old student went to an out-of-state college and was completely unprepared to live away from home. She became depressed and had to leave school. After recovering from her depression, she didn't like the way she looked and lost weight. She went from 110 pounds to 80 pounds and had to be hospitalized to help regain the weight. (Bruch 147)

In order for me to completely understand women's problems with ano- 3 rexia, bulimia, and overeating, I decided to use ethnographic methods to observe a few meetings of Overeaters Anonymous (OA). I had heard about Overeaters Anonymous and decided to get some information about the program. After spending a whole afternoon trying to find a convenient meeting, I arranged to attend a meeting that night at 8:00. I felt extremely nervous, but I just knew that OA was an interesting project.

Background Information

According to a brochure entitled "About OA," Overeaters Anonymous is a 4 group of people from all walks of life who meet in order to help solve their compulsive overeating problem. "About OA" also explains that OA started back in 1960 in Los Angeles with three people meeting to help each other with their eating problems. The OA program is based on the Twelve Steps of Alcoholics Anonymous.

Meetings

I arrived at St. Clement's Church at 7:50 P.M. with a stomach full of nerves. 5 I was panicking; I questioned myself if I could really pull this off without growing a huge "Pinocchio nose" or sweating to death from nerves. After noticing a brave soul exiting her car, I promptly got out of my car and said, "I'm new here. Can you show me where to go?" The woman immediately introduced herself and walked with me to the meeting.

As a researcher, I entered the OA community as a person with an eating 6 disorder; my anonymity was the same as anyone else's in the group. I was expecting to see a bunch of sloppy, fat people who complained about everything; what I thought and what I saw were exact opposites. As I entered the room with my new friend, I sat at the table with about twenty-five people from all "walks of life." One distinctive lady arrived in a brand new BMW sports car, and she was wearing an expensive suit; another looked like she just finished mopping the floor and didn't have time to change clothes. The majority of people dressed casually and were quite talkative among themselves.

"Joyce" (a fictitious name) began the meeting by saying, "My name is 7 Joyce, and I'm a compulsive overeater and bulimic." The group responded, "Hi, Joyce." She methodically ran through the basics of the program such as "The Twelve Steps," anonymity, and the disease of compulsive overeating. The group based its discussion on the second step: "Came to believe that a power greater than ourselves could restore us to sanity." Of course I got a little nervous and thought, "Oh no! What am I going to say? They are going to see right through me."

The section I read was about fasting; luckily, I fast once in awhile so I 8 was able to concoct a response. I froze after I read my paragraph, and I noticed twenty-five people looking me right in the eye. I quickly sputtered out, "I can relate to fasting. After eating a fast food meal, I will fast the next day to burn off the calories." My response was reasonably accurate, and it seemed to be well received.

The book continued to make it around the table. "Joyce," a recovering 9 bulimic, shared that she acted insanely in her past when she was home alone. She would binge and purge all day so she could have food in her mouth constantly. "Kim" said she rummaged through her smelly garbage to salvage a candy bar that was thrown away a couple of days earlier. After the meeting, "Kim" offered me her phone number; she told me that she was having a lot of problems, and when others call her for help, it actually helps her out.

Real People with Real Problems

At the next meeting, the group leader chose the topic of "the difficulty of 10 honesty." The next person to share, "Lisa," began to cry and talk about honesty. She is eight months pregnant, and she found out her husband was dishonest; he was having an affair and wanted a divorce. "Lisa" is scared because she is forced to raise a child alone, and she is hurt because her husband lied to her. She is on the verge of a binge and cries to the group for help, "Please help me. I don't want to go back to purging; I have a child inside of me now, and I don't want to hurt her."

Another person, "Kim," shared a similar experience as "Lisa." "Kim" is 11 also pregnant, and she was served divorce papers from her husband. She is 22 years old, married only two years, and forced to move back in with her parents. "Kim" is overweight, and now she is struggling with compulsive overeating because of this new added stress. She understands that women gain weight when they are pregnant, but in her case, she is not eating wisely. Lately her diet has consisted of Hershey bars, Dunkin' Donuts, Doritos, and Big Macs. She is so hurt and frustrated about her husband's deceit that she says, "I just don't care anymore; I don't even care if my actions are hurting my child. I'd rather us both die."

The saddest story soon followed "Lisa's" and "Kim's." An overweight 12 woman, "Lucy," attended the OA meeting on the advice of her psychiatrist. She is under out-patient psychiatric care for self-mutilation and mental instability. "Lucy" admitted she did not want to attend this meeting, but her doctor told her it would do her some good. "Lucy" explained,

> I have a pagan for a daughter. We were in the Christian bookstore the other day, and she was making horrid comments about Jesus in front of everyone. I told her to leave the store and wait for me outside. My other daughter has epilepsy, and I can never leave her alone. I overeat because I have all these family problems, and I just don't care about how I look. I have attempted suicide twice, and I finally decided I needed help. I tried OA before, but I got too lazy and made excuses for not attending the meetings. Now I'm really going to give it a try. I have to learn to put myself first and not worry so much about everyone else.

After "Lucy" shared, I realized that OA is more than people moaning 13 about eating problems. This group of people is made up of real people with real problems. They talk about their problems so they don't resort back to their destructive eating habits. "Lisa," "Kim," and "Lucy" honestly admitted their problems, and I respect their courage to admit it, rather than covering up their feelings with compulsive overeating.

Conclusion

Many people are confused about people who overeat or purge; I used to 14 believe that fat people and bulimics are grotesque. During my study, I found that 75 percent of the people in the group were not grotesquely obese; the other 15 percent were somewhat overweight; the final 10 percent were anorexics or bulimics.

A person does not have to be fat to have a compulsive eating disorder. 15 Basically, an overeater turns to food as an escape from his or her problems.

Although only women attended the meetings in my case, men can have eating disorders, too. In fact, a man wrote a letter in the OA newsletter about his problem. He was a recovering alcoholic who then turned to food to satisfy his compulsive behavior; now he is an active OA member and an Alcoholics Anonymous (AA) member.

College students can look up Overeaters Anonymous in the phone 16 book, and a helpful person will answer any questions and assist in the process of finding a convenient meeting. I would suggest that college students go to OA rather than weight loss centers or hospitals because there is no expense for the OA program. When people enter a hospital for an eating disorder, the majority of the patients attend some type of support group after their initial therapy is complete. My main goal is to let the public know that compulsive overeaters, anorexics, bulimics, and food addicts are not defective people; they are real people who only want to get their lives back into perspective.

Works Cited

"About OA." Overeaters Anonymous, P.O. Box 92870, Los Angeles, CA. n.d.

Bruch, Hilde. *Conversations with Anorexics.* New York: Basic, 1988.

Powers, Pauline S., and Robert C. Fernandez, eds. *Current Treatment of Anorexia Nervosa and Bulimia.* Switzerland: S. Karger AG, 1984.

Critical Reading Questions

1. How does Cabrero use statistics to both hook her readers' interest and establish a professional tone?
2. How would you define Cabrero's tone in this project? What information does she reveal about herself?
3. In what ways does Cabrero use the narrative voice to organize her report? (Refer to specific passages in your answer.)
4. What is the primary theme that holds this piece together?
5. What makes this piece an ethnography?

In the following selection, Russell Boyce, a student writer, analyzes his experience working for a packaging company. Because he emphasizes his personal experiences, as opposed to the "community," the report moves away from ethnography toward autobiography. Nevertheless, Boyce does quote other workers and compare his experience with that of his colleagues.

Hard Work and Low Pay at RPS
Russell Boyce

A piercing buzzer sounds the beginning of the work shift, and starts the 1 slow movement of the conveyer belt. Two semi-tractor trailers are backed into a bay, and four men begin to methodically unload the hundreds of boxes which are tightly packed within the trailers. They move the boxes single file out of the back of the trucks, and up the double conveyer belt toward the splitters. Here they separate the packages by zip code and place them on a high and low belt. Eventually, the packages will find their way into several vans which line the conveyer belts. This final separation process is the job of the loaders. Drivers then complete the distribution to the final destination of the boxes throughout the city.

I entered into Roadway Package System (RPS) employment on January   2
29, 1991, and ended work on February 20, 1991. I never worked so hard in my life. RPS is a five-year-old, small-package delivery business that has several terminals in Florida. Packages arrive in semis from all over the country to the Florida terminals and are then distributed by smaller vans to specialized areas. The Tampa terminal where I was employed services the Tampa/St. Petersburg/Clearwater area.

Our terminal works two four-hour shifts, one from 11 P.M.–3 A.M., and   3
the other from 3 A.M.–7 A.M. I worked the 11–3 shift, known as a sort, unloading packages. I was a glorified pack mule that worked non-stop for four hours, or until all the packages were unloaded. The life of an unloader is very difficult because the labor is strenuous and intense. Management expects each semi, which is loaded with roughly one thousand boxes, to be unloaded in forty-five minutes. This goal demands that the unloader work at an extremely fast pace. Even working at full speed, two unloaders usually need one hour to unload the first truck of the evening. As the night progresses and fatigue takes its toll, the unloading time increases.

The work is very monotonous, since the packages are unloaded one by   4
one from the trailers and placed onto the conveyer belts. The image that I used to get in my head when working was that of an indentured servant working in a field, propelled by a rhythmic song. We had no music to work to, but the rhythm was there to set the pace. We would set one package down after another onto the rollers, keeping in rhythm to the efforts of the person we were working with.

When I first applied for the unloader's job, the terminal manager asked   5
if I was a student, and explained that RPS hired only students. I was curious about this, and asked him why. He told me that the original founders of RPS had been students, and that the company was dedicated to the furthering of education in the community. He also explained that if a student graduated while at RPS, he would be offered a job in management within the company. This was RPS's version of advancement from within. His statements seemed reasonable at the time, especially since RPS would throw in an extra dollar per hour for education above the seven dollars normally paid. The extra dollar would be held in a fund, and paid to the student's educational institution every three months, once the employees completed at least thirty days at RPS.

Four weeks later I began to suspect that the reason the company hired   6
students was more likely that students are more motivated to earn money at

all costs than average workers. They have the incentive of educational goals to drive them through the intense labor. It also appears that the incentive lasts only so long, because in the one-month period that I was there, our sort went through four unloaders. The only other unloader who survived as long as I did was a guy named Scott. His motivation was that he was only working until the summer.

A major factor in turnover of unloaders besides the intense labor seems 7 to be the evening hours. It is extremely difficult to work until three in the morning, get three to four hours sleep, and then make it to school for a nine o'clock class. I used to pass through school in a dream state, and then get home and try to get a nap before studying and then heading off to work again. I wanted to know if I was the only one who was having difficulty with the evening hours, coupled with early classes. No one seemed to be complaining, so I asked Scott and some of the other unloaders if they were having difficulty. It was as if I had opened up a festering sore. Everyone described the same symptoms I was suffering, along with the addition that their grades were dropping. We all agreed that we just couldn't concentrate after a solid week of sleep deprivation. I really believe that the educational incentive at RPS is nothing more than a hook to get students interested, and that RPS doesn't pay all that much in actual benefits. No one seems to last long enough.

Another thing that gave me a hint about the turnover at the terminal was 8 that nobody ever bothered to learn my name. Scott and I were the only ones on a first name basis. It was sort of a joke, because for some unknown reason I was known to everyone as "Hey." I did receive a name toward the end of my employment, but it was related to what I was wearing. I had on a Boston Celtics t-shirt one night, and so I became Larry Bird. It was ridiculous. It just seemed that people didn't last long enough for anyone to bother to learn names.

The only other unloader that I became even remotely friendly with was 9 a big guy named John. He lasted all of two weeks. John was about 6'4" tall and weighed around 220 lbs. John was a funny case, because he looked so big and strong, but in reality he really had difficulty with the job. It's true that an unloader needs strength, but there is a lot of bending involved in the work, and John was so tall that he used to constantly complain that his back was killing him. He was pretty slow, and no one wanted to work with him, because the work he didn't do had to be made up by his truck-mate. He eventually went the way of all unloaders, which was to quit after barely getting all of his paperwork done for employment.

The management treated the unloaders like slaves. We were constantly 10 being yelled to work faster and to, "Pump it out." We would just swear something under our breath and continue at the same methodical pace. The worst of the management for yelling was a guy named Tom. He was a true company man. He had been with RPS for three years, which I couldn't believe, and the job was his life. Whenever he felt that we weren't working fast enough, he would jump into a trailer with one of us, and set a super-human pace unloading boxes. As soon as he began to tire, he would make some excuse about having to make a phone call and leave. The human body can take just so much physical exertion before it begins to slow and tire. I believe Tom really believed this, but that he was being pressured by the higher-ups to get as much production out of the unloaders as possible. By the time we started unloading the fourth truck of the night, we were just about exhausted. This was when the verbal abuse by management was the most intense. Scott had nicknamed the fourth truck the pride truck. His reasoning was that by the fourth truck you were usually ready to quit, but your personal pride kept you going through it.

After a month, I had decided that I couldn't last and still expect to do   11 well in school. I've always given two weeks notice to employers as a courtesy so they can find a replacement, but a particular incident changed my mind. One of the managers named Jeff found a consulting job with an engineering firm, and put in his two weeks notice. Higher management told him not to bother coming in any more. I was incensed. The two weeks notice is not just for the employer. It also allows the employee to tie up any loose ends before moving up. I felt this was extremely unprofessional, and I decided not to give them any notice. It turned out that this was standard procedure, because an unloader under two weeks notice could not be expected to work as hard as a fresh pack mule.

I learned quite early at RPS that I was considered more part of a   12 machine, like the conveyer belt I was working on, than an employee. The higher-ups that ran RPS understand that they can hold people with their enticing claims for a short period of time only, and after that they will lose a great deal of their employees. It doesn't seem to bother them though, because there is always a huge stack of applications waiting to be activated.

Critical Reading Questions

1. What details about the working environment does Boyce provide to help you visualize conditions at the packaging company?

2. How has Boyce melded the voice of the person going through the experience with the more reflective voice of the person analyzing the experience?

3. Throughout Boyce's report, he summarizes the discussions he had with his coworkers. How else could Boyce have illustrated interpersonal relations at the packaging company?

Evaluating Criticism

1. What have you learned about yourself as a writer as a result of the prewriting, drafting, revising, or copyediting techniques that you experimented with when writing your ethnographic report?

2. Did your perception of yourself as a writer or person change as a result of this assignment?

3. In what ways has writing your research report changed your perception of the research process?

4. If you exchanged criticisms of your peers' work, what did you learn as a result of this experience?

5. If you could begin your ethnography again, what would you do differently?

6. In what ways have your thoughts about the culture or community you studied changed as a result of your research?

7. How were your peers' and teacher's evaluations of your ethnography similar to and different from their evaluations of past writing projects?

Part 3

How to Revise and Edit Your Work

CHAPTER ELEVEN

How to Make Substantive Revisions

Our fast-paced, consumer-driven society is geared to offer us a remarkable number of choices in nanoseconds. If the fast-food chain doesn't deliver lunch within sixty seconds, it's free. With a push of a button, people who live in large metropolitan areas can run through as many as 100 different channels on cable television. You can fly across the United States in hours; in fact, if you have the money, you can take the Concorde and fly from breakfast in New York, to lunch in London, to dinner in Paris.

Clearly, we live in an "information society," an age of smooth, mass-market packaging. We are bombarded with the polished printed word. Newspapers, magazines, junk mail, and interoffice memos surround us like mosquitoes on a hot summer night, buzzing, "Buy me, read me, believe in me." Americans spend over three months of their lives just opening and discarding all of the junk mail stuffed into their mailboxes, 75 percent of which they don't read. Every minute two scientific papers are published, not to mention articles in the humanities or social sciences or popular press. Gifted (and not so gifted) authors spend months polishing proposals and sales letters and then—with the use of photocopiers, fax machines, and computer modems—they send out copies in mass numbers.

The fast pace of our society often seems contrary to the reflective, introspective tone that we must adopt when we are trying to develop and write about ideas. And, perhaps because we are so accustomed to seeing polished final drafts, we expect to create similar texts with little effort. After all, since we are surrounded by printed material, it can seem natural to assume that it can't be that hard to write. Of course, much of what is written is gobbledygook—that is, jargon in search of meaning.

Experienced student and professional writers know that most authors compose multiple drafts before they can produce a manuscript that communicates sophisticated ideas to readers. They know that writing that is easily and enjoyably read, as if the author were sitting with you and discussing his or her ideas, is often the product of many revisions. When difficult concepts are explained simply, you can assume that the author has agonized over them. Kelli Sorrentino, one of my undergraduate students, writes:

> When you first told us about revision in class, it was like some great revelation to me, for some reason. I think I had some sort of mistaken notion

353

about leaving pieces of work "just as they came to me." I believed that there was something magical about inspiration. But now that I've learned to look at my work more critically, I realize that I can improve on all of my so-called "inspired ideas." Revising pieces constantly has taught me to improve on "inspiration," and when I really got into it, it proved to be a godsend. Now I really enjoy picking my writing apart because I've learned that this allows me to produce better writing than I've ever done before.

Experienced, professional writers understand that revision is crucial to successful writing. For example, James Michener writes:

> Getting words on paper is difficult. Nothing I write is good enough in the first draft, not even personal letters. Important work must be written over and over—up to six or seven times.

Perhaps the most pernicious assumption that inexperienced writers make is that polished, A-level essays are the products of an inspired mind, of "a born writer." Just as nonelectricians tend to perceive electricity as a form of magic, inexperienced writers tend to be mystified by the creative process. As Lafcadio Hearn argued in his lectures at Tokyo University between 1896 and 1902, many novice writers wrongly assume that they should wait to be inspired before writing:

> Nothing has been more productive of injury to young literary students than those stories, or legends, about great writers having written great books in a very short time. They suggest what must be in a million cases impossible, as a common possibility . . . It is much more valuable to remember that Gray passed fourteen years in correcting and improving a single poem, and that no great poem or book, as we now have the text, represents the first form [of] the text . . . Almost everything composed by Tennyson was changed and changed and changed again, to such an extent that in almost every edition the text differed. Above all things do not imagine that any good work can be done without immense pains.

Successful writers look and look again at their manuscripts because they know that this constant reworking is one of the most effective ways to discover what they want to say and to find out what they have learned by writing.

> Think before you speak is criticism's motto; speak before you think is creation's.
>
> *E. M. Forster*

> I start my work by asking a question and then try . . . to answer it.
>
> *Mary Lee Settle*

> To rewrite ten times is not unusual.
>
> *Saul Bellow*

> Oh, bother the mss., mark them as much as you like: what else are they for? Mark everything that strikes you. I may consider a thing forty-nine times; but if you consider it, it will be considered 50 times; and a line 50 times

considered is 2 percent better than a line 49 times considered. And it is the final 2 percent that makes the difference between excellence and mediocrity.

George Bernard Shaw

There are days when the result is so bad that no fewer than five revisions are required. In contrast, when I'm greatly inspired, only four revisions are needed.

John Kenneth Galbraith

We write out what we don't know about what we know.

Grace Paley

I mean that generally the more you write—the more times you write it— the better the piece is.

Calvin Trillin

Writing and rewriting are a constant search for what one is saying.

John Updike

I'm working on something. I don't know exactly what.

Eudora Welty

A young author is tempted to leave anything he has written through fear of not having enough to say if he goes cutting out too freely. But it is easier to be long than short. . . . Think of and look at your work as though it were done by your enemy. If you look at it to admire it you are lost. . . . If we look at it to see where it is wrong, we shall see this and make it righter. If we look at it to see where it is right, we shall see this and not make it righter.

Samuel Butler

It's always taken me a long time to finish poems. . . . When I was in my twenties I found poems taking six months to a year, maybe fifty drafts or so. Now I am going over two hundred drafts regularly, working on things four or five years and longer. Too long! I wish I did not take so long.

Donald Hall

I write out of ignorance. I write about the things I don't have any resolutions for, and when I'm finished, I think I know a little bit more about it. I don't write out of what I know. It's what I don't know that stimulates me.

Toni Morrison

Experienced writers understand that the creative process involves juggling a wide array of contrary activities. As a writer, sometimes you are thinking about the voice that you are projecting, sometimes about grammatical issues, sometimes about the topic, sometimes about the deadline, and sometimes about what you want for lunch. At times you can feel pulled in a hundred different directions, and this can naturally be quite frustrating.

Indeed, revising your work can feel like a schizophrenic process, because one of your primary goals—to nurture and develop your ideas like a premature baby in an incubator—works in direct opposition to another primary goal—to refine and polish your ideas. Just as you need to be nonjudgmental in the early stages of writing, you also need to adopt a critical stance—a tough, self-reflexive, questioning stance—once you have given your ideas time to mature.

What makes revising particularly difficult is that each new writing task requires us to juggle the need for nurturing and the need for criticism in totally new ways. As a result, the art of writing (and thinking) cannot be reduced to simplistic formulas. However, based on observations of successful writers at work, we can identify the vital questions and productive strategies that writers use to improve their work.

When you are revising, it is also important that you perceive problems not as mistakes but as essential and natural parts of making meaning. Even if you decide that the first four pages of a five-page document need to be thrown away in the tenth reading of a manuscript, don't tear out your hair and tell yourself that you are a poor writer and a no-good thinker. Instead of regarding revision as a process of correcting errors, try to see it as an opportunity to develop your thinking. Many experienced writers say that they enjoy writing most when a sudden burst of inspiration shatters their preconceptions and plans.

You can enhance your ability to revise by giving yourself time to cool off, time to distance yourself from your ideas. Few of us can really see problems in drafts immediately after we have written them. In addition to soliciting criticisms from peers who are good writers, you may also find that reading your work aloud highlights problems with your tone or content development.

Questions to Ask to Improve Your Manuscript

Throughout the writing portfolio of this book, you used focus questions to revise your work and studied your manuscripts with care to eliminate weaknesses in logical development, faulty transitions, and inadequate use of evidence. As you have learned from fielding your instructor's and peers' criticisms of your work, however, revising is far more complex than answering a few questions and correcting spelling. It is commonplace, for example, for you to assess your work differently each time you reread it. You can ask the same questions at 10:00 P.M. that you did at 9:00 A.M. and come up with remarkably different ideas about how to improve your work. Also, different texts and occasions warrant emphasis on different questions, so you should try to be flexible about which of the questions below you should give most emphasis to when critiquing the substance of your work.

You will eventually want to answer all of these questions, but don't be tempted to face them all at once. Although at first such a critical stance may seem admirable, it is usually counterproductive. Trying to revise a rough draft with every possible critical question in mind is like rushing down a crowded freeway at 85 miles per hour, while fretting over what every car and driver on the road might do, reading all of the passing billboards, and carrying on an important, life-crisis dialogue with a passenger. Clearly, asking every critical question possible may overload your circuits and send you deep into depression and gloom.

Content Questions

- What is my thesis? Have I expressed it, either explicitly or implicitly?
- Will readers understand my reasons for writing? Have I provided the specific examples, concrete language, careful reasoning, and supporting evidence that they need in order to understand my position?
- Have I provided enough background information for readers to understand my opinions and the significance of the subject matter I am addressing?
- Can I make my manuscript more enjoyable to read by incorporating more images and metaphors, by offering more creative examples?
- Have I clarified the credibility of my sources? Have I provided sufficient background information about the studies I have cited?

Audience Awareness Questions

- Have I used any terms or concepts that need clarification?
- Have I expressed my meaning with detail and forcefulness so that my readers will be able to "see" what I have written?
- What additional examples or concrete, sensory details can I provide to help readers understand my message?
- Can I revise any passages to make them less emotionally charged and more sympathetic to my readers' feelings about the matter?
- Are any of the examples and illustrations unnecessary, given the audience's level of knowledge? Are any examples and illustrations redundant?

Tone Questions

- Is the tone appropriate, given my intended audience and purpose? Do I sound like an informed expert, an inquiring scholar, a technocrat, a concerned citizen, a crank? Is this the voice I really want? Would presenting a different persona allow me to convey my meaning more effectively?
- Am I presenting a consistent voice throughout the text? If there are variations in the tone of the document, are they intentional and effective?

Organization Questions

- Does my introduction hook my readers' interest? Does my essay accomplish what the introduction promises?

- Throughout the document, have I offered my reader a deductive overview of my purpose and forecast my organization?
- Could I use a picture, a graph, or a table to visually represent my meaning?
- Is my conclusion an effective summary, restatement, or challenge?

Strategies for Revising Paragraphs*

Unlike punctuation, which can be subjected to specific rules, no ironclad guidelines exist for shaping paragraphs. If you presented a text without paragraphs to a dozen writing instructors and asked them to break the document into logical sections, chances are that you would get twelve different opinions about the best places to break the paragraph. In part, where paragraphs should be placed is a stylistic choice. Some writers prefer longer paragraphs that compare and contrast several related ideas, whereas others opt for a more linear structure, delineating each subject on a one-point-per-paragraph basis.

If your critics have suggested that you take a hard look at how you have organized your ideas, or if you are unsure about when you should begin a paragraph or how you should organize final drafts, then you can benefit by reviewing paragraph structure.

When you are drafting, you need to trust your intuition about where to place paragraphs. You don't want to interrupt the flow of your thoughts as you write to check on whether you are placing them in logical order. Such self-criticism could interfere with creativity or the generation of ideas. Before you submit a document for a grade, however, it makes sense to examine the structure of your paragraphs. The following guidelines can give you some insights about alternative ways to shape paragraphs.

1. Paragraphs often follow a deductive organization that moves from given to new information. Your goals for the opening sentences of your paragraphs are similar to your goals when writing an introduction to a document: in the beginning of a paragraph, you usually want to clarify the purpose of the paragraph. Most paragraphs in academic discourse move *deductively*—that is, the first or second sentence presents the *topic* or *theme* of the paragraph and the subsequent sentences illustrate and explicate this theme. Notice, in particular, how Chris Goodrich cues readers to the purpose of his paragraph (and article) in the first sentence of his essay "Crossover Dreams":

> Norman Cantor, New York University history professor and author, most recently of *Inventing the Middle Ages*, created a stir this spring when he wrote a letter to the newsletter of the American Historical Association declaring that "no historian who can write English prose should publish more than two books with a university press—one book for tenure, and one

---

* This material on paragraphs is adapted from *Publish, Don't Perish: The Scholar's Guide to Academic Writing and Publishing*, by Joseph M. Moxley. Copyright © 1992 by Greenwood Press, an imprint of Greenwood Publishing Group, Inc. Westport, CT.

for full professor. After that (or preferably long before) work only in the trade market." Cantor urged his fellow scholars to secure literary agents to represent any work with crossover potential. And he didn't stop there: As if to be sure of offending the entire academic community, Cantor added, "If you are already a full professor, your agent should be much more important to you than the department chair or the dean."

Notice in Goodrich's paragraph that it is *not* possible for you to simply rearrange the sentences and preserve the same logic. Because the following violates the reader's sense of order, it seems like gibberish:

> As if to be sure of offending the entire academic community, Cantor added, "If you are already a full professor, your agent should be much more important to you than the department chair or the dean." "After that (or preferably long before) work only in the trade market." Cantor urged his fellow scholars to secure literary agents to represent any work with crossover potential.

2. Use an inductive structure for dramatic conclusions or a varied style. While you generally want to move from the *known* to the *new*, from the *thesis* to its *illustration* or *restriction*, you sometimes want to violate this pattern. Educated readers in particular can be bored by texts that always present information in the same way. Note, for example, how Valerie Steele's anecdotal tone and dialogue in the opening sentences to her essay on fashion in academia prepare the reader for her thesis:

> Once, when I was a graduate student at Yale, a history professor asked me about my dissertation. "I'm writing about fashion," I said.
> "That's interesting. Italian or German?"
> It took me a couple of minutes, as thoughts of Armani flashed through my mind, but finally I realized what he meant. "Not *fascism*," I said. "*Fashion*. As in Paris."
> "Oh." There was a long silence, and then, without another word, he turned and walked away.
> The F-word still has the power to reduce many academics to embarrassed or indignant silence. Some of those to whom I spoke while preparing this article requested anonymity or even refused to address the subject.*

3. Paragraphs are usually unified by a single purpose or theme. Regardless of whether a paragraph is deductively or inductively structured, readers can generally follow the logic of a discussion better when a paragraph is unified by a single purpose. Paragraphs that lack a central idea and that wander from subject to subject are apt to confuse readers, making them wonder what they should pay attention to and why.

To ensure that each paragraph is unified by a single idea, Francis Christensen, in *Notes Toward a New Rhetoric*, has suggested that we number sentences according to their level of generality. According to Christensen, we

---

* From "The F-Word," by Valerie Steele in *Lingua Franca: The Review of Academic Life*, 17–18, April 1991. Reprinted by permission of the publisher.

would assign a 1 to the most general sentence and then a 2 to the second most general sentence, and so on. Christensen considers the following paragraph, which he excerpted from Jacob Bronowski's *The Common Sense of Science*, to be an example of a *subordinate* pattern because the sentences become increasingly more specific as the reader progresses through the paragraph:

1. The process of learning is essential to our lives.
    2. All higher animals seek it deliberately.
        3. They are inquisitive and they experiment.
            4. An experiment is a sort of harmless trial run of some action which we shall have to make in the real world; and this, whether it is made in the laboratory by scientists or by fox-cubs outside their earth.
            5. The scientist experiments and the cub plays; both are learning to correct their errors of judgment in a setting in which errors are not fatal.
                6. Perhaps this is what gives them both their air of happiness and freedom in these activities.

Christensen is quick to point out that not all paragraphs have a subordinate structure. The following one, which he took from Bergen Evans's *Comfortable Words*, is an example of what Christensen considers a *coordinate* sequence:

1. He [the native speaker] may, of course, speak a form of English that marks him as coming from a rural or an unread group.
    2. But if he doesn't mind being so marked, there's no reason why he should change.
        3. Samuel Johnson kept a Staffordshire burr in his speech all his life.
            3. In Burns's mouth the despised lowland Scots dialect served just as well as the "correct" English spoken by ten million of his southern contemporaries.
            3. Lincoln's vocabulary and his way of pronouncing certain words were sneered at by many better educated people at the time, but he seemed to be able to use the English language as effectively as his critics.

4. Each paragraph must relate logically to the previous paragraph(s). Readers also expect paragraphs to relate to each other as well as to the overall purpose of a text. Establishing transitional sentences for paragraphs can be one of the most difficult challenges you face as a writer because you need to guide the reader with a light hand. When you are too blatant about your transitions, your readers may feel patronized. To highlight the connections between your ideas, you can provide transitional sentences at the end of each paragraph that look forward to the substance of the next paragraph. Or, you can place the transition at the beginning of a paragraph looking backward, as Valerie Steele does in the following example:

Can a style of dress hurt one's professional career? True to form, most academics deny that it makes any difference whatsoever. But a few stories may indicate otherwise: When a gay male professor was denied tenure at an Ivy League university, some people felt that he was penalized, in part, for his dress. It was "not that he wore multiple earrings" or anything like that, but he did wear "beautiful, expensive, colorful clothes that stood out" on campus. At the design department on one of the campuses of the University of California system, a job applicant appeared for her interview wearing a navy blue suit. The style was perfect for most departments, of course, but in this case she was told—to her face—that she "didn't fit in, she didn't look arty enough."

Another bit of evidence that suggests dress is of career significance for academics is the fact that some universities (such as Harvard) now offer graduate students counseling on how to outfit themselves for job interviews. The tone apparently is patronizing ("You will need to think about an interview suit and a white blouse"), but the advice is perceived as necessary.[*]

The phrase "Another bit of evidence" beginning the second paragraph points out the relationship to the first paragraph. The reader knows where the writer is going.

When evaluating your transitions from paragraph to paragraph, question whether the transitions appear too obtrusive, thereby undercutting your credibility. At best, when transitions are unnecessary, readers perceive explicit transitional sentences to be wordy; at worst, they perceive such sentences as insulting. (After all, they imply that the readers are too inept to follow the discussion.)

5. Vary the length of paragraphs to reflect the complexity and importance of the ideas expressed in them. Different ideas, arguments, and chronologies warrant their own paragraph lengths, so the form of your text should emerge in response to your thoughts. To emphasize a transition in your argument or to highlight an important point, you may want to place critical information in a one- or two-sentence paragraph.

6. Consider the genre of writing and the visual image of the paragraphs. As much as any of the above guidelines, you should consider the genre of your text. For as much as paragraphs are shaped by the ideas being expressed, so are they influenced by the genre of the discourse. For instance, newspapers and magazines produced for high-school educated readers tend to require much shorter paragraphs than those published in academic journals. When evaluating how you have structured your ideas, however, pay attention to whether you have varied the length of your paragraphs. Long chunks of text without paragraph breaks tend to make ideas seem complicated, perhaps even inaccessible to less educated audiences. In turn, short paragraphs can create a listlike style, which intrudes on clarity and persuasive appeal. Because long paragraphs tend to make a document more complicated than short paragraphs, you should question how patient and educated your readers are.

---

[*] Ibid., 20.

7. *Analyze whether paragraphs "flow."* Paragraphs provide a visual representation of your ideas. When revising your work, evaluate the logic behind how you have organized the paragraphs. Question whether your presentation would appear more logical and persuasive if you rearranged the sequence of the paragraphs. Next, question the structure of each paragraph. To see if sentences need to be reordered, determine whether you are organizing information deductively or according to chronology or according to some sense of what is most and least important. Ask yourself these questions:

- How is each paragraph organized? Do I place my general statement or topic sentence near the beginning or near the end of each paragraph? Do I need any transitional paragraphs or transitional sentences? As I move from one idea to another, will my reader understand how subsequent paragraphs relate to my main idea as well as to previous paragraphs?

- Should any paragraphs be shifted in their order in the text? Should a later paragraph be combined with the introductory paragraph?

- Should the existing paragraphs be cut into smaller segments or merged into longer ones? If I have a concluding paragraph, do I really need it?

- Will readers understand the logical connections between paragraphs? Do any sentences need to be added to clarify the logical relationship between ideas? Have I provided the necessary forecasting and summarizing sentences that readers will need to understand how the different ideas relate to each other?

- Have I been too blatant about transitions? Are all of the transitional sentences and paragraphs really necessary or can the reader follow my thoughts without them?

Editing Strategies*

Once you believe a draft conveys the basic information you want your readers to understand, you can begin attacking it at the sentence level. After working hard to develop the substance of a message, you may be weary of it and eager to turn it over to your teacher. If possible, set the draft aside and work on another assignment before trying to edit it. The following techniques may help you critically evaluate your document at the sentence level:

1. Don't try to copyedit a document all at once. Instead, alternate proofreading with other activities.

2. There are three strategies you can use to help ignore the content of your message and concentrate solely on grammatical, mechanical, and formatting errors: First, try reading your document sentence by sentence backwards. Second, place sheets of paper above and below each sentence

---

* This material is adapted from *Publish, Don't Perish: The Scholar's Guide to Academic Writing and Publishing,* by Joseph M. Moxley. Copyright © 1992 by Greenwood Press, an imprint of Greenwood Publishing Group, Inc. Westport, CT.

in the document as you read through it. Third, place slashes between each sentence.

3. If you are using a personal computer, try printing the document with a different font, such as size 14 or size 10 print instead of the normal size 12.

4. Look for mistakes to cluster. When you find one error in paragraph seven, for example, carefully examine the surrounding sentences to see if you had a lapse of concentration when you wrote and copyedited that section.

5. Look for errors that you often make, such as sentence fragments or subject-verb agreement.

Now just as you limited the number of substantive questions when revising your document's content, you should limit the editorial issues you consider when editing your work. For example, rather than considering all six of the following editorial concerns when evaluating a nearly final draft, you may want to read the manuscript with the first three strategies in mind, take a break, and then read it again while stressing the remaining editing concerns.

Use the First Person

"Do not use the first person" is perhaps the most unfortunate writing myth that handicaps inexperienced writers. After all, how can we think without using our experience? Why must we drive a stake through our cerebral cortex before writing? Can we logically assume that we are more objective thinkers when we avoid the first person? What sort of persona do you infer when you read the following passage from an essay that recently appeared in *Evaluation and Program Planning?*

> While some evaluation specialists disagree (Scriven, 1973) this writer believes that a well-planned evaluation effort begins with clearly established goals. Sometimes goals are established by the program staff along with the evaluator well in advance of the program and the planned evaluation. This is the "best case" scenario (Posavac & Carey, 1984). However, in the case of the Very Special Arts Evaluation, programs were already in operation in many locales and had been running for a long period of time. Therefore, it was not possible for the author to be involved in the goal establishment process. In fact, one of the first questions this evaluator posed to Very Special Arts focused on the goals and criteria that were to be the benchmark against which Very Special Arts programs were to be evaluated.

Can you see that the author's prose could be more vigorous, less pedantic, if he used the first person, as suggested by the following revision?

> While I would have preferred to establish goals for evaluating the Very Special Arts programs before their inception, I was unable to do so because the programs had been operating for three years in ten cities. By meeting with personnel from the arts programs, however, I was able to develop significant goals and criteria: etc.

Now it is true that use of the first person can be obtrusive. In the bulk of writing that you do as a student, readers care more about the information and ideas that you are reviewing than about you as an author. Nevertheless, this does *not* mean that your language should lack an occasional personal anecdote. Remember overall that your teachers are people too: like everyone else, they appreciate the human drama, the compassionate moment, the personal involvement.

Use the Active Voice

Passive sentences tend to be wordy, dull, and confusing. One of the best ways to create a vigorous voice is to avoid passive sentence constructions. Essentially, a verb is *passive* when its subject is acted upon by an outside agent rather than doing the action. You can identify passive voice by finding a sentence that uses some form of the verb *to be (am, is, was, were, being, been)* along with a *past participle* (a verb form ending in *-ed, -en,* or some other verb form). The preposition *by* usually follows the *to be* verb and *past participle* or it can be implied, as illustrated below:

Passive: The data were confirmed.

Active: Three independent scholars confirmed the data.

Passive: I was made a better scholarly author by writing regularly.

Active: Writing regularly has made me a better scholarly author.

Passive: She was had by the con man.

Active: The con man had her.

The main problem with passive sentences is that they leave readers unsure of who or what is causing the action. Use of the passive voice tends to create awkward pronoun references and faulty modification. For example, when readers come to the pronoun *it* in the following journal excerpt they have no way of knowing if the *it* refers to *rational behavior* or *purpose*—the subjects of the previous clauses:

> The purpose of this paper will be to define the rational behavior of an academic writer. Once rational behavior is defined, it will be shown that this behavior is consistent with currently observed trends in academic publishing.

Actually, neither of these referents makes much sense because the real referent is the missing subject—the "I" of the author. Nine times out of ten, you should transform passive sentences into active ones. Surprisingly, however, the use of the passive voice is endemic in academic discourse—particularly in the methods section of quantitative research reports. Notice how the revision to the following excerpt from an essay in *Philosophical Magazine* becomes more vigorous and concise once it is transformed into the active voice:

Passive: In this paper the contrast of dislocations in icosahedral quasicrystals is discussed in the framework of the quasilattice model and on the basis of the kinematical theory of electron diffraction. Since, at present, little is known about the structure of quasicrystal dislocations, our treatment is restricted to the derivation of conditions under which the diffraction contrast vanishes and the dislocations become invisible. Some basic structural properties of quasilattices and quasilattice dislocations are first discussed.

Active: We discuss the contrast of dislocations in icosahedral quasicrystals in the framework of the quasilattice model and on the basis of the kinematical theory of electron diffraction. We restrict our treatment to the derivation of conditions under which the diffraction contrast vanishes and the dislocations become invisible because we know little about the structure of quasicrystal dislocations. First we discuss some basic structural properties of quasilattices and quasilattice dislocations.

While the passive voice strangles the life from most academic discourse, it does have some legitimate uses. For example, if you needed to fire someone for inadequate work, you would probably want to say, "The decision has been made to let you go," rather than, "I have decided to fire you."

Eliminate **to be** Verbs

In our daily speech and rough drafts, we tend to rely heavily on the various forms of the verb *to be*. Beyond being boring because of its overuse, the verb *to be* is unlike any other verb because it is *inert*—that is, it doesn't show any action. For example, in the sentence, "The researcher is a professor at Duke" the verb *is* merely connects the subject with what grammarians call the *subject complement*. We could just as easily say "The professor at Duke is a researcher" without changing the meaning of the sentence.

It would be nearly impossible to draft documents without some linking verbs. Yet because you diminish the vigor of a document by using *is* and *are* constructions, you should try to limit their frequency. Finally, note that the *progressive form* of a linking verb—which involves using *to be* as an auxiliary verb with a participle—is much more acceptable. The advantage of the progressive form is that it illustrates action progressing over time, enabling us to shape concise sentences that indicate something is currently happening: *The co-authors are disagreeing about the order in which their names should be listed when the book is published.*

It is and *there are* constructions often lead to sluggish, passive sentences, so you should limit their frequency. Sentences like *It is clearly a fact that the so and so did not invent cold fusion* can invariably be improved by eliminating the weak beginning.

Sample: While it is crucial for us to speak out on behalf of education it is important that we do so in a manner consistent with statute and administrative rule.

Revision: We need to speak out on behalf of education while observing statute and administrative rules.

Sample: According to the certification theory, there is no intrinsic relation between creativity and IQ.

Revision: Certification theory posits no intrinsic relation between creativity and IQ.

Of course, some *it is* or *there are* constructions allow you to be more succinct and avoid repetition of a subject than placing the true subject at the beginning of the sentence, so you should not attempt to eliminate all such constructions.

Select Appropriate Sentence Length and Pattern

Long sentences are not necessarily ineffective or wordy, nor are short sentences necessarily concise. After all, a 70-word sentence, properly constructed, can clarify relationships between ideas. On the other hand, a series of five-word sentences can result in choppiness and poor connections between ideas. Rather than trying to make all sentences a certain length or pattern, you can write graceful sentences by being aware of the demands different sentence patterns make on readers.

Place the Subject in the Beginning of the Sentence. As a general rule, you can improve the readability of your prose by limiting the number of words that come between the beginning of the sentence and its subject. Because the beginning of a sentence is its most emphatic part, you generally don't want to clutter it with unnecessary transitional words or phrases. A second problem with long introductory phrases and clauses is that they strain the reader's short-term memory. Notice, for example, how you need to juggle all of the opening conditions in your mind before you finally come to the subject of this sentence:

> If you write every morning for at least fifteen minutes, if you set aside the urge to criticize early drafts and ideas, if you analyze your rhetorical situation for a document, if you ask critical questions of your drafts, if you share drafts with colleagues, then you will improve quickly as a writer.

Fortunately, most sentences with long introductory clauses can be easily improved; all you need to do is move the concluding words—that is, the *independent clause*—to the beginning of the sentence, as in the following revision:

You will improve quickly as a writer if you write every morning for at least fifteen minutes, etc.

When you copyedit, you should not attempt to eliminate *all* introductory words, phrases, and clauses. A few introductory clauses can help you establish a forceful rhythm. Furthermore, your documents will put your readers to sleep if all of your sentences are shaped in the same way. Occasional transitional words or phrases can also aid readability. *Therefore, however, on the other hand, as a result*—these sorts of words can help you highlight the way ideas relate to each other. Used selectively and logically, these words and phrases actually help readers connect different ideas. Yet these words cannot create logical connections by themselves. Just as a brick house would collapse if the builder used sand rather than mortar to construct it, so will meaning in a document evaporate if you do not provide a logical discussion. Words like *thus, therefore,* and *consequently* are insufficient by themselves to make connections between ideas.

Avoid Excessive Embedding Between the Subject and Verb. Embedding appositives or modifiers between subjects and verbs can enliven what is traditionally considered the least emphatic part of a sentence, the middle. Notice, for example, how the appositive in the following example from an education journal emphasizes the definition of *sentence combining:*

> Research suggests that sentence combining, an instructional technique that provides students with practice in the manipulation of various sentence patterns, is effective in developing the syntactical fluency of writers, elementary through college level.

If we decided to give less emphasis to the definition, we could recast the sentence as follows:

> Research with elementary through college-level writers suggests that practice combining sentences promotes syntactical fluency.

You should use embedding sparingly, however, because this pattern slows down the pace of reading. Such constructions require readers to keep these references in mind until they reach the verb and understand how to apply them. You see, as English speakers we need to link a subject of a sentence to its verb to understand a statement. As a result, we must hold in our short-term memory all of the defining and modifying words—appositives, participial phrases, relative clauses*—that come between the subject and verb. It isn't until we reach the verb that we understand what we are supposed to do with the modifying words.

---

*As you may recall from high school, an appositive is a word or phrase that renames or redefines a noun or pronoun; a participial is a verb form that functions as an adjective; and a relative clause, which usually begins with *that, who,* or *which,* is a dependent clause that offers additional information about a noun.

Maintain a High Verb-to-Noun Ratio

You can imbue your language with a sense of vigor by eliminating unnecessary nouns and choosing powerful verbs. When editing, consider changing Latinated nouns—that is, nouns that end with *ance, ing, ion, tion,* or *ment*—into verbs. For example, transform *introduction* into *introduce; commitment, commit; feeling, feel.* Changing nouns into verbs can result in a more concise and vigorous passage, as illustrated below:

> **Sample:** The assumption that creative ability has a relationship to intelligence warrants further examination.
> **Revision:** We must examine how creative ability relates to intelligence.

> **Sample:** This introduction is a rough conception of the assumptions about the decision-making process underlying the conception: Decisions about belief or action generally occur in the context of some problem and have some basis.
> **Revision:** We can assume that decisions occur in response to problems.

Edit Strings of Prepositional Phrases

When used in moderation, prepositions are invaluable. Few sentences can be written without them. (Notice "in moderation" and "without them" in these two sentences.) Essentially, prepositions work as connecting words: they link the object of the preposition to a word that appears earlier in the sentence. Like linking verbs, however, prepositions do not convey action, nor do they subordinate one thought to another. Instead, they merely link chunks of meaning that readers must gather together in order to understand the sentence. When used excessively, as demonstrated by the following example, prepositional phrases create a choppy, list-like style:

> **Sample:** The major objective of this study was to determine the perceived effects of the union on monetary and on nonmonetary aspects of compensation over the period in which respondents to the survey had been union members.

Because this sentence occurs in the conclusion of a five-page published essay, a careful editor should probably have eliminated this sentence altogether. Let's face it: if the readers still haven't got the point after five pages, there is little hope for them. Nevertheless, the editor and author could have improved the sentence by reducing the number of prepositions:

> This study examines how the union affects monetary and nonmonetary aspects of compensation.

To help identify and eliminate prepositions, isolate them by putting slashes between prepositional phrases and other basic sentence parts as illustrated here:

/Furthermore,/ /*in* response/ /*to* the increased pressure/ /*to* publish/ /*in* academia/ /*in* the past decade/ /and the growing complexity/ /*of* the academic areas and research tools/, /one should expect/ /*to* find/ /increased emphasis/ /*on* cost-cutting techniques/ /*by* academic writers/. /An increase/ /*in* cost/ /can probably be observed/ /by investigating/ /the changing trends/ /*in* the multiple authorship/ /*of* articles/ /*over* time./

Edit for Economy

The following paragraph hurts the eyes and ears of a successful writer.

> Writing that is redundant and states the obvious and says the same thing over and over again is irritating for readers who want writers to get to the point right away. On the other hand, as I am sure you can understand, it is equally important for writers to avoid confusion when they write and to put down as much information—that is, as many words—as the reader needs in order to understand what the writer means when he or she says what he or she says. Also, of course, when you are writing, it is important for you to remember that readers are reading your work and that you need to be somewhat entertaining—even when the subject is technical—when conveying information, so that your readers will keep reading and not go off and do something else like play ice hockey.

Writers abhor wordiness. All of the empty phrases in the above can be translated into one sentence: "Balance conciseness with the reader's need for information and voice." No matter how much you appreciate the sounds of the words you have used, editing for economy may mean cutting the length of your document in half! By using the editing strategies already discussed, you have begun to chip away needless abstractions, unnecessary jargon, awkward passive constructions, weak verbs, tangled sentence patterns, unnecessary nouns, and strings of prepositional phrases. Yet by evaluating the content in light of your audience and the tone that you hope to establish, you can still find ways to eliminate unnecessary transitions, definitions, references, examples. In your search for precision and persuasive appeal, you should also delete unnecessary repetitions—redundant adjectives, repeated phrases, and synonyms. Remember, you add clarity and grace by presenting an idea simply. Cutting away unnecessary deadwood can eliminate much that interferes with communication.

Final Comments

Taken in isolation, each of the strategies discussed in this chapter may seem like nit-picking. Going through a document and reducing the number of linking verbs, for example, will not make a substantial difference in its readability. Yet taken as a whole, these strategies can help you find the truth—the essence of what you want to express. Although at first these strategies may seem awkward or mechanical, they will become natural and automatic after you have worked with them for a while. The end result of practicing these techniques will be smooth prose, the kind that reads easily and pleasurably. You will soon apply these strategies without even thinking about them, editing mentally everything you hear, from television commercials to editorials in the daily newspaper. The end result for your writing will be polished, professional prose.

How to Use Correct Punctuation

Now that you have used the strategies illustrated in Chapter 11 to revise and edit your document, you are probably saying to yourself, "I have been through this a dozen times; it must be perfect!" But there are errors. Lots of them. This is the nature of the beast. In fact, before you evaluate your punctuation, you may want to cycle through the revisions explained in Chapter 11 one more time. If you are confident that the manuscript reflects your best effort, then you are ready to copyedit it. Essentially, copyediting involves identifying and correcting grammatical and mechanical errors. Before submitting your work to your instructor for a grade, you should look especially for errors that classmates and teachers have mentioned that you commonly make. In this final chapter I review some of the perennial problems with punctuation that cause student writers to stumble.*

Punctuation Conventions

A complete review of punctuation is obviously beyond the scope of this chapter. Instead this is a summary of how to punctuate different sentence patterns and how to analyze the likely effect of different syntactical forms on readers' comprehension.

Commas

Commas are like pawns in chess: they seem relatively insignificant and unobtrusive, yet they are actually very important. If properly placed, the lowly pawn can checkmate the king or, once it has reached the end of the board, become a more powerful piece. Commas play an extremely important role in ensuring that your documents are understandable. In fact, failing to insert a comma in the correct spot can cause considerable misreading (and subsequent embarrassment). Beyond a few special circumstances, there are six basic ways to use commas correctly.

---

* This material is adapted from *How to Write the Winning Brief*, by Joseph M. Moxley, pp. 159–170. Copyright 1992 by the American Bar Association, Chicago.

Use Commas to Separate Adjacent Parallel Elements. As demonstrated by the following examples, a series is composed of three or more *parallel* elements, and the series can appear in the beginning, middle, or end of a sentence.

> Stretching, warming up, and cooling down are important to a good exercise program.

> All of the necessary qualities of a good secretary—typing, shorthand, and patience—she had in abundance.

> The three qualities of a good introduction are context, purpose, and organization.

Editors and grammarians are in sharp disagreement about whether a comma should be placed before the last element in a series. The trend in the popular press is *not* to include the comma if the elements in the series are brief. However, many well-known stylists have persuasively argued that conjunctions *connect* and commas *separate*, so it is incorrect in their opinion to judge the comma as redundant punctuation before a conjunction such as *and*. In addition, uninformed readers may perceive the last two elements in the series to be a compound, if the comma is omitted. For example, placement of the comma before *and* in the following example makes it clear that flowering plants are not the same as ornamental bushes:

> The landscaping contract includes several exotic plants, ornamental bushes, and flowering plants.

Occasionally, as dictated by your ear and the rhythm you hope to establish, you may want to insert a comma and forgo the *and*, as in this example:

> We have a government of the people, by the people, for the people.

When you want to slow down the rhythm of your sentence and emphasize a point, you can replace all the serial commas with *and* or *or:*

> He does not like shrimp or crayfish or lobster or anything that turns red when cooked.

> If the abuse of the wetlands continues, we will be without waterfowl and fish and wildlife.

When you must present a long array of parallel elements in your documents, you can avoid listing them by grouping them into logical parts and punctuating accordingly, as demonstrated by the following examples:

> Writing is painful and exhilarating, tedious and inspiring, chaotic and planned.

> Human activities such as coal and oil burning, population growth and increased food demands, clearing and burning forests have caused increases in the release of carbon dioxide and methane.

Finally, note that coequal, consecutive coordinate adjectives that modify the same noun should generally be separated with commas:

Although he appears to have your best interests in mind, he truly is a competitive, combative, cantankerous boss.

However, you should *not* separate two consecutive adjectives with commas if the first adjective is modifying both the following adjective and noun as a unit, as illustrated below:

The competitive track star runs forty miles a week.

Use Commas to Join Two or More Independent Clauses. In most instances, place a comma between two sentences that are joined with a coordinating conjunction—*and, but, or, for, nor, so, yet:*

She was not sure if she had the necessary mathematical abilities to be an engineer, so she pursued a graduate degree in history.

He was surrounded by fifty people, yet he felt all alone.

You do *not* need to place a comma between two independent clauses if they are short and similar in meaning, provided that no misunderstanding will take place, as illustrated in the following example:

Some doctors advertise their services but many doctors find this reprehensible.

The absence of the comma in this sentence is acceptable; it is not necessary to prevent misreading.

Use Commas after Introductory Subordinate Clauses. To avoid confusion, use a comma after an introductory subordinate clause or phrase:

Because the costs of conducting research continue to increase, we need to raise our rates.

As the shrimp boats trawl, sea grass can collect on the trap door, allowing shrimp to escape.

According to the professor, rich women are more likely to have caesarean sections than poor women.

In keeping with the modern trend toward using as little punctuation as possible, some stylists believe that it is not necessary to place a comma after short introductory words *(now, thus, hence)* and phrases *(In 1982 he committed the same crime)*. However, conservative style manuals still call for the comma, so you are better off playing it safe and placing a comma after introductory words and clauses.

Use a Comma after Conjunctive Adverbs and Transitional Phrases at the Beginnings of Sentences. Although our modern style calls for using as few commas as possible, you should generally place a comma after conjunctive adverbs and transitional words because they modify the entire sentence:

> Nevertheless, we must push forward with our plans.

> In other words, you're fired. Hey, I'm just kidding.

Because commas cause readers to pause in their reading, you want to use them sparingly. Although logic would suggest that it makes sense to follow coordinating conjunctions with commas, convention does not call for this usage unless the conjunction is followed by an introductory phrase. Thus, it would be inappropriate to write:

> Yet, I think we should go ahead as planned.

When a short phrase follows the conjunction at the beginning of the sentence, however, it is appropriate—although not absolutely necessary—to place a comma after the conjunction:

> Yet, as I mentioned yesterday, I think we should go ahead as planned.

Use Commas around Nonrestrictive Parenthetical Elements. You should limit the number of times that you interrupt the flow of a sentence by placing modifying words between the subject and its verb. When you do introduce such appositives, participial phrases, or adjective phrases or clauses, you must determine whether the modifiers are *restrictive* or *nonrestrictive*. Essentially, restrictive modifiers add information that is *essential* to the meaning of the sentence, whereas nonrestrictive modifiers add information that is *not essential*. The best way to determine whether a modifier is restrictive or nonrestrictive is to see if taking it out changes the meaning of the sentence.

> **Restrictive:** Lawyers *who work for McGullity, Anderson, and Swenson* need to take a course in copyediting.

In this case the relative clause is essential to the meaning of the sentence. If you embedded the clause in commas, then the meaning would change, suggesting that all lawyers need a course in copyediting.

> **Restrictive:** The lawyer *who has worked on this case for three years* thinks that we have no chance of winning.

In this case the relative clause is essential to the meaning of the sentence. In other words, the sentence refers to only the lawyer who has worked on this case. The discussion is *restricted* to her.

> **Nonrestrictive:** The lawyers, *who have an office downtown*, think that we have no chance of winning.

Because the location of the lawyer's office is superfluous to the gist of the sentence, it should be set off commas.

Use Commas before Nonrestrictive Adverbial Phrases or Clauses at the Ends of Sentences. At the end of your sentence, you need to be especially careful about where you place your commas. In particular, you need to question whether the modifying words are *restrictive* or *nonrestrictive*. For instance, suppose you received a memo from your writing instructor that said,

> You should revise the essay, as I suggested.

You could assume that you were directed to revise the essay in any way you deem appropriate. However, if the instructor omitted the comma, then you would be receiving an entirely different message: revise the essay exactly as prescribed by the instructor.

Below are some additional sentences to give you a sense of how to determine whether your modifying words are restrictive or nonrestrictive:

> **Nonrestrictive:** Reports indicate that a Turtle Excluder Device (TED) costs from $85 to $400 each, depending on the model.

> **Restrictive:** Writers can change readers' outlook on issues provided that they offer sufficient evidence.

In this case, a comma after *issues* could suggest that writers have numerous ways to change readers' opinions and that one of these methods is providing sufficient evidence. In contrast, the lack of a comma means that providing evidence is the one criterion writers need to follow.

Colons

The colon provides a dramatic and somewhat underutilized way to bring a little spark to your writing. Beyond normal business correspondence *(Dear Sir or Madam:)*, you can use the colon before quotations, formal statements, and explanations. The colon enables you to highlight a semantic relationship—that is, a movement from a general statement to a specific clarification. The colon also provides a dramatic way to tease the reader's curiosity:

> As a modern ordeal by torture, litigation excels: it is exorbitantly expensive, agonizingly slow, and exquisitely designed to avoid any resemblance to fairness or justice.

You can also use the colon before an instruction or example:

> An intelligent writer knows how to polish documents: revise the document countless times.

Although usage does differ, most stylists agree that you should not capitalize the first letter after the colon unless the colon is introducing a quotation or formal statement:

You'll be surprised by what his former employees wrote in the character report: "His attitude toward his new associates was rude and pretentious."

Note that a colon must always follow an independent clause. You should *never* place a colon between a verb and its direct object:

> **Incorrect:** Our choices are: rescind our offer; go ahead with our plans; try to renegotiate the deal.

This sentence can easily be revised:

> We have three choices: a, b, c.
>
> Our choices are the following: a, b, c.

Because the colon works as the equivalent to *for example* or *such as*, it would be redundant and incorrect to write

> We have a number of options, such as: a, b, c.

Dashes and Parentheses

Some stylists view the dash with great suspicion—the sort of suspicion that a man in the 1990s who wears a plaid leisure suit to work would arouse. Some people erroneously believe that the dash is acceptable only in informal discourse. However, the dash can provide you with subtle ways to repeat modifiers and dramatic ways to emphasize your point.

Use a Dash after a Series or List of Appositives. When you introduce a long series or list of appositives before the subject and verb, you are placing high demands on the reader's short-term memory. Therefore, use this pattern rarely and only for emphasis. This pattern is particularly appropriate in conclusions, when you are bringing together the major threads of your discussion or argument. Finally, you should place a *summary word* after the dash and preferably before the subject of the sentence, as indicated by the following examples. The most common summary words that writers use are *all, those, this, each, what, none, such, these.*

> Jealousy, lust, hate, greed—*these* are the raw emotions we will explore.
>
> Lying, stealing, cheating, committing adultery—*which* is the greatest sin?
>
> To struggle with meaning, to edit, to combine sentences—*these* activities are well known to the struggling writer.
>
> Wining and dining his friends, stroking people's egos, maintaining a good appearance, and spending money—*all* were part of his scheme to gain influence.

Use Dashes When You Wish to Emphasize a Parenthetical Element.
Commas are usually sufficient punctuation to set off parenthetical elements.

In some instances, however, you can use a dash instead, especially if you want to make the insertion more noticeable:

> The building next to ours—the one with the all-cedar exterior—was engulfed in flames.

When you want to whisper rather than shout, you can place the modifiers inside parentheses:

> The secret I have to tell you (the one I've been hinting about) will surprise you.

Use Dashes to Embed a Series or List of Appositives. A single appositive or modifier can easily be set off from the rest of the sentence in commas, but you must use dashes when you insert a series of appositives or modifiers. After all, how else will the reader know when the series is over?

> The essential qualities of an effective writer—discipline, effort, inspiration—he learned by regular writing.

> With the help of her assistant—a high-speed personal computer—she produced a delightful letter.

Use Dashes to Set off an Emphatic Repetition. You can emphasize an important point by placing a dash or comma at the end of the sentence and then repeating a key word or phrase:

> Hal is a computer, the ultimate computer.

> Mrs. Leavitt is a gambler, a compulsive gambler.

> He was disturbed by the warning—the warning that everyone else ignored.

> All rapists should be severely punished—punished in a way they will never forget.

Semicolons

The semicolon offers a "higher" form of punctuation than the comma or dash. Unlike commas or dashes, the semicolon can correctly be used to separate sentences. If readers tend to pause for a half-second when coming to a comma, they pause for three-quarters of a second when they reach a semicolon. Writers use semicolons two major ways.

Use a Semicolon to Join Two Sentences. You can show that ideas are closely related by using a semicolon rather than a period between them.

> The secretary's fingers burned across the typewriter; the financial statements would be picked up by the client in one hour.

The question, though, is not economics; it is professional objectivity.

Breast cancer used to be the biggest killer for women; now it's lung cancer.

Use a Semicolon to Punctuate a Series or List of Appositives That Already Include Commas. When elements in a series require internal commas to ensure clarity, then semicolons must be used to separate those elements:

A perfect vacation would be long, relaxing, and cheap; include personable, sweet, flexible people; and make everything else seem trivial.

The delegates were from Sacramento, California; Jacksonville, Florida; Providence, Rhode Island; and Ann Arbor, Michigan.

A good proofreader must have good grammar, punctuation, and spelling skills; must like to read; and must have patience.

Note, however, that you are wise to avoid using unnecessary semicolons. Experienced writers and readers would prefer the second sentence because it avoids self-conscious punctuation.

He was dressed in white pants; a white, Mexican wedding shirt; and sandals.

He was dressed in a white, Mexican wedding shirt, white pants, and sandals.

Apostrophes

Of all forms of punctuation, the apostrophe appears to be in greatest peril of extinction. For proof that the apostrophe should be placed on an endangered species list in some grammarian's office, one needs only to consult the popular press or a sample of student themes. However, because of its ability to denote ownership in a concise way (by avoiding the use of a preposition), the apostrophe plays an important role in the English language. Perhaps surprisingly, given the frequency of its misuse, the apostrophe is a fairly simple form of punctuation to master. You can denote ownership to a singular or plural noun and indefinite pronoun by adding an *-'s* if the word doesn't end in *-s:*

They worked on Susan's computer.

The children's toys are cluttering the house again.

You expect me to do a week's worth of typing in two days.

The people's choice was Bill Clinton.

When it is someone else's turn to have his or her writing critiqued by the group, remember to be conscientious.

When a singular noun ends in -*s*, traditional grammarians recommend adding an -'*s*:

> She loves Keats's poems.
>
> The business's direct-mailing campaign worked wonders.
>
> John Adams's letters illustrate his reflective spirit.

However, this usage can be cumbersome. Consequently, the following usage is also correct:

> John Keats' conscience and life spirit energize his poems.
>
> Doris Lessings' ideas are worth examination.

When a plural noun ends in -*s*, you only need to add an apostrophe:

> The judge confiscated the drivers' licenses.
>
> She won two months' free groceries.
>
> The writers' guild meets Monday.

With compound subjects, when you wish to denote individual ownership, you should add an -'*s* to each noun:

> Dr. Wilson's and Mr. Speinberg's law suits were caused by poor communication.

Or, you can demonstrate joint ownership by placing the -'*s* after the second subject:

> Pat and Joe's new car is hot!
>
> This is my father-in-law and mother-in-law's office.

Finally, always use an apostrophe when you form a contraction. The apostrophe is positioned where letters are dropped:

it is	it's
they are	they're
you are	you're
who is	who's
can not	can't
she will	she'll
were not	weren't

I N D E X

381

Instructor's Guide for
Becoming an Academic Writer

Instructor's Guide for
Becoming an Academic Writer
A Modern Rhetoric

Joseph M. Moxley
University of South Florida

Prepared by
Linda Sarbo
University of South Florida

D. C. Heath and Company
Lexington, Massachusetts   Toronto

Address editorial correspondence to

D. C. Heath and Company
125 Spring Street
Lexington, MA 02173

Published simultaneously in Canada.

Printed in the United States of America.

International Standard Book Number: 0-669-24498-8

10 9 8 7 6 5 4 3 2 1

Both beginning and veteran instructors of writing should find this Instructor's Guide to be a helpful tool for teaching with *Becoming an Academic Writer*. It provides sample syllabi for using the text for writing courses with three different foci: expository writing, research writing, and academic writing. The Guide also discusses and offers teaching tips for each chapter of the text.

The Guide concludes with suggestions for responding constructively to student writing and efficiently handling the large number of student papers a writing instructor must typically read and respond to.

I trust that this Guide will support your efforts to teach your students to become successful academic writers.

Linda Sarbo

CONTENTS

Planning Your Course

Becoming an Academic Writer: A Modern Rhetoric is organized in a way that allows you considerable flexibility in planning your writing course. Regardless of your course objectives, you will want to begin with the "Introduction—For the Student" and Chapter 1, which review basic composing strategies, summarize useful rhetorical principles, and begin the process of establishing your classroom as a community of writers. If you intend your students to use library research in any of their writing assignments, your course should also include Chapter 2.

Because the chapters in the Writing Portfolio (Part II) are independent units, you can use them selectively to accommodate a variety of course objectives. Below are suggested syllabi for writing courses with three different overall objectives. The first contemplates a one-semester course in basic expository writing that includes expressive, traditional expository, and persuasive genres. The second emphasizes research reports and includes Rogerian essays and writing based on library research, interviews, questionnaires, and ethnographic methods. The third syllabus presents a sampling of traditional academic genres, including analysis, persuasive essays, and reports based on library research.

Expository Writing Course (Sixteen-week Semester)

Week 1: Introduction to the Course

Reading Assignment: "Introduction—For the Student," "Writing Myths," "How Can You Succeed as a Writer?" and "Talk Over Ideas with Peers and Teachers" (Ch. 1).

Writing Activities: In-class diagnostic writing (Letter of Introduction or Writing Autobiography).

Week 2: Writing and Research Notebook

Reading Assignment: "Maintain a Writing and Research Notebook" up to "Using the New Writing and Research Ideas" (Ch. 1).

Writing Activities: Prompted in-class journal entry writing to begin a Writing and Research Notebooks.

Week 3: Writing and Research Notebooks

Reading Assignment: "Maintain a Writing and Research Notebook" from "The Latest Drafts of Your Reports" to end (Ch. 1).

Writing Activities: Set up Writing and Research Notebooks; conduct biographical research; compose biographical statements.

Week 4: Autobiographies and Biographies

Reading Assignment: "Writing Samples," "Analyzing Pertinent Conventions," and "Writing Assignments" (Ch. 3).

Writing Activities: Journal entry writing prompted by Critical Reading Questions.

Week 5: Autobiographies and Biographies

Reading Assignment: "Prewriting and Drafting Strategies," "Revising and Editing Strategies," and "Collaborative Learning" (Ch. 3).

Writing Activities: Prewriting, drafting, and revising autobiographies and biographies.

Week 6: Analyzing Subjects and Processes

Reading Assignment: "Additional Writing Samples" (Ch. 3), "Writing Samples," and "Analyzing Pertinent Conventions" (Ch. 4).

Writing Activities: Autobiographies and biographies due; journal entry writing prompted by Critical Reading Questions (Ch. 4).

Week 7: Analyzing Subjects and Processes

Reading Assignment: "Writing Assignments," "Prewriting and Drafting Strategies," and "Collaborating Strategies" (Ch. 4).

Writing Activities: Prewriting, drafting, and revising subject and process analyses; Writing and Research Notebook checkpoint.

Week 8: Analyzing Subjects and Processes

Reading Assignment: "Additional Writing Samples" and "Evaluating Criticism" (Ch. 4).

Writing Activities: Peer review and revise analyses; subject and process analyses due; prompted journal entry evaluating criticism.

Week 9: Analyzing Causes and Effects

Reading Assignment: "Writing Samples" and "Analyzing Pertinent Conventions" (Ch. 5).

Writing Activities: Journal entry writing prompted by Critical Reading Questions (Ch. 5).

Week 10: Analyzing Causes and Effects

Reading Assignment: "Writing Assignments," "Prewriting and Drafting Strategies," and "Revising and Editing Strategies" (Ch. 5).

Writing Activities: Prewriting, drafting, and revising cause and effect reports.

Week 11: Analyzing Causes and Effects

Reading Assignment: "Collaborating Strategies," "Additional Writing Samples," and "Evaluating Criticism" (Ch. 5).

Writing Activities: Peer review and revise cause and effect reports; cause and effect reports due; prompted journal entry evaluating criticism.

Week 12: Writing Persuasively

Reading Assignment: "Writing Samples" and "Analyzing Pertinent Conventions" (Ch. 6).

Writing Activities: Journal entry writing prompted by Critical Reading Questions (Ch. 6).

Week 13: Writing Persuasively

Reading Assignment: "Writing Assignments," "Prewriting and Drafting Strategies," and "Revising and Editing Strategies" (Ch. 6).

Writing Activities: Prewriting, drafting, and revising persuasive reports.

Week 14: Writing Persuasively

Reading Assignment: "Collaborating Strategies," "Additional Writing Samples," and "Evaluating Criticism" (Ch. 6).

Writing Activities: Peer review and revise persuasive reports; persuasive reports due; prompted journal entry evaluating criticism.

Week 15: Putting It All Together

Writing Activities: Updated Writing Autobiography (self-evaluation essay); Writing Portfolios due.

Week 16: Final Exam Week

Writing Activities: Writing and Research Notebooks due; Final Exam (in-class essay).

Research Writing Course (Sixteen-week Semester)

Week 1: Introduction to the Course

Reading Assignment: "Introduction—For the Student" and Chapter 1, "The Attitudes and Work Habits of Successful Academic Writers."

Writing Activities: In-class diagnostic writing (Letter of Introduction or Writing Autobiography); prompted journal entries to begin the Writing and Research Notebooks.

Week 2: How to Use the Library and Document Sources

Reading Assignment: Chapter 2.

Writing Activities: Biographical research report.

Week 3: Solving Problems by Negotiating Differences

Reading Assignment: "Writing Samples," "Analyzing Pertinent Conventions," and "Writing Assignments" (Ch. 7).

Writing Activities: Journal entry writing prompted by Critical Reading Questions; freewriting for topic selection.

Week 4: Solving Problems by Negotiating Differences

Reading Assignment: "Prewriting and Drafting Strategies," "Revising and Editing Strategies," "Collaborating Strategies" (Ch. 7).

Writing Activities: Prewriting, drafting, and revising Rogerian argument.

Week 5: Solving Problems by Negotiating Differences

Reading Assignment: "Additional Writing Sample" and "Evaluating Criticism" (Ch. 7).

Writing Activities: Peer review and revise drafts; Rogerian arguments due; prompted journal entry evaluating criticism.

Week 6: Writing Reports Based on Library Research

Reading Assignment: "Writing Samples," "Analyzing Pertinent Conventions," and "Critical Reading Exercise" (Ch. 8).

Writing Activities: Journal entry writing prompted by Critical Reading Questions.

Week 7: Writing Reports Based on Library Research

Reading Assignment: "Writing Assignments," "Prewriting and Drafting Strategies," and "Revising and Editing Strategies" (Ch. 8).

Writing Activities: Research proposal and project schedule; prewriting and drafting of research reports; Writing and Research Notebook checkpoint.

Week 8: Writing Reports Based on Library Research

Reading Assignment: "Collaborating Strategies," "Additional Writing Sample," and "Evaluating Criticism" (Ch. 8).

Writing Activities: Peer review and revise documents; research reports due; prompted journal entry evaluating criticism.

Week 9: Writing Reports Based on Interviews and Questionnaires

Reading Assignment: "Writing Samples," "Analyzing Pertinent Conventions," and "Writing Assignments" (Ch. 9).

Writing Activities: Journal entry writing prompted by Critical Reading Questions; research proposal; project schedule.

Week 10: Writing Reports Based on Interviews and Questionnaires

Reading Assignment: "Prewriting and Drafting Strategies," "Revising and Editing Strategies" (Ch. 9).

Writing Activities: Drafting interview strategy or questionnaire; freewriting on topic; drafting field research report.

Week 11: Writing Reports Based on Interviews and Questionnaires

Reading Assignment: "Collaborating Strategies" and "Evaluating Criticism" (Ch. 9).

Writing Activities: Peer review and revision of field research reports; research reports due; prompted journal entry evaluating criticism.

Week 12: Writing Reports Based on Ethnographic Methods

Reading Assignment: "Writing Samples," "Analyzing Pertinent Conventions," and "Writing Assignments" (Ch. 10).

Writing Activities: Journal entry writing prompted by Critical Reading Questions; research proposal; project schedule.

Week 13: Writing Reports Based on Ethnographic Methods

Reading Assignment: "Prewriting and Drafting Strategies" and "Revising and Editing Strategies" (Ch. 10).

Writing Activities: Prewriting, drafting, and revising ethnographies.

Week 14: Writing Reports Based on Ethnographic Methods

Reading Assignment: "Collaborating Strategies," "Additional Writing Samples," and "Evaluating Criticism" (Ch. 10).

Writing Assignments: Peer review and revise ethnographies; ethnographies due; prompted journal entry evaluating criticism.

Week 15: Putting It All Together

Writing Activities: Updated Writing Autobiography (self-evaluation essay); Writing Portfolios due.

Week 16: Final Exam Week

Writing Activities: Writing and Research Notebooks due; Final Exam (in-class essay).

Academic Writing Course (Sixteen-week Semester)

Week 1: Introduction to the Course

Reading Assignment: "Introduction—For the Student" and Chapter 1.

Writing Activities: In-class diagnostic writing (Letter of Introduction or Writing Autobiography); journal entries to begin Writing and Research Notebooks.

Week 2: How to Use the Library and Document Sources

Reading Assignment: Chapter 2

Writing Assignment: Biography research report.

Week 3: Analyzing Subjects and Processes

Reading Assignment: "Writing Samples," "Analyzing Pertinent Conventions," and "Writing Assignments" (Ch. 4).

Writing Activities: Journal entries prompted by Critical Reading Questions; generate potential topics for analysis.

Week 4: Analyzing Subjects and Processes

Reading Assignment: "Prewriting and Drafting Strategies" and "Revising and Editing Strategies" (Ch. 4).

Writing Activities: Prewriting, drafting, and revising analysis reports.

Week 5: Analyzing Subjects and Processes

Reading Assignment: "Collaborating Strategies," "Additional Writing Samples," and "Evaluating Criticism" (Ch. 4).

Writing Activities: Peer review and revise analysis reports; analysis reports due; prompted journal entry evaluating criticism.

Week 6: Analyzing Causes and Effects

Reading Assignment: "Writing Samples," "Analyzing Pertinent Conventions," and "Writing Assignments" (Ch. 5).

Writing Activities: Journal entry writing prompted by Critical Reading Questions; generate potential topics for cause and effect analysis.

Week 7: Analyzing Causes and Effects

Reading Assignment: "Prewriting and Drafting Strategies" and "Revising and Editing Strategies" (Ch. 5).

Writing Activities: Prewriting, drafting, and revising cause and effect analyses; Writing and Research Notebook checkpoint.

Week 8: Analyzing Causes and Effects

Reading Assignment: "Collaborating Strategies," "Additional Writing Samples," and "Evaluating Criticism" (Ch. 5).

Writing Activities: Peer review and revise cause and effect analyses; cause and effect analyses due; prompted journal entry evaluating criticism.

Week 9: Writing Persuasively

Reading Assignment: "Writing Samples," "Analyzing Pertinent Conventions," and "Writing Assignments" (Ch. 6).

Writing Activities: Journal entry writing prompted by Critical Reading Questions; generate potential topics for persuasive writing.

Week 10: Writing Persuasively

Reading Assignment: "Prewriting and Drafting Strategies" and "Revising and Editing Strategies" (Ch. 6).

Writing Activities: Prewriting, drafting, and revising persuasive reports.

Week 11: Writing Persuasively

Reading Assignment: "Collaborating Strategies," "Additional Writing Sample," and "Evaluating Criticism" (Ch. 6).

Writing Activities: Peer review and revise persuasive reports; persuasive reports due; prompted journal entry evaluating criticism.

Week 12: Writing Based on Library Research

Reading Assignment: "Writing Samples," "Analyzing Pertinent Conventions," and "Writing Assignments" (Ch. 8).

Writing Activities: Journal entry writing prompted by Critical Reading Questions; research proposal and project schedule.

Week 13: Writing Based on Library Research

Reading Assignment: "Prewriting and Drafting Strategies" and "Revising and Editing Strategies" (Ch. 8).

Writing Activities: Prewriting, drafting, and revising library-based research reports.

Week 14: Writing Based on Library Research

Reading Assignment: "Collaborating Strategies," "Additional Writing Sample," and "Evaluating Criticism" (Ch. 8).

Writing Activities: Peer review and revise research reports; research reports due; prompted journal entry evaluating criticism.

Week 15: Putting It All Together

Writing Activities: Updated Writing Autobiography (self-evaluation essay); Writing Portfolios due.

Week 16: Final Exam Week

Writing Activities: In-class final exam; Writing and Research Notebooks due.

Notes on the Text

This section is meant to give an overview of the individual chapters in the text. It provides descriptions of the various elements within each chapter and suggests possible ways to use these features in class.

In the descriptions of Chapters 3–10, which comprise "Part II: The Writing Portfolio," I offer comments on the writing samples, suggestions for using the Critical Reading Questions, and recommendations for implementing collaborative activities for the eight writing projects within these chapters. I encourage you to be flexible in your application of these suggestions. As you become acquainted with your students, you will quickly identify their strengths as well as their needs: some will need help with critical reading tasks, others will blossom in collaborative settings, and still others will find their voice in the solitude of their Writing and Research Notebook. As you and your students work with this text, take advantage of the variety of activities offered to challenge and nurture their abilities.

Because all eight chapters in "The Writing Portfolio" are organized in the same way, planning ahead for the writing assignments is easy. And, by establishing a regular cycle of composing tasks, this format also helps students develop productive writing habits.

Each chapter in "The Writing Portfolio" opens with a brief introduction that identifies a genre and its usefulness for academic writers. Two to four writing samples exemplify the genre, each followed by Critical Reading Questions that help students identify the writers' rhetorical strategies and underlying assumptions. The genre's conventions are then analyzed in more detail and used to critique the writing samples.

For each writing assignment, the topic selection, prewriting, and drafting strategies most appropriate for the genre are explained. A variety of exercises, both self-administered and collaborative, lead students through the steps of revising and editing their documents. I recommend that during this process you provide at least two opportunities for peer review, one responding to an early draft and a second preceding preparation of the formal draft. The additional writing samples, which demonstrate the range of voices and purposes encompassed by the genre, should be read and discussed while students are engaged in revising their drafts. Finally, each chapter concludes by challenging students to evaluate their own writing.

The structure of these chapters suggests convenient segments for planning classroom activities and out-of-class assignments. If, for example, your course includes autobiography and biography writing, you might follow a plan like this one for Chapter 3.

Sample Lesson Plan

Chapter 3. Writing Autobiographies and Biographies

Day 1: (Previous assignment: Read pages 53–63.) Have students define autobiography and biography and identify their private and public purposes. Use the Critical Reading Questions to discuss and respond to "Black Men and Public Space" and "Growing Up."

Day 2: Assign the Critical Reading Questions for "The Invisible Circle" (page 64) as collaborative tasks for small groups. Use Critical Reading Questions 1–3 (page 69) to discuss "Nora Quealey." Ask students to read "Analyzing Pertinent Conventions" (pages 69–72) for the next class.

Day 3: Help students locate instances in the writing samples that demonstrate how the pertinent conventions shaped the document, dictated the authors' decisions, or limited their options in some way. Conclude with journal entry writing in response to Critical Reading Questions 4 and 5 (page 69). Ask students to read "Writing Assignments" and "Prewriting and Drafting Strategies" (pages 72–75) and use the questions on pages 72–73 to generate a topic for autobiographical writing or select a subject for biography writing.

Day 4: Have students freewrite on their writing topics, looping three sessions of ten to fifteen minutes each. Students should use their freewrites to generate a first draft and read "Revising and Editing Strategies" (pages 75–76) for the next class.

Day 5: Let students work in small groups to review drafts using the eight questions on pages 75–76. Ask them to read "Collaborative Learning" (pages 76–80) and revise their drafts for a second round of peer review for the next class.

Day 6: Have students work in small groups to review second drafts using the Peer Review Workshop questions on page 80. For the next class have them read the "Additional Writing Samples" and revise drafts for submission.

Day 7: Collect the writing assignments and discuss the additional writing samples using the Critical Reading Questions. Assign the introduction and writing samples in the next chapter.

Introduction—For the Student

First impressions are crucial, and this introductory section will help you quickly establish your classroom as a place where student writers can improve their writing skills. Here, as throughout the text, the writing process is viewed from the students' perspective. In "Understanding Thinking and Writing Processes" your students will recognize their own frustrations and difficulties with writing, prewriting, and revising. More importantly, they will be invited to join a community of writers and share the strategies successful writers use to overcome these difficulties. "What Controls How We Compose Documents?" considers audience, purpose, voice, tone, and persona, not only as rhetorical terms your students will use to analyze their own writing as well as other texts, but as constraints imposed on all texts by the real world writers work in.

As early as the first class meeting you can reinforce the tone set by the introduction with in-class writing activities that demonstrate your interest in your students' writing processes and underscore the focus of the course. These activities can serve as diagnostic writing samples and will also help you identify any apprehensions or misconceptions your students may have about writing in general and about this course in particular. Below are two possibilities for in-class writing that serve all of these purposes. Their effectiveness will be further enhanced if you participate in them with your students. As with all in-class writing activities, be explicit about how much time you have allotted for the activity and then write with your students.

Sample Assignments

Writing Autobiography: Because our writing process reflects our thinking, our attitudes, and even our emotions, I'd like you to compose your personal writing autobiography. Describe your prior experiences with writing projects. Include people or events that had particularly positive or negative effects on your writing competence or your attitude toward writing.

Letter of Introduction: Write a letter to me introducing yourself and telling me what I need to know about you in order to work with you as a writer. You might want to include, for example, any concerns you have about this course or any conceptions you have of yourself as a writer. Tell me how you would like to improve your writing and what you hope to gain from this course.

Share your Writing Autobiography or Letter of Introduction with the class and invite students to share theirs with each other, but don't insist that they do. Collect and read each writing sample carefully, but in keeping with their purposes, do not grade these activities. I even suggest you refrain from commenting on mechanical errors such as spelling, grammar, and punctuation. Rather, limit your responses to comments that acknowledge the problems, concerns, or experiences the students have identified. Return the autobiographies or letters with your comments and ask students to include them in their Writing and Research Notebooks.

Chapter 1 The Attitudes and Work Habits of Successful Academic Writers

Chapter 1 continues the process begun with the introduction. It asks students to critically examine their writing processes and identify attitudes and habits that may interfere with effective writing. At the same time it offers them accessible strategies that successful writers use to overcome these obstacles and encourages students to appropriate these techniques.

"Writing Myths" will spark a lively class discussion. Don't be surprised if a few students insist that teachers *do* care primarily about grammar, punctuation, and spelling errors, that the first paragraph of every essay *must* contain an explicit thesis statement, or that the use of "I" spells an automatic F. Be prepared for this reaction by presenting several samples of professional writing that dispel these myths. Most students will be relieved to be set free of these constraints and will be eager to model their future writing on the samples you offer. Sharing your personal experiences with planning, drafting, revision, or collaboration will also help dispel many false beliefs students have about these activities. By identifying the frustrations and struggles common to all writers, your example, as well as those provided in the text, will demystify the writing process and help convince students that writing, like playing baseball or the piano, is a skill that can be learned and improved with training and practice.

"How Can You Succeed As a Writer?" suggests concrete and specific guidelines for developing productive writing habits. The quotations lend authenticity to these suggestions and reinforce students' developing sense of membership in a community of writers. Encourage students to collect and share their own favorite quotations from writers—or other experts. For example, one of my favorites is golfer Arnold Palmer's assertion: "The more I practice, the luckier I get."

Talk over Ideas with Peers and Teachers

Use this section as a blueprint for the peer review sessions students will participate in throughout the course. Planning and preparation are essential prerequisites to successful peer group activities. Only when participants clearly understand what is expected of them can group activities be productive experiences for everyone. By carefully reviewing and discussing the ten guidelines presented here, you not only acquaint students with their responsibilities for peer review but also underscore the validity of their responses to peer documents.

Planning for Collaborative Activities

Small groups can engage in many valuable activities in addition to peer reviews. They can perform collaborative writing tasks, solve problems, brainstorm writing topics, analyze texts, and peer-edit documents. Since composition theory tells us that these group experiences are effective teaching tools, the only legitimate constraint on the use of collaborative activities should be their logical connection to the act of writing.

Be forewarned: your first experience with small group activities may leave you feeling either that you have abdicated your role as teacher or that you have abandoned your classroom to chaos. Disregard any feelings of guilt, resist the urge to control the work of the groups, and remain in the background, ready to respond to questions or specific requests for assistance.

In addition to preparing students for their roles in these activities, you can do some advance planning to minimize confusion and promote productivity. Here are some suggestions for you to consider:

1. Small groups of no more than five work best. Having an odd number in each group avoids split decisions.

2. Let students self-select their own groups early in the semester. Particularly the first few times you assign group activities, students may need the security of a friend or familiar face in their group. Remember, too, students often know their needs better than you do.

3. Consider assigning students to groups according to majors. When groups are engaged in selecting or brainstorming topics, grouping students with similar backgrounds may save time by eliminating the need for topic clarification. On the other hand, at later stages of drafting, getting responses from readers with different backgrounds will help writers identify unfamiliar terminology and unclear development.

4. Consider grouping together students who are most likely to help each other. Strong writers can help weaker ones and usually increase the overall quality of the group. A student who is socially reserved may disappear in a group of assertive personalities but may be forced to contribute when paired with equally reticent peers. Be careful not to use strong writers as tutors, however; every student deserves to benefit from the group experience.

5. Consider assigning students to groups randomly using, for example, alphabetical order or seat assignment. Random arrangements can sometimes produce more interesting dynamics than you could have foreseen.

6. Once groups are established, by whatever system you choose, I recommend retaining them for the entire semester. Over time, writing groups can develop into tightly knit units. When there is a high level of trust, members feel free to take chances with their writing and are more honest with each other.

7. Don't overlook the possibility of occasionally assigning students to different groups for different assignments.

8. If you observe a lag in group productivity, consider assigning students to fresh groups for the second half of the semester or quarter.

Maintain a Writing and Research Notebook

The Writing and Research Notebook provides crucial support for the writing goals of this course. Unlike a writing journal, which elicits introspective, expressive writing that often lacks direction or focus, the Writing and

Research Notebook calls for purposeful thinking and writing. It gives students opportunities for self-reflexive writing about their composing habits and methods, promotes regular writing, lets students experience writing as *writers*, and rewards them with tangible evidence of their generative ability. As they see their notebooks expand, students become more willing to be selective and self-critical with their writing.

This section of Chapter 1 introduces students to the project, describes the notebook's purposes, and suggests several possible sections to include. Obviously, the notebook format permits considerable flexibility and can be modified to accommodate your particular course requirements and personal preferences. Advance planning and preparation will ensure that the notebook is a valuable and enjoyable experience for you as well as your students.

Planning for the Writing and Research Notebook

Here are some options for you to consider:

1. Require a minimum number of entries. Two entries per week is a minimum, and four to five per week is a realistic maximum.

2. Consider establishing grading criteria based on the number of entries produced. In a fifteen-week semester, for example, 26 entries would receive a C, 36 a B, and 48 an A.

3. Require that a minimum number of sections be included. This requirement encourages students to develop sections relevant to their research projects and personal interests but permits individual flexibility.

4. Consider setting aside class time for entry writing. Five or ten minutes of writing at the beginning of each class establishes a productive tone and focus. Alternatively, fifteen to twenty minutes of writing following a class discussion can produce thoughtful entries on the discussion topic.

5. Don't evaluate notebooks by the same standards you apply to formal writing. Since the notebook is a place for freewriting, reflection, and experimentation, don't expect entries to be polished or edited.

6. Do evaluate notebooks on the basis of the students' commitment to the project. Their commitment can be measured by the number, thoughtfulness, and regularity of the entries; the number, relevance, and development of the sections included; and the extent to which they have integrated work on their writing or research projects into the notebook.

7. Establish checkpoints. At least once prior to midterm, collect notebooks and evaluate them. This policy encourages regular entry-writing and identifies those students who may be having difficulty with the project.

8. Consider using the Critical Reading Questions or your own questions as prompts for journal entries.

9. Be specific about what you expect from students. The more explicit your expectations are, the more satisfied you will be with the results.

Once you have decided upon notebook requirements, prepare a written policy statement in the form of a handout or devote a separate section in your syllabus to the Writing and Research Notebook. Provide students with copies and follow the policies throughout the course.

Chapter 2 How to Use the Library and Document Sources

Students will use Chapter 2 as a ready reference when they begin work on their research projects, but in the absence of a concrete research-writing task, library resources and source documentation formats quickly become hopelessly abstract. Since adding such a requirement to those of an already complex writing project can overwhelm and discourage many students, I recommend that you introduce students to the guidelines in Chapter 2 by means of a relatively simple writing task: biographical research.

Organize the class into teams or small groups and ask them to use a variety of library resources to discover the identity and significance of five or six individuals they select from a list of names you provide. Ask them to compose two- or three-paragraph statements describing each individual's significance and to prepare a bibliography in MLA format of the sources they consulted.

Compile your own list of individuals, solicit possible names from students, or use the list below. The objective is to include figures who will appeal to a variety of interests and who are significant enough to be reported in biographical resources but are not widely recognized by college students. Here are some examples to start with:

Spiro Agnew	Nelson Mandela
Grace Paley	Margaret Sanger
Thomas Kuhn	Rosalind Franklin
Barry Commoner	Sojourner Truth
Alvin Toffler	Malcolm X
Kenneth Clark	James Galway
Raymond Loewy	Zora Neale Hurston
John Ashbery	Margot Fonteyn
Czeslaw Milosz	Boris Pasternak

If your college or university library offers an orientation program for students, by all means take advantage of it. If a formal orientation program is not available, the reference librarian may be willing to provide your class with a tour of the library and an introduction to the reference department's resources. In either event you will probably need to schedule this activity with the librarian well in advance, so contact the library early and plan to reinforce the field trip to the library with a hands-on research activity like the one suggested above.

Chapter 3 Writing Autobiographies and Biographies

"The Writing Portfolio" begins with genres that are generally considered to be the least demanding forms of academic writing: autobiography and biography. While the two are presented as alternate writing assignments, they differ substantially, and you should be aware of several important considerations as you plan and present this writing assignment.

Autobiographical writing is an appealing opening assignment for several sound reasons. Writing based on personal reflection and revelation can help establish a positive relationship between teacher and student. Autobiography requires no library research and when students write about emotionally charged experiences, their writing is often vivid, compelling, and rich in detail. With their energy focused on self-expression, most students can produce effective essays. And, as the introduction to this chapter points out, self-examination can make a valuable contribution to personal growth and development. The usefulness of autobiographical writing is obvious. But before you present this genre to your students, you should be aware of other implications of this assignment and the ethical issues it raises.

The first of these ethical considerations involves the difficulty (if not impossibility) of objectively evaluating autobiographical writing. That is, emotionally wrenching accounts of physical or sexual abuse or the loss of a loved one tend to receive better grades than essays about an unusual vacation or a favorite aunt. Since we cannot entirely divorce our judgments from our personal values, we must also consider the potential impact of race, ethnicity, class, and sexual orientation on grades. Even gender comes into play. Women students are more likely than men to have been the victims of rape, incest, and sexual abuse, and they most often choose to write on topics that focus on interpersonal relationships. In contrast, given the prevailing socialization process, men are more likely to disavow emotions and to choose to write on topics that valorize the self, such as accounts of physical challenges. Unwittingly, we may let our own gender influence our judgments about which essays are more interesting or valuable and, therefore, more grade-worthy.

Another major issue involves the coercive element in writing assignments. Regardless of our intent, we cannot divest ourselves of authority when we give an assignment. When we ask students to write about "a significant moment in your life," we are making a demand for self-revelation that may have serious consequences. Our students may have difficulty judging how much to reveal and to whom. Victims of sexual abuse in particular have difficulty establishing appropriate personal limits. Confronted with an intrusive writing assignment, they often feel powerless to avoid the topic but shamed and degraded by their revelations. For students who have survived traumatic childhood events, the assignment may evoke a flood of painful memories. Many students feel uncomfortable about sharing any "significant" event but believe they have no choice. Because of socially imposed power and status inequities, women students receiving the assignment from a male teacher are especially vulnerable. In any case, when you assign autobiographical writing, you ask students to surrender even more control to someone who already has emotional and social power over them.

Ultimately, sensitivity to your students' feelings and respect for their privacy offer the best protection from the undesirable aspects of auto-biographical writing assignments. Before presenting these assignments or evaluating autobiographical essays, examine your own gender-linked prefer-ences. (Notice that neither the Writing Samples nor the suggestions for writ-ing assignments favor one gender's mode of self-reflection over the other.) Explicitly reassure students that you respect their privacy and that they should never say or write anything that makes them feel uncomfortable. And, above all, present biographical writing as an equally valuable alternative.

You can avoid any appearance of preferring autobiography over biogra-phy by introducing them as two forms of self-examination. Then challenge conventional distinctions between the two. Show students how writers manipulate voice and persona to blur the boundaries: biography can be writ-ten in first person voice and authors of autobiography are often masked by persona. Point out, for example, that writers can view another's life experi-ence through their own eyes or write about their own experiences from the perspective of someone of the opposite sex or from a different racial or eth-nic background. And don't overlook one of the most useful forms of self-examination, autobiography written *prospectively*, that is, contemplating the future rather than the past.

Thoughtfully presented, biographical writing need not impose addi-tional research burdens. If your course schedule includes Chapter 2 and your students completed the research activity suggested there, they already have a good start on a biographical essay. Using the suggestions on page 17 in this guide, students can develop essays based on their own research or on the research reported by classmates. If you did not assign the research activity in Chapter 2, you can offer its subjects as potential topics. Finally, remember to give students who choose to write biographies as much encouragement and support as those writing autobiographies.

Writing Samples

In "Black Men and Public Space" Brent Staples brings autobiographical in-sights to bear on larger issues of racial politics. Open class discussion of this essay by helping students identify Staples's unusual figuration and its unify-ing function.

Critical Reading Questions (page 57)

1–5. Use these questions to analyze Staples's purpose, audience, voice, persona, and tone. (See Chapter 1 for a detailed discussion of these terms.) Until students have experience with this kind of analysis, don't expect much more than is called for by the questions.

Introduce the excerpt from Russell Baker's autobiography by asking students to compare it to the previous writing sample. Take this opportunity to challenge the assumptions about men's and women's experience that underlie this essay. How would Baker's sister Doris have recounted the anecdote?

Critical Reading Questions (page 63)

1. To help students identify the unifying theme, ask what the essay is about or what Baker's purpose is.

2–3. As students analyze Baker's tone and his use of dialogue and specific details, encourage comparisons with the previous writing sample.

Consider opening class discussion of "The Invisible Circle" by comparing it to "Black Men and Public Space." While Staples uses personal insight to illuminate racial stereotypes, Bernice Geradts lets an impersonal TV talk-show topic lead her to a startling personal revelation.

Critical Reading Questions (page 64)

1–3. Since the strategies used in student writing samples are often more accessible to analysis than those of professional writers, your students may need less help with analysis of this essay. Consider assigning these questions as collaborative tasks for small groups.

Based on interviews and written in first person, "Nora Quealey" demonstrates how writers manipulate the boundaries between autobiography and biography. Students can adapt Jean Schroedel's methods for the writing assignment in this chapter.

Critical Reading Questions (page 69)

1. Reconstructing the questions behind Schroedel's interview helps prepare students for interviewing subjects for their own biographical essays.

2–3. These questions call for close reading and attention to detail. You can use them to emphasize the choices the author made and the strategies she employed to control the tone and depth of the essay.

4–5. Because both these questions call for critical speculation, they work well as prompts for journal entries or in-class writing.

Analyzing Pertinent Conventions

Students should read this section outside of class. Although examples of each convention are presented in the text, have students locate other instances in the writing samples that demonstrate how these conventions shaped the documents, dictated the authors' decisions, or limited composing options in some way.

Writing Assignments

Students should read proposed assignments outside of class and use the questions to generate a topic for autobiography writing or to select a subject for biography.

Prewriting and Drafting Strategies

Students should also read this section outside of class. In the next class have students freewrite on their topics, looping three sessions of ten to fifteen minutes each. During the initial stages of drafting, many students have difficulty defining the focus of their topic. Self-reflexive writing in the form of journal entries can help. Consider using the following questions as prompts for out-of-class journal entry writing:

1. Does the person or event seem interesting?
2. Can I deal with the topic in a short essay?
3. Do I have enough information about or experience with the topic to provide concrete, sensory details?
4. Exactly why am I writing about this person or event?
5. What tone and voice are suitable for this topic?

Revising and Editing Strategies

Students should read pages 75–76 outside of class. The revision strategies presented here are designed to be self-administered but can also be used as the basis for peer review. I recommend that you plan two rounds of peer review for each writing assignment. Schedule the first early in the drafting process to help students contend with problems of voice and tone and to discourage procrastination.

Collaborative Learning

The sample peer revision in this section provides a model for your students to follow in their small group peer review sessions. Have them read pages 76–80 outside of class. During the next class, review the guidelines suggested in the Peer Review Workshop on page 80; then have students work in small groups to review their drafts using the questions in the Peer Review Workshop.

Additional Writing Samples

Assign these samples for students to read while they are engaged in revising their drafts. Then divide class time between discussing the Critical Reading Questions and peer group review of drafts.

Evaluating Criticism

If this is the first writing assignment your students have completed in the course, you will need to defer the activities in this section until you have evaluated and returned their essays. On the day you return the essays, set aside some time in class for students to take advantage of the suggestions in this section.

Chapter 4 Analyzing Subjects and Processes

Analysis (that is, dividing something into its components in order to understand it better) is a fundamental thought process that your students have been using for most of their lives. The analyses that they undertake in the course of making everyday decisions, however, are largely intuitive and certainly not rhetorically self-conscious. And although these analyses may have practical consequences, they seldom need to withstand the scrutiny of others. On the other hand, in academic situations students are called upon to demonstrate their analytic abilities self-consciously and publicly. Familiarity with the rhetorical conventions that shape analytic writing will help students demonstrate their analytic abilities more effectively. At the same time, the varied voice, audience, and tone illustrated in the writing samples presented here encourage student writers to avoid the pitfall of reducing analytic writing to the mechanical replication of a rhetorical form that is divorced from their actual thought processes.

A good way to introduce analytic writing is by asking students to recall occasions when they have used analysis in their writing. Then explore the other private and public uses of this genre with them.

Writing Samples

The student essay by Michael Miller can be used to prompt students' awareness of how they use analysis in their composing process, and Miller's concern with clarity will strike a responsive chord in most students.

Critical Reading Questions (pages 89–90)

1. Use this question as a springboard for examining how purpose and audience affect our composing process. Ask students to recall a previous

writing task that required analysis. How did you use analysis to understand the subject or process? Did your analysis help you remember the subject or process better? How did your analysis shape or organize your writing? How did your prewriting, drafting, or revising strategies for that essay differ, for example, from those for the writing assignment in Chapter 3?

2–3. Since these questions call on critical reading skills that play an important role in peer review, use them for collaborative group activities. Divide students into small groups and assign each group one or the other of the questions. Each group should designate a secretary to record and report their findings to the class.

4. This question makes an excellent prompt for a journal entry or in-class writing activity. Students are more likely to be honestly self-critical in the privacy of their journal than in a public class discussion.

Alfie Kohn's "Girl Talk—Guy Talk" will open students' eyes to the profound but subtle ways in which our gender influences our use of language, and they will be eager to react to the essay's propositions. Kohn's engaging tone and the controversial nature of his topic tend to draw students' attention away from his use of analysis. So after allowing some time for students to react to the essay's content, ask them to locate sections of the essay where Kohn explicitly relies on analysis to develop his thesis.

Critical Reading Questions (page 93)

1. This question highlights the use of concrete details and specific examples to *show* rather than *tell*. Although students will probably recognize this device as a means for supporting a more general claim, in this essay Kohn's use of directly quoted dialogue also functions as a tone-setting strategy.

2–3. These questions work well as the basis for class discussions. Students, who are accustomed to accepting the written words of "experts" at face value, may need help untangling the complex interplay among social status, occupational status, and power status and gender. Ask them to tap their experience and imagine themselves in conversations first with, for example, a teacher, parent, or close friend of the same sex. Then ask how those conversations would be different if they were with individuals of the opposite gender. Students are unlikely to reach any definite conclusions, but they will become more sensitive to their own patterns of discourse as well as to the effects of audience on discourse.

4. Students may quickly point out that the imaginary dialogue that opens the essay helps set its informal, conversational tone. But you can direct their attention to other stylistic strategies the author uses to maintain

that tone: How does Kohn present research findings? What information does he fail to include? How carefully does he define terms? What words does he use to qualify or limit his statements? What can you infer from his tone about his intended audience?

This excerpt from Gail Sheehy's *Passages* provides a model of analytic writing that is anything but academic or abstract. Notice how the author's rather complex analytic structure is clarified and intensified by her use of concrete, figurative language.

Critical Reading Questions (page 99)

1. Class discussion of these questions will bring Sheehy's stages to life as students place themselves, friends, or relatives within the patterns she describes.

2. These questions prompt close reading and direct students' attention away from the content of Sheehy's analysis and toward her rhetorical assumptions. Have students identify undocumented generalizations and unsupported insights, then remind them that this text has been excerpted from a book.

3. Use this question to demonstrate how quotations, like other specific, concrete details, can function as support for generalizations.

4. Since this question calls for introspection and self-reflection, it is an appropriate prompt for a journal entry or in-class writing.

5. Use these questions, which require imaginative speculation, as collaborative tasks for small groups or as journal entry prompts.

Analyzing Pertinent Conventions

Students should read about the conventions of analytic writing outside of class; then, in class, help them locate instances in the writing samples that demonstrate how these conventions shaped the documents, dictated the authors' decisions, or limited their composing options in some way.

Writing Assignments

Have students read the assignments and use the questions to generate one or two topics for analysis.

Prewriting and Drafting Strategies

Have students also read pages 107–109. During the next class meeting let them work in small groups for fifteen to twenty minutes brainstorming with peers to narrow their selection to one topic. Then students can work individually developing an informal outline, pie diagram, or some other form of "itinerary" for their analysis that they will use to develop a first draft for the next class meeting.

Collaborating Strategies

The sample peer revision in this section presents a model for your students to follow in their small group peer review sessions. Have them read pages 110–111 on their own. Briefly discuss the guidelines suggested in the Peer Review Workshop on page 111; then have students work in small groups to review drafts using the questions provided.

Additional Writing Samples

Assign these samples for students to read while they are engaged in revising their drafts. Then divide class time between discussing the Critical Reading Questions and peer group review of drafts.

Evaluating Criticism

It is important to set aside some class time for students to take advantage of the suggestions in this section. The day the writing assignment for this chapter is due is an appropriate occasion for self-evaluation in the form of a journal entry or in-class writing.

Chapter 5 Analyzing Causes and Effects

While the analysis of subjects and processes entails dividing something into its parts, analyzing causes and effects involves making logical connections, often between things that are not obviously related. Most college students possess the cognitive skill to make logical connections, but many lack the discursive ability to express complex relationships clearly. Their thinking often appears illogical when in fact their writing is merely clumsy. As with other forms of academic writing, knowledge of relevant conventions is crucial for success.

Introduce cause and effect analysis by having students define the process and explore its private and public uses. You should also review the specialized vocabulary introduced and encourage students to use these terms in their discussions.

Writing Samples

"Another Kind of Victory," an entertaining account of a personally painful but profitable learning experience, will neutralize the initial anxiety many students feel about cause and effect analysis. Van Lenten's analytic process is implicit, so students must probe to uncover it.

Critical Reading Questions (pages 127–128)

1. This question requires students to recognize the first sentence as a snatch of directly quoted, internal monologue. They should also perceive the first sentence as a rhetorical device the author selected in order to achieve a specific effect.

2. This question pushes students to uncover the analysis implicit in Van Lenten's essay.

3. Students will have little difficulty locating instances of figurative language but may be unable to explain clearly how the language contributes to tone. Rereading these portions of the text with the colorful figures omitted will illuminate their effect.

4. This question gives students an opportunity to personalize the author's experience and prepares them for the self-reflection called for in the next question.

5. This question works well as a prompt for journal writing.

Shelli Boyd's "What Causes Date and Acquaintance Rape?" was probably written for an audience very much like your class, and the relevance of the essay's voice, tone, and topic will likely elicit a vigorous discussion. In light of Boyd's statement that one in ten college women believe they've been the victim of date rape, however, undirected class discussion could provoke painful emotions in some of your students. Be alert to this possibility and keep discussion task-oriented and focused on the essay as an example of cause-effect analysis. Or, bypass large-group discussion of this essay altogether and follow the suggestions below.

Critical Reading Questions (page 130)

1–4. For a change of pace, use the first three questions as collaborative tasks for small groups. Have each group report their conclusions to the class. Then practice peer review techniques by having students work independently to compose written responses to question 4.

Joseph Skinner's "Big Mac and the Tropical Forests" presents a classic cause-effect analysis in a voice that is compelling and human. The following questions lead students through an examination of both aspects of the essay's effectiveness.

Critical Reading Questions (page 136)

1–3. Questions 1, 2, and the first part of 3 call for descriptions of the essay's purpose, audience, and tone. As they gain experience with this kind of analysis, students should be developing a vocabulary of rhetorical terms they can use to describe these features. (See Chapter 1 for a detailed discussion of these terms.)

3. Involve the entire class in the project of uncovering the structure of Skinner's cause-effect analysis by reconstructing on the blackboard the author's "itinerary" or prewriting. Encourage students to be creative in devising graphic schemes to represent the connections Skinner makes in his essay.

4. This question offers an opportunity to practice the specialized vocabulary introduced in this chapter.

Analyzing Pertinent Conventions

Assign pages 136–141 for out-of-class reading; then take some time in class to review the examples that are included under each convention. Finally, help students find instances in the writing samples where these conventions shaped the documents, dictated the authors' decisions, or limited their composing options in some way.

Writing Assignments

Have students use the questions to generate topics for cause-effect analysis. Since these questions contemplate a wide range of writing projects from personal essays to library-based research papers, you will need to specify any limitations you intend to impose on this assignment.

Prewriting and Drafting Strategies

Student writers tend to choose topics that are either poorly focused or too broad for the project at hand. So once students have identified their topics, give them time in class to freewrite. Three looped sessions of ten to fifteen minutes each are desirable, but even one freewrite will often help narrow a writer's focus to areas of genuine personal interest. I recommend that you also provide class time for students to generate an informal plan or outline for their analysis using the questions on pages 143–144. With this plan in hand, they are ready to begin drafting.

Revising and Editing Strategies

Have students use the suggestions and questions in this section to revise their drafts before submitting them for peer review. They should also review the pertinent conventions and consider their influence in the revising process.

Collaborating Strategies

Have students use the questions in the Peer Review Workshop to critique each other's drafts. For a change of pace, consider having students work in teams for this peer review session rather than in small groups. Although team review limits the range of response to a draft, it can also lead to a more detailed examination of the analysis, a process students may benefit from on this writing assignment.

Additional Writing Samples

Assign these two writing samples for out-of-class reading while students continue to review, revise, and polish their drafts. Use the Critical Reading Questions as the basis for class discussions. For practice with peer review techniques, have students compose a written response to question 3 on page 148.

Evaluating Criticism

By this time students should have in hand peer and teacher evaluations of the previous writing assignment(s), as well as peer responses to the present one. Set aside class time for them to consider the questions in this section and to prepare a list of the major problem patterns their critics have identified in their writing. Then use this self-reflection as a prompt for journal entry or other in-class writing.

Chapter 6 Writing Persuasively

As with other genres in the Writing Portfolio, persuasive writing is presented as an extension of skills students already possess. Argumentation is introduced by a rich catalog of examples drawn from common experience, and students are encouraged to apply their experience with oral arguments to the demands of written argumentation. Consideration of the crucial elements of argumentation (such as audience and emotional, ethical, and logical appeals) evolves naturally as students struggle to adjust the familiar strategies of oral argument to the rigors of a new context: persuasive writing.

Since students have all had experience with informal oral argument, concentrate on identifying the features that distinguish written argumentation. Don't assume that these differences are obvious. Even if students can articulate the distinctions easily, the articulation process itself alerts them to the most significant difficulties they will encounter in writing persuasively.

Writing Samples

Most of your students probably have no experience with analyzing written arguments; therefore, plan to discuss "Making the Population Connection" together in class. (If your course includes Chapter 5, you might begin the discussion by asking how the Ehrlichs' essay is an analysis of cause and effect.)

Critical Reading Questions (page 166)

1–5. Use these questions to direct the class discussion. When students identify the authors' purpose, primary claims, and thesis, they will quickly recognize the piece as *persuasive* rather than *analytic*. On this initial foray into persuasive writing, however, don't expect much more from students than the questions call for.

Students will find Sandra Serrano's essay a manageable subject for critical analysis. Although the personal tone and narrow focus of her argument are less formidable than the more complex strategies of the Ehrlichs' piece, continue to have the class work together on the analysis.

Critical Reading Questions (page 169)

1. This question probes the use of persona for persuasive purposes (ethical appeal).

2–5. In response to these questions students examine Serrano's claims, the evidence she provides to support them, and the counterarguments she anticipates (logical appeals).

6. Finally, students are asked to identify the emotional tone of the essay and evaluate its effectiveness (emotional appeals).

7. At this point students will likely be ready to make suggestions for improving the essay. Conclude the discussion with their suggestions or ask them to compose written peer reviews of the essay for the next class.

Analyzing Pertinent Conventions

Students should read pages 170–175 outside of class; then in class help them locate instances in the writing samples that demonstrate how these conventions shaped the documents, influenced the authors' decisions, or limited composing options in some way.

Writing Assignments

Have students use the suggested questions and activities outside of class to generate topics for persuasive writing.

Prewriting and Drafting Strategies

The strategies presented in this section are designed to be self-administered and can be assigned as out-of-class work. Alternatively, schedule time in class for prewriting activities such as freewriting, brainstorming in small groups, or journal entry writing. In either event you should allow enough time for students to take advantage of the suggested strategies but also impose a reasonable deadline for completion of first drafts.

Revising and Editing Strategies

As in the previous section, the strategies presented here are designed to be self-administered and can be completed outside of class. The questions on page 178 address the most crucial features of persuasive writing. In addition, two new strategies are introduced with examples of each. Since the benefits of these strategies will become apparent through their use, I recommend that you require students to reformat and critique their texts and to self-evaluate their texts using the criteria-based evaluation. Students should revise their drafts in response to these self-evaluations before moving on to collaborative activities.

Collaborating Strategies

Persuasive writing demands increased critical skills from peer reviewers. In order to heighten your students' critical awareness, have them complete the exercise presented in the sample peer writing workshop before they review peer drafts. Then schedule class time for a peer review in small groups. For this first round of peer review, since drafts are already formatted for double entries, reviewers' comments can be recorded in the right column. After revisions, schedule a second round of peer review with drafts formatted conventionally.

Additional Writing Sample

Assign this sample for students to read while they are engaged in revising their drafts. Then divide class time between discussing the Critical Reading Questions and peer group review of drafts.

Evaluating Criticism

Although persuasive writing is generally a demanding genre, you may find that some students revel in the opportunity to assert their opinions and beliefs. Encourage students to recognize their writing strengths as well as their weaknesses when they evaluate their progress. Set aside class time for students to respond to the questions on page 192 and expand their self-reflection in journal entries or other in-class writing.

Chapter 7 Solving Problems by Negotiating Differences

Negotiation is fast becoming the rhetoric of choice for accommodating differences and solving problems in our postnuclear, postmodern society. As planetary survival becomes increasingly dependent on successfully dealing with competing priorities, confrontation must give way to negotiation. Moreover, academic discourse is responding to demands for ethnic and gender diversity. In their academic and professional careers students will likely encounter more contexts that affirm consensus and compromise over confrontation and competition. Likewise, they will engage in persuasive writing that negotiates rather than argues.

Students will quickly accept the usefulness of Rogerian problem-solving methods but may have more difficulty envisioning concrete examples. So once they grasp the essential dynamics of the genre, move on to the writing samples.

Writing Samples

Rachel Richardson Smith's essay, "Abortion, Right and Wrong," presents a compelling, accessible demonstration of Rogerian methods. Open discussion of the piece by asking students what Smith's goal is. How does her goal differ from advocating either antagonistic position?

Critical Reading Questions (page 197)

1–5. These questions prompt a step-by-step analysis of the essay's Rogerian method. The first question leads students to uncover evidentiary support for both sides of the abortion issue. The questions in 2 and 3 focus on audience and tone. (See Chapter 1 for a detailed discussion of these terms.) Use questions 4 and 5 to compare the effects of persona, tone, and other emotional appeals with those of logic.

Leslie Milne's essay introduces a prewriting strategy that is crucial to the success of Rogerian methods: formal analysis of the communication situation. Ask students to evaluate Milne's success on the basis of her analysis, which precedes the essay.

Critical Reading Questions (page 200)

1–4. Having analyzed the previous essay, students should be ready to exercise their critical judgment. These questions encourage students to evaluate the effectiveness of Milne's strategies and to suggest revisions. Question 4 can also be used as a prompt for a journal entry or an in-class writing activity.

Analyzing Pertinent Conventions

Students should read this section outside class. Although sample arguments are presented to illustrate the pertinent conventions, plan class time to help students locate instances in the writing samples that demonstrate how these conventions shaped the documents, dictated the authors' decisions, or limited composing options in some way.

Writing Assignments

Because of the interpersonal dimensions of Rogerian argument, students will need frequent opportunities for feedback from peers during this writing assignment. Working on their own, students should use the questions on page 205 to generate two or three possible topics for a negotiation essay. Provide class time for them to work in small groups brainstorming the issues and the audiences associated with the competing positions. When they have identified topics that both interest them and offer opportunity for negotiation, they can begin prewriting.

Prewriting and Drafting Strategies

The strategies presented here are designed to be self-administered, leading students step by step through the prewriting and drafting process.

Revising and Editing Strategies

Once students have generated a first draft, encourage them to review the pertinent conventions and undertake honest self-evaluation of their work. They should use the questions on page 205, the criteria-based evaluation on pages 205–206, and the suggestions on page 205 to identify the weaknesses in their draft. These strategies are designed to be self-administered but can also be used collaboratively. Depending on your course schedule and the time available, you could, for example, have students use the questions on page 205 for self-evaluation and initial revision, plan one round of peer review using the criteria-based evaluation, and schedule a final round of peer review using the Peer Review Workshop.

Collaborating Strategies

Because tone and balance are so important to negotiation, peer review is especially helpful with this writing assignment. The sample peer review session presented here should dispel any lingering doubts students may have about the benefits of the review process or the necessity for revisions. Assign pages 206–213 as outside reading; then have students work in small groups, using the questions in the Peer Review Workshop to critique each other's drafts.

Additional Writing Sample

Assign the additional selections for outside reading while students are engaged in revising drafts. Then divide class time between discussing the Critical Reading Questions and peer group review of drafts. King's letter provides an excellent opportunity for you to discuss the use of figurative language in persuasive writing. Point out one example; then ask students to identify and analyze the effects of other instances in the letter. You should also remind them to review the pertinent conventions as they revise their drafts.

Evaluating Criticism

I recommend that you follow the suggestions in this section. When you return their negotiation essays, schedule time, either in or outside class, for students to respond to the questions in this section in their Writing and Research Notebooks.

Chapter 8 Writing Reports Based on Library Research

If you did not assign Chapter 2 ("How to Use the Library and Document Sources") earlier in the course, you should do so now, before you begin the work in this chapter. Chapter 2 provides the resource and documentation guidelines students will refer to when they work on their library-based research reports.

Writing based on library research allows you considerable flexibility. Let your course goals and time schedule shape this assignment's precise form. You may elect to devote about the same amount of time to library-based research reports as to other genres in the Writing Portfolio. Students can gain valuable experience with library research and produce a report in approximately two to three weeks, provided you limit the scope of their projects and the number of sources consulted. ("The Fast Food Diet" by Tracey Williams, for example, cites only one source.) On the other hand, if library-based research writing is a major component of your course, you will find Chapter 8 provides a generous amount of material and activities from which your students can develop more extensive research projects.

In either case, library-based research reports are excellent vehicles for collaboration. Consider having students work on this writing assignment in small groups. For example, have each group select a topic; then have each group member research and prepare a report on one aspect of the topic. Individual reports are then collated by the group into a coherent research paper on the topic, which can be published and shared with the rest of the class. Students gain valuable experience from coordinating their research projects with the work of their peers, but they are still responsible for and evaluated on their individual efforts.

Most students have encountered some form of library-based research in high school and will have no difficulty suggesting its academic purposes. They may be surprised, however, to discover the genre in nonacademic print media. Encourage them to share with the class any examples they encounter in popular periodicals or general-audience books.

Writing Samples

Roy Brooks' use of a variety of secondary sources to establish credibility and to lay the groundwork for his analysis makes "Formal Equal Opportunity" an excellent introduction to the genre.

Critical Reading Questions (page 236)

1–3. Use these questions to test your students' comprehension and to help them identify the primary claims of Brooks' argument. As they respond to these questions, encourage their recognition of Brooks' text as a carefully crafted argument.

4. If your course includes Chapter 6 and 7, challenge students to call on their experiences with persuasive writing and Rogerian methods in response to these questions. If those chapters are not included in your course, have students reconstruct Brooks' audience analysis before describing the tone of the text.

5. Prompted by these questions, students should now be able to examine Brooks' strategic use of secondary source documentation to accommodate critical readers without disrupting the ethical and emotional appeal of his argument.

Beverly Naminsky's "Who Is Winning in the Battle with the Bugs?" will encourage and reassure students. Naminsky's report provides students with a modest but successful example of library-based research. More importantly, they will see how her peers' comments helped shape and improve her report.

Critical Reading Questions (pages 241–242)

1–3. These questions, which lead students through a systematic analysis of audience, tone, and voice, work well as the basis for class discussion. (See Chapter 1 for a detailed discussion of these terms.)

4. Conclude the class discussion with a critique of Naminsky's report, or, alternatively, ask students to compose a written response to this question outside of class.

Analyzing Pertinent Conventions

Assign pages 242–255 for outside reading. (If your course does not include Chapter 2, refer students to relevant sections for guidance with researching and citing secondary sources.) Because this section is long and the conventions are complex, set aside sufficient class time to review each convention and answer any questions. Notice that these conventions are presented, not as rule-bound academic mannerisms, but as necessary and reasonable accommodations to critical readers. The connection between critical reading and documentation conventions is reinforced by the samples of student writing in double-entry format and by the Critical Reading Exercise on pages 255–256. I recommend that you critique at least two or three excerpts in this exercise as an in-class activity. With a little practice students will become adept critics. You can then assign the remaining excerpts to small groups and have each group summarize their critique for the class.

Writing Assignments

Be prepared to provide your students with specific guidelines for this writing assignment. Even before they select topics for their reports they will need to know (1) approximately how long the report should be; (2) approximately how many library sources they should consult and cite; (3) whether they should argue an opinion or position in their reports; (4) whether they should propose solutions or policy changes; (5) whether the report must address a formal academic audience or whether students may choose their audience; (6) when their report is due; and (7) if there are any restrictions on their topic selection. Once you have determined what limitations you intend to impose, tell students clearly and explicitly what you expect. I recommend that you prepare and distribute a brief written policy statement for this assignment. This tactic helps you think through the assignment thoroughly in advance, saves you time in the long run, and avoids confusion and repetitious policy clarification. And students will appreciate having written guidelines they can refer to as their work progresses.

However you conceive this writing assignment, I urge you to avoid any external limitations on topic selection. Encourage students to use this assignment to explore topics they care about; their research reports will be more interesting and better written if they do. The suggestions on page 258 will help them identify potential topic areas.

Prewriting and Drafting Strategies

The scope of the research project will determine how much time students need for prewriting and drafting. If the research project is extensive, they will need help planning their work load and scheduling their time. The project will become more manageable if you divide it into steps and establish timely checkpoints for each segment. I recommend that instead of arbitrarily imposing due dates for these checkpoints, you have the class generate a schedule similar to the sample on page 261. Dates should be established for (1) reviewing tentative topics in peer groups; (2) submitting research proposals to peer groups for review; (3) submitting a brief annotated bibliography for instructor review; (4) at least two rounds of peer review workshops; and (5) final submission of documents. Once this schedule is generated, copy and distribute it to the class.

Revising and Editing Strategies

The critical questions and criteria-based evaluation are designed to be self-administered but can also be used as the basis for peer review workshops. For more extensive writing assignments, schedule a peer review workshop early in the drafting process to help students contend with problems of voice and tone and to discourage procrastination.

Collaborating Strategies

During the drafting process, schedule additional peer review workshops using the questions on pages 264–265.

Additional Writing Sample

"The Fast Food Diet" by student Tracey Williams is an excellent illustration of a brief library-based research report. Assign this sample for students to read while they are engaged in revising their drafts. Then divide class time between discussing the Critical Reading Questions and peer group review of drafts.

Evaluating Criticism

It is important to set aside some class time for students to take advantage of the suggestions in this section. The day the research report is due is an appropriate occasion for self-evaluation in the form of a journal entry or in-class writing.

Chapter 9 Writing Reports Based on Interviews and Questionnaires

Original research based on interviews and questionnaires is introduced as a natural extension of library-based research. If your students have just completed Chapter 8, they will be eager to build on their library research skills and take on a more active research role. As with library-based research reports, consider having students work on this research writing assignment in small groups. (See suggestions for collaborative projects on page 33 in this guide.)

Aside from defining interviews and questionnaires, you need to give this genre little introduction, and you can move on quickly to the samples of student writing.

Writing Samples

Joseph Scaglione takes advantage of the special opportunities interview-based reports offer for writers to develop unique persona, voice, and tone. "Into the Wilderness—Victimization and the Criminal Justice System" also illustrates a balanced blending of library-based and original research.

Critical Reading Questions (page 278)

1. If students have difficulty describing Scaglione's tone and persona, refer them to his analysis of his communication situation. Remind them that

tone refers to the reader's perceptions of the author's feelings toward the subject, and persona is a mask the author wears to achieve certain purposes. (See Chapter 1 for a detailed discussion of these terms.)

2. This question leads students to examine Scaglione's use of language to lend emotional impact to his logical argument.

3. Students must recognize the author's strategic use of quotations. In order to evaluate the effectiveness of this strategy, they should consider what other options were available for presenting the information Scaglione gathered in interviews.

4. Like the previous one, this question requires students to recognize that the document reflects one of several possible strategic options. They must first identify what choices the author made and then propose and evaluate possible alternatives.

Notice that "View from the Bread Box: Race Issues on Campus" was produced by a collaborative effort such as the one described on page 33 in this guide. Compiling, administering, and interpreting a survey is time-consuming work that requires a range of talents and abilities. Small groups can divide responsibility for the work in a variety of ways and produce a more thoughtful and interesting report than one person could alone.

Critical Reading Questions (page 286)

1. Ask students to describe the authors' tone in the first paragraph. Then compare the tone in the first paragraph with the tone of the second. Ask them to account for any differences they discover.

2. In order to respond to this question, students will need to study the survey results carefully and judge how accurately the results were reported, a process that may take too much time for an in-class discussion. You can accomplish the same results by assigning a different survey item to each student for evaluation and discussing only those items they find to be inaccurately reported.

3. Use this question as a prompt for journal entry writing.

4. Have students locate instances where the authors referred to secondary sources and speculate on the purposes of the reference.

5. Student response to this question will probably be related to their personal experience with the issues. Consider linking this question with question 3 above, perhaps as a conclusion to their entries.

Analyzing Pertinent Conventions

Students should read pages 286–293 outside of class. (If your course does not include Chapters 2 and 8, refer students to relevant sections for guidance with researching and citing secondary sources.) Because these conventions are complex and flexible, plan sufficient class time to review each convention and answer any questions.

Writing Assignments

Be prepared to provide your students with specific guidelines for this writing assignment. (See the section on Chapter 8 in this guide for detailed recommendations.) Regardless of the limitations imposed, encourage students to use this assignment to explore topics they care about. The prompts on pages 294–295 will help them identify potential topic areas.

Prewriting and Drafting Strategies

The scope of the research project will determine how much time students need for the prewriting and drafting process. (See the section on Chapter 8 in this guide for detailed recommendations on planning and scheduling research projects.) Guidelines for conducting research based on interviews or surveys are presented on pages 297–306. You need to supplement this information with in-class opportunities for peer group reviews of topics, research proposals, interview methods or surveys, and drafts of reports.

Revising and Editing Strategies

The critical questions and criteria-based evaluation are designed to be self-administered but can also be used as the basis for peer review workshops. For extensive research writing projects schedule a peer review workshop early in the drafting process to help students contend with problems of voice and tone and to discourage procrastination.

Collaborating Strategies

During the drafting process schedule additional peer review workshops using the suggested questions.

Evaluating Criticism

It is important to set aside some class time for students to consider the questions in this section. The day the writing assignment for this chapter is due is an appropriate occasion for self-evaluation in the form of a journal entry or in-class writing.

Chapter 10 Writing Reports Based on Ethnographic Methods

Ethnography constitutes a fitting conclusion for the Writing Portfolio since it incorporates features of the other academic genres. When your students engage in ethnographic research and writing, they use library and field research methods; they analyze data and search for connections between causes and effects; and they present their observations engagingly and persuasively, weaving the autobiographical threads of their experiences with the biographies of their research subjects. In a sense, they return in ethnography to a more personal form of writing, armed with a sophisticated arsenal of writing skills.

Don't be surprised or concerned if few of your students are familiar with ethnography. The writing samples will quickly provide them with a working definition of the genre.

Writing Samples

Generally, students are pleased and excited to learn that Doug Harper's *Good Company* represents legitimate research. Because voice and tone distinguish ethnography from other research forms, the Critical Reading Questions focus attention on these features.

Critical Reading Questions (page 313)

1–4. Since this excerpt may be your students' first encounter with ethnography, use these questions as the basis for class discussion. Each question suggests characteristics of the ethnographer's writing style, research methods, or attitudes.

Suzanne Farber's research report, which presents interesting contrasts in tone, subject, and audience, helps deepen students' definition of ethnography. Students will appreciate her efforts to blend her academic and work experiences.

Critical Reading Questions (page 318)

1–4. Once students have described Farber's tone, have them contrast it with Harper's tone in the previous writing sample and suggest reasons for the differences.

Because Todd Taylor's research report comes closer to your students' experience and potential writing ability, it serves as an example for their own research projects.

Critical Reading Questions (page 328)

1–3. Use these questions, which direct attention toward considerations of methods, as the basis for class discussion.

Analyzing Pertinent Conventions

Students should read pages 328–333 outside of class. Schedule class time for reviewing the conventions presented here, discussing the examples and answering questions. Notice that these conventions not only govern how ethnographies look and sound but also constitute methodological guidelines students will follow when they conduct their research projects.

Writing Assignments

In ethnography the selection of an appropriate culture is crucial to the success of the project. Have students read the suggested assignments outside of class and use the questions to identify one or two possible subject groups for their study. During the next class meeting have them work in small groups for fifteen or twenty minutes brainstorming with peers to narrow their selections. Follow this small group work with looped freewriting sessions for students to react to peer comments and develop their research ideas.

Prewriting and Drafting Strategies

The prewriting and drafting strategies presented here are designed to be self-administered, but you should plan in-class activities to reinforce them. As with other research projects, I recommend that the class generate a schedule for the project. (See the section on Chapter 8 in this guide for detailed recommendations on planning and scheduling research projects.) For example, checkpoints should be established for defining the culture or community to be studied, developing a research proposal, accessing the community, concluding field observations, and drafting and revising the research report.

If your students have already developed a Writing and Research Notebook, they will find it to be an invaluable tool for organizing their field notes, interpreting their observations, and generating the narratives that will become the first drafts of their ethnographies. If your students are not maintaining a Writing and Research Notebook, you should require a field notebook for this research project. (See Chapter 1 of the text and the section on Chapter 1 in this guide for detailed recommendations for keeping a Writing and Research Notebook.)

Plan to schedule opportunities for students to meet with their peer groups during the prewriting and drafting process. Long before first drafts are due, students need feedback on their research proposals, and they will want to share their preliminary impressions and discuss problems they may be encountering.

Revising and Editing

The critical questions and criteria-based evaluation presented here are designed to be self-administered but can also be used as the basis for peer review sessions. Schedule a peer review workshop early in the drafting process to help students contend with problems of voice and tone and to discourage procrastination.

Collaborating Strategies

Schedule additional peer review sessions during the drafting process using the suggestions in the Peer Review Workshop.

Additional Writing Samples

Assign these samples for students to read while they are engaged in revising their drafts. Then divide class time between discussing the Critical Reading Questions and peer group review of drafts.

Evaluating Criticism

It is important to set aside some class time for students to consider the questions in this section. The day the student ethnographies are due is an appropriate occasion for self-evaluation in the form of a journal entry or in-class writing.

Chapter 11 How to Make Substantive Revisions

You may wish to assign this chapter at any point in your syllabus for reading outside of class, followed by in-class discussion. Alternatively, you can use the chapter as needed with individual students or peer review groups whose work indicates a need for more focused study of paragraph- and sentence-level revision.

Encourage students to view writing as a recursive, yet progressive, process. Thus, after they have completed a first draft of any particular writing project, they may revise it as many times as they find necessary, and as time allows, to achieve what they consider a final draft. During their successive rounds of revision, students can use the suggestions in this chapter first to revise areas such as content, audience awareness, tone, and organization that affect the entire paper (pages 357–358); then to revise paragraphs and transitions (pages 358–362); and finally to edit and improve sentences.

An alternate strategy is to have students focus on specific paragraph and sentence issues with each new writing assignment to progressively refine and improve their writing style.

Chapter 12 How to Use Correct Punctuation

Encourage students to use this chapter, perhaps along with a writer's handbook, as they undertake the final, copyediting/proofreading revision of any writing project. Remind students that the use of correct grammar, spelling, and punctuation, while perhaps the most mechanical revision activity, is also the clearest mark of careful academic writing. Invite students to imagine the results for a scholar who submits a carefully researched and well-written senior thesis, doctoral dissertation, or book manuscript that is full of spelling and punctuation errors! The lower grade that you, no doubt, would give a paper with such errors might look like a lenient penalty compared to what a more advanced scholar could expect for such carelessness.

Responding to Student Writing

Thanks to a growing body of research, we know a great deal about how teacher response to student writing affects writing improvement. We know, for example, that red-flagging mechanical errors fails to improve student writing and that assigning a grade to a document forestalls further revision. Yet we operate in an academic community that imposes on us responsibility for eliminating error and assigning grades. While nothing can entirely eliminate the onus of evaluating student writing, the following suggestions will help you transform the evaluation process into a teaching process. They will also save you valuable time.

1. Provide helpful rather than judgmental evaluations. In other words, instead of justifying a grade, your comments should respond to the writer's intentions. Since your ultimate concern is to teach students to ask the critical questions that successful writers ask when revising, you need to pose these questions and propose alternative solutions when your students' writing fails to realize its purposes.

2. Praise positive attributes in each paper. Like everyone else, students respond to encouragement and positive reinforcement.

3. Avoid overburdening students with advice and criticism. Identify only one or two significant *patterns* of error at a time. Try to respond primarily to the substance and significance of the writing rather than to its line-by-line correctness.

4. Avoid abstract, formulaic, "textbook" language in your comments. Students do not modify their writing patterns in response to vague comments such as "awk" or "wordy." Instead, suggest more effective options.

5. Play the role of the students' intended audience. By such role-playing, you demonstrate that writers compose for an audience rather than perform for a grade.

6. Require multiple drafts. To transform grading papers into a learning process, allow students to revise their work in light of your criticism. Otherwise, they will tend to ignore your comments, no matter how helpful your responses may be.

7. Encourage students to view revision as an opportunity to clarify and discover their meaning rather than as punishment for not getting it right the first time.

43

8. An effective way to accomplish #6 and #7 above is to omit grades on individual papers. Instead, have students keep a portfolio of papers, continue to revise them, and select a few to be graded at the end of the semester.

9. Avoid appropriating students' texts. That is, your job is not to reconstruct the text but to direct the writer's attention to discrepancies between intentions and results. Leave final decisions about revisions to the student.

10. If one-on-one conferences are impossible, do the next best thing: respond orally via a tape recorder to your students. Taped responses allow you to provide more commentary in less time than written notes, and they are more personal.

11. Solicit feedback from students regarding the helpfulness of your comments. Throughout the semester you can determine what sorts of comments students find useful by asking them to freewrite or write journal entries about your remarks. For example, you can ask, "What comments on your last writing assignment did you find most useful?"

12. We know from composition research that students improve as writers when they are challenged to assess their own writing. As a result, I recommend that you require students to complete the self-evaluation activities that conclude each chapter. If you ask students to do this in their Writing and Research Notebook, they can assess their growth as writers during the course of the semester.

Handling the Paper Load

There's no way around it. You will have an avalanche of paperwork to manage. If you value your students' writing process, you'll want to see, not just their finished manuscripts, but their prewriting, peer review comments, and revisions for each assignment. If you are using portfolio grading, students need to keep all their work for each writing assignment in hand until the end of the semester. There is no way to eliminate the mountainous paper load; however, here are some practical suggestions for keeping it under control:

1. Require students to purchase inexpensive portfolio folders at the beginning of the course. These folders can be used when students submit each writing assignment for evaluation and for submission of final portfolios, and they provide a cumulative record of your evaluation of each student's work.

2. Don't grade every assignment. Monitor the completion of freewrites, prewriting activities, rough drafts, and other out-of-class writing, but don't grade them. A check mark or brief notation is sufficient response.

3. All writing assignments should be submitted to peer review before being submitted to you for evaluation.

4. Limit the amount of time you spend responding to each completed writing assignment. Read the entire essay through before you respond. React to the essay holistically, identifying global strengths, weaknesses, and significant patterns of error.

5. Evaluate but don't assign a grade to every completed writing assignment. Instead allow students to select and submit portfolios of their best writing for a grade at the end of the course.

6. Cancel classes and schedule individual conferences at appropriate times during the course. Use these conferences to respond to topic selection, initial drafts, or recurring writing problems.

7. On the day writing assignments are due, set aside time for students to read their work to the class. Experiencing peer reaction to their work helps students develop a sense of audience for their writing. In addition, hearing other students' work provides grounding for self-evaluation.

8. Have students evaluate their writing before submitting completed assignments to you. Then enter into a dialogue with them in your response to their writing.